THE BREAD TRAY

THE BREAD TRAY

NEARLY 600 RECIPES FOR HOMEMADE BREADS, ROLLS, MUFFINS AND BISCUITS

by

LOUIS P. DE GOUY

with a Foreword by Dorothy Thompson

DOVER PUBLICATIONS, INC.
NEW YORK

Published in Canada by General Publishing Company, Ltd., 30 Lesmill Road, Don Mills, Toronto, Ontario.
Published in the United Kingdom by Constable and Company, Ltd., 10 Orange Street, London WC 2.

This Dover edition, first published in 1974, is an unabridged republication of the work originally published in 1944 by Greenberg Publisher.

International Standard Book Number: 0-486-23000-7
Library of Congress Catalog Card Number: 73-88329

Manufactured in the United States of America
Dover Publications, Inc.
180 Varick Street
New York, N. Y. 10014

THIS BOOK IS FONDLY DEDICATED

TO THE MEMORY OF

LOUIS P. DE GOUY

(1876-1947)

BY HIS DAUGHTER

JACQUELINE S. DOONER

FOREWORD

BY DOROTHY THOMPSON

All my life I have found cook books among the most fascinating of reading matter. No literature comes closer to living experience. Whatever our other activities may be, we all eat, most of us three meals a day. Why we eat what we do, what it does for us or to us, how others eat—other peoples, and other cultures—how to extend and refine our tastes and our appetites, and how to prepare the food that we put into our mouths, not only for our nourishment, but for our delight—these are matters of prime importance to all civilized persons.

This book deals with the basic human food: Bread. Its author is a great gourmet and an incomparable chef. It is the most complete guide to bread-making that I know of.

It has always astonished and annoyed me that even the most voluminous cook books, that instruct in everything from the preparation of rare game to the concoction of the most intricate desserts, including hundreds of recipes for cakes, ignore or telescope into a few inadequate pages the culinary science and art of baking bread. Even excellent cooks and bakers show, in this generation, an almost complete lack of knowledge of bread—of bread flours and bread mixtures.

So lost an art is that of home bread-baking that families who scorn a bakery cake suffer daily the sliced loaf that passes itself off over the grocery counter as the Staff of Life. In my mother's household, the sickly, bleached-blonde, airy, quick-staling, crustless, sweetish, sticky mass would have been dumped in the garbage can as unfit for human consumption.

For those who, scorning the afternoon cocktail, look forward to a cup of five o'clock tea, the paper-thin bread and butter, preferably white and brown, rolled around watercress, in summer, or tissue-thin cucumbers, or accompanied by wild strawberry jam, is an unknown luxury. The bakers' loaf is already cut and were it not, no one could shave from its bodyless consistency, the millimeter slice.

Were it not for our immigrants, who come to our shores with the taste of real bread still on their tongues, we should probably have become a breadless nation, and as such, unique among mankind. The dieter takes our pseudo-bread off her list—the dieter is usually female—with less regret than any other food, because she has seldom eaten good bread. Actually, as this author tells us, a piece of good bread and butter is not high in caloric content in proportion to other foods. But the average baker's bread is just low in sensory pleasure.

Yet one woman has already demonstrated that if you can bake a better loaf than the big firms, the world will beat a path to your door. Baking an old-fashioned loaf in her own kitchen, and selling it first to a few friends, she rapidly built up a big business, with a loaf of average size and costing twice as much, simply because, with it, people rediscovered bread as such.

A return of home baking would be a challenge to the commercial bakers of a mass product and should therefore be encouraged, in the interest of their reform.

But even those who must shop for bread, having no time to make it, should read this book, as a guide to buying. Its revelation concerning the enormous varieties of bread may encourage people to search for something resembling them, in the not too obvious places. As I have said, good bread is always easier to find in communities or districts where there is a "foreign" colony. Up in the country, I owe it to a colony of Italian-Americans in a nearby industrial town, that I can get the round, crusty, nutty dark loaf that one cuts in hunks to eat with meats and vegetables.

But even the bakers cannot supply the home with that aroma sweeter than all the perfumes of Araby that issues from the oven when the fresh loaves are taken out. They cannot supply you with the irreplaceable deliciousness of the fresh yeast-raised roll, straight out of the oven, into which the hard, sweet butter melts most toothsomely. Nor can they supply you with the disproportionate sense of accomplishment and triumph which accompanies the turning out of a perfect brace of loaves. I do not know why this is so, because it is not hard to make bread. But the housewife who does it enjoys extraordinary praise, and especially from her husband.

One does not slice the bread one makes oneself, in wanton waste, into a basket or onto a plate. It appears at the table on a white-scoured board, with a gleaming knife at its side. It is custom-made and cut to order. It goes back into the bread box, carefully wrapped in a spotless linen tea-towel. It is treated with respect. In it one feels the sun on wheatfields; one smells the freshness of earth; one savors the fragrant sweetness of honey; it brings a message of friendly labor—the labor of men on the soil, under the sun, and of a competent good-tempered woman, serene in her own kitchen. It is not anonymous bread, but strictly personal.

Only one warning must be uttered. The expert bread-maker tends to smugness. So intense is the satisfaction with the product that it promotes self-satisfaction. If you don't believe this, watch the expression on a woman's face, when she announces, "It's home made."

CONVERSION TABLES FOR FOREIGN EQUIVALENTS

DRY INGREDIENTS

Ounces	*Grams*	*Grams*	*Ounces*	*Pounds*	*Kilograms*	*Kilograms*	*Pounds*
1	28.35	1	0.035	1	0.454	1	2.205
2	56.70	2	0.07	2	0.91	2	4.41
3	85.05	3	0.11	3	1.36	3	6.61
4	113.40	4	0.14	4	1.81	4	8.82
5	141.75	5	0.18	5	2.27	5	11.02
6	170.10	6	0.21	6	2.72	6	13.23
7	198.45	7	0.25	7	3.18	7	15.43
8	226.80	8	0.28	8	3.63	8	17.64
9	255.15	9	0.32	9	4.08	9	19.84
10	283.50	10	0.35	10	4.54	10	22.05
11	311.85	11	0.39	11	4.99	11	24.26
12	340.20	12	0.42	12	5.44	12	26.46
13	368.55	13	0.46	13	5.90	13	28.67
14	396.90	14	0.49	14	6.35	14	30.87
15	425.25	15	0.53	15	6.81	15	33.08
16	453.60	16	0.57				

LIQUID INGREDIENTS

Liquid Ounces	*Milliliters*	*Milliliters*	*Liquid Ounces*	*Quarts*	*Liters*	*Liters*	*Quarts*
1	29.573	1	0.034	1	0.946	1	1.057
2	59.15	2	0.07	2	1.89	2	2.11
3	88.72	3	0.10	3	2.84	3	3.17
4	118.30	4	0.14	4	3.79	4	4.23
5	147.87	5	0.17	5	4.73	5	5.28
6	177.44	6	0.20	6	5.68	6	6.34
7	207.02	7	0.24	7	6.62	7	7.40
8	236.59	8	0.27	8	7.57	8	8.45
9	266.16	9	0.30	9	8.52	9	9.51
10	295.73	10	0.33	10	9.47	10	10.57

Gallons (American)	*Liters*	*Liters*	*Gallons (American)*
1	3.785	1	0.264
2	7.57	2	0.53
3	11.36	3	0.79
4	15.14	4	1.06
5	18.93	5	1.32
6	22.71	6	1.59
7	26.50	7	1.85
8	30.28	8	2.11
9	34.07	9	2.38
10	37.86	10	2.74

CONTENTS

A SHORT HISTORY OF BREADS

In the Middle Ages, the kind of bread eaten indicated a family's standing. White bread, called *manchett* in feudal Europe, was first used only in church services, but once when there was a surplus of unconsecrated bread, the clergy sold it to the nobility, who, up to that time, had been subsisting on dark bread as everyone else did, irrespective of station. The white bread made an immediate hit with the nobility—they refused to go back to eating dark bread. Ovens were removed forcibly from the convents and monasteries where the nuns and friars hitherto had done all the baking. All the bread for the entire estate then was baked in the manor ovens. The royal family ate fresh bread daily.

Although it is one of the oldest and most important foods in the human diet and the story of bread runs through the story of civilization itself, science continues to discover new and interesting things about the Staff of Life and new reasons why man, since primitive days, has used it in his daily fare.

As a result of their observations, doctors agree that it isn't only the dizzy pace of the jazz-age that tires the modern woman. It is her lack of food energy caused by fads and her persistent but mistaken methods of trying to stream-line her figure, not only by cutting down on breads, but also by putting the taboo on other energy foods such as candy, potatoes, milk and cake which she mistakenly believes are in themselves fattening. Here, as ever, moderation and balance should be the golden rule.

Nefertiti, the most beautiful woman who ever lived, Cleopatra, Hat-Shepsut and other queens of ancient Egypt didn't have swing bands, movies and other modern distractions to keep them on the go, but according to historians their days usually were just as occupied as those of the modern girl, and they always had a reserve of energy. One of the most important reasons for this may have been the vital part which bread played in their daily diet.

Bread was so important in ancient Egypt that even after death it was placed in the tomb of the deceased so that the combined spiritual body and soul, the "KA," would have food enough to supply energy for the trip to heaven.

The Egyptians are credited with having organized the baking industry. Every Egyptian village had its public ovens, and every king and noble had his private bakery to supply him with fresh bread. By the time of the Pharaohs, two kinds of bread, the leavened and the unleavened products, were in use. Leavened bread was made with a fermented yeast, while unleavened bread, eaten ceremonially by the ancient Hebrews during Passover Week, was made of flour, water and salt baked into a round, hard flat cake, as is still done today.

An Egyptian housewife would give her husband three loaves of leavened bread for a meal, and she herself ate nearly as much. This practice particularly interests modern dietitians in view of the limited amount of bread which some misguided present-day women eat for fear of getting fat. If bread really did add to the waistline, the researchers want to know how the Egyptian women got away with it, inasmuch as nearly all ancient records and pictures of Egyptian men and women show them to be strikingly slender and graceful.

Food experts and dietitians, as well as archeologists, were excited when in 1936 the Metropolitan Museum of Art Expedition headed by Ambrose Lansing and William C. Hayes, while excavating in the Asasif Valley on the site of the Ramesside temples, discovered several loaves of bread, thirty-five centuries old. Some of it was unearthed from the tombs of Ra-Mose and her husband Hat-Nufer, the mother and father of Sem-Nut, the architect who had been a favorite of the Egyptian queen Hat-Shepsut. The rest of it was found in the tomb of Amen-Hotep, a relative of the Pharaoh who had reigned prior to Hat-Shepsut.

When the scientists examined this bread, they almost expected to find secret ingredients unknown to present-day dietitians. Instead, they found that some of the loaves had the physical characteristics of modern rye bread. One specimen was like present-day honey cake or honey bread. Another was on the order of plum pudding; while still another piece, shaped like an éclair, was made of ordinary grain.

Thus it appeared that, while they did not have what we now call a scientific knowledge of nutrition, the Egyptians of 2500 years ago did know that bread supplied a most immediate need of the body—*food energy*. And the ancient Egyptian housewives, surrounded as they may have been by many other superstitions, were free from the fanaticism of modern women in excluding bread and other items wrongly believed to be fattening in themselves.

When the Beautiful Queen Nefertiti "broke bread" with her husband Akhnaton, while they were building the beautiful city of Akhetaton, or that very active Queen Hat-Shepsut dined with Sem-Nut, her favorite, after a tiring chariot ride, they renewed their energy by eating plenty of the Staff of Life.

Fully 85 per cent of the food we eat today can be used to supply energy, and the energy produced by the human organism should be derived from fats and carbohydrates. The ancient Egyptians probably did not know that "fats burn in the flame of carbohydrates" and that we all need food that releases its energy most effectively and continues to supply it during periods of muscular work.

The Egyptians evidently found such food largely in bread, which, like a coal fire, gives out abundant heat. It is also easily digestible, leaves no harmful residue and puts no overload on the digestive organs.

INSTINCT GUIDED THE STONE AGE MAN

Even centuries before the Egyptians, the Stone Age man of 10,000 years ago instinctively sensed these elementary facts about the Staff of Life. When the Stone Age woman knelt before a hollowed-out stone and with a smaller stone in her hands pulverized into a coarse flour the grain which she had planted and reaped on the slopes near her cave, she produced the earliest loaf of bread. So tough and impervious to decay was this primitive food that hard, flat and charred bits of the loaves baked in the Stone Age have been found in the 10,000-year-old ruins of the Swiss Lake Dwellers.

Archeologists who made the discovery found that the loaves contained bits of grit, pulverized rock and sand from the grinding stones. Stone Age skulls, when unearthed, exhibited worn-off teeth, proving that primitive man must have eaten considerable quantities of this hard "bread."

Just how the Stone Age man discovered that the bread he ate supplied him with a source of energy is, of course, not known. With his limited brain power, he probably didn't reason it out. He may have eaten bread instinctively, just as some wild animals eat certain grasses, herbs and plants which are good for them. Since the harvest was meager, the first dough may have been baked in order to preserve the wheat. So much the scientists can only guess, just as they surmise that the first leavened bread was made when a primitive baker let his dough stand long before baking, and fermentation accidentally took place.

DISCOVERY OF FERMENTATION OF BREAD DOUGH

In the course of time it was learned, probably quite by chance, that if a portion of well-raised dough was added to a fresh batch of ground grain and water, fermentation was more likely to take place. A simple thing, but it took a primitive genius to grasp this new and revolutionary idea, and ages passed before its general adoption by the Egyptians.

BREAD SUPERSTITIONS

As bread was used through the ages, it became surrounded by many superstitions, but as dietitians point out, until the American woman began to develop harmful food fads and fancies, these superstitions were all in favor of the Staff of Life. Even today some Dutch mothers place a piece of stale bread in their babies' cradles to ward off disease. In Morocco, stale bread is considered an excellent cure for stuttering, and present-day Egyptians believe that licking a stale crust will cure indigestion. The Normans, though burly men, turned from the coarse black bread then in vogue elsewhere and insisted upon being served Wastel, a well-baked white bread of excellent quality and flavor, which was supposed to give them courage. In Labrador, it is considered a breach of etiquette to pass a neighbor's house without stopping for some bread and tea. In Medieval England, bread served as both food and plates for all but the wealthy. Food was served in hollowed-out bread loaves. The juice-soaked loaves were the forerunner of "bread and gravy." English housewives scratched a cross in a loaf of bread before baking it, so it wouldn't be bewitched and "turn out heavy." The Capitol in Washington, D. C. was once a bakery. During the Civil War ovens were set up under the Senate wing and 16,000 loaves of bread were baked there daily for the Union Army.

Neither bread nor any other single food is fattening when it is part of a well-balanced diet. If a woman keeps her total diet within proper bounds, she may eat and enjoy good bread, butter, potatoes, pure milk, ice cream, some cake, pie, candy and other foods often erroneously considered to cause overweight. Fat is stored when too much of such foods is eaten in proportion to other foods and to the amount of energy expended. But the trick lies in eating foods that give you the most satisfying and varied nutrition.

WHY THIS IS

Since the body is a working mechanism, even when it is apparently at rest, it requires a certain amount of fuel for necessary energy. This fuel comes from food and is measured in heat units known as calories.

The normal person usually needs about 3000 calories a day, although the precise number depends upon age, sex, build, activity, mode of life, the climate and other factors. A person who is reducing can get along on 1200–1500 calories a day, while a hard-working laborer may need as many as 5000. Active children often require more calories than adults who lead sedentary lives.

One slice of white bread (3″ × 3½″ × ¼″) furnishes only 25 (whole grains about 35) calories. Butter (2 teaspoons level) on the bread will provide about 67 calories. For fats yield 2¼ times more calories per gram than the feared carbohydrates. Hence dry toast! A medium-sized baked potato adds 100 calories and a glass (8.5 oz.) of whole milk yields 170 calories.

It is obvious, then, that two slices of bread and butter and a glass of milk would contribute 354 calories to a meal, or about one-eighth of the day's total requirements; and it is economic well-balanced nourishment. It is only when all the foods in the daily diet exceed the body's demand for energy that the excess is stored up as fat.

After a decline which set in seven or eight years ago, the consumption of bread turned upward recently. Window displays of some thousands of bakeries bear testimony to the variety of loaves now being used, and inside the shops there is further evidence that the bread tray on the family table need never be monotonous.

White bread consumption declined sharply when the Hollywood figure became the ideal and slimming diets were widely followed. The millers and the bakers took counsel, and the results of their efforts have never been more inviting than they are today. Home economics research workers in the miller's laboratories and nutritionists in university dietetic clinics can claim credit, along with the producers of flour, for the appetizing varieties of bread now available.

At any rate, white bread is still with us, made by the millions of pounds every day of the year, for those who prefer this long-established food. Today's *bread tray* boasts many varieties which our grandmothers never knew.

Breads, like people, have national characteristics. They have personality. There are the long bread sticks of Italy; the crisp, sturdy bread loaves of France; and the flavorful black breads of Russia. There are the tender *ole koek* of the Dutch, the English crumpets served with tea and the glazed tapering rolls of Vienna.

A book of recipes reflects the tastes and products of the country from which they come. For instance, pork and corn meal were among the few staples left in the South during the lean years following the Civil War. So Crackling Bread, a mixture of corn meal and crisp bits of pork, was invented in Southern kitchens—crisp and flavorful little breads when made correctly. Hoe Cake and Johnny Cake—both could be baked under almost any crude conditions—were handed down from our Colonial ancestors. Bread made with molasses, such as Boston Brown Bread, also found origin during Colonial days when molasses, known as "long sweetening," was more plentiful than sugar, and the cold climate of New England inspired an urge for sweet foods. Southern breads, on the other hand, are less sweet. Even a teaspoon of sugar in bread of some types is scorned by a Southern cook.

. . . Back of the loaf is the snowy flour,
Back of the flour the mill,
And back of the mill is the wheat and the shower
And the sun and the Father's will. . . .

LOUIS P. DE GOUY

GENERAL INFORMATION

(1) BREAD MAKING

It has been well said that the quality of the bread used by the inhabitants of any country is a fair measure of their prosperity. Flour is prepared from various grains by crushing and grinding processes. The grains consist of (1) an outer layer, the husk or skin, which is woody, fibrous, and indigestible, and which in the milling process is separated into "bran"; (2) the kernel within the husk, which is composed of gluten, fats, and salts; (3) the starch.

To appreciate the important details of bread making it will be necessary to first review the structure and composition of the grain from which the bread is derived.

The wheat kernel is subdivided into four layers. The first or outermost layer consists of two or three strata of elongated cells the long diameters of which correspond with the long axis of the grain. From these cells slender filaments or tapering, hair-like processes project outward. The cell margins are irregular in outline, and appear somewhat beaded.

Immediately beneath the outer hairy layer lies the second layer, consisting of more or less quadrangular cells, with rounded angles, which are more uniform in size than the others, and grow at right angles to them. The third layer consists of a delicate, transparent membrane-like structure. The fourth or internal layer is composed of large, almost rectangular, cells arranged in one or two strata, and which contain a dark granular material which may be easily separated from the cell walls.

The grains of other cereals conform in a general way to the structure of the wheat grain, although they differ in the thickness of the several layers, the number of their strata, and the size of the individual cells.

(2) BRAN

Bran contains carbohydrate material which is only partly digested in the human alimentary canal, but the cellulose is useful as roughage in promoting elimination. The nutritive salts of wheat are chiefly contained in the bran and the vitamins in the germ; for this reason, if bread constitutes the principal food for a time, it is best to eat that which contains some bran or the whole grain. But if too much is consumed in too coarse a form, it may unduly hasten peristalsis, so that nutrition suffers because the food is hurried out of the alimentary canal before absorption is complete. When bread is eaten as part of a well-balanced diet, white bread can well be one-half of the total used.

(3) GLUTEN

Gluten is separated in the process of making starch from wheat and other grains. It is a valuable nitrogenous food product, consisting of 60 to 70 per cent gliadin and 30 to 40 per cent glutenin. The greater part of the gluten is held in the central four-fifths of the grain. The gliadin adheres to the glutenin, retains the gas in dough, and in excess it makes the flour soft and sticky; soft wheat yields a flour with high percentage of gliadin, but hard wheat has a low percentage.

Gluten is capable of considerable expansion independently of the development of CO-2, and, as this power varies with different flours, it affects the quality of lightness of the bread. Some glutens expand four or five times as much as others.

(4) COMPOSITION OF BREAD

Bread is really a mixed food, in that it contains so many classes of ingredients—fat, protein, salts, sugar, and starch—and this, together with its bland taste, is probably the explanation of the fact that its daily use never cloys the appetite. Although it contains some fat, it has not much, and hence the almost universal custom of spreading butter on bread; the butter also aids in mastication and deglutition.

Good bread contains, on the average, protein, 9.57 per cent; fat, 1.5 to 2 per cent; carbohydrates, 55 per cent; the remainder being largely water, with a trace of salts in white bread and about 1.8 per cent in whole grains. In round numbers, bread contains about two-thirds nutrient material. A pound of bread is made from approximately three-quarters of a pound of flour by the addition of 25 per cent of water or milk, and leavening agents with salt and fat. Some flours will take up 10 per cent more water.

(5) GRAINS AND FLOUR

DESCRIPTION AND COMPOSITION OF GRAINS—Grains or cereal grains are the seeds of such plants as wheat, corn, oats, rye, buckwheat (buckwheat is not really a cereal), etc. Grain seeds, as such, or in some manufactured form, constitute one of the most important food items of man and animals. While they vary somewhat in composition, they all contain—

Carbohydrates—Carbohydrates include starch, and sugar used by man to provide the energy necessary for activity such as working, walking, etc.

Protein—Protein is used by man to build up and replace muscle and other body tissue. It is necessary to growth and replaces worn-out cell structure.

Fat—Fat is used by man as a reserve energy supply and is stored in the body in that form. When the quantity of carbohydrate food eaten is insufficient to supply the energy required for the activities of man, the stored up fats are used to supply this deficiency.

Mineral matter—Mineral matter is used by man for teeth and bone building, and is essential to body functions. Every cell needs calcium; the blood uses iron and copper. Much more mineral matter is contained in the whole grain than in white flour, because in the manufacturing process most of the mineral matter in hulls and bran is removed.

Water—Water in a considerable amount (4 to 6 glasses a day) is needed to promote elimination, perspiration, circulation of the blood, and many other functions of the body. The water contained in grains, or manufactured products thereof, which man ordinarily consumes, is insufficient to meet his requirements. To a certain extent, the eating of cereal foods, such as bread, encourages the drinking of water.

MILLING OF GRAIN—The preparation of grain for white flour, commonly called milling, involves the removal of the germ, hull and bran coats from the kernel and the grinding, sifting, bolting, and separation into various grades of the endosperm (starch granules). If the grinding is limited to rather coarse particles, the product is known as meal, such as corn meal. If grinding is continued until a powdery product is produced, it is called flour, such as wheat flour, rye flour, rice flour, etc.

(6) WHEAT

Wheat is by far the most important of the grains, especially in the United States. It is grown in all temperate climates; when manufactured into flour, it makes better and more palatable bread than flour from other grains which, to a large extent, does not possess the qualities which make well-risen loaves of bread.

CLASSIFICATION—There are many classifications of wheat, but for purposes of this book the author will confine himself to the descriptions of—

Winter Wheat—Winter wheat is wheat sown in the fall and harvested the following summer.

Spring Wheat—Spring wheat is wheat sown in the spring and harvested in the fall.

Hard Wheat—Hard wheat may be either winter or spring wheat and has kernels that are hard, tough, and difficult to cut. It contains from 10 to 12 per cent protein. The gluten of hard wheat flour is tough, resistant, generally of good quality, and best suited for bread making.

Soft Wheat—Soft wheat is composed of kernels that are soft and of a starchy appearance when cut and usually contain from 6 to 10 per cent protein. It produces a soft and weak gluten, does not make a good loaf of bread, but is suitable for biscuits, muffins, pastry, crackers, and cakes.

PRODUCTS OBTAINED FROM MILLING—The chief products obtained from the milling of wheat are—

Bran—Bran is the coarse particles of the outer coatings. It is used largely as animal feed and to a limited extent as a breakfast cereal.

Shorts Germ—Shorts is the fine particles of the outer coatings and germ of wheat. Like bran, it is used largely as animal feed.
Flour—For various grades of flour obtained from milling we have:

(7) WHEAT FLOUR

Wheat flour is made of several classes. Within each class, each of the grades described in flour grading may be obtained. Flours are classified according to the kind of wheat from which they are obtained, as follows:
Hard spring flour—This is flour milled from wheat grown in Minnesota, North and South Dakota, and nearby territory. It has a rich, creamy color and a large amount of gluten of the best quality, and makes a good, well-risen loaf of bread when properly handled. It is sharp or granular to the touch and is an excellent bread flour.
Hard winter flour—This flour, milled from wheat grown in Kansas, Nebraska, Oklahoma, and other western States, has a good color, an excellent flavor, and a good strong gluten. Although its gluten is not generally as strong as that of hard spring wheat, it is an excellent bread flour if properly handled.
Soft winter flour—This flour comes from the more humid central States and the Pacific coast. Its gluten is low in quantity and it has poor tensility. It is white, has a soft and fluffy texture, and an excellent flavor. It is used for pastry and biscuits.
Durum flour—Durum flour is milled from durum wheat, grown mostly in the northwest section of the United States. It has a yellowish creamy color and a large amount of very hard and tough gluten. It is not satisfactory for bread making purposes unless blended with a weaker flour.

(8) FLOUR GRADING

Low grades—About 3 per cent of the total flour obtained at first and last stages when milling wheat is *low-grade* flour. It is dark in color, contains some bran specks and dirt and does not make a satisfactory loaf of bread. It is used for purposes other than bakery products, such as sizing, paste, etc.
Patent—Patent flour is sometimes further divided into short and long patent, and constitutes from 40 to 90 per cent of the flour; that

is, that portion which contains the smallest quantity of bran and is capable of producing an excellent quality of gluten desirable for bread making purposes. Short patent flour is a higher or better grade than long patent.

Clear—Clear flour is sometimes divided into first clear and second clear, and is that portion remaining after the patent flour and low-grade flour are separated from a run of flour. First clear is a higher or better grade than second clear, as the first clear is that portion remaining after separation of a short patent, and a second clear is that remaining after separation of a long patent. Clear flour does not make satisfactory white bread as it imparts a dark color to the crumb, but it may be used advantageously when making part whole wheat or rye bread, the dark color of crumb not being objectionable in such products.

Straight—Straight flour is the total produced from a run of wheat, excluding the low-grade; that is, the product obtained by combining the patent and the clear flour. Federal specifications provide for the purchase of straight flour for Army ration purposes. Although generally not so fine or white as a patent flour, straight flour is capable of producing an attractive, palatable and highly nutritive loaf of bread if properly handled.

Cut straight—Cut straight flour is a straight flour from which a portion of the best or patent flour has been removed.

Stuffed straight—This is a straight flour to which an additional amount of clear flour from another run of flour has been added.

(9) ADDITIONAL FLOUR

In addition to the white flours described in No. 8, there are several other flours frequently used in making bread and other bakery products. These flours are highly desirable, especially in restricted diets, since they provide more complete nutrition as well as variety. Among the more important are:

Whole wheat—Whole wheat flour is the product made by grinding the entire wheat grain to a powdery consistency. It contains not only starch granules, but also most of the bran or outer coats of the wheat. Whole wheat flour may be used by itself as the flour component of bread or it may be blended with either patent, straight, or clear flours or a combination thereof. Bread produced from whole wheat flour is brown in color and high in vitamin, mineral and roughage content as compared with bread produced from all patent, straight, or clear flours. Whole wheat breads add nourishment as well as variety to the ration.

Rye—Rye flour is lacking in gluten-forming protein, which quality is essential to the formation of a loaf of bread having a good volume and smooth, porous texture. For this reason it is generally used in proportions of 10 to 40 per cent rye flour and the remainder wheat flour. Bread made from 100 per cent rye flour would be small in volume, soggy, compact and unpalatable to the average American. There are three types of flour obtained from the milling of rye, as follows:

(1)—*White*—While darker in color, this flour corresponds to the short patent wheat flour. It is nearly white and has a small percentage of ash, but is deficient in gluten-forming protein.

(2)—*Dark*—Dark rye flour corresponds to the clear grade wheat flour. It is very dark, has a branny taste and is used to obtain a dark rye loaf of bread.

(3)—*Medium*—Medium rye flour corresponds to the straight grade of wheat flour. It is a blend of the dark and white rye flours. It possesses more of the true rye taste than the white rye and for this reason is the type mostly used when making rye bread.

Other flours—These are flours made from corn, rice, barley, potatoes (bleached or unbleached), rice, soybean, etc. They are best used in combination with wheat flour. They are practically devoid of gluten-forming protein and for this reason will not produce a satisfactory loaf of bread when used by themselves. With the exception of soybean, up to 20 per cent of these flours or a combination thereof, the balance to be wheat flour, may be used successfully. Soybean flour is very high in protein and low in starch. If used in excess of 5 per cent it tends to produce a compact small volume loaf lacking attractiveness and palatability.

Self-rising flour—This is a flour which is mixed with baking powder in the proper proportions so as to produce a satisfactory raised product after mixing with water or other liquid. It is in convenient form for the household, especially for the preparation of hot cakes and quick breads, but is of no particular merit in the bakery. Most pancake flours on the market are self-rising.

(10) BLEACHED FLOUR

Flour improves with age under proper storage conditions, up to one year, both in color and quality. However, some flour is shipped from the mill before it is naturally aged. In lieu of natural aging flour is often bleached. Bleaching has the effect of whitening and artificially aging flour. There is no objection to the purchase of bleached flour, providing it is carefully done and the bleaching agent is used solely for the purpose of aging the flour and not to cover up inferior qualities such as original dark color, off odors, etc.

(11) NEW FLOUR

New flour is freshly milled flour from recently harvested wheat. Such flour is unstable and presents difficulties in bread making until it matures. This is due to the fact that the proteins of the wheat must undergo certain changes before they combine to form a satisfactory gluten. A warm, dry storage is the best means of aging the flour and developing the gluten qualities. Under good storage conditions new flour may be considered as sufficiently aged for use after a period of one month. If new flour must be used before it is aged, it is best to mix it with an equal quantity of flour that has been on hand for some time. If no aged flour is available, good bread may be made with new flour by giving a rapid fermentation at a slightly higher temperature than that ordinarily used, making a stiff dough, and using a larger quantity of yeast and salt.

New flour should not be confused with green flour, which is flour obtained from milling wheat that is unsweated or insufficiently sweated. Proper sweating of wheat is obtained by leaving wheat in stacks 10 days to 8 weeks before threshing. Green flour will not produce a satisfactory loaf of bread even if allowed to age.

(12) STORAGE OF FLOUR

Flour should be kept in a dry, well-ventilated storeroom or closet at a fairly uniform temperature. A temperature of about 70° F., with a relative humidity of 65 per cent, is considered ideal. Flour should not be stored in a damp place. When milled, flour contains moisture up to 15 per cent but it will take up additional moisture when stored in damp places. Moist storerooms accompanied by temperatures greater than 75° F. are very conducive to mold growth, bacterial development and rapid deterioration of the flour. The storage room or closet should be well-ventilated, as flour absorbs and retains odors. For this reason, flour should not be stored in the same room or closet with supplies, such as cheese, onions, garlic, coffee, flavoring extracts, etc. which give off strong odors.

(13) TESTING OF FLOUR

The testing of flour to determine the quantity of carbohydrates, protein, moisture, and ash contained therein requires the services of an experienced chemist and technical equipment. However, there are several tests which can be made at home which will give a good indication of the quality and characteristics of the flour on hand.

Soundness and odor—The odor of flour should be sweet and similar to that of freshly ground wheat. Flour which is in unsound condition or has a musty, garlicky or other objectionable odor will not make a well-flavored bread.

Granulation (feel)—Rub the flour between the thumb and fingers. Good hard wheat flour has a somewhat granular or gritty feel. A soft, smooth or slippery feeling denotes a soft wheat flour or a blend of soft and hard wheat flours. Hard wheat flours retain their form when pressed in the hollow of the hand and fall apart readily when touched. Soft wheat flour tends to remain lumped together after pressure.

Color (pekar test)—Place a small quantity of flour on a smooth glass or porcelain plate and "slick" with a steel flour trier, spatula, or table knife to form a firm smooth mass about 2 inches square, the thickness running from about one-half inch at back of plate to a thin film at the front. This test should be made in comparison with a flour of known grade and quality, both flours being "slicked" side by side on the same plate.

A bright, rich, creamy-white color indicates a hard flour of good gluten qualities. A dark or grayish color indicates a poorer grade of flour or presence of dirt. Bran specks indicate a lower grade of flour; a dead, chalky-white color indicates a soft wheat flour of excessive bleach. After making color comparison on the dry samples, dip the plate obliquely in a vessel of clean water, remove, and allow to partially dry. Variations in color and presence of bran specks are more pronounced in the damp samples. Owing to the custom of bleaching flours, color is not always a reliable guide. Bleaching will, however, not improve the dull appearance of a poor flour and will not conceal dirt and bran specks. Unless overdone or to conceal inferiority, bleaching is legally approved.

Absorption—Absorption is, roughly speaking, the amount of water that should be added to a flour to produce a dough of the proper consistency; that is, a dough that is smooth and soft and yet not sticky. The absorption ability of a flour will usually be between 55 and 65 per cent. The absorption factor can be determined by the following procedure:

(1)—Place a small quantity of the flour (a few ounces) in a cup or bowl. Add water gradually from a beaker or graduated cup containing a known quantity (ounces). As water is added, stir with a knife, spatula or handle of a spoon until a dough of the desired consistency is obtained. Do not use the fingers for mixing, as some of the dough will stick to them or they will either absorb or give off moisture through the pores of the skin, thereby giving inaccurate results. Care must be taken to mix the flour and water thoroughly so that no dry particles remain on the outside or inside of the dough. When no loose flour or water remains, it may be taken in the fingers for final mixing and determination of consistency. Weigh the unused water. Divide the weight of used water by the weight of the flour used and the result is the absorption ability expressed in terms of percentage.

EXAMPLE: Weight of flour used........................10 ounces
Weight of water used........................6¼ ounces

Therefore $\frac{6\frac{1}{4}}{10}$ or ....0.625 or 62.5 per cent.

(2)—For accurate work, the greater part of the water should be added at once and then a few drops at a time until the desired consistency is reached. This may be checked by a second determination in which all the water is added at once. If the moisture content of the flour either increases or decreases as a result of storage conditions, the absorption ability of the flour will vary accordingly. It is, therefore, essential to make an absorption test on the flour being used at least once each month in order to determine its proper absorption at time of use. The per cent of absorption being known, the quantity of water to be added to any given quantity of flour used in a dough is readily calculated.

Gluten test—The grade and baking qualities of a flour depend largely upon the quantity and quality of its gluten-forming ability. The gluten test should always be a comparative one, that is, the gluten of an unknown grade or kind of flour is compared with the gluten of a known or previously used flour, in order to determine by comparison the kind and grade of the unknown flour and how dough made with it should be handled in the making of bread. The following procedure should be followed to obtain gluten from flour: Carefully weigh out small samples (a few ounces) of previously known and unknown flours and place each sample in a cup or bowl. Add water to each sample until dough of the proper consistency is obtained by the method described for the absorption test. Allow the doughs thus obtained to stand submerged in water at room temperature for 30 minutes in order to permit the formation and setting of the gluten within the dough. Knead each dough gently in a thin stream of cool water until the starch and all soluble matter is removed. To determine if the gluten is starch-free, let a few drops of the wash water, obtained by squeezing the gluten, fall into a glass containing clear water. If starch is still present, a cloudiness appears. If gluten is practically starch-free, no discoloration appears in the water. Allow the gluten thus obtained from each sample of flour to stand in water for 30 minutes.

If weight comparison is to be made, small scales should be used. For practical purposes the weight of the wet gluten may be considered as being three times that of dry gluten; that is, the dry gluten (all moisture removed by heat) will be one-third of the weight of the wet gluten. As gluten content is always expressed in terms of dry gluten, divide the weight of the wet gluten by 3 and the result thus obtained by the weight of flour used to make sample. This result is the amount of gluten in flour expressed in percentage terms.

Baking test—The final and conclusive test of any flour is the kind of bread that can be made from it. A single loaf should be baked and compared with a loaf baked from a known flour. To make baking tests of value all conditions should be standardized. Definite weights of flour, sugar, salt, yeast, and shortening should be used and water added in accordance with the absorption ability. The same materials, except flour, should be used in each dough. A definite procedure must be followed using identical times and temperatures for all operations.

(14) REASONS FOR MAKING FLOUR TESTS

The kind and grade of flour used in a dough is the most important factor in the appearance and qualities of the finished loaf of bread. Using a certain formula and procedure with dough made from one batch of flour may produce an excellent loaf of bread, while the identical formula and procedure with another batch of flour will produce a poor loaf. If the kind, grade, absorption ability, and quality of gluten in the flour to be used are known in advance, the housewife may readily adjust formula and procedure so as to produce the best results obtainable from that flour.

(15) LEAVENING AGENTS

YEAST—Next to flour, yeast may be considered as the most important ingredient used in bread making. The quality of the finished loaf of bread is dependent to a large extent upon the kind, quality, and condition of yeast used in the dough. Although flour is a highly nutritious substance, it is not suitable for human food until it has been made into a form which is palatable and really acted upon by the digestive juices of the human system. Cooking or baking alone causes certain changes to take place which make the product more palatable and digestible; unleavened products, such as hard bread, crackers, etc., are not usually relished as a steady diet. Incorporating yeast in a flour dough results in a leavened product or an expansion, and a modification of the starch cells which greatly improves the palatability and digestibility of flour foods.

Description of Yeast—A yeast cell is a minute vegetable substance which cannot be seen with the naked eye. Yeast cells are constantly floating about in the air and settling on food substances. With proper food, air, moisture, and temperature conditions, yeast will grow and reproduce rapidly. Light is not necessary for its growth. When yeast is exposed to unfavorable conditions it may go into spore form, a condition in which the cells are temporarily inactive but still possess the ability to become active again as soon as favorable

(16) CONDITIONS NECESSARY FOR EFFICIENT FUNCTIONING OF YEAST

Yeast, in order to grow, multiply, and act efficiently as a leavening agent, requires proper air, moisture, temperature and food conditions. Like all other living organisms, yeast requires a certain amount of oxygen (obtained from air) and moisture in order to live and thrive. In a slack dough its activity is increased whereas in a stiff dough its action is retarded. Yeast works best in temperatures of 78 to 82° F. As temperature increases beyond this point, action is accelerated; but the chances of obtaining undesirable fermentation, such as acetic and wild yeast, are greater. At about 120° F. the action of yeast is killed. Similarly, as temperature of dough containing yeast is lowered from 78 to 82° F., the action of yeast is retarded until at about 45° F. activity practically ceases. Food in the form of carbohydrates (starch, sugar, malt) must be present before yeast will cause fermentation.

(17) FERMENTATION

Fermentation may be considered as the chemical action that takes place in certain substances, caused by the action of micro-organisms (bacteria, yeasts, molds) under favorable conditions. Common fermentations are:

Alcoholic—A conversion of sugar to approximately equal parts of carbon dioxide (a gas) and alcohol, caused by the action of yeast. This is the type of fermentation desired in bread making.

Acetic—A conversion of dilute alcohol to acetic acid (vinegar) caused by the action of acetic bacteria. At high temperatures (above 90° F.), or on prolonged fermentation, acetic fermentation may take place in an alcoholic fermentation of yeast action on sugar. If this happens, sourness of bread results.

Lactic—A conversion of sugar (cane sugar, beet sugar, milk sugar) to lactic acid caused by the action of lactic bacteria. It is this fermentation that causes the souring of milk and, to a certain extent, it may be formed in connection with yeast fermentation of sugar in bread making, thereby imparting a lactic acid flavor to bread.

conditions are provided. Dried yeast is a good example of yeas spore form. The absence of sufficient moisture in dried yeast p hibits growth and development until such time as it is mixed w water and flour or other carbohydrate substance. When so mixed, t yeast changes from spore to active form.

Kinds of Yeast—There are numerous varieties and strains of yea all capable of fermenting sugar, but each is best suited to certa conditions and substances. While these all produce alcohol an carbon dioxide, the quantities produced and the character of th other products formed are such that many of them are inefficient o undesirable for baking purposes. Bread yeast is generally obtaine from manufacturers who carefully grow selected pure strains and sell them in practically pure condition. The use of a cultivated yeast eliminates much uncertainty as to the results of fermentation. Wild yeasts are present in nature and are the cause of many natural fermentations. These organisms are undesirable in bread making.

Compressed Yeast—Compressed yeast is a pure culture of bread yeast grown on a large scale, collected and compressed into cakes. It may be mixed with not more than 5 per cent starch to absorb the excess moisture and give it body. For household use, it is put up in ½-ounce packets or cakes wrapped in tinfoil. It is very perishable and spoils quickly when removed from cold storage and exposed to warm temperatures. For this reason it must be refrigerated.

Good compressed yeast should feel firm, tough and springy and should break with a clean fracture resembling broken plate glass. It should have a fresh yeasty odor and be practically tasteless. Yeast's color is not a safe guide in determining its quality. Spoiled yeast is soft and has a sour or putrid odor. DO NOT USE IT.—A quick test is to roll a small amount into a firm ball about 1 inch in diameter and drop it into a glass containing a dilute solution of sugar. Note the time required for the ball to float to the surface. A good sample will rise to the surface in a few minutes; a poor or doubtful one will take a much longer time. The time required will vary according to the temperature of the water and the amount of sugar dissolved in the water.

Dried Yeast—This kind of yeast is less used in the home, but is perfectly practicable and more available in some localities. Being largely in spore form it requires more time to develop growth when mixed with water and other ingredients.

(18) ACTION OF YEAST IN A DOUGH

Yeast secretes four substances known as enzymes. The enzyme diastase breaks down some of the starch in flour into compound sugar. Invertase breaks down compound sugars to simple sugars. Zymase breaks down simple sugars to carbon dioxide gas and alcohol. The enzyme protease has a softening effect on the gluten, thereby giving it more expanding power.

It may be seen that it is not necessary to add sugar to a dough in order to secure fermentation by yeast, as part of the flour may be converted into sugar by the enzyme diastase and subsequently acted upon to produce carbon dioxide and alcohol. However, it is advisable to use some sugar (cane, beet, or corn sugar, malt, syrup, honey, etc.) as yeast food in a dough in order to prevent extensive fermentation periods and possible breaking down of gluten by the enzyme protease to the point where only small volume is obtainable.

The carbon dioxide gas, formed by the action of yeast on sugar, is the element which it is desired to retain in a dough. The alcohol formed is usually vaporized during baking. It is the expanding of the carbon dioxide gas (caused by heat) within and between the cells of the dough that causes it to rise and expand and form the silky, spongy texture which aids materially in making bread appetizing and palatable.

(19) BAKING POWDER

Baking powder is a gas-forming or leavening agent produced by the action of an acid reacting material on sodium bicarbonate (baking soda) which causes the formation of carbon dioxide gas. This is the same gas as that produced by yeast in its action on sugar. While both the acid reacting material, such as tartaric acid phosphates, compounds of aluminum, etc., and the baking soda are present in baking powder as purchased, the carbon dioxide gas cannot be formed until sufficient water is present to cause the gas formation. When baking powder is added to a dough or batter, sufficient water is present to cause this gas formation.

There are several kinds of baking powder available commercially, some of which must be handled differently to obtain the best results.

For this reason it is essential that instructions as to quantity to be used and the method to be employed, as given on the label of containers, should be strictly followed.

While baking powder is an excellent agent for quickly leavened products, such as griddle cakes, biscuits and cake, it cannot be used to produce a palatable and attractive loaf of plain bread. In order to obtain the desired flavor and consistency of real bread, a gradual formation of gas and expansion of gluten, such as is produced by yeast, is necessary. There are, however, "quick rolls," and small fancy loaves of bread such as the orange and sesame loaves, that are delicious.

(20) WATER

Water is an essential ingredient in bread making. Without water, the formation of a dough would be impossible. When mixed with wheat flour, water unites with the protein substances of flour called glutenin and gliadin and forms the substance known as gluten; this is essential to produce a well-risen loaf. The presence of water in comparatively large quantities is also necessary to cause fermentation by use of yeast. Before being incorporated in a dough, the yeast should be dissolved separately in a portion of the water to be used in mixing. When so treated, the yeast is uniformly distributed throughout the entire mass, resulting in a much better and more uniform fermentation. Water plays an important part in the fermentation, eating qualities and freshness of bread, mainly from the following standpoints:

Without water, yeast activity would cease.

The presence of water makes possible the pliable and expansible properties of the dough so that in this form it can be raised by the carbon dioxide gas resulting from yeast activity.

The presence of water aids materially in imparting good eating qualities to the loaf of bread. A dough containing insufficient water when baked would give a dry, brittle product. Conversely, too much water remaining in a baked loaf of bread results in a soggy, unpalatable product and makes it readily susceptible to mold development.

Water in bread imparts the characteristic of freshness. The

evaporation of the water contained in a loaf of bread is the principal cause of staleness.

Milk may be used, in whole or in part, and adds to the nutritive value.

TYPES AND EFFECT IN BREAD MAKING—All water used in bread doughs should be of a purity equal to that of drinking water.
Hard water—Hard water is water which, after falling as rain, seeps through the soil and while so doing absorbs minerals such as carbonates and sulphates of calcium and magnesium. If water is hard, it is difficult to form a lather with soap. Medium hard water is desirable for bread making purposes as it provides the essential mineral matter necessary to activate yeast in a dough. Excessively hard water retards the progress of fermentation by toughening the gluten; it may be softened by boiling prior to use.
Soft water—This is water which is relatively free of mineral matter. Soft water readily forms a lather with soap. Very soft water, when used for bread making, has a tendency to soften the gluten and result in a soft sticky dough. If soft water must be used, this softening of gluten and stickiness of dough may be remedied by using larger quantities of salt. The mineral matter contained in the salt will supply the mineral deficiency of the water.
Alkaline water—This is water which contains in solution an alkaline substance such as sodium carbonate. In rare cases water may be sufficiently alkaline to require special treatment before using in a dough. Excessively alkaline water will either neutralize or change to the alkaline side a dough that should be slightly acid for best yeast activity and fermentation. If alkaline water must be used, its ill effects may be overcome by adding to it a small quantity of vinegar.

QUANTITY OF WATER TO BE USED—The quantity of water to be used in a dough is determined by the flour absorption test (see No. 13). The use of slack or stiff doughs may be desirable under certain conditions, but it must be remembered that the quantity of water to be used in any case should be such as not to materially affect the quality of the finished bread. From a commercial standpoint, the retention of more water in a loaf of bread is beneficial to the baker as it results in increased profits from weight and the fact that it does not become stale so soon; but for the home, there is no advantage gained by the use of more water than is necessary to produce a palatable and attractive product.

(21) SALT

Salt used in bread making is the kind universally used as table salt; that is, a chemical compound of the elements of sodium and chlorine. *Salt, flour, yeast* and *water* constitute the essential ingredients of a bread dough. In other words, a good leavened bread may be made by the use of these ingredients only. Other ingredients such as sugar, milk, and shortening, when added to a dough improve the attractiveness and nutrition of the finished product but they are not essential to the production of a good quality of leavened bread.

Salt is used primarily to impart a desirable flavor to bread. Without salt, the bread would be flat and insipid. In addition to imparting flavor, salt to a large extent may be considered as a time factor in fermentation. As the amount of salt used in a dough is increased, the proper fermentation time for that dough is increased, and vice versa.

EXAMPLE: *If 2 per cent is the normal amount of salt used in a dough and it is desired to shorten the fermentation period, reducing the amount to 1 per cent is one way of accomplishing the desired result. Conversely, if it is desired to lengthen the fermentation period, increasing the amount of salt to 3 per cent will accomplish this result.*

In order to insure equal distribution, the salt and sugar should be dissolved in a part of the water before being added to the dough. The salt *should never be mixed with the yeast nor added to the yeast and water solution,* as this high concentration of salt with yeast will *invariably seriously weaken, if not kill, yeast activity.*

Normally, 2 per cent salt, based on weight of flour used, will give the best results. Amounts above and below this percentage may be used to meet special situations but in no case should the amount exceed 5 per cent, based on weight of flour. Amounts in excess of 5 per cent will *seriously injure* the quality and flavor of bread.

(22) SUGAR AND SUBSTITUTES

The word "sugar," without qualification, means the sugar obtained from sugar cane or sugar beets. For all practical purposes there is no difference between cane and beet sugar. The chemical name for cane or beet sugar is *sucrose.* The sugar obtained by chemically treating cornstarch is known as corn sugar. Its chemical name is *dextrose.* The chemical name for sugar contained in milk is *lactose* and that obtained from the malting of grains is *maltose.* Other sweetening agents such as brown sugar, corn syrup, cane syrup, molasses, honey, etc., may be used in bakery products in lieu of sugar. For bread making purposes fine granulated sugar is most desirable.

Function of Sugar in Bread and Bread Products—Sugar is added to a bread dough primarily to provide immediate food for yeast. It is the sugar in a dough that is acted upon by yeast to produce the carbon dioxide gas resulting in a leavened product. Its second important function is to provide a sweet flavor to the finished loaf. It also gives to the crust of a loaf of bread that golden color which adds materially to its attractiveness. For this reason, more than just enough sugar to act as yeast food should be incorporated in a bread dough; if no sugar remains in the dough upon completion of fermentation, the resultant product will have an unattractive, light-colored crust.

In order to be fermentable by yeast, sugar must be in simple form. The starch of flour may be broken down from its complex form through compound sugar to simple sugar by the action of enzymes secreted by yeast. Sucrose, or cane and beet sugar, is a compound sugar and must be broken down to simple sugars by the yeast enzyme invertase before it is fermentable. Dextrose, or corn sugar, is a simple sugar and is, therefore, directly fermentable by yeast. The conversion of a compound sugar to a simple one within a dough is so rapid that no difference in fermentation time need be considered in using cane sugar or corn sugar. Lactose, or milk sugar, is *not fermentable* by yeast. Therefore, any lactose present in a dough will remain as such during fermentation and, as a result of caramelization caused by high heat of oven, will tend to give a golden brown color to the crust of bread.

Amount of Sugar to be Used—The amount of sugar used depends on the kind of bakery product desired. For ordinary bread doughs, the amount of sugar generally ranges from 2 to 4 per cent, based on the weight of flour used. The same weight of either sucrose or dextrose may be used, even though the latter is only three-fourths as sweet as sucrose. Unless the fermentation period is rather extended, or the amount of yeast used is more than 2 per cent, the incorporation of from 2 to 4 per cent of sugar will give satisfactory results as to flavor and color of crust, provided the dough has been otherwise properly handled. When there is a long fermentation period (over 5 hours) or the amount of yeast used exceeds 2 per cent, the amount of sugar used should be correspondingly increased.

Amount of Substitutes to be Used—The use of molasses, syrup, brown sugar, malt, etc., in lieu of white sugar is satisfactory and *often desirable,* especially in dark-colored products such as rye bread, whole wheat bread, or dark-colored cake. It must be borne in mind, however, that syrups, molasses and malt contain from 25 to 35 per cent moisture, while white sugar contains practically no water, so that an additional quantity of the substitute must be used to obtain an equivalent proportion of sugar in a dough. When used in the production of white bread substitutes for white sugar have a tendency to transmit their dark color to the crumb of the finished loaf.

(23) SHORTENING

Shortening is the fat or oil added to a dough. It gives the finished product "shortness," that is, the property of breaking and crushing easily, and produces a soft, velvety crumb.

KINDS—If liquid at ordinary room temperature, a shortening is called an oil; if solid at room temperature, it is called a fat. Among the oils are cottonseed, peanut, corn, and olive. Among the fats are lard and lard substitutes (such as the hydrogenized vegetable fats or margarines). Lard is rendered hog fat. Lard substitute is either all vegetable fat or a combination of vegetable and animal fats. Butter is also considered as a shortening but its high cost in comparison with other shortenings precludes its use in commercial bread making, although it makes a delicious product.

Use in a Bread Dough—Shortening in a solid form (fat) is preferred to shortening in oil form for the reason that measurements are more easily and accurately made. In liquid form, part of the shortening tends to adhere to the sides and bottom of the measuring container. There is very little preference between lard and lard substitutes. It is thought by some that lard imparts a superior flavor to bread, but the quantity ordinarily used is so small that any superiority is difficult, if not impossible, to detect by the average consumer. If lard substitutes can be obtained at a cheaper cost than lard, they should be used as the shortening for bread doughs.

Effect On Bakery Products—Shortening imparts desirable chewing quality to bread. The smooth, pleasing crust and the soft velvety crumb are to a certain extent obtained by the proper use and handling of shortening in a dough. A finished loaf of bread containing shortening will retain its freshness for a longer period of time than one without, as the presence of shortening tends to lessen the loss of evaporation of water from baked goods. Shortening is the most concentrated food known, therefore, its incorporation in a bread dough increases the energy value of the bread.

Quantity To Be Used—The quantity of shortening to be used depends upon the product to be baked. For soft rolls, sweet doughs, pies, etc., the quantity of shortening used is much greater than for bread. Conversely, for hard rolls, the quantity is lessened. For bread doughs, from 1½ to 3 per cent is ordinarily used; 2 per cent (based on the weight of the flour) being considered the most desirable for home bread. Shortening should be the last ingredient added when mixing a dough as its incorporation at an earlier stage will tend to prevent thorough incorporation of other ingredients, thereby retarding active and uniform fermentation.

Every precaution should be taken to prevent shortening from becoming rancid and to preclude the use of rancid shortening in doughs.

(24) MILK

Milk is one of the few almost complete natural foods. When a notable amount is incorporated in a bread dough, it increases its nutritive value. Whole grain bread becomes very nearly a balanced diet in itself when milk is used in the dough, and the new "reinforced" breads carry this a step further, adding vitamins. Milk also improves the flavor of bread, its appearance (by imparting a golden brown color to crust), and its keeping qualities. Milk may be used not only in its original liquid state, but also in various concentrated forms such as evaporated, sweetened condensed, dried whole and dried skim.

AVERAGE COMPOSITION OF VARIOUS FORMS OF MILK

(Expressed in terms of percentage)

	Water	*Butter-fat*	*Protein*	*Milk Sugar*	*Other Sugars*	*Mineral Matter*
Liquid whole milk	88	3.5	3.25	4.5		0.75
Evaporated milk	72	8	7.25	10.5		1.75
Sweetened condensed milk	31	8	7.25	10.5	41	1.75
Dried whole milk	1.5	27.5	27	38		6
Dried skim milk	2.5	1.5	36.5	51.5		8

From Department of Agriculture, Washington, D. C.

(25) IMPROVERS

Fruits, such as prunes, apricots, oranges, raisins, etc., and other products, such as peanut butter, are occasionally added to a dough to provide variety and impart additional flavor and nourishment to the products. When added to a dough, they should be used in the proportion of from 20 to 30 per cent, based on the weight of flour. The use of smaller quantities would practically nullify the purpose for which they are added and larger quantities might have a deleterious effect on fermentation, loaf volume and texture.

(26) TERMS USED IN BAKING AND THEIR MEANING

BAKING—Cooking in a dry heat.

BATTER—Several ingredients beaten together to form a semiliquid mixture suitable for baking or cooking.

BREAD—The sound product made by baking a dough consisting of a leavened or unleavened mixture of ground grain and/or other clean, sound, edible farinaceous substance, with potable water, and, with or without, the addition of other edible substances.

BUNS—Small cakes or breads, generally round or oval in shape and frequently spiced.

CAKE—Leavened flour mixtures with egg, fat and sugar added.

CARAMEL—A syrup made from scorched sugar used for coloring food products.

CARAWAY SEED—A highly aromatic seed used whole for flavoring rye bread of certain types. Also used in cooking.

CORN BREAD—A bread prepared from corn meal, with flour, sugar, lard (or substitute), and baking powder.

CRULLERS—Ring-shaped cakes of dough, usually sweetened and fried brown in smoking fat.

CRUMB—The soft inner part of the loaf as distinguished from the crust.

CRUST—The outside of a loaf of bread. It is formed by the intense baking heat and consequent drying of the surface. This drying and a certain chemical change in the starch are known as caramelization. In the crust the gluten has hardened or gummed and the starch has changed into a more digestible form.

CURRANT BUNS—Buns with currants added.

DOUGH—A name given to the unbaked product resulting when flour, water, yeast, salt, and other ingredients are combined by mixing.

DOUGH MIXER—A machine for mixing ingredients. It should be kept thoroughly cleaned.

DOUGHNUTS—A sweet, round dough composition with center cut out, fried in deep fat.

DREDGE—To sprinkle, as with pepper and salt, or rub in, as with flour, etc.

FERMENTATION—A chemical change in organic substances caused by micro-organisms.

FERMENTATION PERIOD—The period elapsing between the time dough is mixed and the time it is sent to the oven.

FLOUR—Bolted grain meal.

GEMS OR MUFFINS—Hot breads made from white flour, graham, or corn meal and baked in gem pans. Usually eggs are added.

GLUTEN—That constituent of wheat flour dough which enables the dough to expand and thus retain the fermentation gases. Two elements of flour, distinct from each other in a dry state, unite upon the addition of water to form gluten.

GRITS—Grains, as of wheat, corn, or oats, coarsely ground.

HOMINY—Cracked Indian corn from which the outer husk has been removed.

HOPS—The cured, kiln-dried blossoms of the hop vine, a perennial, climbing plant cultivated in Europe and on the Pacific coast for its blossom. The flavoring element is known as lupulin and can be extracted by boiling 10 or 15 minutes.

ICING—A glazing or coating of sugar, usually mixed with white of egg and suitable flavoring, and applied to cakes. Sometimes called frosting.

INGREDIENTS—A general term describing the factors that constitute a substance. For example, ingredients of bread include flour, water, yeast, salt, sugar, shortening, and in some instances milk, hop tea or malt.

LEAVEN—A piece of old dough used as a ferment in making bread by the left-over process.

LOAF—The characteristic shape of the bread after it has been molded and the baking process is completed.

MAKE-UP PERIOD—The length of time between end of fermentation period and time molded and panned dough is placed aside for raising.

MOLDING—Shaping bread into forms suitable for baking.

NO-TIME DOUGH—A straight dough that has no fermentation period. As soon as the dough is mixed it is molded and panned and then placed in a warm place for proofing.

OVEN—The closed, insulated section of a stove in which bread is baked.

PASTRIES—Food preparations such as cakes, pies, jelly rolls, lady fingers, cookies, plum duff, etc. Sugar, butter, eggs, baking powder and extracts are generally employed in their preparation. Also a short paste, as for pie crusts.

POPPY SEED—The seed of the black or white poppy. Contains about 50 per cent oil. Used for enriching rolls and loaves of Vienna style bread.

PROTEIN—A complex constituent of foods that builds body tissues and muscle. Lean meats, fish, eggs, peanuts and soy beans contain a complete protein. Cereals, peas, beans and lentils have an incomplete protein.

SCALD—As applied to flour, potatoes, etc., to submerge or wet with water at a temperature of 160° F. or more, which is sufficient to dissolve the bands of the starch cells and expose the individual grains composing it to the action of the yeast plant.

SHORT-TIME DOUGH—A dough which, by reason of increased amount of leavening agent and/or temperatures of mixed dough or fermentation, requires a shorter fermentation period than usual.

SHORTENING—Lard, butter, or other fats or oils mixed in bakery products to make them more friable, richer and more crumbly in texture.

SLACK DOUGH—A dough that contains more water or other liquid than is required to make a dough of the proper consistency. It has a tendency to flatten out and to stick to the hands or the mixer.

SPONGE—A dough that contains part of the flour, part of the water, all or part of the yeast and all, part, or none of the other ingredients to be used in making baked products.

SPONGE AND DOUGH PROCESS—A process resulting from the combining of a fermented sponge with the remainder of the ingredients to be used and mixing same. A sponge and dough necessitates at least two mixing periods, that is, the mixing of the sponge ingredients and the mixing of the fermented sponge with the other ingredients to form the sponge and dough.

STIFF DOUGH—A dough that contains less water or other liquid than is required to make a dough of proper consistency. It is hard to handle, especially when hand-mixed. Generally used to overcome deficiencies in flour.

STRAIGHT DOUGH PROCESS—A process whereby a dough is obtained by mixing together at one time all the ingredients to be used.

TEMPERATURE—"The degree or intensity of sensible heat." A condition that pertains to heat or cold; that is, the relative degree of each. This is one of the most important factors in bread making and must be taken into consideration in connection with the yeast, water, dough, sponge, fermentation development or retardation, bake ovens, etc.

UNFERMENTED BREAD—This includes all breads made without yeast, such as aerated bread, crackers, baking powder biscuits, etc.

(27) METHODS OF MIXING AND THE RISING OF HOMEMADE BREAD

THE SPONGE—Local tradition and taste peculiarity determine the character of many homemade breads. New England has its steamed Boston brown and its extra crusty spider corn bread, made in an old-fashioned frying pan. The South has its batter bread, sometimes baked according to Chief Justice Marshall's family recipe. The "Tall-Corn Belt" smacks its lips over fresh corn bread (and many sections recall pioneer days with hoe cakes no longer baked on the blade of a hoe). But the entire nation of homemakers unites in making the palate-proved favorite, old-fashioned white bread.

In the last few decades "store breads" have almost entirely replaced home-baked bread, particularly in urban communities. But the era of Wednesday and Saturday bread making has not entirely passed; America's private kitchens, especially in rural districts where "rising time" does not weigh so heavily on the housewife's conscience, still regularly witness the sacred rites of bread making.

The "makings" are simple—white flour, water, salt, yeast, and sometimes milk instead of, or mixed with, water. Although the methods have differed, that formula has been used for ages by bakers, both at home and in shops. Yet the domestic entrepreneur among her ingredients today, in spite of gas, electric or coal stove ovens, really has no more assurance of success than did her great-grandmother. Bread making is a skill, and its results are the logical outgrowth of the cook's deftness in mixing, kneading, letting rise and baking.

A warm bowl receives the sifted flour and salt. The yeast is creamed separately in warm water. Then the skilled housewife pours the yeast into a hollow made in the flour, stirs in enough flour to make a thick batter, sprinkles a little more on top, and sets the sponge in a warm place to rise, always covered with a dry, clean, light cloth. When the sponge has risen and bubbled, she mixes in the rest of the flour and enough warm water or milk to make a soft dough. She flours a board and flours her hands. The dough is ready for the kneading, the process that thoroughly distributes the yeast, breaks up the bubbles, and works the leavening gas evenly through the dough to make a fine-grained bread.

The covered dough is set aside again in a warm place until it is twice its original size or bulk, and has little cracks all over the surface, after which it is ready for a second light kneading before being shaped into loaves and put in greased tins.

If the homemaker is especially wise, she will know that new baking tins should be baked blue in the oven before they are consecrated to their use.

Baking requires as meticulous care as mixing and kneading. The bread should continue to rise for fifteen minutes after being placed in the hot oven; then it should begin to brown. After twenty minutes of browning (or thereabouts, according to directions), the oven's heat must be reduced. The last fifteen minutes fill the kitchen with that new-baking smell which is sweeter than the aroma of Elysium's finest flowers. Then the crusty brown loaves are taken from the oven and allowed to cool. The baking is done. The bread is ready for the waiting family and guests.

Yeast breads must be allowed to take their time; never make them in a hurry. Unless you have experimented you cannot realize the difference in the flavor, volume, tenderness and texture between a bread dough allowed to rise slowly and gently and a dough quickened by the use of too much yeast or heat.

For normal plain homemade yeast breads, four to six hours should be allowed from mixing time to serving time; one cake of yeast should be allowed to 3 to 6 cups of flour; the room temperature should be around 80 to 85° F. Many kitchens, during the working day, have this as a steady temperature, but if your kitchen is drafty or really cool, place the bowl containing the yeast dough in a bowl of warm water, about 90° F. (the same temperature as the milk you heat for rennet custard) during the rising period. But do not set it over a too-hot oven or on a very hot radiator, or you will never realize the goodness of yeast bread.

Baking Powder Biscuit Recipes

MABEL

. . . She is not gracious as my mammy was,
I am not "Lamb" or "Honey" child to her,
And sullen blood runs strong in her because
She is not now a queen in Africa.
Still she ranks high with me as a magician
For her hot biscuits, chicken pie and crullers
Are just as much an art as that of Titian,
Her cooking would have satisfied Lucullus.
—*Harriet Gray Blackwell*

BISCUIT RECIPES

(28) A FEW GOOD HINTS ABOUT BISCUITS

Butter always gives a characteristic flavor that most gourmets find palatable. If the cost of butter is prohibitive, it is possible sometimes to use half butter and half other fat.

The shortening in biscuit dough is cut into the flour mixture with a fork, two knives or a pastry blender until the mixture resembles coarse meal, or it may be blended in with tips of the fingers. It is important to have the mixture cool. If it is warm the fat melts and melted fat makes less tender products. Flakiness and tenderness depend upon the shortening being distributed in very thin layers between the layers of flour. This is best accomplished when cold fat is used.

Generally biscuit dough which is stirred up in a few minutes is the best. Just enough milk, fruit juice or even water to hold the mixture together nicely, should be added quickly. The dough then is put on a floured board and patted out or kneaded only two or three times to make it smooth enough to handle.

All hot breads, such as biscuits, should be served as soon as they come out of the oven if they are to be at their best.

In making biscuits the flour is sifted before measuring. It is then combined with the salt and baking powder and sifted again so that baking powder and salt are evenly distributed in the flour.

The quality of baking powder biscuits is determined largely by the kneading of the dough. The least possible handling (stirring for drop biscuits, just enough to moisten the ingredients and then dropping the dough on a baking sheet) produces tender, crisp biscuits.

The same dough spread on a board, cut and baked, produces even, crusty, flat biscuits. Dough which receives 15 to 18 strokes of kneading produces tall, light, flaky, tender biscuits. Too much kneading results in tough, flat, close-grained biscuits because the gluten in the flour is developed to the point of toughness. Some of the leavening is lost. Folding and rolling the dough several times produces flakier biscuits than kneading it on the board. The less flour added to the dough on the rolling board the better.

Biscuit dough may be varied many ways. Try adding grated cheese . . . or a couple of tablespoons of minced parsley, minced cress, minced onion . . . or chopped pimiento . . . or substitute one-half cup of hot mashed potatoes for a half cup of the flour in the basic recipe . . . or use tomato, spinach, beet or any other kind of juice as the liquid in making biscuit. Cut biscuit dough in rounds or with a doughnut cutter; or cut into pie-shaped wedges, squares, diamonds or any fancy shape desired.

To reheat biscuits put them into a wet paper bag, tie up tightly and place in a moderate oven.

To a biscuit, add sugar, fruit, jam or candied citrus peel—and you have a quick and good dessert. Add cheese—and you have a salad accompaniment or an afternoon snack.

Baking powder biscuits should be placed two-thirds to an inch apart on the baking pans. This gives them room for expansion during rising and baking.

To make tasty tea biscuits add chopped candied fruit or peel to your regular biscuit dough. The fruit may be placed inside or on top of the mixture before it is baked. Candied ginger, too, may be used.

To make biscuits for breakfast or after-school snacks, sprinkle a sugar and cinnamon mixture generously over the top of them before placing in the oven. Watch them disappear.

Cut an extra pan of biscuits when baking and place in the refrigerator; cover with wax paper and the next morning you can slip them into your oven while preparing breakfast. A real treat with no precious minutes lost in preparation.

When baking biscuits for tea time, by way of variety press into center of each a sugar dot which has been dipped in fruit juice, marmalade, jam or preserve.

Biscuits need a hot oven and naturally the smaller they are the quicker they will bake. As soon as they are out of the oven they should be served, so that the butter will melt when they are split and buttered.

The best amount of shortening or butter for biscuits is two level tablespoons for each cup of flour. Do not be stingy; even three tablespoons will do no harm.

You may add a half cup of cut seedless or seeded raisins before milk is added. Cheese added to a biscuit mixture should be finely grated or sieved or added to flour with shortening.

For shortcakes and dumplings, increase shortening to five level tablespoons and add one-quarter cup sugar to each two cups flour. To prepare shortcakes (old-fashioned), divide dough in half and pat into two rounds to fit pie pan, individual tartlet molds or shallow pan. Butter and put other half on top. After baking, the two rounds, or what have you, can be separated easily.

Sprinkle poppy seeds over baking powder biscuits. First brush with slightly beaten egg whites.

Too much has been said, too many jests have been repeated about the bride's biscuits. The considerate bride will experiment in private, keeping any unfortunate results a secret between herself and the ashcan; but, in the meantime, there is no reason why she may not serve hot bread, since most good biscuit recipes cannot fail, if followed to the letter, with special attention to oven temperature (450° F. hot oven) for 12–15 minutes.

Brown biscuits may be made by spreading the rolled biscuit dough with melted butter and then with brown sugar. Roll up like a jelly roll and cut in one-inch slices. Place in a buttered pan and bake in a quick oven (425° F.) for 12 to 15 minutes. Serve as hot as possible.

Add one cup mashed bananas to any biscuit recipe, using two cups whole wheat flour, and adding raisins or nuts. You have a delicious little cake to eat with stewed fruit, or for breakfast, especially on Sunday.

BAKING POWDER BISCUIT RECIPES

(29) AFTERNOON CHEESE-DATE BISCUITS

Mix a Standard Baking Powder Biscuit Recipe No. 36. Roll the biscuit dough lightly to ¼-inch in thickness. Cut in rounds and spread with butter, grated cheese and chopped seeded dates. Fold over, press edges together, brush tops with milk and bake as for plain biscuits.

(30) AFTERNOON MACE BAKING POWDER BISCUITS

Mix a Standard Baking Powder Biscuit Recipe No. 36, adding a blade or two of mace (¼–½ teaspoon) to the dough. Shape and cut and bake as directed.

(31) AFTERNOON TEA DATE AND HONEY BISCUIT SLICES

Approximately 12 slices. Oven temperature: 425° F.
Baking time: 20 minutes.

2 cups sifted bread flour
2 teaspoons baking powder
¾ teaspoon salt
¼ cup shortening
¾ cup milk (about)
Filling as below

Sift flour once; measure; add baking powder and salt and sift once more. Cut in shortening using a pastry blender or a fork. Add milk gradually and mix lightly. Turn dough onto a lightly floured board and knead gently about 15 times. Roll dough to ¼-inch in thickness and spread with honey-date filling. Roll up like a jelly roll and cut in ¾-inch slices. Place cut side down on greased baking sheet and bake in a hot oven as directed.

Honey-Date Filling—Cream together ¼ cup butter and 2 tablespoons of honey. Stir in ¼ cup of nut meats, coarsely ground, and ½ cup sliced dates. Spread on the dough and roll up as directed.

(32) AFTERNOON TEA MOLASSES-NUT BISCUITS

Approximately 8–10 biscuits. Oven temperature: 400° F.
Baking time: 15 minutes.

3 tablespoons melted butter
½ cup molasses
¼ teaspoon cinnamon
½ cup pecans
2 cups sifted bread flour
3 teaspoons baking powder
½ teaspoon salt
¼ cup shortening
¼ cup milk

Combine melted butter, molasses and ground cinnamon and put ½ tablespoon in eight muffin pans. To the flour add baking powder and salt and sift once. Cut in the shortening to make a coarse grained mixture; then add cold milk gradually, and stir it rapidly. Turn out on lightly floured board and knead about 25 seconds. Roll into an oblong 6 × 12 inches. Spread with remaining molasses mixture and sprinkle with chopped nuts. Roll up from the long side and cut roll into 1½-inch lengths. Place cut side down in greased muffin pans. Bake in a hot oven as directed.

(33) AMERICAN CHEESE BAKING POWDER BISCUITS

Approximately 24 biscuits. Oven temperature: 450° F.
Baking time: 10–12 minutes.

2 cups sifted bread flour
2 teaspoons baking powder
⅝ teaspoon salt
2 tablespoons shortening
1 cup grated American cheese
¾ cup milk (about)

To the flour add baking powder and salt and sift together. Cut in shortening and cheese, then add milk gradually until dough is soft. Turn dough onto floured board and knead 25 seconds. Roll out ¼-inch in thickness and cut with floured biscuit cutter. Bake on ungreased baking sheet in a hot oven as directed.

Very fine to serve hot with a green salad.

(34) AMERICAN CHEESE BISCUIT WREATH

Approximately 6 servings. Oven temperature: 425° F.
Baking time: about 25 minutes.

2 cups sifted bread flour
3 teaspoons baking powder
5/8 teaspoon salt
1/2 teaspoon curry powder
1/2 cup butter or margarine
1/2 cup milk
3/4 cup grated American cheese

To the flour add baking powder, salt and curry powder and sift twice. Cut in butter or margarine, then add milk to make a soft dough. Knead about 20 seconds on lightly floured board. Roll out to 1/2-inch in thickness. Sprinkle generously with grated American cheese, then carefully roll up like a jelly roll, and bring the two ends together forming a wreath or ring. Place on baking sheet, and with sharp scissors, cut the roll in sections about 2 inches apart, cutting from the outside of the ring 2/3 of the way toward the center. Turn over each section so that the cut side is placed on the baking sheet, resembling a Swedish yeast tea ring. Bake in a hot oven as directed. Serve as hot as possible.

(35) BACON BAKING POWDER BISCUITS

Approximately 16 biscuits. Oven temperature: 450° F.
Baking time: 15 minutes.

Mix a Standard Baking Powder Biscuit Recipe No. 36, doubling the amount of ingredients. Roll biscuit dough very thin and cut into large rounds. Place half a strip of bacon on each one. Moisten edge and turn dough over bacon, pressing together with the tines of a fork. Brush with milk and bake on ungreased sheet in a hot oven as directed. Serve sizzling hot. Fine for breakfast, afternoon tea or with a green salad.

(36) BAKING POWDER BISCUIT—STANDARD RECIPE

Approximately 15 biscuits. Oven temperature: 450° F.
Baking time: 12 to 15 minutes.

2 cups sifted bread flour
3 teaspoons baking powder
1/2 teaspoon salt
1/4 cup shortening
3/4 cup milk (about)

To the flour add the baking powder and salt and sift together. Cut in shortening with two knives or pastry blender until the consistency of coarse corn meal. Stir in the milk to make a soft dough; then turn dough out on slightly floured board and knead for ½ minute. Roll out to about ½ inch in thickness. Cut in 2-inch rounds with floured biscuit cutter and bake on ungreased pan in a hot oven as directed.

(37) BAKING POWDER BISCUIT HEARTS

In the Standard Baking Powder Biscuit Recipe (No. 36), add to the dough, before adding the milk, 1 teaspoon each of finely minced parsley, chives and green onion tops. Proceed as directed for recipe and bake as indicated after cutting the rolled dough with a small heart-shaped cutter.

Appropriate for St. Patrick's Day with a green salad.

(38) BAKING POWDER DROP BISCUITS

Number varies with size of biscuits dropped.

Proceed as indicated for Standard Baking Powder Biscuit Recipe No. 36, having the dough slightly softer (⅞ to 1 cup milk). Drop from teaspoon or tablespoon onto ungreased baking sheet and bake 12 to 15 minutes in a hot oven (450° F.).

(39) BAKING POWDER SWEET POTATO BISCUITS

Approximately 15 biscuits. Oven temperature: 450° F.
Baking time: 15–20 minutes.

A fine way to use left-over cooked sweet potatoes.

¾ cup cooked mashed sweet potatoes
⅔ cup milk
¼ cup butter, melted
1¼ cups sifted bread flour, resifted
4 tablespoons baking powder and
1 tablespoon brown sugar, and
⅝ teaspoon salt

Combine potatoes, milk and melted butter and blend thoroughly. To the flour add the remaining ingredients and sift together, then blend with the potato mixture, making a soft dough. Turn onto lightly floured board and toss until smooth. Roll out to ½-inch in thickness; cut with floured biscuit cutter; place on ungreased baking sheet, and bake as directed.

(40) BISCUITS BAKED AT TABLE

Make a Standard Baking Powder Biscuit No. 36, a trifle softer and richer than usual. Preheat waffle iron about 6 minutes. Drop a spoonful of dough on each grid and bake 3 minutes. Serve hot. For variety, add 1/4 cup grated cheese to the dough with the flour. A fine biscuit recipe for late supper.

(41) BRAN BUTTERMILK BISCUITS

Approximately 1 dozen biscuits. Oven temperature: 450° F.
Baking time: 12–15 minutes.

Add 1/2 cup of breakfast bran to 3/4 cup of buttermilk and let stand while assembling other ingredients:

1 1/2 cups sifted bread flour
1 teaspoon baking powder
3/4 teaspoon salt
1/2 teaspoon soda
1/3 cup shortening
Buttermilk mixture

To the flour add baking powder, salt and soda and sift again. Cut in the shortening until mixture resembles fine meal; then add the buttermilk-bran mixture and mix until the dough follows the wooden spoon around the bowl. Turn out onto lightly floured board and knead lightly for about 20 seconds. Roll out one-half inch thick and cut with floured biscuit cutter. Bake on a lightly greased baking sheet in a hot oven as directed.

Should you like them a little sweet, you may add to the dry ingredients before sifting, 1 tablespoon of sugar. Should you prefer to use sweet milk instead of buttermilk, omit soda and increase baking powder to 3 teaspoons.

(42) BUCKWHEAT AFTERNOON TEA BISCUITS

Approximately 18 biscuits. Oven temperature: 400° F.
Baking time: 20–25 minutes.

These biscuits are made with yeast and should be served very hot.

1 yeast cake
1/2 cup water, lukewarm
1/4 cup butter, melted
2/3 cup milk, scalded, cooled
2/3 cup water, lukewarm
2 tablespoons molasses
1 1/2 cups sifted buckwheat
3 1/2 cups sifted bread flour
2 tablespoons sugar
1 1/4 teaspoons salt
Melted butter
Chopped nut meats

Crumble yeast cake in the ½ cup lukewarm water. Combine melted butter with lukewarm milk, the ⅔ cup lukewarm water and molasses, and blend thoroughly, then stir in the dissolved yeast. Keep in a warm place.

Combine buckwheat flour, bread flour, sugar and salt and sift twice. Now combine the first liquid mixture with the dry one and mix thoroughly. Toss upon lightly floured board and knead 1 minute or until smooth and velvety. Place in greased bowl, cover with a dry cloth and let rise to double its bulk. Punch down and let it double again. Punch again, then pinch small balls about 1½ inches in size, roll in floured hands, then in melted butter. Place close together on ungreased baking sheet; let rise and bake in hot oven as directed above. Remove from the oven and immediately brush tops with egg whites, slightly beaten, and sprinkle finely chopped nut meats (any kind, even almonds) over tops. Place under the flame of broiling oven and brown slightly.

(43) BUTTERMILK BISCUITS

Approximately 1½ dozen biscuits. Oven temperature: 450° F. Baking time: 12 minutes.

2 cups sifted bread flour
2 teaspoons baking powder
¼ cup shortening
¾ cup buttermilk
½ teaspoon salt
¼ teaspoon soda

To the flour, add baking powder, salt and soda. Sift once. Cut in shortening until mixture resembles coarse meal. Make a depression in center and add buttermilk; mix lightly with fork to make a soft dough. Toss and knead dough on lightly floured board until smooth (about half a minute). Roll out dough ½-inch thick; cut with floured biscuit cutter; place on ungreased baking sheet and bake in a hot oven as directed. Serve warm with butter, jam, marmalade or preserves.

(44) BUTTERSCOTCH BISCUITS

Approximately 1 dozen biscuits. Oven temperature: 450° F. Baking time: 12–15 minutes.

Make a Standard Baking Powder Biscuit as in recipe No. 36. Roll out and spread with a mixture made of ¼ cup butter and ¾ cup brown sugar; fold over and roll again to ½ scant inch in thickness; cut with floured biscuit cutter and bake in a hot oven as directed.

(45) CARAWAY SEED BISCUITS

Approximately 1 dozen biscuits. Oven temperature: 450° F. Baking time: 12–15 minutes.

Make a Standard Baking Powder Biscuit as in recipe No. 36. Roll out very thin; cut with floured biscuit cutter, brush each round with melted butter and sprinkle half of the rounds with caraway seed. Cover with the unseeded rounds; sprinkle caraway seed on top and bake in a hot oven as directed.

(46) CHEESE BISCUITS

Cheese biscuits are no more than the usual baking powder biscuit with a teaspoon of cheese and butter melted together and placed on top of each one before baking. Or add 1 cup grated cheese to flour blended with shortening. These biscuits require no butter when served, and this also recommends them for passing with salads at late suppers or whenever something piquant and dainty is needed to accompany a dish.

A good suggestion is to cream equal amounts of butter, cream cheese, and a few ground nut meats and drop by spoonfuls on top of biscuit rounds. Chill in refrigerator a few hours. Bake 12 to 15 minutes in a hot oven (450° F.).

(47) CHEESE AND RAISIN BISCUITS

Approximately 1 dozen biscuits. Oven temperature: 400° F. Baking time: 15 minutes.

⅔ cup seedless raisins
2 cups sifted bread flour
4 teaspoons baking powder
½ teaspoon ground mace
½ teaspoon salt
6 tablespoons grated Swiss cheese
3 tablespoons lard
1 cup milk
1 teaspoon prepared mustard

Wash raisins in hot water; then scald them until plump and drain thoroughly. Sift flour with baking powder, mace and salt. Add raisins and Swiss cheese, and cut in lard as for Standard Baking Powder Biscuits (No. 36). Now add the cold milk mixed with the mustard. Knead a few seconds upon lightly floured board; roll out to ½-inch in thickness; cut with floured biscuit cutter and bake on ungreased baking sheet as directed. Serve warm.

(48) CHIVES BISCUITS

FRENCH METHOD

Approximately 24 biscuits. Oven temperature: 450° F.
Baking time: 15 minutes.

4 cups sifted bread flour
4 teaspoons baking powder
2 teaspoons (scant) salt
6 tablespoons butter
5 tablespoons minced chives
1⅓ cups rich milk

To the flour add baking powder and salt and sift once. Cut in the butter, alternately with finely minced chives. Add milk, to which has been added a tiny bit of garlic (or the container may be rubbed with a cut clove of garlic), gradually and slowly, mixing just enough to make a soft dough. Toss out on lightly floured board. Pat and roll out about ½-inch in thickness. Cut with floured biscuit cutter and bake in a hot oven as directed.

Delicious with cheese, especially Camembert, Roquefort, Gorgonzola or Brie.

(49) CLABBER RYE BISCUITS

Approximately 16 biscuits. Oven temperature: 425° F.
Baking time: 20–25 minutes.

NOTE: No baking powder is used; the soda does the work.

1½ cups sifted rye flour
½ cup sugar
1 scant teaspoon salt
⅞ teaspoon soda
2½ cups clabber (pot cheese)
1½ cups sifted white flour

To mixed rye and white flours add sugar, salt and soda and sift twice. Make a hole in center of the dry mixture and pour in the clabber; gradually bring in the flour mixture, using a fork, then beat until well mixed. The batter should be soft. Drop by tablespoonfuls upon slightly greased baking sheet, and bake in a hot oven as directed. Serve warm.

(50) COOKED MEAT BISCUITS

The problem of utilizing left-overs to avoid waste is one that bothers many homemakers. It is almost impossible when planning meals to calculate so closely that no odds and ends of meats remain.

In fact, many homemakers count on them. Late snack sandwiches may be hearty or delicate, according to the taste of your family or guests, but the following biscuits are "tops," and you may prepare them ahead of time, and when ready to serve heat them a little, or in hot weather eat them cold. Here's how:

Make the regular Standard Baking Powder Biscuits No. 36. Knead gently for 30 seconds. Roll out on lightly floured board to ¼-inch in thickness. Brush with melted butter and spread with ground cooked meat, any kind or even several kinds mixed (or use some of the canned spreads). All in all, use 1 cup of ground meat. Roll as for jelly roll and cut in one-inch slices. Place on buttered baking pan and bake in moderately hot oven as directed. You may bake the slices in greased muffin pans.

(51) CORN MEAL BREAKFAST BISCUITS

Approximately 16 small biscuits. Oven temperature: 450° F.
Baking time: 15 minutes.

¾ cup sifted corn meal
1¼ cups sifted bread flour
4 teaspoons baking powder
1 teaspoon salt
¼ cup shortening
¾ cup milk (about)

Combine corn meal and bread flour with baking powder and salt (a half teaspoon sugar may be added) and sift once. Cut in shortening, using fork or 2 knives or pastry blender, until mixture is coarse and all the dry ingredients are moistened. Add enough milk to make a soft dough. Turn onto lightly floured board and knead 30 seconds. Roll out ½-inch thick. Cut with a 2-inch floured biscuit cutter; place on a greased baking sheet, and bake in a hot oven as directed. Serve hot with butter.

(52) COTTAGE CHEESE BISCUITS COUNTRY STYLE

Approximately 12 biscuits. Oven temperature: 450° F.
Baking time: 10–12 minutes.

1 cup cottage cheese, sieved
2 tablespoons thin cream
1 egg, beaten
A pinch of ground thyme
2 tablespoons butter, softened
2 cups sifted bread flour
½ teaspoon salt
4 teaspoons baking powder

Cream together cottage cheese, butter, egg and cream. Combine the flour with salt, ground thyme and baking powder. Make a hole in the flour mixture and damp in the cottage cheese mixture. Gradually blend, starting from the center and bringing down the flour mixture from the edge, making a soft dough. Turn out on lightly floured board, knead 30 seconds, then roll out to ½ inch in thickness. Cut with floured biscuit cutter; place on ungreased baking sheet, and bake in a hot oven as directed. Serve warm.

(53) CREAM BISCUITS

Approximately 1½ dozen biscuits. Oven temperature: 425° F. Baking time: 12 minutes.

NOTE: In this recipe no shortening is used, the richness of the whipped heavy cream taking its place. These rich biscuits may be served for afternoon tea or coffee, and you may sprinkle the tops with shaved maple sugar before baking.

2 cups sifted bread flour
3 teaspoons baking powder
¾ teaspoon salt
1 cup heavy cream, whipped

To the sifted flour add baking powder and salt and sift twice into a mixing bowl. Make a hole in center, pour in the whipped cream and fold thoroughly into the flour as you would in folding whipped cream into a cake mixture. Turn upon a floured board; knead 30 seconds. Pat or roll out ½ inch in thickness. Cut with a 2-inch floured biscuit cutter, place on an ungreased baking sheet and bake in a hot oven as directed. Serve warm with jam, marmalade, preserves or jelly.

(54) CREAM CHEESE BISCUITS

Approximately 18 small biscuits. Oven temperature: 425° F. Baking time: 15 minutes.

This recipe is quite different from No. 46, the cream cheese being mixed into the dough before baking. For a variation, you may add a heaping tablespoon of chopped almonds or mixed candied fruit when kneading the dough. Then these rich biscuits become a real sweetmeat. No baking powder used.

1 cup sifted bread flour
½ teaspoon salt
1 three-ounce package cream cheese
½ cup butter

Add salt to the flour; then sift twice. Add cream cheese, creamed or sieved with the butter and blend thoroughly. Toss upon lightly floured board and knead 30 seconds. Shape into a flat cake and roll out to ¼ inch in thickness. Cut with floured biscuit cutter; place on ungreased baking sheet and bake in a hot oven as directed. Serve warm.

(55) CREAM BISCUITS CLUB STYLE

NO BAKING POWDER IS USED IN THIS RECIPE

Approximately 15 biscuits. Oven temperature: 400° F.
Baking time: 15 minutes.

1 cup sifted bread flour
1 teaspoon salt
1 teaspoon soda
2½ teaspoons cream of tartar
1½ cups unwhipped sweet heavy cream
Additional sifted flour as needed

To the flour add salt, soda and cream of tartar and sift twice. Stir into this the unwhipped sweet heavy cream, adding more sifted flour if necessary to make a soft dough that can be handled. Toss upon lightly floured board and knead 30 seconds. Pat and roll to ⅜ inch in thickness. Cut out with floured biscuit-cutter; arrange on an ungreased baking sheet; brush with cold milk and bake in a hot oven as directed.

(56) CURRIED BISCUITS

DROPPED BISCUITS

Approximately 18 small biscuits. Oven temperature: 425° F.
Baking time: 12 minutes.

Exceedingly fine with lamb cooked in any style, shortcakes made of left-over meat, etc.

1 cup sifted bread flour
1½ teaspoons baking powder
½ teaspoon salt
1 generous teaspoon curry powder
2 generous tablespoons butter
½ cup sweet milk (about)

To the flour add baking powder, salt and curry powder, and sift twice. Cut in the butter to a coarse-grained meal and add the milk. (The original recipe requires coconut milk, so if you have some on hand you may use it.) Blend to a soft dough and drop by spoonfuls onto a greased baking sheet. Bake in a hot oven as directed. Serve hot. Split the hot biscuits, butter generously and fill with a mixture of creamed meat, poultry, mushrooms, etc.

(57) DATE GRAHAM BISCUITS

DROPPED BISCUITS

Approximately 1 dozen biscuits. Oven temperature: 425° F.
Baking time: 12–15 minutes.

1 cup sifted bread flour
3 teaspoons baking powder
½ teaspoon salt
2 tablespoons brown sugar
1 cup graham flour, unsifted
6 tablespoons shortening
¾ cup dates, pitted, chopped
¾ cup milk (about)

To the flour add baking powder and salt and sift once. Combine brown sugar and graham flour and add to bread flour mixture. Cut in shortening until mixture is as fine as corn meal. Add chopped dates and mix well. Stir in milk with a fork, adding enough to make a soft, sticky dough. Drop from teaspoon onto lightly greased baking sheet an inch apart and bake in a hot oven as directed. Serve warm.

(58) DATE AND NUT BISCUITS

Approximately 14 biscuits. Oven temperature: 450° F.
Baking time: 12–15 minutes.

Make Standard Baking Powder Biscuits No. 36. After stirring in the milk, add ½ cup each of chopped dates and nut meats previously floured. Bake in very hot oven as directed.

(59) ENGLISH TEA BISCUITS

Approximately 15 biscuits. Oven temperature: 450° F.
Baking time: 12–15 minutes.

2 cups sifted bread flour
1½ teaspoons baking powder
½ generous teaspoon salt
5 tablespoons butter
½ cup rich milk (about)
1 rounded teaspoon grated orange rind
1 egg yolk, beaten
4 tablespoons orange juice (about)
Melted butter

To the flour add baking powder and salt and sift twice. Cut in the butter until mixture is as fine as corn meal. Remove about ⅓ of the dough from the mixing bowl and set aside. Into the remaining two-thirds, gradually stir just enough (about ½ cup) milk to make a soft but not sticky dough. Toss onto lightly floured board; knead about 30 seconds, then roll out to ½-inch in thickness.

Into the third part set aside, stir the grated orange rind, mixed with the egg yolk and orange juice (just enough to make a soft dough). Roll this third part upon a lightly floured board to ½ inch in thickness and place in center of the plain biscuit dough. Fold ends over to cover the yellow third of dough, envelope-style, then roll out to ½ inch in thickness. Cut with floured biscuit-cutter, place on ungreased baking sheet and brush tops with melted butter. Bake in very hot oven as directed. Serve hot. These delicious biscuits are very popular in England and are usually served for afternoon tea with jam, marmalade or jelly.

(60) HAM AND CORN BISCUIT SQUARES LUNCHEON

A REAL NOON MEAL

Approximately 6 servings. Oven temperature: 450° F. Baking time: 18–20 minutes.

2 cups sifted bread flour
4 teaspoons baking powder
½ teaspoon salt
¼ cup shortening
6 tablespoons cold celery water
6 slices boiled ham
9 tablespoons canned whole kernel yellow corn
1 tablespoon butter
¼ teaspoon salt
A pinch of pepper
1 rounded tablespoon butter
1 rounded tablespoon flour
1 cup milk
1 teaspoon prepared mustard
2 tablespoons grated cheese

To the flour add baking powder and salt and sift once; cut in the shortening in the usual way and add enough cold celery water (obtained from cooking celery) to make a soft dough. Toss onto lightly floured board and knead 30 seconds. Roll out to ½ inch in thickness and cut into six squares. Heat the canned corn with the butter and season to taste with salt and pepper. Place one slice of boiled ham on each square; spread 1½ tablespoons corn over each; fold the biscuit dough over the ham and corn to form a pocket, pressing tightly around the edges with the tines of a fork. Place on an ungreased baking sheet and bake in a very hot oven as directed. Serve with a cheese-mustard sauce made with the five remaining ingredients. A savory, quickly made luncheon.

(61) HONEY BISCUITS—FARMER'S STYLE

Approximately 1 dozen biscuits. Oven temperature: 450° F. Baking time: 12–15 minutes.

Make Standard Baking Powder Recipe No. 36. Bake as directed. When done, quickly split biscuits in two and spread lower halves with strained honey and upper halves with butter. Put halves together and let stand a few minutes so that the flavor permeates the biscuits.

(62) JAM TEA BISCUITS

Approximately 2 dozen small biscuits. Oven temperature: 450° F. Baking time: 8–10 minutes.

Sift bread flour once, take 2 cups, add 2 teaspoons baking powder and 1/2 teaspoon salt and sift twice. Cut in 4 tablespoons of butter; add gradually 1/2 cup milk, mixed with 1/4 cup orange juice (unstrained), until soft dough is formed. Toss upon lightly floured board and knead 30 seconds. Roll out to 1/4 inch in thickness and cut with small biscuit-cutter (1 3/4 inch) dipped in flour. Place on ungreased baking sheet. Make deep depression in center of top of each biscuit; fill with your favorite jam and bake in a hot oven as directed. Serve hot.

(63) LEMON TEA BISCUITS I

Approximately 2 1/2 dozen biscuits. Oven temperature: 450° F. Baking time: 8–10 minutes.

2 cups sifted bread flour
2 teaspoons baking powder
1/2 teaspoon salt
5 tablespoons butter
1 1/2 teaspoons grated lemon rind
2/3 cup milk
1/4 cup sugar
1 1/2 teaspoons grated lemon rind
1/2 teaspoon *unstrained* lemon juice

To the flour add baking powder and salt and sift twice. Cut in butter in the usual way; add the first lemon rind and blend thoroughly. Now, add the milk gradually and stir until all flour is dampened. Then stir vigorously until mixture forms a soft dough and follows spoon around the bowl. Turn out immediately on slightly floured board and knead 30 seconds. Roll out 1/4 inch thick and cut with 1 1/2 inch floured biscuit-cutter.

Combine sugar, remaining lemon rind and lemon juice to make a crumbly mixture. Place half of biscuits in greased muffin pans, spread them with melted butter and the sugar-lemon mixture and top with remaining biscuits, pressing lightly together. Bake at once in a hot oven as directed.

(64) LEMON TEA BISCUITS II

Approximately 2 dozen biscuits. Oven temperature: 450° F. Baking time: 15 minutes.

In this recipe more unstrained lemon juice is needed and the biscuits are baked on ungreased baking sheet after being brushed with melted butter to which has been added a pinch of cinnamon.

3 cups twice-sifted bread flour
5 teaspoons baking powder
½ teaspoon baking soda
1 tablespoon sugar
1 teaspoon grated lemon rind
4 tablespoons butter
¾ cup rich milk, scalded, cooled
⅓ cup *unstrained* lemon juice
1¼ teaspoons salt

To the flour add baking powder, salt, baking soda and sugar and sift twice again. Stir in the grated lemon rind, then cut in the butter (or margarine) in the usual way. Add combined milk and unstrained lemon juice and stir rapidly to form a soft dough. Turn onto lightly floured board; knead 30 seconds and roll out ½ inch thick. Cut with small floured biscuit-cutter; place upon ungreased baking sheet and bake 15 minutes in a hot oven as directed. Serve warm.

(65) LEMON YEAST BISCUITS—ENGLISH METHOD

Approximately 2 dozen biscuits. Oven temperature: 425° F. Baking time: 18–20 minutes.

1 cup sweet milk, scalded
½ generous teaspoon salt
½ cup sugar
2 tablespoons butter
½ yeast cake
¼ cup water, lukewarm
1 whole egg, well-beaten
3½ cups twice-sifted bread flour
½ generous teaspoon lemon extract
½ cup currants, washed, seeded, dried and floured
Additional bread flour, sifted twice
1 beaten egg yolk

Scald the milk with salt, sugar; cool a little, add butter and let stand until lukewarm. Dissolve ½ yeast cake in lukewarm water and add to milk mixture. Then, stir in beaten egg. Now, stir in the bread flour and mix thoroughly. Flavor with lemon extract and add the prepared currants. Place the dough in a greased bowl; cover with a light dry cloth and let rise in a warm place until doubled in bulk (about 5 or 6 hours). Turn out on lightly floured board and knead 30 seconds, adding enough additional flour to handle the dough easily. Let rise for about 1 hour, then punch, pat and roll to about 1 inch in thickness. Let rise once more for 45 to 50 minutes, then cut with biscuit-cutter, place about 2 inches apart on greased baking sheet and let rise until double in bulk (about 1½ hours). Brush with beaten egg yolk diluted with a little milk and bake in a hot oven as directed. Serve warm or cold.

(66) MARYLAND BEATEN BISCUITS

Approximately 2½ dozen biscuits. Oven temperature: 350° F.
Baking time: 35–40 minutes.

No leavening of any kind is used in these biscuits which when made in the old-fashioned method will keep perfectly fresh for almost a week. Preferably Winter wheat should be used, although any kind will serve. The dough should be wrapped in a clean towel and beaten mercilessly for a half hour with a hatchet, stick, flat iron or solid rolling pin—hard work, but it's what "makes" the biscuits. Down in Maryland, every Saturday morning about 8 a.m. one can hear the thump, thump, as the folks start beating their biscuit dough. Almost every family has a biscuit block, similar to meat blocks seen in butcher shops, only a little smaller. When the dough is beaten out flat, it is folded up again and again and beaten for 25 to 30 minutes, until you can hear the dough snap and crackle. Then it is made into small, round biscuits, the wrist gives them a little push to dent the top and they are pricked with the tines of a floured fork and baked for a long time in a moderate oven.

Here is a modernized method for these delicious biscuits:

2 cups sifted bread flour
½ teaspoon salt
Ice water or chilled milk (as little as possible)
1 tablespoon leaf lard

Add salt to flour and rub in the lard with the hands. Add the iced liquid (water or milk, or equal part of each) to make a very stiff dough, kneading all the time. Wrap the stiff dough in a strong, clean, dry towel and beat hard with either a hatchet, a heavy stick or flat iron, for 25–35 minutes or more, the time depending on the snapping and crackling of the dough. Cut into small biscuits and prick tops with the tines of a fork dipped in flour. Place on ungreased baking sheet, and bake in a moderate oven as directed. Serve hot or cold, usually the latter.

(67) MASHED POTATO BISCUITS

Approximately 1½ dozen biscuits. Oven temperature: 400° F. Baking time: 12–15 minutes.

1 cup cold mashed potatoes
1 cup sifted bread flour
3 tablespoons baking powder
1 scant teaspoon salt
2 tablespoons butter
½ cup cold milk

To the flour add baking powder and salt and sift once. Work in the butter (a little more butter will make the biscuits richer); add the potatoes and blend thoroughly, being careful not to leave any lumps. Then add enough cold milk to make a soft dough. Toss upon a lightly floured board and knead a few seconds (about 12 to 15). Roll out the dough lightly to about ½ inch thickness. Cut with biscuit-cutter and bake on ungreased baking sheet in a hot oven as directed. Serve warm.

(68) MOLASSES DIPPED BISCUITS

Approximately 1 dozen biscuits. Oven temperature: 400° F. Baking time: 12–15 minutes.

Make a batch of Standard Baking Powder Biscuits No. 36. Cut with floured biscuit cutter and proceed as follows:

Combine ½ cup molasses with 2 tablespoons melted butter and mix thoroughly. Turn into a medium-sized shallow baking pan, then arrange the 12 biscuits in the molasses mixture. Bake as directed in a hot oven and serve hot. What happens? During the baking process the molasses mixture is absorbed by the biscuit dough and these biscuits when baked are soft like a molasses bun.

You may substitute honey or maple syrup for molasses if desired.

Speaking of molasses, it is interesting to know how our American molasses is made.

In October, when the cane joints gleam reddish-purple, cane cutting begins. Leaves are stripped from the stalks which are carted to the mills by an army of Negroes sweating, swaying to the rhythm of old plantation songs. Once in the mill, modern machinery does the rest.

Crushers squeeze the juice from the stalks. Only the fiber is left and this is so deprived of its life blood that it comes forth dry as a cactus bed. The juice, impregnated with the very soul of the sugar cane, is purified, then concentrated, different mills using different methods for evaporation. Once the natural sugar crystallizes, the molasses is driven off or in some mills "spun" out. Molasses from this first boiling, amber-clear, is the finest grade.

The molasses subject will be dropped for the moment. Grandma used to spread good homemade bread with butter, then with apple butter "wet up" with molasses. "School days, school days—"

(69) MUSTARD CHEESE BISCUITS

NO BAKING POWDER USED

Approximately 12 biscuits. Oven temperature: 450° F.
Baking time: 15–20 minutes.

2 cups sifted bread flour
1 scant teaspoon baking soda
2 teaspoons cream of tartar
¾ teaspoon salt
¼ teaspoon dry mustard
4 tablespoons butter
1 scant cup grated American cheese
½ teaspoon Worcestershire sauce
⅞ cup milk

To the flour add baking soda, cream of tartar, salt and dry mustard and resift twice. Cut in the butter in the usual way; then add grated cheese and blend thoroughly. Combine Worcestershire sauce and cold milk and stir gradually into the mixture. Mix with a fork until dough barely sticks together. Drop by spoonfuls into greased muffin tins; sprinkle a little grated American cheese over the tops and bake in a very hot oven as directed. Serve at once.

Fine biscuits for a Sunday supper.

(70) NEW ENGLAND HASTY PUDDING BISCUITS

Approximately 2½ dozen biscuits. Oven temperature: 400° F.
Baking time: 20 minutes.

Prepare a Hasty Pudding (Corn Meal Mush) as follows:

1 cup granulated corn meal
1½ cups boiling water
½ cup cold water
¼ teaspoon salt

Make a paste of the corn meal and cold water, stirring until there are no lumps. Pour gradually into the rapidly boiling water, slightly salted, stirring until mixture is thick. Place in top of double boiler and cook over hot water for from 2 to 2¾ hours, stirring frequently from the bottom of the pan.

For the biscuits follow these directions:

4 cups of thick, lukewarm Hasty Pudding
1 yeast cake
½ cup lukewarm water
1 egg, well-beaten
1 tablespoon melted butter
½ teaspoon ground cinnamon
½ teaspoon ground ginger
½ cup molasses
4½ to 5 cups sifted bread flour

Dissolve the yeast cake in lukewarm water; add to the lukewarm Hasty Pudding and mix well. Then stir in the combined beaten egg, butter, spices and molasses. Stir briskly, taking care that there are no lumps. Add enough flour to make a stiff dough. Knead well. Let rise overnight, in a cool place, covered with a towel.

Next day toss onto a lightly floured board; roll out ½ inch in thickness; place on ungreased baking sheet and let rise to twice its bulk. Bake in a hot oven for 10 minutes; brush biscuits with milk, and bake 10 minutes longer until delicately brown. Serve hot.

(71) NEW ORLEANS SHRIMP BISCUITS

Approximately 1 dozen biscuits. Oven temperature: 450° F.
Baking time: 12–15 minutes.

Prepare a batch of Standard Baking Powder Biscuits No. 36 and bake in the usual way, making the biscuit a little larger and thinner than usual. Place on half of the biscuits 2 or 3 tablespoons of creamed shrimps; cover with another biscuit and serve covered with white sauce sprinkled with grated cheese.

(72) OLD-FASHIONED MAPLE SKILLET BISCUITS

Approximately 8 biscuits. Oven temperature: 450° F.
Baking time: 15 minutes.

2 cups sifted bread flour
4 teaspoons baking powder
½ teaspoon salt
4 tablespoons butter
¾ cup milk (about)
1 cup soft maple sugar
2 tablespoons butter, melted
Shaved maple sugar

To the flour add baking powder and salt and sift twice. Cut in the butter, then stir in the milk gradually, adding only enough to make a dough that can be handled easily. Break up the soft maple sugar and add to the dough, working it in as you would the shortening. Toss upon lightly floured board and knead 25 seconds; then roll out to ½ inch in thickness; cut with biscuit cutter; place in a greased skillet closely together, brush with melted butter, and sprinkle with the shaved maple sugar. Bake in a hot oven as directed.

You may fit the rolled dough in one piece into the skillet, if desired, and proceed as above. If maple sugar is not available, slightly lumpy brown sugar may be used.

(73) ORANGE BISCUITS I

Make Standard Baking Powder Biscuits No. 36. Roll out the dough to ¼ inch in thickness, then cut into 1½ inch strips. Grate orange rind over strips and sprinkle with a little sugar. Roll up as you would for jelly roll, place on ungreased baking sheet and bake in a moderate oven (375° F.) for 8 to 10 minutes. Serve with fruit compote or for afternoon tea or coffee.

(74) ORANGE BISCUITS II

Approximately 20 small biscuits. Oven temperature: 450° F.
Baking time: 12–15 minutes.

Make Standard Baking Powder Biscuits No. 36. Cut with small biscuit-cutter. Dip 20 small pieces of square lump sugar in 2 tablespoons of orange juice. Press a piece of sugar into center of each biscuit; sprinkle tops with a bit of grated orange rind and bake in a very hot oven as directed. Serve hot with stewed fruit or custard.
NOTE: You may dip sugar cubes into strong coffee instead of orange juice, if desired. Or, if for a special party, into almost any kind of liqueur.

(75) PARK AVENUE VIRGINIA HAM BISCUITS

Approximately 12 biscuits. Oven temperature: 450° F.
Baking time: 15–20 minutes.

2 cups sifted bread flour
4 teaspoons baking powder
½ scant teaspoon salt
½ cup Virginia ham, ground
3 tablespoons butter
¾ cup milk (about)

To the flour add baking powder and salt and sift twice; mix in the ground Virginia ham thoroughly, then gradually stir in the cold milk, handling as little as possible. Toss onto lightly floured board and knead 25 seconds. Roll out to ½ inch in thickness; cut with floured biscuit-cutter; place on ungreased baking sheet, and bake until golden brown, in a very hot oven as directed.

(76) PEANUT BUTTER BISCUITS I

Approximately 12 biscuits. Oven temperature: 350° F.
Baking time: 12–15 minutes.

2 cups sifted bread flour
4 teaspoons baking powder
½ teaspoon salt
1 tablespoon granulated sugar
1 tablespoon butter
3 generous tablespoons peanut butter
2 whole eggs, well-beaten
Cold milk to make a soft dough

Add baking powder, salt and sugar to the flour and resift twice. Cut in the butter and peanut butter to a coarse meal, then stir in the beaten eggs and enough cold milk to make a soft dough. Blend well, then toss upon lightly floured board and knead 20 seconds. Roll out to ½ inch in thickness and cut with floured biscuit-cutter. Place on ungreased baking sheet, close together, brush tops with beaten egg yolk, and bake in a moderate oven as directed.

Another recipe, much less rich, is as follows:

(77) PEANUT BUTTER BISCUITS II

Use 3 tablespoons butter and 3 tablespoons peanut butter and omit the eggs. Bake as indicated above.

(78) PIMIENTO AND PARSLEY BISCUITS

Approximately 12 biscuits. Oven temperature: 450° F.
Baking time: 12–15 minutes.

In the Standard Baking Powder Biscuit recipe No. 36, add 1½ tablespoons each of minced finely sieved, canned pimiento and parsley to the milk before adding to the dough. Bake as directed.
NOTE: By cutting the dough with a doughnut-cutter and placing the rings on top of stew, you will have a delicious covering and dumpling at the same time.

(79) PIMIENTO CHEESE BISCUITS

Approximately 1 dozen biscuits. Oven temperature: 425° F. Baking time: 12–15 minutes.

Make the Standard Baking Powder Biscuit recipe No. 36 and after placing the cut biscuits on baking sheet, top each biscuit with part of the following mixture:

Mix 4 ounces pimiento cheese with 4 tablespoons butter and melt without browning. Spread over biscuits and bake as directed. About 1 teaspoon should cover the top of each biscuit.

(80) PINWHEEL TEA BISCUITS

Approximately 1 dozen biscuits. Oven temperature: 450° F. Baking time: 12 minutes.

1½ cups sifted bread flour
½ generous teaspoon salt
3½ teaspoons baking powder
3 tablespoons butter
1 egg yolk, beaten and mixed with
½ cup milk
Melted butter

To the flour add salt and baking powder and resift twice. Add butter and mix with tips of fingers. Add beaten egg yolk to milk and stir into the mixture. Mix lightly. Turn out on lightly floured board and knead for 30 seconds, or until smooth. Roll about ¼ inch in thickness; spread with softened, but not melted, butter (peanut butter will give a nutty flavor). Roll up like a jelly roll. Cut in 12 equal slices and bake in muffin pans in a very hot oven as directed.

(81) PIONEER BISCUITS

Approximately 12 biscuits. Oven temperature: 425° F. Baking time: 15 minutes.

1 cup sifted bread flour
1 cup sifted corn meal
4 teaspoons baking powder
½ teaspoon salt
3½ tablespoons bacon fat (solid)
1 whole egg, well-beaten
½ cup cold milk

Combine flour and corn meal; add baking powder and salt and sift once. Cut in the solid bacon fat (bacon drippings solidified) and mix well. Combine egg with milk and add gradually, stirring until all flour mixture is dampened. Turn onto lightly floured board and knead 25 seconds; roll out to 1/3 inch thick; cut with biscuit-cutter; place on ungreased baking sheet, and bake in a hot oven as directed.

(82) RAISIN BISCUITS

*Approximately 12 biscuits. Oven temperature: 425° **F.***
Baking time: 12–15 minutes.

2 cups sifted bread flour
3/4 teaspoon salt
4 teaspoons baking powder
1 cup small seedless raisins
3 tablespoons butter
2 tablespoons lard
3/4 cup cold milk (about)
Melted butter

Combine flour, salt and baking powder and sift once. Cut in butter and lard alternately; then mix in the washed, drained, dried raisins, floured to prevent their falling. Stir in the cold milk gradually, mixing lightly. The dough should be soft and easy to handle. Toss dough onto lightly floured board and knead 15 seconds. Roll out to about 1/3 inch in thickness; cut with floured biscuit-cutter; place on ungreased baking pan; brush with melted butter, and bake in a hot oven as directed.

Many foods shrink during the cooking process, but the dried fruits are a notable exception. The following figures show you how much a pound of the different dried fruits swell and will help you to figure out the amount necessary for their different uses in cookery.

Dried apricots, figs, prunes and raisins double in weight. Dried peaches and pears are almost tripled, and dried apples absorb enough water or liquid to make their cooked bulk five times the original pound.

(83) ROQUEFORT AND MUSTARD BISCUITS

Approximately 12 biscuits. Oven temperature: 450° F.
Baking time: 12–15 minutes.

2 cups sifted bread flour
4 teaspoons baking powder
1/2 generous teaspoon salt
1/2 teaspoon paprika
3 tablespoons butter
1/2 cup crumbled dry Roquefort cheese
2/3 cup of cold milk
2 teaspoons prepared mustard

Combine flour, baking powder, salt and paprika and sift twice. Cut in the butter and add crumbled Roquefort cheese. Mix lightly but thoroughly. Add the milk to which has been added the prepared mustard. Blend well to make a soft dough. Knead 25 seconds on lightly floured board; roll out to ½ inch in thickness; cut with floured biscuit-cutter; place on ungreased baking sheet and bake in a hot oven as directed.

Delicious at the cocktail hour. Split in two after being reheated (if prepared in advance) and fill with a thin slice of smoked salmon or any other smoked fish.

(84) SAVORY SUPPER BISCUITS

Approximately 12 biscuits. Oven temperature: 450° F. Baking time: 12–15 minutes.

Prepare Standard Baking Powder Biscuit No. 36. Before stirring in the milk, add 1 cup cooked, finely chopped, cold, mixed meats or poultry. Then proceed as directed.

(85) SHAMROCK CHEESE BISCUITS

Approximately 12 biscuits. Oven temperature: 400° F. Baking time: 18–20 minutes.

Shamrocks may also be put into the menu by making your hot biscuits and rolls in that shape. A shamrock cookie or biscuit cutter (or the "clubs" cutter from your bridge cookie set) will add a festive touch to the St. Patrick's dinner or luncheon. For more reality, follow this recipe:

2 cups sifted bread flour
4 teaspoons baking powder
½ generous teaspoon salt
4 tablespoons shortening
½ cup grated cheese
2 tablespoons minced parsley
2 tablespoons minced green pepper
¾ cup of milk (about)

To the flour add baking powder and salt, then sift twice. Mix in shortening with fork or pastry blender; add grated cheese, parsley and green pepper, and mix thoroughly. Stir in enough milk to make a soft dough. Roll out on lightly floured board. Pinch off dough and shape into small balls of uniform size. Rub muffin pans with shortening and in each one put three small balls of biscuit dough. Brush with milk, butter or egg yolk. Bake in a hot oven as directed. Serve warm.

(86) SODA BISCUITS—COWBOY FASHION

Approximately 12 biscuits. Oven temperature: 450° F.
Baking time: 12–15 minutes.

As a vital force in the building of the West, the cowboy has ensconced himself in a definite place in American history. He is recognized as an essential citizen of the land, a mainstay of early civilization. Before the era of baking powder, baking soda was the only means of leavening bread. Following is a cowboy recipe for biscuits:

2 cups sifted bread flour
¾ teaspoon soda
½ teaspoon salt
¼ cup lard
¾ cup thick sour milk or buttermilk
1 level teaspoon sugar

To the flour add soda, salt and sugar and sift once. Cut in the lard until well mixed, using two knives or a pastry blender. Slowly add the sour milk or buttermilk until a soft dough is formed. Roll out dough on lightly floured board; cut with floured biscuit-cutter; place on ungreased baking sheet and bake in a very hot oven as directed. Serve warm.

(87) SOUR CREAM BISCUITS—COUNTRY STYLE

Approximately 12 biscuits. Oven temperature: 450° F.
Baking time: 12–15 minutes.

NOTE: ¼ cup chopped seedless raisins, dates or figs can be mixed with the flour, in which case a little more liquid may be needed.

2 cups sifted bread flour
¾ teaspoon salt
3 teaspoons baking powder
1 tablespoon lard
1 cup light sour cream
½ teaspoon soda

To the flour add salt, baking powder and sift once into mixing bowl. Rub in the lard with finger tips dipped in flour; stir in combined light sour cream and soda, then mix with a fork. If too dry, add a few spoonfuls of milk until dough is soft enough to be handled easily. Place on lightly floured board, roll into a smooth sheet about ¾ inch thick; cut with floured biscuit cutter; place close together on a greased baking sheet so they almost touch and bake in a very hot oven as directed. Serve warm.

Half of this recipe makes the old-fashioned shortcake if baked in a 9-inch pie pan.

(88) SQUASH BISCUITS MADE WITH YEAST

Approximately 14 biscuits. Oven temperature: 450° F.
Baking time: 18–20 minutes.

NOTE: Cooked, sieved pumpkin may be substituted for squash, if desired.

1½ cups cold, cooked, sieved squash
¼ cup sugar
¾ teaspoon salt
2 tablespoons melted butter
1 cup milk, scalded, cooled to lukewarm
½ yeast cake, dissolved in
2 tablespoons lukewarm water
2 cups sifted bread flour (about)

Combine squash, sugar, salt and butter and mix well. Stir in lukewarm milk. Blend thoroughly. Add dissolved yeast and enough flour to make a soft dough. Place in greased bowl; cover with light, dry, clean towel, and let rise to double its bulk. Punch down; roll out on lightly floured board and knead 30 seconds. Shape into biscuits either by hand or with floured biscuit-cutter. Place on greased pan and let rise to double its bulk. Bake in a very hot oven as directed. Serve warm. Very delicious.

(89) SWEET POTATO BISCUITS—SOUTHERN METHOD

Approximately 16 small biscuits. Oven temperature: 450° F.
Baking time: 15–20 minutes.

1 cup sifted bread flour
3 teaspoons baking powder
¾ teaspoon salt
2 generous tablespoons butter
1 cup mashed sweet potatoes, cold
Enough cold milk to make a soft dough

Combine flour, baking powder and salt and sift into mixing bowl. Cut in butter, rubbing it in with tips of the fingers. Add sweet potatoes, then enough milk to make a soft dough (the amount will vary from 2 to 4 tablespoons according to moisture of potatoes). Turn dough upon lightly floured board and knead 30 seconds. Pat lightly into a sheet ½ inch thick. Cut with floured biscuit-cutter about 2¼-inches in diameter. Place biscuits on lightly oiled baking sheet and bake in a very hot oven as directed.

These crusty biscuits should be served very hot, split and spread with butter.

(90) SWISS CHEESE DEVILED BISCUITS

Approximately 14 biscuits. Oven temperature: 425° F.
Baking time: 12–15 minutes.

2 cups sifted bread flour
3 tablespoons baking powder
½ generous teaspoon salt
¼ teaspoon dry mustard
¾ teaspoon paprika
⅛ teaspoon cloves
⅛ teaspoon ground thyme
A few grains of cayenne pepper
⅛ teaspoon ground mace
5 tablespoons butter
½ teaspoon Worcestershire sauce
⅔ cup cold milk (about)
1 cup grated Swiss cheese

To the flour add baking powder, salt, dry mustard, paprika, cloves, thyme, cayenne pepper and mace and sift twice. Cut in butter with pastry blender. Stir in enough milk to make a smooth dough. Knead on lightly floured board about 25 seconds, then roll out into a sheet, six by eight inches. Sprinkle dough with grated Swiss cheese. Roll up dough as for jelly roll and slice crosswise. Put slices close together in a generously buttered pan. Sprinkle with a little paprika mixed with an equal part of ground cinnamon and bake in a hot oven as directed until light brown. Serve hot.

(91) TOMATO JUICE DROP BISCUITS

Approximately 18 biscuits. Oven temperature: 450° F.
Baking time: 10–12 minutes.

2 cups sifted bread flour
4 teaspoons baking powder
¾ teaspoon salt
6 tablespoons shortening
¾ teaspoon Worcestershire sauce
1 cup tomato juice (about)

Combine flour, baking powder and salt and resift once. Cut in shortening with 2 knives or pastry blender; add Worcestershire sauce to tomato juice and add to dough, mixing lightly to a soft dropping dough. Drop from tablespoon onto ungreased baking sheet, and bake as directed in a hot oven. For smaller biscuits, drop from tip of teaspoon. This will make about 2 dozen biscuits.

(92) WATERCRESS BISCUITS

Approximately 1 dozen biscuits. Oven temperature: 450° F.
Baking time: 12–15 minutes.

Color is one of the tests in selecting cress. It should be green, and a deep green at that, all through the bunch. It should look crisp and even lively. To be kept that way until it is used, it needs to be washed right away in icy-cold water, wrapped in a wet towel and placed in the refrigerator. It must be hidden from light and air.

Watercress has a past as well as a present. Ancient recipes made frequent reference to the green herb. It was believed that this green, eaten with vinegar, would cure a deranged mind. This gave rise to a Greek proverb, "Eat cress and get more wit." There may be something to this notion. At any rate it is rich in minerals and vitamins A and C. Fresh cress munched while drinking is rumored to keep the drinker sober.

2 cups sifted bread flour
3 teaspoons baking powder
½ teaspoon salt
A few grains of cayenne pepper
½ generous cup chopped watercress
5 tablespoons shortening
¾ cup milk (about)
½ teaspoon onion juice

To the flour add baking powder, salt and cayenne pepper and sift together. Chop cress very fine and press very gently in a dry clean towel, just enough to remove excess moisture, and blend into the flour mixture as thoroughly as possible. Cut in shortening with two knives or pastry blender; combine onion juice and milk, add to flour mixture, using enough to make a soft dough. Roll out on a lightly floured board to ½-scant inch in thickness; cut with floured biscuit-cutter and place on an ungreased baking sheet. Bake in a very hot oven as directed.

Very fine with almost any salad, fish, meat, poultry, etc.

(93) WHOLE WHEAT HARD BISCUITS

ENGLISH, CRACKER STYLE

Approximately 12 biscuits. Oven temperature: 450° F.
Baking time: 12–15 minutes.

1 cup unsifted whole wheat flour
1 cup sifted bread flour
4 teaspoons baking powder
1 scant teaspoon salt
4 tablespoons butter or margarine
¾ cup milk (about)

Combine bread flour, baking powder and salt and sift in mixing bowl; mix in the unsifted whole wheat flour; cut in butter or margarine (another kind of shortening may be used), blending thoroughly. Add enough milk to make a soft dough; roll out on lightly floured board to ½ inch in thickness; cut with floured biscuit-cutter; place on a greased baking sheet and bake as directed. Serve hot.

For variation you may sprinkle with poppy seeds; brush the biscuits with lightly beaten egg white and bake.

Breads

"... Three may partake as well as two,"
  Ilderim softly said,
"The portion of the birds will be
No less," and bowed his head.
And when down through the centuries
  The hour of feasting comes,
Men ask their God to bless their bread,
  And give the birds the crumbs.
    —*Hildegarde Walls Johnson*

BREADS

(94) A FEW GOOD HINTS ABOUT BREADS

Young growing bodies need the energy and nourishment provided by bread. Keep their natural appetite for bread alive by serving a variety of breads. Choose different breads when you buy or bake—serve different breads from meal to meal—put two or three kinds of bread on the same tray or plate—and watch your family sit up and take notice.

Thousands of women have, without realizing it, fallen into the "one bread habit." It is an easy habit to break. Frequent change and a variety of breads heighten interest in the whole meal.

Bread should be cooled thoroughly before it is stored. In hot weather, especially, each loaf should be inspected daily—for mold. The bread box also should be cleaned and aired frequently and kept in as cool a place as possible.

If you haven't time to make regulation patty shells, cut bread in two-inch slices, hollow out the center, and then fry in deep fat until a golden brown, or place in the oven until crisp and brown. A splendid substitute.

How did that dark, moist bread receive its name? Napoleon, on one of his campaigns had been given the coarse bread with his dinner. The little Corporal had sniffed at it and had then remarked scoffingly, "Bon pour Nickel." Nickel was his horse. Thereafter the bread, through local corruption of the French words, came to be known as "pumpernickel."

The Arabs say that wheat and other grains, including millet, rye (doura) and barley (oats are unknown except in a very limited region in Syria) came down from heaven in seven mandeels or handkerchiefs, and that it must always be respected since Allah took so much trouble to keep it clean and pure from all defilement. All who know the life of the East have listened with reverence to the cry of the breadseller going his early round. "Allah Karim!" is his cry. "God is merciful." Bread is recognized as His special gift—it is life—El Aish. It is not treated as ordinary food. There was a time not so long ago when bread could not be sold. It must always be given or exchanged—gift for gift.

To freshen dry bread or rolls, moisten with cold water and place in a hot oven until thoroughly heated, or in a paper bag in the oven for a few minutes.

Summer calls for diligent cleaning and airing of bread and cookie jars and boxes, since these foods mold easily when it's hot.

When making bread remember it should be kneaded until perfectly smooth and so elastic that any indentation made with the finger will fill up again instantly.

Often a crust forms on rising dough. To avoid that spread a little fat over the dough and cover it with a dry clean cloth.

To keep yeast fresh press into bottom of cup or bowl, invert and place in a saucer containing a little cold water.

To prevent corn bread from sticking to pan, grease well, then sprinkle with sifted corn meal.

Corn bread, that simplest of all fare, but, alas, seldom prepared as it should be, is also known under different "aliases" or disguises—"johnny cake," "corn pone," "bumble puppy" or "hush puppies," etc.

Brush your loaf of bread with melted shortening to get a fine even brown crust. By the way, do you know that a one-pound loaf of bread will make fifteen slices?

When compressed yeast is used in bread, if potato water should be used for the liquid instead of milk, it will remain moist much longer.

Graham bread takes its name from Sylvester Graham, Suffield, Connecticut, temperance lecturer, who preached vegetarianism as well as temperance in the early eighteenth century.

When removing homemade bread or rolls from the oven dip a piece of waxed paper in butter and rub the tops. It gives a luster to the crusts, making them appear more tempting.

If you have trouble with bread molding in hot weather, wrap it securely in waxed paper and store in the refrigerator.

Butter slices of bread and cut off the crusts, then cut the slices into half inch cubes. Toast these quickly on a baking sheet in a hot oven and serve piping hot at breakfast time to "dunk" into soft cooked eggs.

Fine breads, perhaps, are the best test of good cooking. They require quick, accurate workmanship and a dash of imagination to lift them from the commonplace. A fine cook goes about her mixing and baking with an endless zest. Such cooks are bold, creative artists, blending everyday staples into tender-textured, crisply-browned culinary masterpieces—with as skilled a hand as an orchestra leader's.

Toasted corn bread is tasty with creamed meats, fish or vegetables. Toast on both sides.

Bread is economical because it gives a high return in calories and some protein (energy-giving and body-building elements) for what it costs.

Dry bread crumbs are used as a topping for scalloped dishes, for coating croquettes and in place of all or part of the flour in steamed puddings, muffins, unbaked pie shells, etc.

The safest place for bread in warm humid weather is in a cool dry place. In average weather, the keeping of bread is not a problem unless it is kept too tightly sealed from the air.

Coarse bread crumbs fried in butter make an acceptable garnish for any vegetable or for alimentary pastes.

If you get crumbed food, as croquettes, ready some time before frying, scatter crumbs on a board and set the croquettes, or whatever, on these. And how they take it!

"Soft bread crumbs" means crumbs from soft or fresh bread out of the inside of the loaf, no crust included. They may or may not be soaked in water, milk or other liquids, but usually only dry bread is soaked. For Brown Betty, the bread should be grated; for bread puddings or dishes for which crumbs are soaked, you may break in very small pieces unless the recipes state otherwise.

To make buttered crumbs, melt ¼ cup of butter or substitute and stir in one cup of bread crumbs, mixing gently over low heat until butter is absorbed and crumbs delicately browned. Such buttered crumbs are used as a filling, a topping, for scalloped dishes or "au gratin dishes" when combined with grated cheese.

Save the bread for crumbs in a paper bag; keep it tied and hanging so that the air can circulate through it rather than in the bread box or a closed jar where it soon becomes moldy. *Don't store away* buttered pieces of bread as the butter becomes rancid and the taste is far from pleasing. For fine, dry crumbs, put bread in a cloth bag and roll on board with rolling pin. Sift and re-roll the coarse crumbs. Crumbs of this type may be kept days before using. If you use grinder, fasten a large paper or cloth bag over the end to catch all of the crumbs.

Whether a little sugar goes into your corn bread or not is a matter you must decide. Experiments show that small amounts of sugar encourage browning without adding apparent sweetness.

Slice crust off of one loaf of bread. Slice thin, butter generously, put together in loaf form again. Place in steamer and put in low oven for an hour. Serve very hot. You have here a delicious, rich bread.

Kneading of bread will take from three to five minutes. To test, cut the dough with a sharp knife and if there are no large bubbles the kneading has been sufficient. The hands may be greased or floured; this depends largely upon the natural warmth of the hands. The time for kneading bread may be cut by lifting the dough—baker fashion—and dropping it on the surface to break the bubbles.

BREAD RECIPES

(95) AFTERNOON TEA CANDIED ORANGE BREAD

Makes 1 loaf. Oven temperature: 350° F.
Baking time: 45–50 minutes.

2 tablespoons butter
¼ cup sugar
1 whole fresh egg, well-beaten
1½ cups sifted bread flour
3 teaspoons baking powder
½ generous teaspoon salt
½ cup candied orange peel, finely chopped
½ cup milk
¼ cup fresh orange juice

Cream butter with sugar. Add well-beaten whole egg and beat vigorously until smooth. Mix flour with baking powder and salt and sift once more. Mix in candied orange peel and add to butter-sugar mixture, blending well, alternately with mixed milk and orange juice. Set aside and let stand for about 25 minutes. Turn into greased loaf pan, and bake in a moderate oven as directed.

(96) ALSATIAN ONION BREAD

Approximately 15 individual breads or biscuits. Oven temperature: 450° F. Baking time: 12–15 minutes.

Coarsely chop 2 cups onions, and fry in ¼ cup of lard until soft and transparent but do not allow to brown, stirring almost constantly. Season to taste with salt and freshly ground black pepper and turn mixture into a shallow baking pan. Keep warm.

2 cups sifted bread flour
3 teaspoons baking powder
¼ cup lard or other shortening
¾ cup cold milk (about)
½ teaspoon salt

To the flour add baking powder and salt and sift again. Cut in shortening as you would for baking powder biscuit, that is until mixture is of the consistency of coarse corn meal. Stir in the milk to make a soft dough. Turn dough out on lightly floured board and knead for ½ minute or so. Roll out to ½ scant inch in thickness and spread the sheet over the onions in the pan. Over the dough pour the following mixture:

Beat together 1 cup thin sour cream (or 1 cup evaporated milk soured with 2 tablespoons of good vinegar) and 3 egg yolks. Season highly with freshly ground black pepper and salt and bake in a very hot oven as directed. To serve, cut into squares the size of biscuits, or spoon out if preferred.

This delicious bread is usually served with roast meat or fowl, like Yorkshire pudding.

(97) APPLE CORN BREAD

Serves about 8. Oven temperature: 375° F.
Baking time: 18–20 minutes.

¾ cup sifted bread flour
¾ cup sifted corn meal
3 teaspoons baking powder
½ teaspoon salt
1½ tablespoons granulated sugar
1 whole fresh egg, slightly beaten
¾ cup cold milk (about)
2 tablespoons shortening, melted
¾ cup, almost a cup, finely chopped apples

Combine the flour and corn meal and sift once again. Measure, then add baking powder, salt and fine granulated sugar, and sift once more. Combine egg and cold milk, mixing well, and stir into the flour mixture. Beat vigorously till thoroughly blended and smooth, adding the melted shortening, alternately with chopped apples. Turn dough into greased, shallow pan or muffin pans, and bake as directed. This will make 8 medium-sized muffins. Fine with roast pork.

Pears, peaches, prunes, dates, figs, etc. may be substituted for apple, if desired.

(98) APRICOT BREAD I

Makes 1 loaf. Oven temperature: 375° F.
Baking time: 40 minutes.

1 whole fresh egg, well-beaten
¾ cup cold milk
1 tablespoon shortening, melted
2 teaspoons baking powder
½ teaspoon salt
¼ teaspoon soda
1 teaspoon grated orange rind
1 cup sifted bread flour
½ cup fine granulated sugar
½ cup whole wheat flour, unsifted
½ cup dried apricots, shredded
½ cup dates, shredded

Beat the egg with the milk thoroughly, then stir in the melted shortening and grated orange rind. Mix flour, sugar, baking powder, salt and baking soda and sift once. Add to the egg-milk mixture and blend well; then stir in the whole wheat flour, alternately with shredded apricots and dates, mixing well. Turn mixture into a greased, floured loaf pan, and bake in a moderate oven as directed. This bread should be served only when cold.

(99) APRICOT BREAD II

Makes 1 loaf. Oven temperature: 375° F.
Baking time: 45 minutes.

- ¾ cup dried apricots, chopped
- ¾ cup boiling milk (or water)
- 1 tablespoon butter
- ½ cup sugar
- ½ generous teaspoon salt
- 1 egg, well-beaten
- ½ teaspoon orange extract or lemon extract
- ½ cup unsifted whole wheat flour
- ¾ cup sifted bread flour
- ½ teaspoon baking soda
- ½ cup chopped blanched almonds

Put apricots through food chopper, add to boiling milk (or water), alternately with butter, creamed with sugar and salt. Set aside to cool and mellow. When cold, stir in the beaten egg (flavored with extract) alternately with whole wheat flour, and bread flour sifted with baking soda. Beat briskly to blend thoroughly and quickly; then stir in the almonds. Turn into greased and floured loaf pan and bake in a moderate oven as directed.

Any kind of chopped nuts may be substituted for almonds.

(100) BACON CORN BREAD

Serves 6–8. Oven temperature: 400° F.
Baking time: 20 minutes.

- 1 egg, well-beaten
- ¼ cup sugar
- ½ cup all-bran
- 1 cup corn meal
- 1 cup milk
- 1 cup sifted bread flour
- ¼ teaspoon salt (generous)
- 1 teaspoon baking powder
- ¾ lb. sliced bacon, chopped

Combine all-bran, corn meal and milk. Combine egg and sugar. Sift flour with salt and baking powder. Then mix all together and beat well. Turn batter into greased shallow pan and sprinkle chopped bacon over top. Bake in a hot oven as directed. If crust and bacon do not brown sufficiently, place pan under the flame of broiling oven for a few minutes.

(101) BACON AND ONION BREAD ROLL

BOHEMIAN METHOD

Makes 1 roll serving 12. Oven temperature: 300–325° F.
Baking time: 30 minutes.

3½ cups scalded milk
¼ cup sugar
¼ cup butter or margarine
1 cake compressed yeast
4½ cups sifted bread flour
2 eggs, well-beaten
2 or 3 tablespoons strong, cold black coffee
6 cardamon seeds, crushed
4 cups sifted bread flour
¾ lb. bacon, chopped fine
3 cups minced onions
¾ teaspoon salt
Pepper and paprika to taste (about ¼ teaspoon pepper and 1 teaspoon paprika)

Dissolve sugar, salt and butter in scalded milk; cool to lukewarm; add crumbled yeast and let stand 5 minutes. Then stir in the 4½ cups flour and mix until very smooth. Add the combined eggs, crushed cardamon seeds and remainder of flour. Mix to a stiff dough and knead until elastic. Place in a large, greased bowl and let rise until doubled in volume. Then turn out on lightly floured board, knead ½ minute, roll out to one-inch thick. Cut in two; spread one piece with minced bacon, mixed with chopped onions, salt, pepper and paprika. Cover with the other half, pressing edges together and roll up like a jelly roll. Let stand until double in volume. Brush all over with cold, strong coffee and bake in a slow oven as directed. Serve warm.

(102) BAKING POWDER BRAN BREAD

QUICK METHOD

Makes 1 loaf. Oven temperature: 350° F.
Baking time: 1 hour.

2 cups sifted bread flour
2 teaspoons baking powder
1 teaspoon soda
1 scant teaspoon salt
2 cups all-bran
½ cup seedless raisins (or nuts)
1 egg, well beaten
⅔ cup molasses
3 tablespoons melted shortening
1½ cups sour milk

Brush a loaf pan with shortening and set aside. To flour add baking powder, soda and salt and sift together; stir in the all-bran, mixing well.

Beat egg, molasses, melted shortening and sour milk together, add the raisins. Combine with flour mixture and stir thoroughly. Turn dough into greased loaf pan, having the sides higher than the center. The pan should be only two-thirds full. Let stand about 15 minutes to mellow and ripen. Bake in a moderate oven as directed. Remove from oven, invert upon a rack, let cool before slicing very thin.

(103) BAKING POWDER NUT BREAD

QUICK METHOD

Makes 1 loaf. Oven temperature: 350° F.
Baking time: 1 hour.

In making this easy and quick nut bread, two points should be kept in mind. First, the dough must stand fifteen minutes in the pan before being baked. Second, the baked loaf must be allowed to cool before it is sliced. This will require several hours standing upon a rack. You may vary the bread by using half whole wheat or graham flour and half bread flour. Brown sugar may replace the white sugar.

2⅔ cups sifted bread flour	1 cup chopped dates
4 teaspoons baking powder	1 whole fresh egg, well-beaten
½ generous teaspoon salt	½ cup granulated sugar
1 cup broken nut meats	1 cup fresh, cold milk

To the bread flour add baking powder and salt and sift together. Add the broken nut meats and shredded dates, incorporating well in the flour mixture. To the beaten egg add the sugar and beat till sugar is dissolved and mixture is fluffy and creamy. Then pour in the cold milk, beating well. Add this to the flour mixture, stirring only until thoroughly blended. Turn batter in a buttered loaf pan; let stand 15 minutes to mellow and ripen, and bake in a moderate oven as directed. When well cooled, slice very thin.

(104) BANANA BRAN BREAD

Makes 1 loaf. Oven temperature: 375° F.
Baking time: 1 hour.

1½ cups sifted bread flour
2 teaspoons baking powder
½ teaspoon baking soda
½ teaspoon salt
A pinch ginger (may omit)
2 tablespoons orange juice or water
½ cup nut meats, chopped
½ cup sugar
4 tablespoons butter, margarine or lard
1 egg, well-beaten
1 cup all-bran
½ teaspoon vanilla extract mixed with
¼ teaspoon almond extract
1½ cups mashed, sieved bananas

To the flour add baking powder, soda and salt and sift together. Add nut meats and blend well. Cream shortening and sugar together, adding sugar gradually and creaming till fluffy. Stir in the beaten egg, adding alternately with all-bran. Combine flour mixture with creamed shortening-mixture, alternately with bananas flavored with extracts. Turn batter into greased loaf pan, and bake in a moderate oven as directed. Cool before cutting.

(105) BANANA BREAD

Makes 1 loaf. Oven temperature: 350° F.
Baking time: 1¼ hours.

What is called the "Quick loaf bread" is very familiar to many homemakers, who use it at tea-time, as afternoon snacks for school children, or as a sandwich spread for the lunch-box. In technique, such "quick breads" are mixed as is a muffin.

½ scant cup of shortening
1 scant cup sugar
2 eggs, well-beaten
2 cups sifted bread flour
½ teaspoon salt
½ teaspoon baking soda, dissolved in
2 tablespoons sour milk
1 cup mashed, sieved bananas (about 3)

Cream shortening; add sugar slowly, creaming until fluffy. Now add the eggs and beat well. Combine flour, salt and baking soda (dissolved in sour milk) and add to shortening mixture, alternately with bananas. Beat briskly for a minute or two. Turn batter into a greased loaf pan, and bake in a moderate oven as directed. Cool before cutting.

Another recipe calls for the addition of 1¼ teaspoons of cream of tartar. This may or may not be added.

(106) BANANA NUT BREAD

Makes 1 loaf. Oven temperature: 350° F.
Baking time: 1 long hour.

1¾ cups sifted bread flour
3 teaspoons baking powder
½ teaspoon salt
1 cup dates, coarsely ground
½ cup chopped nut meats
⅓ cup butter, margarine, or lard
⅔ cup granulated sugar
2 eggs, well-beaten
1 cup mashed bananas (2 large or 3 small)

To the flour add baking powder and salt and sift together. Mix ¼ cup of the flour mixture with dates and nut meats. This is to prevent them from falling to the bottom. Cream shortening; add sugar slowly, creaming until fluffy. Now, stir in the eggs and beat all together until well blended. Combine flour and shortening mixtures alternately with bananas. No liquid is necessary; the bananas furnish the moisture. Last, stir in the floured dates and nut meats, stirring just enough to blend well. Quickly turn batter into a greased loaf pan, and bake in a moderate oven as directed. This is much more delicious if used the day after baking as the banana flavor is improved and the bread slices better. The addition of ½ teaspoon of vanilla extract also is good.

(107) BANANA BRAN NUT BREAD I

Makes 1 loaf. Oven temperature: 375° F.
Baking time: 1 hour.

¼ cup shortening
½ cup sugar
1 egg, well beaten
1 cup all-bran
1½ cups sifted bread flour
2 teaspoons baking powder
½ teaspoon salt
½ teaspoon baking soda
½ cup nut meats, chopped
1½ cups mashed, sieved bananas (about 3)
2 tablespoons orange juice or water
1 scant teaspoon vanilla extract

Cream shortening and sugar until fluffy. Add egg alternately with all-bran. Blend well. To the flour, add baking powder, salt and baking soda. Mix chopped nut meats and flour mixture and add alternately with bananas to which orange juice or water has been added. Stir in vanilla extract. Pour into a greased loaf pan and allow to stand 30 minutes to mellow and ripen. Then, bake in a moderate oven as directed. Let cool before cutting.

(108) BANANA BRAN NUT BREAD II

Makes 1 loaf. Oven temperature: 375° F.
Baking time: 1 hour.

Combine 1 egg, well-beaten with 1½ cups mashed, sieved bananas (about 3 large ones), ¼ cup melted butter, margarine or lard and 1 cup all-bran. Sift 1½ cups bread flour once, measure, add 2½ teaspoons baking powder, 1 teaspoon baking soda, ½ teaspoon salt and ½ cup granulated sugar (brown, rolled and sifted sugar may be substituted for granulated, if desired) and sift once. Add ½ cup of broken nut meats and mix well, then add to the banana mixture, stirring only enough to dampen all flour. Pour into greased loaf pan and bake in a moderate oven as directed. Let cool before cutting.

(109) BANANA NUT BREAD

Makes 1 loaf. Oven temperature: 375° F.
Baking time: 50–55 minutes.

This delicious sandwich bread may be eaten warm.

Sift 2 cups bread flour once, measure, add ½ teaspoon baking soda, ½ generous teaspoon salt, ¼ teaspoon ground nutmeg, and a generous pinch of ground ginger (may be omitted). Stir in ½ generous cup broken nut meats (any kind) and ½ cup of bran. Cream ¼ cup butter, margarine or lard; slowly add ¼ cup sugar mixed with ¼ cup rolled, dark brown sugar. Blend well, until mixture is fluffy and light, then beat in 2 well-beaten eggs. Now add the dry ingredients and blend thoroughly, alternately with 1½ cups mashed, sieved bananas (about 3) mixed with 2 tablespoons thick sour cream. Turn mixture into greased loaf pan, and bake in a moderate oven as directed. Serve warm.

(110) BANANA RAISIN BREAD

Makes 1 loaf. Oven temperature: 325–350° F.
Baking time: 1¼ hours.

½ cup butter, margarine or lard
¾ cup (generous) granulated sugar
2 eggs, well beaten
⅔ cup mashed, sieved bananas
2¼ cups sifted bread flour
1 scant teaspoon baking soda
½ scant teaspoon salt
¼ cup sour, rich milk
½ cup seedless raisins, parboiled, drained
⅓ cup broken nut meats

Brush a loaf pan with butter, margarine or lard; line the bottom with waxed paper. Cream shortening; slowly add sugar and cream until fluffy; then beat in the eggs, alternately with the mashed, sieved bananas. Mix flour with baking soda and salt and sift together. Combine raisins and nut meats and blend with ¼ cup of the flour mixture; then add flour and raisin mixture to sour milk (made by stirring ½ teaspoon of lemon juice into milk). Blend quickly and thoroughly; then turn into prepared loaf pan. Bake in a 325° F. oven until well risen and beginning to brown; increase the heat to 350° F. and bake until a cake tester comes away clean (about 1¼ hours). Remove from oven; let stand a few moments; take from the loaf pan; strip away the paper. Let cool on rack. Do not try to slice before it's cold.

(111) BARLEY PEANUT BUTTER BREAD

Makes 1 loaf. Oven temperature: 350° F.
Baking time: 45–50 minutes.

1 cup barley flour, sifted
½ cup rice flour, sifted
4 teaspoons baking powder
¾ teaspoon (scant) salt
⅛ teaspoon ground nutmeg
½ cup bran flakes
½ cup peanut butter, well-beaten
¾ cup milk
1 egg, well-beaten
¼ cup corn syrup

Mix sifted flours with baking powder, salt and nutmeg and sift together. Blend in the bran flakes thoroughly. Cut in the peanut butter, then add cold milk, mixed with the egg and corn syrup. Beat briskly to blend thoroughly, and turn into greased loaf pan. Bake in a moderate oven as directed. Cool before slicing.

(112) BOHEMIAN BREAD (Houska)

PRONOUNCED HOSKA

Makes 3 loaves. Oven temperature: 400–350° F.
Baking time: 40–45 minutes.

1 cake of compressed yeast
2 tablespoons sugar
2 cups milk, scalded
8 cups (2 quarts) bread flour, sifted
1¼ teaspoons salt
¼ teaspoon ground mace
1 cup lard or other shortening
3 eggs, well-beaten
1 cup seedless raisins, parboiled, drained
½ cup chopped blanched almonds

Make a sponge with crumbled yeast, 2 tablespoons sugar, ½ cup milk and 2 tablespoons sifted flour. Mix well and allow to rise until doubled in bulk. Sift remainder of bread flour once, add salt and mace and sift together three times; cut in shortening. Add remainder of sugar to remainder of milk; stir into mixture. When dissolved, add the eggs, blending well, and turn this into the yeast sponge. Combine parboiled, drained and dried raisins with almonds and sift over them 2 tablespoons of flour; combine with flour sponge mixture. Allow to rise until double in bulk. Divide dough into three even sections and divide each section into three even strips. Make one braid out of each three strips and place in greased loaf pans. Let rise to double its bulk and bake in a hot oven (400° F.) for 15 minutes. Reduce heat to moderate (350° F.) and continue baking 20–25 minutes longer.

(113) BOSTON BROWN BREAD I

A COMPANION TO BAKED BOSTON BEANS

Makes 3 loaves. Steaming time: 3 hours. Oven temperature: 250° F.
Baking time: 25–30 minutes.

NOTE: The loaves which are not used at once should be wrapped in waxed paper and stored in bread box and then resteamed in the molds until hot.

1 cup corn meal, sifted
2 cups whole wheat flour
2 teaspoons baking soda
1½ teaspoons salt
½ cup seedless raisins, parboiled
¾ cup molasses
2 cups buttermilk or sour milk

Combine corn meal and whole wheat flours with baking soda and salt and sift together; stir in parboiled, drained and dried raisins.

Blend well. Combine molasses and milk and add to flour mixture, mixing thoroughly. Steam in three well-greased covered one quart molds, filled ⅔ full, to allow for expansion, for 3 hours. Uncover and bake in a very slow oven as directed.

(114) BOSTON BROWN BREAD II

YEAST METHOD

Makes 2 loaves. Steaming time: 4 hours. Baking time: 250° F. for 5 hours.

For this special homemade bread, it is wise to weigh the flours.

½ lb. corn meal
1 cup boiling water
1 cup molasses
1¼ teaspoons salt
¾ ounce yeast
½ lb. graham flour
½ lb. whole wheat flour

Scald the corn meal by pouring the boiling (really boiling) water over it. Add molasses and salt and blend well. When lukewarm add the crumbled yeast, then the combined graham and whole wheat flours. Toss upon a lightly floured board and knead lightly. Place in large greased bowl and allow to rise six hours, at room temperature, covered with a light towel. Knead again until glossy; cut into two loaves of equal weight; place in high round molds and let rise again for about 30 minutes. Cover tightly and steam for 4 hours or place molds in several inches of hot water and bake in a 250° F. oven for 5 hours. Delicious, and keeps moist several days.

(115) BOSTON BROWN BREAD III

RYE FLOUR METHOD

Makes 3 small loaves. Steaming time in covered soup kettle, 4 hours. Oven temperature: 250°–275° F. Baking time: 30 minutes.

1 cup corn meal, sifted
1 cup rye flour, sifted
1 cup graham flour
1 cup molasses
1½ cups sour milk
1 teaspoon baking soda
1¼ teaspoons salt

Mix all ingredients together thoroughly. Put rounds of buttered paper in bottom of 3 baking powder tins or the like, and divide the mixture equally between them (⅔ full). Cover tightly and steam for 4 hours in a covered soup kettle, half full of hot water. Add more boiling water, as needed. Remove molds from water, remove lids and place in a slow oven (250–275° F.) for about 30 minutes to dry out somewhat.

(116) BRAIDED BREAD—COUNTRY STYLE

Makes 3 braids. Oven temperature: 375° F.
Baking time: 30 minutes.

2 compressed yeast cakes	½ scant cup sugar
¼ cup lukewarm water or milk	1 teaspoon salt
1 cup milk, scalded	2 whole fresh eggs, beaten
¼ cup butter	5 cups sifted bread flour

Crumble yeast cakes into lukewarm milk. Stir in the cup of scalded milk; add butter, sugar and salt and cool to lukewarm, stirring well. To the flour, add the yeast mixture, using enough flour to make a thick batter. Then, add beaten whole fresh eggs and beat briskly. Turn out on lightly floured board and knead until satiny. Place the dough in greased bowl, cover with a light dry towel and let rise until double in bulk (about 2 hours). When light, divide in half and cut each half of dough into three equal pieces. Roll each piece until about eight inches long; cross three of the rolls in the center, braid to each end and fasten. Place on greased baking sheet. Braid remaining rolls. Place on top of first braid; cover and let rise until doubled in bulk. Brush with beaten egg yolk and sprinkle with rock sugar. Bake as directed.

(117) BRAN-BACON CORN BREAD

Makes 1 pan serving 6. Oven temperature: 400° F.
Baking time: 18–20 minutes.

2 eggs, slightly beaten	1 cup cold milk
¼ cup sugar	¾ cup bread flour, sifted
½ cup bran	¼ generous teaspoon salt
1 cup yellow corn meal	2 teaspoons baking powder

¼ lb. coarsely chopped bacon

To the eggs add sugar and stir in alternately with mixed bran, corn meal and milk, until dissolved. Blend thoroughly. To the flour add salt and baking powder and sift together. Beat flour mixture into the first mixture, gradually and thoroughly. Pour batter into a greased baking pan (9 × 12 inches) and sprinkle coarsely chopped bacon over the top. Bake in a hot oven as directed; then slip pan under the flame of the broiler for 3 or 4 minutes to golden brown the top and crisp bacon. Serve hot.

(118) BRAN BREAD—HOME METHOD

A LIGHT AND TENDER BRAN BREAD

Makes 1 pan serving 6. Oven temperature: 375° F.
Baking time: 20 minutes.

1/4 cup butter or margarine	1 cup bread flour, sifted
3/4 cup sugar	1/2 cup yellow corn meal, sifted
3 eggs, unbeaten	2 teaspoons baking powder
3 cups of bran	1/2 generous teaspoon salt
1 1/2 cups milk	1 scant cup seedless raisins, parboiled

Cream fat; add sugar gradually and continue creaming until mixture is light and fluffy; add eggs, one at a time (beating briskly after each addition) alternately with the bran. To the flour and corn meal add baking powder and salt, and sift together; then add gradually to first mixture alternately with milk and floured raisins. Pour batter into greased shallow pan to 1/3 inch and bake in moderate oven as directed. Serve hot. Raisins may be omitted. To parboil raisins, place in a pan, cover with boiling water and allow to simmer 8 to 10 minutes; drain, then dry in folded towel.

(119) BRAN HONEY BREAD

Makes 1 loaf. Oven temperature: 375° F.
Baking time: 1 1/4 hours.

A long and interesting story could be told about honey, one of the oldest sweets known to mankind. Centuries ago it was held in high esteem by peoples of all races. The Old Testament describes the ideal living place as one "flowing with milk and honey." Romans and Greeks referred to honey as a "food fit for the gods."

The Norsemen wrote about the wonders of honey. As a food it is a delight to people, young and old, of many lands. Just as the honeybee intrigues the imagination of artists, writers, poets and scientists of every land, this nectar-sweet liquid, of more-or-less pronounced flavor, compels the interests of every connoisseur of foods.

Honey has many uses in cookery, particularly in making bread, cakes, cookies and confections. Many Old World Christmas cakes, breads and cookies using honey are extremely popular, and have a most remarkable lasting quality, because baked foods made with honey will keep moist longer than those made with sugar. Honey has much the same consistency as molasses and may be used in place of it, measure for measure, in bread, gingerbread, steamed puddings, brown bread, etc. It contains less acid than molasses, so use one teaspoon of baking powder for each quarter teaspoon of soda in substituting honey for molasses.

Honey contains some water. This affects the amount of liquid used in a recipe when honey is substituted for sugar. The liquid must be reduced, however, more than the difference between the water content of the honey and sugar and also according to the proportion of honey used. For example, if medium-thick honey is substituted for *one-half the sugar* in cake or quick-bread recipes, reduce the liquid *one-fourth.* If honey is substituted for *all the sugar,* reduce the liquid *one-half.* If honey is very thin or very thick, this proportion may have to be altered.

In making honey cakes and quick breads, mix the honey with the liquid called for in the recipe and bake at the lowest temperature possible. This prevents loss or change of flavor of the honey and also avoids too rapid browning.

As to the care of honey in the home, always store it, particularly comb honey, in a warm place, and *never* in the refrigerator, as low temperatures make honey crystallize or become cloudy, and high temperatures make it turn dark and browner. To liquefy a jug or jar of honey which has become solid or crystallized, set in a dish of moderately hot (140° F.) water—not higher, or it will lose its flavor. Honey, which is a summer-made sweet, needs warmth in winter, too; so just keep it on the kitchen shelf, or the dining-room buffet.

OTHER USES—Many homemakers have learned that the distinctive flavor of honey makes a delicious sandwich filling when creamed with butter and mixed with chopped nuts or grated orange peel, or used in combination with cream cheese, peanut or almond butter, or chopped dried fruits.

Substituting honey for half the sugar in hard sauce, or serving it as a sauce for ice cream and other desserts, produces results appealing to most palates. A good frozen dessert may be made with a cup of honey dissolved in two cups of water, to which the juice of half a medium-sized lemon is added. The mixture may be frozen like ordinary ice cream if it is done rapidly; or it may be chilled and hardened by the addition of finely powdered ice, which is stirred in gradually until the mixture is of the proper consistency.

Honey and half-honey jellies add distinction to a breakfast table and honey custards and puddings appeal as much to the healthy member of the family as to the invalid. Sweet potatoes and other vegetables candied with honey are a wholesome variation and half a cup of honey poured over a baking ham enhances both its flavor and appearance. In making candies like fondant, nougat and caramels, honey is often substituted for corn syrup. Now for the recipe:

RECIPE

Beat 1 egg, adding gradually 1/4 cup brown sugar alternately with 1/2 cup honey and melted butter, margarine or lard. Stir in 1 cup of bran, blending well. Sift 2 1/2 cups of bread flour once, measure, then add 3/4 teaspoon baking soda, 2 teaspoons baking powder and 1 scant teaspoon salt. Sift together over 1 cup of chopped figs (stems removed) and 1/2 cup chopped nut meats (either pecans, walnuts, peanuts, hazelnuts or Brazil nuts). Next stir the flour mixture into the egg-sugar-honey-butter mixture, alternately with 1 1/2 cups of cold milk. Blend thoroughly; then pour into a greased loaf pan and bake as directed. Cool before slicing.

(120) BRAN RAISIN BREAD

Makes 1 loaf. Oven temperature: 350° F.
Baking time: 1 hour.

The two varieties of raisins with which most of the homemakers are familiar are the Thompson and the Muscat. The Thompson raisin grows without seeds and the Muscat, while it contains seeds when harvested, usually reaches the home with the seeds removed, except for fruit which is left on the stems and sold at holiday time Both raisins are made from grapes by the same sun-drying process. Because of the high flavor of seeded raisins they are preferred by many for various types of baking and cooking.

There are two main reasons for using raisins. One is that their luscious taste and texture "make common foods uncommonly good"; and the other is that their nutritional value is extremely high. This combination of values puts raisins away up on the "Must" list of foods to be kept handy on the pantry shelf.

Although raisins are appropriate and appreciated all the year-round, winter, when fresh fruits are less available and more limited, is a fine time for their greater use. And no matter how inexpensive the package, raisins always remain a luxury food because of the quality they give to any baked or cooked dish to which they are added.

As a winter sauce or breakfast fruit, figs, dates and raisins could be more widely used. Each and all of these are particularly wholesome and high in food and calorie value as well as full of taste.

Practically all foods shrink during the cooking process but the dried fruits are a notable exception. The following figures show how much a pound of the different dried fruits swell and will help you in deciding how much to use:

Dried apricots, figs, prunes and raisins double in weight; dried peaches and pears are almost tripled, and dried apples absorb enough water to make their cooked bulk five times the original weight.

There are so many ways of using raisins that homemakers will have no difficulty in thinking up raisin dishes. Seedless raisins may be added whole, by the cupful to almost any recipe for bread, cake, candy, cookies, muffins and puddings. They are also good in stuffing for meat or poultry and in meat and dessert sauces. The fruity flavor of raisins, perhaps more than anything else, makes them very zestful in sauces. For raisins provide a sauce fit for a gourmet—one which gives tone and contrast to roast poultry, baked meats, etc. They should be cut with the scissors, however, before being added to a thin, light cake batter or to icing. Put them sliced on the breakfast table in a pretty bowl and let the children, and grown ups, sprinkle them on the cereal before adding the sugar and cream. And don't forget the raisins in the old stand-by custards and puddings—be it bread, cottage, or rice—of which the family is apt to tire if they are not dressed up a bit. One should not need to hunt for the raisins! Be liberal.

1 egg, well-beaten
¼ cup molasses or honey
¼ cup sugar
1 cup buttermilk or sour milk
2 tablespoons shortening, melted, cooled
2½ cups sifted bread flour
2 teaspoons baking powder
1 generous teaspoon salt
½ teaspoon baking soda
½ cup chopped, seedless raisins, parboiled
1 cup bran

To the egg, add molasses, sugar, buttermilk or sour milk, shortening and bran and blend thoroughly. Let stand until most of the moisture is taken up (about 15 minutes). To the flour, add baking powder, salt and soda and sift together. Add to the first mixture, reserving 2 tablespoons to blend with chopped raisins, added last. Stir only until flour disappears; turn into a greased loaf pan, lined with greased or waxed paper on bottom only. Bake in a moderate oven as directed. Cool before slicing.

(121) BRAZILIAN EASTER SWEET BREAD

CALLED ALSO: "EASTER SURPRISE BREAD"

Makes 3 loaves. Oven temperature: 375° F.
Baking time: 30 minutes (about).

9 cups twice-sifted bread flour
2 teaspoons salt
1 teaspoon ground cinnamon
1 teaspoon grated lemon rind
6 whole fresh eggs, well beaten
½ cup ground Brazilian nut meats
4 cups granulated sugar
1¾ cups butter, melted, then cooled
1½ cakes compressed yeast
¼ cup water, lukewarm
¾ cup rich milk, lukewarm
6 hard-cooked eggs, shelled

To flour, add salt and cinnamon and sift together. Stir in 1 teaspoon grated lemon or orange rind. Into the eggs stir the butter alternately with ground nuts and sugar. Blend thoroughly until smooth and add to it the yeast cakes, which have been crumbled into lukewarm water. Mix thoroughly; then combine with the flour mixture, a little at a time, blending well after each addition. Work this for about 15 minutes in a large mixing bowl; set aside, covered with a clean cloth and allow to rise until doubled in bulk. Then knead down and let rise again, two or three times. Do this the night before you want to bake. The following day form into 3 small loaves, after reserving a little dough for last use. Place two of the hard-cooked eggs in each loaf. With the reserved dough, make for each loaf 2 strips about the size of a banana and place over the eggs, covering well. Now let rise again in a warm place until each loaf is double its size; brush tops with beaten egg yolk, diluted in a little milk, and bake as directed in a moderate oven. Cool before slicing.

(122) BROWN NUT BREAD I

USING BROWN SUGAR

Makes 2 loaves. Oven temperature: 325° F.
Baking time: 1 hour or more.

2 cups brown sugar	1¾ cups graham flour
2 whole fresh eggs, beaten	¾ teaspoon salt
1 cup sour milk	1 teaspoon baking powder
¾ teaspoon baking soda	1¾ cups sifted bread flour
1 teaspoon water, warm	1 cup broken nut meats

To the eggs add brown sugar gradually, beating well after each addition, then stir in sour milk to which has been added the baking soda, dissolved in the warm water. Combine all the dry ingredients and sift once. Add to the first mixture gradually, stirring briskly until mixture is smooth, adding last the broken nut meats (any kind desired). Turn dough into greased loaf pans, and bake in a slow oven as directed.

(123) BROWN NUT BREAD II

USING MOLASSES

Makes 1 loaf. Oven temperature: 325° F.
Baking time: 1 hour or more.

Molasses-making and the production of sugar is older than the Bible. Hindu mythology indicates that the first molasses and sugar were produced in India. Other ancient writings refer to that country's "honey-bearing" reeds. The prophet Jeremiah in the Bible speaks of "incense from Sheba and the sweet cane from a far country." History is vague regarding how cane spread into the Mesopotamian Valley. Yet by the fifth century A.D. it was growing there abundantly. By the tenth century the manufacture of crude sugar and molasses was large enough to attract traders from many distant lands. In the thirteenth century Marco Polo found the Chinese making sugar and molasses by open-kettle methods. Today cane is grown in a wide tropical and subtropical belt that encircles the world.

It was in 1750 that the first cane, as introduced in America, was planted in New Orleans. Today molasses is used principally for flavor rather than as a sweetening.

About molasses Dr. James A. Tobey says: "People used to take pink pills. Now they take foods rich in iron, which drive away their languor and give them the rosy glow of good health. Anemia, or a deficiency of red blood, is easy to prevent and yet too many persons suffer from this malady. It is estimated, in fact, that fully half of our child population is anemic in some degree, and that numerous adults are similarly afflicted.

"When bread and molasses was a favorite food and was served at every meal, there was much less nutritional anemia than exists today. The reason was because plain old-fashioned molasses is an outstanding source of the type of iron that the body can best use for making red blood. The old custom of dosing the family with sulphur and molasses in the spring served to cure the anemia that often developed during the winter. It was the molasses that did it, not the sulphur, which made the mixture sharp and disagreeable, but merely passed through the body. The best old-fashioned molasses sold today never contains sulphur."

When molasses is eaten with bread, even more iron is utilized. Bread contains a little iron itself, but more significant is the fact that white bread made with milk is fairly high in calcium and phosphorus, which help the body to assimilate its food-iron. (Molasses, which is made from sugar cane, is of course not the only food that will help to prevent anemia, although it is probably the least expensive. Other foods high in available iron are liver, raisins, egg yolk, dried apricots, figs, prunes, red meats, and whole wheat bread.) Along with iron, these excellent foods also contain small amounts of copper, which aid in producing hemoglobin in the blood. Since the blood carries oxygen to the muscles and other body tissues, good red blood likewise helps to prevent fatigue.

In using molasses as a flavoring, remember it has sweetening power. In cookery a *cupful of high-grade molasses furnishes about the same sweetening contained in three-quarters of a cup of granulated sugar.* When substituting molasses for sugar, take into account that *a cupful of molasses carries about 2½* fluid ounces of liquid into the formula and compensation should be made, especially in baking recipes, *by decreasing the water, milk or other liquid ingredient accordingly.*

In baking, the soda neutralizes the acid in the molasses, thereby providing the leavening gas. This action is similar to the effect obtained by using sour cream, buttermilk or sour milk with soda. It aerates and raises cakes and bread and controls the spread and spring of cookies.

1½ cups graham flour
¾ cup sifted bread flour
½ teaspoon salt
1½ cups fresh milk
⅓ cup molasses
¼ cup broken nut meats
1½ teaspoons baking soda

Combine flours, salt and baking soda and sift together. Add fresh cold milk to molasses, blending well, and stir into the flour mixture. Last, stir in the nut meats. When smooth, pour batter into a greased loaf pan and bake in a very moderate oven as directed. Let cool before slicing.

(124) BUTTERMILK SPOON BREAD

Makes 6 servings. Oven temperature: 350° F.
Baking time: 50 minutes.

1 cup sifted corn meal
1½ teaspoons baking soda
1½ teaspoons salt
1 quart buttermilk
1 generous tablespoon melted butter
2 whole eggs, well beaten

Mix corn meal with salt and baking soda and sift together. Gradually stir in the combined fresh eggs and buttermilk and last the melted butter; mix until smooth. Turn batter into a buttered casserole and bake in a moderate oven as directed.

(125) CAMPER'S BREAD

CALLED ALSO: "CORKSCREW BREAD"

Makes 8–10 servings. A good bed of coals.
Baking time: until brown.

8 cups (2 quarts) sifted flour
2 tablespoons baking powder
2 teaspoons salt
¼ cup (4 tablespoons) lard or butter
1 cup cold milk
1 cup cold water (about)

To the flour add baking powder and salt and sift together. Cut in lard, butter, or other shortening, and rub in well, as you would for baking powder biscuits. Add combined milk and water, gradually, using only enough to make a rather stiff dough. Have ready a good bed of coals and the usual two forked sticks to hold whatever utensil is used. On a green stick, an inch or more in diameter, wind the dough. Rest the end on the forked sticks and turn frequently until brown and crisp on all sides. Pull out the stick and the bread is ready for eating.

(126) CANADIAN TRAPPER'S GRAHAM BREAD

CALLED ALSO: "FLAPPER BREAD"

Serves 6. Over a bright flame.

Baking time: until brown on both sides.

NOTE: 4½ oz. powdered milk or 3½ oz. dried skim milk plus 1½ oz. butter are equivalent to one quart whole milk.

½ cup sugar
1 generous tablespoon lard
2 cups graham flour
1 cup sifted bread flour
1 tablespoon baking powder
½ teaspoon salt
1 cup powdered milk
Cold water
4 good sized slices of salt pork

Cream sugar and lard; then blend in the graham flour. To the flour add baking powder, salt and powdered milk and sift together over the first mixture. Blend the whole thoroughly and add enough cold water to make a spreading dough. Try the pork slices over a low flame and when all the fat has been tried out, set aside the cracklings and turn the batter (which should be soft enough to be spread with a spoon) into the fat and cook very slowly until brown enough to turn; then flip and cook the other side until brown, pancake-fashion. The cracklings may be eaten with the bread, if desired.

(127) CANDIED FRUIT BREAD

VERY APPROPRIATE FOR AFTERNOON TEA

Makes 1 loaf. Oven temperature: 375° F.
Baking time: 1 hour.

2 cups bread flour, sifted twice
4 teaspoons baking powder
¾ cup sugar
⅓ teaspoon salt
¼ cup chopped candied citron
¼ cup seedless raisins or currants
2 tablespoons chopped candied cherries
2 tablespoons chopped candied lemon peel
¼ cup chopped almonds
¼ cup chopped pecans
2 eggs, well beaten
1 cup milk
3 tablespoons lard or butter, melted
¼ level teaspoon ground cinnamon

To the flour add baking powder, sugar and salt and sift together over well-mixed fruit and nuts. Blend thoroughly. Beat the eggs into the milk, stir in the melted butter, and mix with the flour-fruit combination, together with the cinnamon, stirring just enough to moisten it evenly. Pour into a generously buttered loaf pan and let stand for at least 30 minutes to mellow and ripen; then bake in a moderate oven as directed. Let cool before slicing very thin.

(128) CARAWAY BREAD

Makes 2 loaves. Oven temperature: 350° F.
Baking time: 45 minutes.

3½ cups sifted bread flour
1 tablespoon baking powder
½ scant cup granulated sugar
1 teaspoon salt (scant)
1½ cups cold milk
1 whole fresh egg, well beaten
1 cup seedless raisins
1 tablespoon caraway seeds
1 tablespoon melted lard or butter

To the flour add baking powder and salt and sift together, sifting a little over the parboiled, drained and dried seedless raisins. Combine the eggs with milk and sugar; then stir into flour mixture, blending well, and adding the floured raisins alternately with caraway seeds and melted lard or butter. Knead a few seconds, then allow to stand for about 30 minutes. Divide the dough between two greased loaf pans; let stand 20 minutes in a warm place before baking in a moderate oven as directed. Let cool before slicing. You may stir into the dough or the milk mixture ½ to ¾ teaspoon of vanilla extract.

(129) CHEESE SHORTBREADS

APPROPRIATE WITH ANY KIND OF SALAD

Makes about 50 tiny balls. Oven temperature: 400° F.
Baking time: 8–10 minutes.

¾ lb. American cheese, grated
¾ cup butter, creamed
A pinch of cayenne pepper
1½ cups bread flour, sifted twice with
½ scant teaspoon salt

Blend grated cheese with creamed butter thoroughly, using a wooden spoon; then blend in the flour with salt and cayenne pepper. Roll into small balls one inch in diameter. If mixture becomes too soft, put in refrigerator to chill. Place the balls on an ungreased cookie sheet and bake in a hot oven as directed until delicately brown. Serve warm.

(130) CHRISTMAS BREAD

Makes 2 loaves. Oven temperature: 350° F.
Baking time: 40 minutes (about).

1 9-oz. package dry mincemeat
½ cup water
2 cups bread flour, sifted twice
1 cup all-wheat flour (unsifted)
¾ cup fine granulated sugar
4 teaspoons baking powder
1 scant teaspoon salt
1 whole egg, slightly beaten
1 cup cold rich milk

Break the mincemeat in small pieces into a saucepan, add the water and cook, stirring it constantly, until lumps are thoroughly broken and dissolved. Bring to a brisk boil and boil for 3 minutes, as indicated on the package of mincemeat, or until mixture is practically dry. Cool. Combine sifted bread flour and all-wheat flour with sugar, baking powder and salt and mix together. Mix well the slightly beaten egg with the milk and add to the flour mixture, beating vigorously to make a smooth dough. Then fold in the mincemeat thoroughly. Pour dough into two greased loaf pans and bake in a moderate oven as directed. Preferably served cool, although it may be eaten warm, if desired.

(131) COCONUT BREAD

Makes 1 loaf. Oven temperature: 350° F.
Baking time: 45–50 minutes (about).

3 cups bread flour, sifted twice
1 tablespoon baking powder
½ teaspoon salt
1 cup shredded coconut
1 egg, well-beaten
1 cup milk
1 scant cup sugar

NOTE: If you wish, you may substitute 1 cup of whole wheat flour for 1 cup of bread flour.

To flour, add baking powder, salt and sugar and sift together over shredded coconut. Mix well. Combine egg with milk, and stir into the flour mixture, blending carefully. Let stand for 20 minutes to mellow and ripen then pour batter into a loaf pan, and bake in a moderate oven as directed. Let cool before slicing.

(132) CODFISH CORN BREAD

CALLED ALSO: "FRIDAY CORN BREAD"

Serves 6–8. Oven temperature: 425° F.
Baking time: 20–25 minutes.

¾ cup corn meal, sifted
1 cup bread flour, sifted
1 tablespoon sugar
¼ scant teaspoon dry mustard
5 teaspoons baking powder
1 cup milk
2 tablespoons shortening, melted
¼ scant teaspoon salt
1 whole egg, well beaten
½ cup salt codfish, parboiled

To the corn meal and flour, add sugar, dry mustard, baking powder and salt (more or less depending on how salt the fish is) and sift together twice. To the cold milk, add melted shortening and egg. Then stir in codfish, parboiled, squeezed dry in a clean, dry towel and put through food chopper, using the finest blade. Blend flour and milk mixtures thoroughly. Pour into a greased shallow pan, and bake until brown, in a hot oven as directed. Very appropriate for breakfast.

CORN BREAD

Legend tells us that when Columbus discovered this New World and found growing in the West Indies a high green grass with yellow "ears" of ripened grain, he called it "Indian Corn." Early explorers of every race found "corn" growing in this new land. The Frenchman Cartier reported in his journal tall corn almost hiding the huddled Indian village which later came to be known as Montreal, Canada; Spanish adventurers, voyaging the then little-known river of the Mississippi, brought back such glowing tales of the fertility of the rich, black, bottom lands, that Eastern settlers picked up their belongings and families and pushed rapidly West to seek in the untilled acres a new type of treasure known as "prairie gold."

Closely connected as it is with the rise in our industrial history and the development of foods and other notable products now produced from the corn plant, nevertheless many of the present housekeeping uses of the corn kernel were appreciated long before the Christian era. It is authentically proved that the belles and showgirls of Egypt employed cornstarch powder as "make-up," that "corn oil" was long and favorably known from Biblical times onwards, and that probably the "oil" of Arabia and adjoining sections, later used as a money exchange, was pressed from corn kernels.

Queen Elizabeth of England, who was as shrewd as she was homely, set a style in court fashions by wearing an upstanding lace collar or ruff made stiff with starch, designed to hide her all-too-scrawny neck. This fashion was also introduced for men by Elizabeth's courtier, Sir Walter Raleigh, who wore the stiff ruff which thus, shortened into a plain linen band, became the familiar stiff collar worn by men today.

Corn, according to the dictionary, is an Anglo-Saxon word that means "grain, a small seed of a certain grass such as rye, wheat, etc., or collectively, the seeds of any cereal grass used as food," and when corn is mentioned in the Bible, it probably means wheat, for at that time the word was used in its original meaning and did not refer to the Indian cereal whose real name is maize.

. . . Till at length a small green feather
From the earth shot slowly upward,
Then another and another,
And before the summer ended
Stood the maize in all its beauty,
With its shining robes about it,
And its long, soft, yellow tresses;

And in rapture Hiawatha
Cried aloud, "It is Mondamin!
Yes, the friend of man, Mondamin!"
—*The Song of Hiawatha*

And maize, as it is pretty generally called in Europe, has traveled to many countries in flinty kernels and fine ground meal, but the green corn remains peculiarly American.

According to myth the story is something like this. Once upon a time there was an Indian youth who went to the woods to fast in honor of his approaching manhood. He built himself a hut and wandered about it, praying that the Great Spirit might acknowledge him by sending him a gift for his people, who were in great need. Finally, after several days of absolute fasting, he was too weak to walk further and so lay on the ground looking at the sky. On the third day of this idleness a spirit appeared before him, dressed with flowing green plumes. The young spirit youth commanded the Indian to rise and wrestle with him if he wished to get his heart's desire. After the exercise he was exhausted and before he revived the spirit left. This was repeated for four days, and then the spirit said that he would return once more on which occasion the youth would overcome him, after which he was to strip off the green clothes and bury them in the ground. The mound over the clothes was to be tended and kept free from weeds. If this were done, so said the spirit, the young Indian would get his desire.

The lad did as he was told and one day a corn stalk grew up from the spot where the plumes had been buried.

(133) CORN BREAD—TENNESSEE MANNER

Serves 6–8. Oven temperature: 425° F.
Baking time: 18–20 minutes.

- 1 cup bread flour, sifted
- ½ cup corn meal, sifted
- 3 tablespoons granulated sugar
- 1 tablespoon baking powder
- ¾ cup bran flakes
- 1 whole fresh egg, well-beaten
- 1 cup milk
- 3 tablespoons melted butter
- ½ teaspoon salt

To the mixed flour and corn meal add sugar, baking powder and salt and sift together. Stir in the bran flakes. Combine beaten egg and cold milk and add to dry ingredients, stirring just enough to blend. Melt butter in a shallow square pan (8 × 8 inches); add the butter to the batter; pour the batter into pan and bake in a very hot oven as directed. Serve hot in squares with plenty of butter.

(134) CORN BREAD—KENTUCKY MANNER

USING WHOLE SWEET KERNELS

Serves 6. Oven temperature: 425° F.
Baking time: 30 to 35 minutes.

1 cup bread flour, sifted
2 teaspoons sugar
1¼ teaspoons salt
2½ teaspoons baking powder
2½ cups scraped sweet corn kernels
1 whole fresh egg, well-beaten
¼ cup shortening, melted

To the flour add sugar, salt and baking powder and sift together over the corn, mixing thoroughly. Stir in egg alternately with melted shortening—no liquid is necessary, the moisture being given by the scraped corn. Turn into a generously greased shallow pan (8 × 8 inches) and bake in a very hot oven as directed. Serve hot with plenty of butter.

(135) CORN BREAD—FARMER'S METHOD

VERY RICH AND MELLOW BREAD

Serves 6–8. Oven temperature: 425° F.
Baking time: 18–20 minutes (about).

4 cups white corn meal
2 cups boiling water
4 whole fresh eggs, well-beaten
1 cup evaporated milk
1 cup hot water
2 teaspoons salt
¼ cup bacon or ham drippings

Pour boiling water over meal and stir well. To the eggs add combined drippings, evaporated undiluted milk, hot water and salt; blend well; then mix thoroughly with white corn meal. Turn batter into two greased shallow pans (8 × 8 inches). Bake one pan in a very hot oven as directed, and while this is being served bake the other pan in the same way. Serve with plenty of butter and molasses.

(136) CORN BREAD—ALABAMA METHOD

Serves 6. Oven temperature: 425° F.
Baking time: 25 minutes (about).

Small squares of bacon stirred into the batter of white or yellow corn meal flavor the corn bread during its period in a hot oven. The bread emerges brown and inviting, needing only butter and perhaps a touch of sweetness in the form of honey, jam, marmalade or molasses to complete its appeal at breakfast or midday luncheon.

- 1 cup corn meal, sifted
- ¼ cup bread flour, sifted
- 1½ teaspoons granulated sugar
- ½ teaspoon baking soda
- ½ teaspoon salt
- ¼ teaspoon ground mace
- 1 whole fresh egg, well-beaten
- ½ cup fresh sweet milk
- ½ cup buttermilk
- 2 or 3 slices bacon, cut small, partially fried
- 1 tablespoon bacon fat
- ½ cup top milk

To the corn meal and flour, mixed together, add sugar, soda, salt and ground mace (may be omitted) and sift together. Combine the egg, first ½ cup of milk and buttermilk, and beat together, then stir into the dry ingredients, beating slightly, adding as you go along the partially fried bacon. Heat a square pan (8 × 8 inches) and grease with bacon fat, then pour batter into it. Lastly pour the remaining ½ cup rich milk over the top, but do not stir in. Bake in a very hot oven as directed or until the bread browns on top, is firm and shrinks slightly from the sides of the pan. Serve as hot as possible.
NOTE: All the above corn bread recipes may be formed into small pones or cakes, placed upon a greased, heated iron griddle and baked in a quick oven (400–425° F.). In that case the bread should be served uncovered so as to let the steam escape.

(137) CORN BREAD LOAF—MONTANA METHOD

Makes 1 loaf. Oven temperature: 350° F.
Baking time: 1 hour (about).

This bread should be prepared the night before baking in order to let it ferment well. Proceed as follows:

Stir 2 cups rapidly boiling water into enough corn meal to make it thick enough to drop off spoon. Let this stand till lukewarm, then stir in 2½ cups lukewarm water, and thicken again with corn meal.

Let stand overnight to ferment well, covered with a light, clean cloth. Into the fermented mixture, sift 2 cups of bread flour, ½ cup granulated sugar, ¾ teaspoon baking soda, and 1 teaspoon salt, and blend thoroughly. Now add 2 generous tablespoons of butter or margarine and turn dough into a well-greased loaf pan. Bake as directed. Serve warm or cold.

The Roman goddess Ceres was patron deity of all growing vegetation and it is from her name that the word cereal *is appropriately enough derived. Here is one kind of bread-meal made from that precious cereal, the corn:*

(138) CORN BREAD SOUFFLÉ—MA FAÇON
("My Way")

A MEAL IN ONE DISH

Serves 4. Oven temperature: 350° F.
Baking time: 20 minutes.

1½ cups milk
¼ cup white corn meal
4 egg yolks, beaten thick
½ teaspoon salt
4 egg whites, stiffly beaten
1 lb. link sausage, parboiled
1 generous tablespoon butter
4 fresh whole eggs
Pepper to taste

Cook the milk and corn meal in a double boiler, stirring until smooth. Beat egg yolks with salt and a little pepper to taste, then beat this into the hot mush. Cool. When cold, fold in the stiffly beaten egg whites. Turn mixture into a generously buttered baking pan (8 × 8 inches). Quickly parboil the sausages, no longer than one minute; drain and press them lengthwise throughout the mush; dot with extra butter and bake in a moderate oven as directed. Quickly make four depressions in top of the corn bread soufflé with a spoon; drop a whole egg into each; return to the oven and bake until eggs are set, about 10 minutes. Serve immediately.

(139) CORN BREAD RING—CREOLE MANNER

Serves 6. Oven temperature: 350° F.
Baking time: 20 minutes.

May be served as is and very hot, or filled with creamed foods, as codfish, chicken, vegetables, etc. If the ring is filled let stand 10 minutes after baking and unmold on a large hot platter.

¾ cup corn meal
2 cups milk, cold
1 cup water, cold
1 medium-sized onion
10 whole cloves
1 tablespoon butter
2 whole fresh eggs, well beaten
½ teaspoon salt
⅛ teaspoon white pepper
⅛ teaspoon ground thyme

Stick cloves in onion and place in saucepan, add milk and water and slowly bring to a boil. When boiling briskly, sprinkle corn meal into the mixture, and cook for 20 minutes, stirring frequently. Remove the onion after taking pan from the fire and stir in butter and eggs with salt, pepper and thyme. Turn mixture into a well-greased ring mold and bake in a moderate oven as directed. Serve hot with or without creamed food mixture.

(140) CORN CREAM BREAD

Serves 6. Oven temperature: 375° F.
Baking time: 1 hour (about).

This rich corn bread should be served as hot as possible with jam, marmalade, jelly, or molasses. A fine breakfast or luncheon bread.

1¾ cups white or yellow corn meal
1¾ cups briskly boiling water
½ teaspoon salt
⅛ teaspoon summer savory
1 tablespoon butter or margarine
3 eggs, well beaten
3 cups buttermilk
1 scant teaspoon baking soda

Drop the corn meal, rain-like, into the salted briskly boiling water, stirring vigorously; stir in butter. Combine eggs, buttermilk, soda and summer savory and mix thoroughly with rotary egg beater. Slowly add to corn meal, mixing well with a wooden spoon. Pour batter into a well-greased baking pan and bake until firm in a moderate oven as directed.

CORN HOMINY

Because hominy is so very mild, though distinctive in flavor, it will combine with other foods most successfully, as well as play its role alone. As you know, hominy is made from corn. The whole kernels are soaked in lye to remove the husks, and are then cooked until tender. There are several excellent brands from which to choose of both the grits (the finer form more popular in the South) and the large hominy or samp. Hominy combined with tomato sauce and grated cheese is a favorite casserole dish in the Middle West. Good with fried meat patties and buttered greens, such as kale, string beans, dandelions, cooked lettuce, etc. Molded grits, when sliced and fried in butter, are a fine substitute for potatoes and may be used for garnishing meat, poultry and game. Hominy fritters, hominy au gratin, scalloped hominy, hominy gems, creamed hominy, hominy ring filled with creamed spinach, meat, poultry—all these are favorite dishes in America. Boiled hominy, well salted and buttered and made pink with paprika, vies with wild rice to accompany duck and game.

HOW TO MAKE HOMINY AT HOME—This is a very old pioneer recipe which may come in handy for a thrifty homemaker when there is abundance of corn. You may use baking soda instead of lye. The results are the same with either. Select sound corn, shell and put into an iron or enamelled vessel. To each quart of corn, allow 4 tablespoons of baking soda. Soak the corn overnight. Put it over a low flame and heat, gradually adding the soda and enough water barely to cover. Let boil slowly until the hulls will slip off readily when you try a few kernels. Then wash the corn thoroughly in clear, cold water until free from hulls and cook until tender. If the corn is very dry you may need more baking soda. The hominy grits are ready to prepare in many a delicious way as indicated above. Browned hominy ties in perfectly with pork chops for dinner instead of potatoes.

(141) CORN HOMINY BREAD

Serves 6. Oven temperature: 375° F.
Baking time: 35 minutes (about).

1 cup freshly boiled hominy grits
2 tablespoons butter
½ cup white corn meal
1 cup rich milk, hot
½ teaspoon salt
2 eggs, well beaten

Add butter to the hot hominy, stir until melted, and add alternately the hot milk and corn meal. Add salt to eggs and stir briskly into the mixture. Turn batter into a greased baking dish and bake in a moderate oven as directed.

(142) CRACKLIN' BREAD—SOUTHERN MANNER

Serves 6 generously. Oven temperature: 400° F.
Baking time: 35–40 minutes.

Cracklings are crisp, lightly browned bits of pork fat that remain after the lard has been tried out. For next to nothing your butcher will sell you the pig fat next to the skin. Cut it into 3 or 4 inch squares and render it (try it out) in a large frying pan over low heat. The squares will shrink considerably in the process. When a good brown, drain them thoroughly on absorbent brown paper, sprinkle with salt and pepper and serve with hominy grits. Really delicious. To make cracklin' bread proceed as follows:

3 cups sifted white corn meal
2 cups milk
2 egg yolks, well beaten
1 cup cracklings
½ generous teaspoon salt
1 teaspoon sugar
4 teaspoons baking powder
2 stiffly beaten egg whites

To the corn meal add sugar and salt and pour in half of the milk. Blend to a smooth paste. Then beat in egg yolks, one at a time (beating well after each addition) alternately with remaining cup of milk. Beat briskly for 1 minute, adding while beating, the baking powder, alternately with cracklings. Do not add salt or pepper again. Lastly fold in the stiffly beaten egg whites; turn into a well-greased baking pan, previously heated in the oven, and bake in a hot oven as directed. Serve hot.

(143) CRACKLING BREAD—NEW YORK MANNER

Serves 6. Oven temperature: 425° F.
Baking time: 30 minutes (about).

1½ cups corn meal, sifted
¾ cup bread flour, sifted
½ teaspoon salt
½ teaspoon baking soda
1 cup sour milk, cold
1 cup cracklings (see No. 142)

Mix corn meal and flour with salt and soda and sift together. Stir in sour milk, alternately with cold cracklings, made as indicated for No. 142. Blend thoroughly. Turn mixture into a well-greased baking pan, or form into individual oblong cakes and bake in a very hot oven as directed. Serve hot. Try it with a green salad.

(144) CRACKLING BREAD—PENNSYLVANIA MANNER

Serves 6 generously. Oven temperature: 425° F.
Baking time: 25 minutes.

2 cups briskly boiling water
2 cups water ground corn meal, sifted
2 eggs, well-beaten
½ teaspoon baking soda
½ teaspoon salt
1 cup buttermilk
1 cup cracklings (see No. 142)

To the corn meal, add salt and soda (a level teaspoon sugar is optional) and sift over briskly boiling water, stirring quickly until free from lumps. Mix eggs and buttermilk thoroughly and add gradually to corn meal paste, stirring constantly. Lastly stir in the cracklings, made as indicated for No. 142. Turn mixture into a greased, shallow baking pan and bake in a very hot oven as directed. Serve hot.

CRANBERRIES

Who gives a second thought to the luscious "cranb'ry sars" that somebody in days long gone said, put the "hanks" in Thanksgiving? —Yet what would that festive dinner be without cranberries? Ask almost anybody what he knows about cranberries and their ways and about all he will admit is that they grow. He may have seen where they grow, but because there's nothing especially inviting about cranberry bogs, the memory doesn't linger. And it's possible, with huckleberries in mind, that he may be under the impression that an army of pickers invades the bogs with baskets or buckets and picks each berry by hand. But autumn out in the open—provided your mind is open to every new thing—is a revelation.

If there is Yankee blood in your veins a close-up view of the harvesting process itself conjures up visions of a table laden with all sorts of good things to eat with a huge roast turkey in the center and hard by a great big dish of cranberry sauce. That is what those bleak bogs will do to your appetite if you're there at the proper season.

"Easy money," you say to yourself as bushel after bushel of the berries goes into the packing house. Not at all, says the man whose money is invested in the industry, for that is what it is, just as over in the Connecticut Valley, tobacco growing looks a matter of simply raking in the dollars. Cranberries, like tobacco, don't just grow. Nature, in fact, takes over only a relatively small share of the labor that goes into production.

There is even more science involved in providing the berries with just the right amount of water than in irrigating the beet and alfalfa fields of Colorado and New Mexico and the other arid states. It's not with any possible water shortage that the cranberry industry has to cope, for water is almost always to be had. It's the proper amount. And while the bogs are taking that treatment they have to be watched and carefully tended. If the weather bureau comes along with a frost warning the water must be turned on. If an army worm is lurking in the neighborhood, that calls for a flood. And, in turn, the water must be allowed to escape at exactly the right time in order to maintain normal conditions.

Sand also is a requisite, even though that may sound like an anomaly, farmers generally rating sand as a foe. Just as fertilizer is important to most growing crops, sand is important to cranberry culture. The underlying soil is a rich peat. Over it, three inches or so of sand are required for the bush to root in, but it must have something more substantial to feed on. The sand also serves as a protection against worms and a pest called *the girdler,* not to mention the frost.

These are the processes that have been developed after more than three hundred years' study. The Indians recognized the value of cranberries and showed the Pilgrims some things they never knew before in bringing them gifts of wild turkey and cranberries. No wonder the Pilgrims were thankful.

Those who have looked upon the blossoming cranberry vines in the month of June declare that nothing in the floral kingdom can equal the living, blush-tinted counterpane woven of myriad tiny, four-petaled flowers shimmering in soft breezes from the sea. With the birth of the berries, the pattern changes to a soft maroon, and after the gathering each patch looks like a red squirrel pelt spread out to dry.

From the standpoint of preparation, too, cranberries have excellent recommendations. They are clean, smooth, firm berries which require only light rinsing. The sorting is made easy by the fact that their usefulness can be judged by the "feel" in most cases. Thus, they are the least possible trouble to prepare.

In muffins, jelly roll and other breads, the cut berry also makes a pleasing color contrast to the white or ivory tone of the baked dough or cake. For small pastry tarts, too, as well as for a large Winter "mock cherry pie," the cranberry supplies a decorative epilogue in the form of a rich, bright filling behind the bars or lattice strips of pastry.

For the following recipe, raw cranberries are used. As for the nut meats, any kind may be used, including Brazil nuts and almonds.

(145) CRANBERRY NUT BREAD

Makes 1 loaf. Oven temperature: 350° F.
Baking time: 1 hour (about).

1 cup washed cranberries
1 cup sugar
3 cups bread flour, sifted
4 teaspoons baking powder
½ cup chopped nut meats
Grated rind of a large orange
1 whole fresh, slightly beaten egg
1 cup milk
2 tablespoons butter or margarine, melted
1 level teaspoon salt

Put cranberries through food chopper and mix with ¼ cup of the sugar. To the flour add remaining sugar, baking powder and salt and sift together. Then stir in the grated orange rind and chopped nut meats, rolled in a little of the flour mixture, and combine with cranberries. Mix thoroughly the egg, milk and melted butter and stir into the flour mixture. Turn batter into a well-greased loaf pan and bake in a moderate oven as directed. Let cool before slicing.

(146) CZECH BREAD OR HORN BREAD

ROHLIKY BREAD OR CRESCENTS

Makes about a dozen. Oven temperature: 400° F.
Baking time: 15–20 minutes.

3½ cups bread flour, sifted
2 tablespoons sugar
¼ cup lard or butter
1 teaspoon salt
1 cake of compressed yeast
Caraway seeds
1¾ cups milk (about) scalded and cooled

To the flour add salt and sift together over a large mixing bowl. Make a depression in the flour and put in the combined sugar and lukewarm milk, then crumble in the yeast cake. Let stand for about 5 or 6 minutes, or until yeast is dissolved, then stir in the melted butter or lard. Gradually mix all together, starting from the center, so as to form a sponge. Cover with a light cloth and let rise to double its bulk, in a warm place. Turn the dough upon a lightly floured board and knead lightly for about ½ minute. Place in a large bowl and let rise for about 15 minutes. Toss upon lightly floured board, flour your rolling pin and roll out into a large circular piece ¼-inch thick. Cut into long, narrow pie-shaped wedges. Roll up each wedge beginning at wide end of triangle. Curve ends to give crescent shape. Moisten tops slightly with either water or milk and sprinkle with mixed salt and caraway seeds. Place on greased baking sheet; let rise until double its bulk, and bake in a hot oven as directed. Serve warm or cold.

(147) CZECH BREAD AND VARIATIONS

BOHEMIAN CZECH KOLACHKY

Makes about 6 dozen. Oven temperature: 375° F.
Baking time: 25 minutes.

These little breads, more like our buns, are great favorites in Bohemia. The recipe was introduced into this country by Bohemians who settled in America especially in Minnesota. The recipe varies as to fillings. Each home has its own particular recipe, handed down through generations, but the standard shape remains the same. As in almost all breads made in the Balkans, yeast is used. Here is how:

1 yeast cake
¼ cup water, lukewarm
½ cup good butter
¾ cup granulated sugar
2 whole large eggs or 3 small ones
2 cups sweet milk, scalded and cooled
6 or more cups bread flour, sifted twice
1 teaspoon salt
Powdered sugar

Dissolve crumbled yeast cake in lukewarm water. Cream butter, then add sugar gradually, creaming until light and fluffy, adding the salt. Turn the dissolved yeast cake into the lukewarm milk. Mix well; add 3 cups of the flour and beat briskly until well blended. Then add creamed butter and beat until there are no lumps. Add the whole eggs, one at a time, beating well after each addition.

Gradually add the remaining flour, spoonful by spoonful, until the dough is smooth enough to handle. Turn upon a lightly floured board and knead (adding more flour if necessary) until dough is elastic and glossy, rather on the soft side, but not sticky. Place again in a well-greased mixing bowl, cover with a light towel and let rise to double its bulk (about 2½ hours). Now turn the dough upon a warmed board, slightly floured, pat down a little (½ minute), roll out to ¼-inch in thickness and cut into 2-inch squares. Place a tablespoon of any desired filling (indicated below) on each square, gather up the four corners carefully and fold one over the other square-envelope fashion. When folded correctly, the filling will peek through the four sides. Place the *kolachky* or buns on a greased cookie sheet, about 2 inches apart, and allow to rise to double in bulk, in a warm place (¾ of an hour or so). Bake in a moderate oven as directed. When cool, sprinkle generously with powdered sugar.

KOLACHKY FILLINGS

APPLE FILLING—Peel and slice 4 large apples and cook with ⅓ cup water and 3 tablespoons red cinnamon candies, until the apple slices are soft, but not mushy.

APRICOT PRUNE FILLING—Wash and boil together until tender ½ lb. each of prunes and dried apricots. Pit prunes, then chop both fruits finely; sweeten to taste, and mix well with ½ cup chopped nut meats and 1 teaspoon grated orange or lemon rind. Flavor with a ½ teaspoon of vanilla extract, if desired.

DATE AND BUTTER FILLING—Cook 2 cups of washed, pitted dates with ⅓ cup sugar and ¼ cup butter, stirring constantly to prevent scorching or burning, adding ¼ scant cup water and a tiny pinch of salt. When thick, flavor with ⅓ teaspoon vanilla or ¼ teaspoon almond extract.

DATE AND NUT FILLING—Pit and boil ¾ lb. dates for about 15 minutes in scant ½ cup water with ½ teaspoon grated orange rind. Remove from the fire; beat slightly; sweeten with 1 tablespoon brown sugar and stir in ½ scant cup of chopped nut meats (any kind).

FIG NUT FILLING—Proceed as indicated for Date and Nut Filling, substituting figs for dates and flavoring with ¼ teaspoon almond extract.

POPPY SEED FILLING—Cook 2 cups ground poppy seeds in ½ cup sweet milk, ¼ cup corn syrup and 2 tablespoons granulated sugar for about 5 minutes: stir in 1 teaspoon butter and ¼ teaspoon cinnamon.

PRUNE CINNAMON FILLING—Clean and boil 1 lb. prunes in enough water barely to cover until tender (about 15 minutes) with 2 slices of lemon. When tender, drain and coarsely chop. Flavor with ¼ teaspoon cinnamon and 1 teaspoon grated orange rind.

RAISIN NUT FILLING—Parboil 1 lb. seedless raisins for about 5 minutes; drain and coarsely chop. Combine with ½ cup chopped nut meats (any kind) and sweeten to taste with either brown or granulated sugar. You may add also ¼ teaspoon vanilla.

In fact these delicious sweet breads may be filled with almost any mixture used for pies or cookies.

DATES

There is no "closed season" on dates. Dates are fresh, tasty and available all the year round and fit into the balanced menu at all seasons. Golden dates, dried right on the tree by the sun, which seals in their goodness and turns their natural sweetness to easily digested invert sugar, are concentrated sources of energy and put no tax on digestion! They also contain iron for the blood and calcium for the teeth and bones and the vitamins A and B.

Many a dull meal is brightened by the addition of dates. Sliced dates perk up the cereal; stuffed dates make a confection second to none; dates straight from the carton with a big glass of milk are a lunch fit for any mother's daughter or father's son. Cookies, salads, pudding, cake, fruit cups, ice cream, gelatine molds—how will you have your just and rightful dates?

Some of the dried fruits of the date palm have a natural sugar content as high as 80 per cent, combined with other carbohydrates, proteins and fats. They figure as one of the world's most important staple foods yet we know them best as an occasional treat for the children, and the practical confectioner, with unconscious irony, dresses them up in jackets of sugar—quite literally, "sweets to the sweet."

Probably there are persons in this part of the world who have never given the date a thought, never bought a pound of dates, never tasted a date, but always in the rural general store or the urban corner grocery the open box of dates reposes just below the inevitable bunch of bananas, and those familiar companions may have appeared, just as they do today, in the first corner grocery that was opened in the Massachusetts Bay colony. In Jericho, the city of palm trees, the date is commonplace and it was a staple commodity in Babylon, Nineveh, Palmyra and Tyre, yet we of the western world have never taken the trouble to cultivate its acquaintance, though it has been bread and meat to millions, and is one of nature's most impressive gifts.

We know little enough of the Arabian desert, beyond the gallant exploits of the late Colonel Lawrence and some counterfeit presentments arranged for us on Hollywood lots, but we are inclined to wonder how and why any people whatsoever should voluntarily pass their lives in such an arid and dusty place—just as we marvel at the Eskimo's evidently placid family life in an igloo erected on a cake of ice. But the Arabs and their faithful camels are there and were there when America was inhabited by the first copper-colored aborigines. It is something to think about—not casually, but with earnest attention to first causes and the solemn problems of the human race—that in that far-flung howling wilderness of shifting sand, eternally scorched and baked by a fiery sun, mysterious Nature graciously provided the date palm to furnish a fruit that is one of the most sustaining rations known to man. "Some call it Evolution, and others call it God."

That prodigy of energy and endurance, the Arab, can cheerfully subsist for days, weeks and months upon handfuls of dried dates; and the trees, which sometimes reach a height of a hundred feet, provide him not only with food but with his favorite building material. His house, if he has one, is made of palm timber, thatched with palm leaves, and palm fiber is in his furniture, baskets, ropes and household appliances. Dates, some authorities have asserted, constitute the national wealth of Arabia, the fruit and by-products amounting to an average of half of the annual exports, and though our dates now come from Arizona and California and from European countries along the Mediterranean, in significant volume, the Arabic people still ship over a hundred million pounds of date products to Europe and America every year.

There is quite a ceremony attached to the harvesting of the dates. Before the clusters are to be cut, the climbers and other natives join in a chant thanking Allah for the harvest. After the bunches have all been cut off, and before they come down from the trees, the boys lead the crowd in an invocation to Allah, saying, "May Allah in his loving kindness preserve this palm from all harm and permit it to bear a good harvest in the season that is to come."

(148) DATE BREAD

Makes 1 loaf. Oven temperature: 350° F.
Baking time: 50–55 minutes.

2 cups chopped dates
1 teaspoon baking soda
1 tablespoon butter
½ teaspoon salt
1 egg
1 cup boiling water
1 teaspoon vanilla extract
1 cup sugar
½ cup chopped pecans
1½ cups bread flour, sifted twice
½ teaspoon baking powder

Sprinkle soda over dates; add boiling water. Let stand until cool. Beat egg with salt, sugar, butter, nuts and vanilla extract; then mix well with the dates and water. To the flour add baking powder and sift together; add to first mixture and blend thoroughly. Turn batter into a generously greased loaf pan, and bake in a moderate oven as directed. Allow to cool before slicing.

(149) DATE BROWN BREAD

STEAMED

Makes 2 small loaves. Steaming time: 3 hours (about).

A fine bread to serve steaming hot with baked beans, lima beans, cole slaw or bean salad.

2 cups whole wheat flour, sifted
1 cup bread flour, sifted
1 cup yellow corn meal, sifted
1¼ teaspoons baking soda
1¼ teaspoons salt
1 cup Grandma's molasses (very dark)
2 cups buttermilk
1 cup shredded dates

Brush the bottom and inside of 2 quart molds or pound coffee cans with melted fat. Have the water boiling briskly in the steamer, or in a large kettle equipped with a trivet to receive the molds. Combine whole wheat and bread flours with yellow corn meal, add soda and salt, then sift together into a large mixing bowl. Stir in Grandma's molasses and add enough buttermilk to make a batter that will pour. Add the dates, rolled in flour (raisins, figs, prunes, apricots, or any kind of dried fruit may be substituted), and mix rapidly. Pour batter into greased molds or cans, filling them about 2/3 full to allow for expansion; cover with waxed paper, adjust the lids securely; place in steamer or kettle with boiling water coming up about half way on the molds. Cover tight and steam steadily for about 3 hours. Smaller molds, about 1/2 lb., will steam in half of the time. When done, remove the lids and waxed paper; cool slightly. Slice thin or thick, using a string or a knife dipped in hot water. Serve as hot as possible, although when cold it is delicious, too.

(150) DATE AND CHEESE BREAD

Makes 1 loaf. Oven temperature: 350° F.
Baking time: 1 hour.

4 cups of bread flour, sifted
5 teaspoons baking powder
1/2 teaspoon baking soda
1 scant teaspoon salt
1/2 cup grated American cheese
3/4 cup molasses
3/4 cup sterilized dates, coarsely chopped
1 1/2 cups cold milk
2 tablespoons butter or margarine

Measure the flour; add baking powder, soda and salt, and sift three times, sifting a little over chopped dates. Cream together American cheese (other hard cheeses may be used) and butter; then rub the dates into this mixture; add the flour mixture, alternately with combined milk and molasses, mixing thoroughly. Turn batter into generously buttered—not greased—loaf pan, and bake in a moderate oven as directed. Remove immediately from oven and rub top with butter. Allow to cool in the pan before slicing.

(151) DATE, HONEY AND NUT BREAD

Makes 1 loaf. Oven temperature: 325° F.
Baking time: 1 long hour.

1 cup sterilized dates, chopped
1 cup boiling water
2 tablespoons butter or margarine
1 cup thick honey
1 egg, well beaten
1 1/2 cups bread flour, sifted
1 cup nut meats (any kind), chopped
1 scant teaspoon salt
2 teaspoons baking powder

Parboil dates for 5 to 6 minutes in boiling water, then beat to a paste and allow to cool. Combine honey and shortening, creaming well, adding the beaten egg; then combine with date paste, alternately with chopped nut meats. To the flour add salt and baking powder, and sift twice. Combine flour mixture with the first mixture blending well. Turn dough into generously greased loaf pan, and bake in a moderately low oven as directed. Let cool before slicing.

(152) DATE, MAPLE AND NUT BREAD

NO MILK USED

Makes 1 loaf. Oven temperature: 325° F.
Baking time: 1 short hour.

1 cup sterilized dates, chopped
1 cup boiling water
½ cup maple sugar
1 whole fresh egg, well-beaten
1 cup bread flour, sifted twice
1 cup whole wheat flour
1 teaspoon baking powder
1 teaspoon (scant) salt
1 tiny pinch of ground ginger
½ teaspoon baking soda
1 tablespoon melted butter or margarine
½ cup nut meats, chopped
2 tablespoons maple syrup

Parboil chopped dates in boiling water for 5 minutes. Cool; add egg and maple sugar and beat to a paste. Combine the two flours. Add baking powder, salt, ginger and soda, and mix together, adding a little over the nut meats. Stir in the butter or margarine alternately with the nuts and add to first mixture, stirring only until blended. Turn dough into a generously buttered loaf pan and bake in a moderately low oven as directed. Brush top with maple syrup while hot and let cool before slicing. Sprinkle finely chopped nut meats over maple sugar, if desired.

(153) DATE MOLASSES BREAD

Makes 1 loaf. Oven temperature: 325° F.
Baking time: 1¼ hours (about).

¾ cup cold water
½ cup light brown sugar
½ cup molasses
¾ cup cold milk
1 cup bread flour, sifted
2 cups whole wheat flour
¾ teaspoon salt (scant)
1 scant teaspoon baking powder
¾ teaspoon baking soda
¾ cup chopped sterilized dates
½ teaspoon orange grating
1 tablespoon butter, melted

Dissolve brown sugar in cold water; then stir in the molasses, mixed with cold milk, blending thoroughly. To the combined flours add salt, baking powder and soda and mix together adding a little over chopped dates; then stir in the orange rind. Add flour mixture to first mixture, alternately with floured, chopped dates, blending well. Turn dough into greased loaf pan, and bake in a moderately slow oven as directed. When removing from the oven, turn out on a rack and brush top with melted butter. Let cool before slicing.

(154) DATE MOLASSES YEAST BREAD

KEEPS MOIST FOR SEVERAL DAYS

Makes 3 loaves. Oven temperature: 350° F.
Baking time: 55 minutes (about).

3 cakes compressed yeast
¼ cup lukewarm water
½ cup molasses
1½ teaspoons salt
1½ cups lukewarm milk
1½ cups lukewarm water
4 tablespoons melted butter or margarine
3 cups quartered pasteurized dates
10 to 12 cups entire-wheat flour

Dissolve yeast cakes in the quarter-cup lukewarm water and combine with molasses, salt, milk and the 1½ cups lukewarm water, melted butter or margarine and dates. Mix slightly to blend. Beat in the entire-wheat flour until mixture is of the consistency to knead, and knead about five minutes, or until dough is elastic and does not stick to the board, which should be lightly floured. Cover with a light, dry cloth; let stand in a greased pan, placed over warm water to rise until doubled in bulk. Toss upon lightly floured board, kneading lightly for about a minute; then form into three loaves. Transfer the loaves to well-greased loaf pans; cover and let rise again until doubled in bulk. Bake in a moderate oven as directed or until firm in the center and brown on top. Rub over with butter after baking. Let cool before slicing.

(155) DATE NUT BREAD

USING BAKING POWDER

Makes 1 loaf. Oven temperature: 350° F.
Baking time: 1¼ hours.

½ lb. dates, chopped
1 cup boiling water
¼ cup butter, margarine or lard
1 scant cup sugar
1 teaspoon salt
1 whole egg, well beaten
2½ cups bread flour, sifted
2½ teaspoons baking powder
½ cup chopped nut meats (any kind)

Parboil chopped dates in the boiling water for 3 or 4 minutes; stir in shortening, sugar and salt; blend well and allow to cool. When cold, stir in the beaten egg, alternately with flour, mixed with baking powder. Sift a little over the chopped nut meats and add them alternately with the flour mixture, blending thoroughly. Turn dough into generously greased loaf pan and bake in a moderate oven as directed. Let cool before slicing.

(156) DATE NUT BREAD

USING BROWN SUGAR AND MILK

Makes 1 loaf. Oven temperature: 350° F.
Baking time: 1 hour.

- 3 cups bread flour, sifted
- 3 teaspoons baking powder
- ½ generous teaspoon salt
- ½ cup brown sugar
- 1 cup sterilized dates, chopped
- ½ cup broken walnut meats
- 1 whole fresh egg, well-beaten
- 1 cup cold milk
- ¼ cup melted butter or margarine
- 1 tablespoon butter

To the flour add baking powder and salt and sift together; stir in the brown sugar, then the dates and walnut meats, mixing only enough to flour and separate them. Combine egg with milk and stir into the flour mixture. Blend well. Turn dough into a buttered loaf pan after stirring in the melted butter or margarine, and bake in a moderate oven as directed. Remove from oven; let stand 5 minutes or so before turning out of pan. Cool before slicing.

If desired, substitute 1 cup of graham flour for one cup of bread flour.

(157) DATE NUT YEAST BREAD

Makes 1 loaf. Oven temperature: 400° F.
Baking time: 45–50 minutes.

- 1 cup lukewarm milk
- 1 cake compressed yeast
- 1 tablespoon granulated sugar
- 1¼ cups bread flour, sifted
- 2 tablespoons lard or butter
- ⅓ cup granulated sugar
- ½ generous teaspoon salt
- 1 egg yolk
- 2 cups bread flour, sifted (about)
- ¾ cup chopped nut meats (any kind)
- ⅓ cup chopped, sterilized dates

Scald milk and cool to lukewarm. Crumble the yeast cake into a mixing bowl, add sugar and a little lukewarm milk, stir and when dissolved, add the remainder of the milk; then stir in the 1¼ cups of flour. Beat vigorously until sponge is smooth. Cover, and set over a pan containing hot water to rise until light and bubbling on the surface (about 15 minutes).

Cream lard or butter with the sugar; add salt and egg yolk, and when smooth stir into the yeast mixture. Beat well. Now add the 2 additional cups of flour, or enough to make a dough, soft enough to handle. Mix in the chopped nut meats and dates. Toss upon a lightly floured board and knead until dough is elastic and not sticky, using a little more flour if needed. Return dough to a greased bowl, cover and set in a warm place to rise to double in bulk (about 2½ hours). Shape into a loaf; place in well-greased loaf pan; cover and let rise again to double its bulk (about one hour). Bake in a moderately hot oven as directed. Let cool before slicing.

(158) DATE ORANGE BREAD

Makes 1 loaf. Oven temperature: 350° F.
Baking time: 55 minutes (about).

1½ cups bread flour, sifted
1 tablespoon baking powder
1 scant teaspoon salt
1½ cups whole wheat flour
1 generous tablespoon sugar
1 cup sterilized dates, sliced
1 generous tablespoon chopped candied orange peel
1 whole egg, well-beaten
1½ cups sweet milk

To the flour add baking powder and salt and sift together. Stir in whole wheat flour and sugar. Add dates and chopped orange peel and mix well. Combine egg and cold milk and beat into the flour mixture. Turn dough into a generously buttered loaf pan, and bake in a moderate oven as directed. Let cool before slicing.

(159) DRIED APRICOT BRAN NUT BREAD

LIGHTLY SPICED

Makes 1 loaf. Oven temperature: 350° F.
Baking time: 1 hour (about).

1 cup dried apricots, coarsely cut
1 cup boiling water
¼ cup butter or margarine
⅓ cup sugar
1 egg, well beaten
2 cups bread flour, sifted
4 teaspoons baking powder
½ generous teaspoon baking soda
½ teaspoon salt
¼ teaspoon ground nutmeg
1¼ cups sour milk
1 cup bran
½ cup chopped nut meats (any kind)

Scald chopped apricots with boiling water and allow to stand 10 minutes, covered. Cream butter or margarine; gradually add sugar, creaming thoroughly. Add beaten egg and beat until mixture is light and fluffy. Drain apricots and roll in a little bread flour, then add to creamed mixture, blending well. Combine flour with baking powder, soda and nutmeg, and add alternately with sour milk to first mixture, mixing thoroughly. Now add combined bran and nut meats and beat until batter is smooth. Turn into generously greased loaf pan, and bake in a moderate oven as directed. Let cool before slicing.

(160) DRIED APRICOT GRAHAM BREAD

Makes 1 loaf. Oven temperature: 325° F.
Baking time: 1 hour (about).

- 1 cup boiling water
- 1/3 cup light brown sugar
- 1 cup dried apricots, coarsely chopped
- 2 eggs, well-beaten
- 2/3 cup brown sugar
- 1 cup graham flour
- 1 generous teaspoon salt
- 1 tablespoon baking powder
- 1/2 teaspoon baking soda
- 3/4 cup chopped walnuts and almonds (equal parts)
- 1 3/4 cups bread flour, sifted twice

To the boiling water add the 1/3 cup light brown sugar and stir until dissolved, then stir in the chopped apricots; cover and allow to cool. To the eggs, add the remaining brown sugar and beat until light; stir into the cooled apricot mixture, blending thoroughly. Combine the two flours with salt, baking powder and soda and sift together; sift a little over the mixed walnuts and almonds. Beat the flour mixture into the first mixture, then add floured walnuts and almonds. Blend well, pour into greased loaf pan, and bake in a moderately slow oven as directed. Let cool before slicing.

(161) DRIED APRICOT ORANGE NUT BREAD

Makes 1 loaf. Oven temperature: 350° F.
Baking time: 1 1/4 hours.

- Soaked dried apricots to make 3/4 cup when ground
- 2 cups bread flour, sifted twice
- 1 cup whole wheat flour
- 1 tablespoon baking powder
- 1/4 teaspoon baking soda
- 1/2 generous teaspoon salt
- 1 egg, well-beaten
- 1/2 cup each brown and granulated sugars
- 2 tablespoons melted butter or margarine
- 1/2 cup unstrained orange juice
- 1/2 cup apricot water
- 3/4 cup chopped Brazil nut meats

Soak enough dried apricots in cold water for 30 minutes to make ¾ cup when drained and ground, reserving water. Combine bread flour with baking powder, soda and salt and sift together. Then stir in whole wheat flour, blending well. Cream sugar with egg and melted shortening and add to apricot-flour mixture, alternately with combined orange juice and apricot water, mixing well. Last add chopped Brazil nut meats. Turn batter into greased loaf pan, and bake in a moderate oven as directed. Let cool before slicing.

(162) DRIED FRUIT NUT BREAD

Makes 1 loaf. Oven temperature: 350° F.
Baking time: 50–55 minutes.

Put ½ cup each of dried apricots and prunes through food chopper, using coarse blade. Add fruit to ¾ cup of boiling water into which has been stirred 1 tablespoon butter, ½ cup granulated sugar, and ½ teaspoon salt. Mix well; then cool. When cold, add 1 egg, well-beaten, to ½ cup whole wheat flour. Sift twice ¾ cup bread flour and add to it ¾ teaspoon soda and 1 teaspoon baking powder; sift together over ½ cup chopped walnut meats; add this to first mixture. Flavor with 1 teaspoon orange extract; mix quickly and turn into greased loaf pan. Bake in a moderate oven as directed. Let cool before slicing.

(163) DUTCH APPLE BREAD

Makes 1 loaf. Oven temperature: 350° F.
Baking time: 55 minutes.

½ cup butter
1 cup sugar
1 egg, well-beaten
2 cups bread flour, sifted twice
½ teaspoon salt
1 teaspoon baking soda
½ teaspoon ground cinnamon
1 cup peeled, sliced apples, packed solid
½ cup sweet milk
¼ cup chopped raw cranberries

Cream butter; add sugar and cream well, then add egg. To the flour, add salt, soda and cinnamon and sift together over apple and cranberries. Mix well and add to first mixture, alternately with cold milk, stirring thoroughly. Turn batter into generously greased loaf pan, and bake in a moderate oven as directed. Let cool before slicing.

(164) DUTCH PRUNE BREAD

YEAST METHOD

Makes 2 loaves. Oven temperature: 350° F.
Baking time: 55 minutes.

- 2 cups milk, lukewarm
- 1 teaspoon salt
- 2 cakes compressed yeast
- 2 cups bread flour, sifted
- ½ scant cup granulated sugar
- 3 whole fresh eggs, well-beaten
- ½ cup melted butter
- 1 teaspoon ground cinnamon
- 1 teaspoon grated lemon rind
- 2 cups cooked prune pulp, sieved
- 6 cups bread flour, sifted
- Melted butter for top

Scald milk and cool to lukewarm. Add salt; crumble in yeast cakes and stir in the first 2 cups of flour to which has been added the sugar. Mix thoroughly. Cover and allow to rise in a warm place or over warm water until sponge is light (about ¾ hour). Then beat in melted butter mixed with cinnamon, lemon rind and prune pulp. Gradually beat in the flour. Blend well and knead until dough is elastic and smooth. Return to greased pan, cover with a dry cloth and allow to rise to double its bulk, then knead for a half minute. Turn dough into two greased loaf pans, let rise until it again doubles in bulk. Bake in a moderate oven as directed. Remove from oven and brush top with melted butter. Cool before slicing.

(165) EASTER BREAD—ARGENTINA METHOD

PAN DE PASCUASE

Makes 2 loaves. Oven temperature: 350° F.
Baking time: 30 minutes.

- 3½ cups bread flour, sifted twice
- 1 teaspoon salt
- ½ cake compressed yeast
- 1 cup sweet milk, lukewarm
- 3 tablespoons butter
- 4 eggs, unbeaten
- 1 cup seedless raisins
- ⅓ cup mixed, chopped candied orange and lemon or citron peel in equal parts
- 5 tablespoons sugar

Crumble yeast into lukewarm milk. To the flour add salt and sift together over the yeast mixture, gradually, stirring well with a wooden spoon after each addition. Cover and leave in a warm place overnight. The following morning cream butter, add sugar and cream until light and fluffy; then add the eggs, one at a time, creaming well after each addition, and add to the sponge, using more flour if needed. Knead on a lightly floured board for a few minutes, or until dough is glossy, elastic and not too stiff, adding while you are kneading the combined seedless raisins and candied fruits. Turn dough, divided in half, into two greased loaf pans, and set aside to rise for 2 hours, or until it doubles in bulk. Bake in a moderate oven as directed. Cool before slicing.

(166) EASTER BREAD—FRENCH METHOD

YEAST METHOD

Makes 2 loaves. Oven temperature: 375° F.
Baking time: 35 minutes (about).

2 compressed yeast cakes
1 cup rich milk, lukewarm
4 egg yolks, well-beaten
4 cups bread flour, sifted twice
¾ teaspoon salt
½ cup sugar
½ scant cup melted butter
1 tablespoon finely chopped citron
1 tablespoon finely chopped angelica
1 tablespoon finely chopped orange peel
½ cup white raisins

Crumble yeast into a large mixing bowl; add scalded milk, cooled to lukewarm, and stir until yeast is dissolved. Beat in the egg yolks; then gradually add flour, mixed with salt and sugar and sifted again, mixing well after each addition. Combine melted butter and fruit thoroughly. Turn out on lightly floured board; knead 2 or 3 minutes until dough is smooth and elastic. Put in a greased bowl, cover with a dry towel and let rise over hot (not boiling) water until doubled in bulk. Divide the dough in half; form into small loaves, place in greased loaf pans; brush with melted butter and let rise over hot (not boiling) water to almost double in bulk. Brush tops with egg yolk diluted in a little milk or water and bake in a moderate oven as directed. Let cool before slicing.

(167) EASTER BREAD—SWEDISH METHOD

STOLLEN

Makes 2 coffee loaves. Oven temperature: 350° F.
Baking time: 55 minutes (about).

This bread is also served as a coffee cake, buttered or plain. When toasted it makes a delicious afternoon tea or coffee treat with jam, marmalade or jelly.

1 quart rich milk, lukewarm
1 cake compressed yeast
1 scant cup granulated sugar
2 cups bread flour (about), sifted
1 lb. butter
1 cup sugar
4 cups bread flour (about), sifted
1 teaspoon salt
1 generous teaspoon ground cardamom
¼ cup chopped candied citron
¼ cup chopped candied orange peel
¼ cup chopped candied lemon peel
½ cup chopped, blanched, toasted almonds
½ cup chopped walnut meats

Crumble yeast cake into lukewarm milk and when dissolved, add sugar. Beat in the 2 cups (more or less) of flour to make a soft sponge. Blend well. Cover and set over hot (not boiling) water and let rise until bubbles on top of sponge begin popping. Then add creamed butter with the second cup of sugar. Now add the 4 cups of flour, sifted with salt and cardamom, alternately with candied fruit and nuts. Knead gently on a lightly floured board; place in a greased mixing bowl, cover with a dry cloth and let rise over hot (not boiling) water until doubled in bulk. Pat a few seconds; divide into halves and place in two greased loaf pans. Let rise again (brushed with melted butter) until doubled in bulk. Bake in a moderate oven as directed. Just before removing from the oven, brush tops with egg yolk diluted in a little water. Let stand one day before slicing.

(168) EMERGENCY BREAD DOUGH

FOOLPROOF

Makes about 3 loaves.

This dough will keep fresh for at least 8 to 10 days in a good refrigerator, and may be used in case of emergency, for bread, rolls, coffee cakes, etc.

Scald 4 cups of milk, and let cool to lukewarm. Add 1 cup shortening (any kind), 1 cup granulated sugar and 1 cup freshly cooked, mashed potatoes, cooled to lukewarm. Blend thoroughly. Now crumble into the mixture 1 yeast cake, with 1 teaspoon baking soda, 2 teaspoons baking powder and 1 teaspoon salt, sifted with 2 quarts (8 cups) of sifted bread flour. Beat mixture until it bubbles (about 20 minutes). Place over hot (not boiling) water and allow to rise until double in bulk. Now, add about 8 more cups of sifted bread flour and mix thoroughly. Knead on a lightly floured board until dough is smooth, elastic and doesn't stick. If more flour is needed, add some after sifting it, but be careful not to put in too much, as this will spoil the flakiness of the bread, rolls or what have you. Place the dough in a greased bowl; cover with waxed paper, then with a clean, dry towel and keep in refrigerator until needed.

(169) FARMER'S WHOLE WHEAT BREAD

Makes 2 large loaves. Oven temperature: 350° F. Baking time: 45 minutes (about).

2 cups milk, lukewarm
3 tablespoons light brown sugar
2 generous teaspoons salt
3 tablespoons butter
1 cake compressed yeast
5 to 5½ cups whole wheat flour
1 cup seedless raisins

Combine milk, sugar, salt and butter; add crumbled yeast and stir to blend thoroughly. Gradually, stir in about 3 cups of the flour, beating briskly after each addition. When free from lumps, stir in the remaining whole wheat flour, to get a dough that can be handled. Toss on a lightly floured board and knead until smooth, elastic and satiny. Place the dough in a greased bowl; brush with melted butter to prevent cracking, cover with a clean, light, dry towel, and let rise over warm water (not boiling) until double in bulk. Turn dough upon lightly floured board. Knead a half minute; divide in halves; shape into round loaves; place on ungreased baking sheet sprinkled with flour; dust tops with a little flour; make several gashes on top with a sharp pointed knife and let the loaves rise until double in bulk (about 55 minutes). Bake in a moderate oven as directed. Let cool before slicing.

(170) FARMER'S SHREDDED WHEAT NUT BREAD

Makes 3 loaves. Oven temperature: 350° F. Baking time: 1 hour (about).

3 shredded whole-wheat biscuits
1 cup hot water
3 cups milk, hot
2 tablespoons lard
2 scant teaspoons salt
1 compressed yeast cake
¼ cup lukewarm water
⅓ cup Grandma's molasses
12 cups (3 quarts) bread flour, sifted
1 cup broken nut meats

Break shredded wheat biscuits into combined hot water and milk. Mix well; then stir in lard, salt and molasses. Blend, and when lukewarm crumble yeast cake into lukewarm water and stir into the shredded wheat mixture. Gradually beat in 8 cups (2 quarts) of the flour and when thoroughly blended, beat in the remaining 4 cups of flour, gradually (about ¼ cup at a time) with the broken nuts. Turn out on lightly floured board and knead until smooth, elastic and not sticky. Place the dough in a large, greased mixing bowl; brush with melted lard and let rise over warm water (not boiling) covered with a clean towel, until double in bulk. Cut it down; then let rise again. Form into three equal round loaves; place upon a floured baking sheet, let rise to almost double in bulk; sprinkle tops with flour and bake in a moderate oven as directed. May be eaten warm or cold.

(171) FIG BREAD

Makes 1 loaf. Oven temperature: 350° F.
Baking time: 1 hour (about).

2½ cups bread flour, sifted
4 teaspoons baking powder
½ teaspoon salt
½ cup sugar
1¼ cups of dried figs, coarsely chopped
1½ cups cold milk
2 whole eggs, well-beaten
¼ cup lard or butter, melted

Combine flour with baking powder, salt and granulated sugar and sift over chopped figs. Blend well, so as to coat figs with flour mixture to prevent their falling to bottom of bread. Combine eggs with cold milk and add to flour-fig mixture, mixing thoroughly, adding as you go along the melted lard or butter. Turn dough into generously greased loaf pan. Let stand 25 minutes to mellow and ripen, and bake in a moderate oven as directed. Let cool before slicing.

(172) FIG, RAISIN, HONEY BREAD

Makes 1 loaf. Oven temperature: 325° F.
Baking time: 1¼ hours.

This delicious afternoon tea or sandwich bread will keep moist for a few days.

¾ cup finely chopped dried figs
¾ cup seedless raisins, chopped
2 tablespoons lard or butter
1 cup honey
1 whole egg, well beaten
2¾ cups bread flour, sifted
½ teaspoon baking powder
¾ cup sweet milk, cold
¼ cup sour milk
½ teaspoon baking soda
1 cup nut meats, chopped (any kind)
½ teaspoon salt

Cream together shortening and honey with beaten egg. Combine flour with salt and baking powder and sift over mixed figs, raisins and nut meats; add alternately with combined milks and soda to shortening and honey mixture. Blend thoroughly. Turn batter into generously greased loaf pan, and let stand 20 minutes to mellow and ripen. Then bake in a moderately low oven as directed. Let cool or, still better, let stand 24 hours before slicing.

(173) FIG AND NUT YEAST BREAD

Makes 1 loaf. Oven temperature: 350° F.
Baking time: 1 hour (about).

½ cup boiling water
½ cup scalded milk
2 tablespoons shortening
1 tablespoon Grandma's molasses
½ generous cup chopped dried figs
2 compressed yeast cakes
½ cup bread flour, sifted
3½ cups entire wheat flour
1 teaspoon salt (scant)
½ generous cup chopped walnuts

Combine boiling water, milk, shortening and molasses and stir until shortening dissolves. Cool until mixture is lukewarm. Add crumbled yeast cakes and stir until dissolved. Combine bread flour, entire wheat flour and salt and beat into sponge, using a wire whisk or slotted spoon. Turn onto a board, dusted with a little flour, and knead until smooth and elastic, after adding chopped figs and chopped nuts previously rolled in a little flour. Rub all over with melted shortening and transfer to a large mixing bowl rubbed with shortening. Place in a shallow pan containing enough warm water to heat the bottom of the bowl or mixer. Cover and keep in a warm place. Let rise until doubled in bulk. Now turn onto a board dusted with flour. Knead again a few minutes and turn into a well-greased loaf pan. Set again in warm water, cover and let rise until doubled in bulk. Bake in a moderate oven as directed, until brown on top and the loaf can be tipped out of the pan without sticking. Rub top with a little butter or lard. Let cool before slicing.

(174) FRENCH BREAD STYLE

Makes 1 long loaf. Oven temperature: 400° F.
for 15 minutes, then 375° F. for 30 minutes.

1 cake compressed yeast
2 teaspoons sugar
1¾ cups lukewarm water
1 teaspoon salt
6 cups bread flour, sifted

Rub yeast and sugar together until liquid. Add lukewarm water and salt. Make a hollow in the center of the flour. Add liquid mixture and mix to form a smooth elastic dough, starting from center and gradually reaching the edge. Rub or brush with butter and let stand until dough has doubled in bulk, over a pan containing hot (not boiling) water. Now toss upon lightly floured board, and knead slightly. Return to the pan or mixer and let rise again. Shape into a loaf about 15 inches in length and three inches in height and place on lightly floured baking sheet. Brush again with butter and let rise until doubled in bulk. Bake in a hot oven as directed. Ten minutes before bread is done brush with the following mixture:

(175) FRENCH BREAD GLAZE

Mix together 1 tablespoon cornstarch, 1 tablespoon sugar and 2 tablespoons of cold water.

Sometimes, you may like to bake a loaf or so of bread and to use the rest of the mixture for sweet rich rolls. In this case, you may knead in a little softened butter, which has been mixed with sugar and nuts or raisins, after the first rising. The texture will not be quite so fine, as when the sugar and butter are added in the first place, but the results will be very acceptable. Or you may roll some of the dough into a thin sheet, brush it with butter, sprinkle it with brown sugar and perhaps nuts or raisins, and roll up and slice it. From the dough mixture you may make a variety of fancy breads merely by changing the shape and spreading them with egg yolk or white; sprinkling them with sugar, edible seeds as cardamom, caraway, or cumin; or by filling them with a sugar mixture. There are many other variations in bread-making and these are left to the ingenuity of the homemaker.

(176) FRENCH SAVARIN BREAD

YEAST METHOD

Makes 1 ring mold for 6 servings. Oven temperature: 350° F. Baking time: 55 minutes.

Savarin is one of the favorite breads of France and is usually baked in a ring mold or tube pan. It is particularly light and tender with a rich flavor of butter and almonds. When served with whipped cream piled in the center of the ring and strewn with chopped nut meats or almonds, or chopped candied citron, orange or lemon peel, it is truly a food for the American gourmet. Or it may be served with a hot syrup made by boiling together one cup sugar with one-half cup water for five minutes, adding lemon or orange juice for flavoring.

1 cup rich milk, lukewarm
1 cake compressed yeast
1/4 cup sugar
1/2 cup bread flour, sifted
3 1/2 to 4 cups bread flour, sifted
1 scant cup butter, melted (not hot)
6 whole fresh eggs, unbeaten
1 1/4 cups shredded blanched almonds
1 scant teaspoon salt

Scald the milk, cool to lukewarm and add crumbled yeast cake and sugar. Stir until yeast and sugar are dissolved, then beat in the half cup of bread flour, beating briskly. Cover and place over a pan of hot (not boiling) water for about 30 minutes or until the mixture is light and spongy. Now, beat in gradually from 3 1/2 to 4 cups of flour (sifted once and measured with salt added and sifted again) alternately with melted butter and eggs added one at a time. Beat well after each addition until mixture is smooth. Lastly, add the shredded blanched almonds and beat briskly for ten minutes using a large wooden spoon. Return to the mixing bowl; place over hot water and let stand for 30 minutes or so until batter is light and almost doubled in bulk. Now beat lightly and pour into well buttered ring mold or tube pan and set aside to rise over hot water until again doubled in bulk. Bake in a moderate oven as directed or until bread leaves sides of the pan. Cool before filling or serve as is.

(177) FRUIT NUT BREAD

VERY RICH BREAD

Makes 3 small loaves. Oven temperature: 300° F.
Baking time: 70 minutes (about).

Occasionally the homemaker has use for a baked fruit and nut bread. The quick bread (so-named because its leaven acts more quickly than the yeast used in regulation bread) resembles an inexpensive cake and for those who do not care for sweets is a good family dessert. In the following bread neither yeast nor baking powder is used.

½ lb. raw prunes, pitted, chopped	2 cups boiling water
1 cup seedless raisins, parboiled then drained and sponged	1 cup sugar
	2 whole fresh eggs, lightly beaten
1 cup pitted dates, chopped	2 teaspoons vanilla extract
¼ lb. walnuts, chopped	3 cups bread flour, sifted twice
¼ lb. blanched almonds, shredded	2 teaspoons baking soda

Combine the cut fruits, walnuts and almonds in a bowl; pour boiling water over them; let stand until cold, stirring occasionally. Add sugar, beaten into the eggs with vanilla extract, mixing thoroughly. To the flour, add soda and sift together into the first mixture, stirring until well mixed with the fruit and nuts. Fill three greased pound coffee cans, or similar mold, half full and bake in a slow oven as directed or until a cake tester comes away dry. When cold, cut into thin slices and serve with cream, fruit sauce, stewed fruit or cottage or cream cheese.

The only type of yeast-raised bread that can be made without wheat flour is a rye bread. For rye and wheat are the *only* flours which contain enough gluten (or other elastic substance) to make a loaf raised with yeast. Other flours such as corn, rice, potato, etc., may be used for yeast breads *only* if at least 60 per cent of wheat flour is combined with them. Baking powder breads and muffins, however, can be made with these gluten-free flours.

(178) GRAHAM MOLASSES BREAD

NO BAKING POWDER OR YEAST USED

Makes 1 loaf. Oven temperature: 375° F.
Baking time: 1 hour (about).

2 cups entire wheat flour	1¼ teaspoons baking soda
½ cup bread flour, sifted	½ cup molasses
1 teaspoon (scant) salt	¼ cup butter or lard, melted

1½ cups sour milk

To the entire wheat and bread flours, add salt and baking soda and sift together. Combine molasses (use old-fashioned, dark molasses preferably unsulphured) with melted shortening and sour milk and mix thoroughly. Beat this into the flour mixture as briskly as possible until smooth. Turn into greased loaf pan and bake in a moderate oven as directed.

(179) GRAHAM NUT BREAD

BAKING POWDER AND BROWN SUGAR USED

Makes 1 loaf. Oven temperature: 325° F.
Baking time: 45–50 minutes.

2 cups graham flour
1 cup bread flour, sifted
1 generous teaspoon baking soda
1 scant teaspoon salt
1 tablespoon baking powder
⅔ cup brown sugar
2 cups buttermilk
1 cup broken nut meats (any kind)

Combine the graham and bread flours; add soda, salt, baking powder and brown sugar and blend thoroughly. Stir in the broken nut meats, then the buttermilk, mixing well. Turn into a greased loaf pan, cover with a dry cloth and let stand 30 minutes to mellow and ripen. Bake in a moderately slow oven as directed. Let cool before slicing.

(180) GRAHAM BREAD ROLL

YEAST METHOD

Modern times have brought new and simpler methods of making yeast breads. With this good fortune, bread—be it plain or fancy—is resuming a more important place in the menu. Try the following delicious roll:

For the bread itself:

1 cup milk, scalded
½ cup lard or butter, softened
1 cup honey
1 teaspoon salt
1 cake compressed yeast dissolved in
¼ cup lukewarm water
2 cups bread flour, sifted
2 whole fresh eggs, well-beaten
1 cup *unsifted* whole wheat flour

Scald milk; stir in lard or butter, honey and salt and stir well to blend and melt the shortening. When lukewarm add compressed yeast cake dissolved in lukewarm water. Add then 2 cups of sifted bread flour and mix thoroughly. Cover and set in a pan of hot (not boiling) water to rise until light. Then, beat in the eggs, alternately with whole wheat flour. Cover again and let rise until light, placing the mixing bowl over hot water. Knead lightly in the mixing bowl, then toss upon a lightly floured board; roll out very thin (about ⅛-inch) and spread with the following filling:

Filling:

½ cup butter, softened
½ cup seedless raisins, parboiled, puffed, drained and thoroughly sponged
1¼ cups pitted, cooked prunes, chopped
½ cup brown sugar

Directions: Spread butter over the rolled dough. Combine raisins and prunes, and spread over butter. Roll up like a jelly roll and press brown sugar against sides and bottom. (If desired, press some chopped almonds or walnuts over the brown sugar.) Cut in slices one inch thick and press against sides and bottom of gem pans, placing one slice topside down in each ring. Cover and let rise until light and doubled in bulk. Bake 25 minutes in a hot oven (400° F.). Remove from oven, invert rolls on plate to cool.

When the holidays come, plan to make the bread a special note. Any homemaker who can manage to whip up two kinds of bread is sure to send her Easter-present-rating sky high.

For a loaf of Greek apricot bread proceed as follows:

(181) GREEK APRICOT BREAD

Makes 1 loaf. Oven temperature: 350° F.
Baking time: 1 hour (about).

1 cup dried apricots, chopped
1⅓ cups sour milk
3 tablespoons butter
⅓ cup sugar
1 egg, well beaten
1½ cups bran
2 cups bread flour, sifted
2 teaspoons baking powder
½ teaspoon baking soda
¼ teaspoon ground nutmeg
¼ cup chopped blanched almonds
¼ cup chopped seedless raisins
1 tablespoon chopped candied angelica
1 tablespoon chopped candied citron
1 tablespoon chopped candied orange peel
½ teaspoon salt

Soak chopped apricots in sour milk for 15 minutes. Cream butter with sugar, then add the beaten egg. Cream until light and fluffy. Now beat in the bran, the apricots and the sour milk in which they were soaked. Let this stand until most of the moisture is taken up. To the flour, add baking powder, soda, salt and nutmeg and sift part of it over almonds combined with the raisins, angelica, citron and orange peel. Add to the first mixture, alternately with the remaining flour mixture, stirring only until flour is absorbed. Turn dough into a buttered loaf pan, lined with waxed paper at bottom.

(Do not use any other kind of shortening for this bread but good butter.) Bake in a moderate oven as directed. Let cool before slicing very thin.

(182) GREEK FRUIT BREAD

YEAST METHOD

Makes 3 small loaves. Oven temperature: 375° F.
Baking time: 45–50 minutes.

- ½ cup milk
- ½ cup butter
- ½ teaspoon salt
- ¼ cup sugar
- 2 cakes compressed yeast
- 2½ cups bread flour, sifted twice
- 2 eggs
- ¼ cup shredded blanched almonds
- 1 tablespoon chopped candied angelica
- 1 tablespoon chopped candied lemon peel
- 1 tablespoon chopped candied pineapple
- 1 tablespoon chopped candied apricot

Scald milk; stir in butter and salt mixed with sugar. When lukewarm add crumbled yeast and half of flour to make a sponge, beating vigorously to a smooth batter. Now, beat in eggs, alternately with remaining flour, mixed with candied fruit and almonds. Toss dough upon lightly floured board, and knead until elastic, smooth and not sticky. Transfer to a greased mixing bowl; brush with softened butter; cover with a dry towel and let rise over hot water until it doubles in bulk. Shape into three round loaves and place on greased baking sheet in form of a three-petaled flower. Brush with butter and let rise again to double its bulk. Bake in a moderately hot oven as directed. Remove from the oven; brush with butter and let cool before slicing, after separating the three petals.

Another delicious petal-shaped Greek bread, also a favorite during Easter is:

(183) GREEK EASTER BREAD

YEAST METHOD

Makes 3 small round loaves. Oven temperature: 350° F.
Baking time: 1 hour.

- ½ cup rich milk, scalded
- ½ cup butter
- ½ teaspoon salt
- ¼ cup sugar
- 2 cakes compressed yeast
- ¼ cup lukewarm water
- 2½ cups bread flour, sifted
- 2 whole fresh eggs, well-beaten
- 1 generous teaspoon grated lemon rind

To the scalded rich milk add butter, salt and sugar. When lukewarm stir in yeast cakes dissolved in the lukewarm water, and half of the flour. Beat to a smooth batter while stirring in the eggs, alternately with the remainder of the flour. Let rise to double its bulk over hot water, covered with a dry towel. Turn dough upon lightly floured board and knead until smooth, and satiny. Return to the mixing bowl; brush with butter and let rise again to double its bulk, covered. Toss upon floured board; shape into three round loaves and place on generously greased baking sheet in form of a three-petaled flower. Brush with butter; cover; let rise again to double its bulk. Now, brush top with egg yolk diluted with a little water and bake in a moderate oven as directed or omit the brushing, bake as directed, and when done and cold, ice with your favorite cooked frosting and decorate with fancifully cut candied fruits (angelica, apricots, citron, etc.) interspersed with almonds and nut meats.

(184) GROUND APPLE BREAD

Makes 1 loaf. Oven temperature: 350° F.
Baking time: 1 hour.

½ cup butter or lard
½ cup sugar
½ cup brown sugar (dark)
½ cup milk
1 whole fresh egg, well-beaten
2 cups bread flour, sifted
½ generous teaspoon salt
1 scant teaspoon baking soda
1 teaspoon baking powder
½ teaspoon ground cinnamon
1 cup ground fresh apples

Cream butter or lard with combined sugars. Combine beaten egg with cold milk and add to creamed mixture, stirring well. To the flour, add salt, soda, baking powder and cinnamon and sift together over the unpeeled, cored, fresh ground apples. Blend well and combine with the first mixture, stirring just enough to dampen the flour. Turn dough into well-greased loaf pan. Let stand about 20 minutes to mellow and ripen, then bake in a moderate oven as directed. Let cool before slicing.

Bread was introduced in England by the early Phoenicians who traded it for tin. Rye, however, was used in place of wheat and continued to be the common bread flour in England until the eighth century.

(185) HOMEMADE BREAD

YEAST METHOD

Makes 2 loaves. First rising time: 2 hours, or until double in bulk.
Second rising time: 1 hour, or until double in bulk.
Oven temperature: 450°–350° F.
Baking time: 55–60 minutes.

The recipe for two large loaves calls for six to seven cups of bread flour, one pint liquid (milk, milk and water or water and powdered milk), a little sugar, a little salt and, last but not least, yeast. For the very short process two cakes compressed yeast to the pint of liquid is the rule and the bread will be mixed and baked in three to four hours. One cake of yeast produces bread in five to six hours, and one-fourth to one-half yeast cake, by the overnight rising method, which some homemakers may find more convenient.

Follow the directions carefully if you are making bread for the first time; experienced bread-makers will of course vary the recipe to suit themselves.

2 cups (one pint) milk, scalded
2 tablespoons granulated sugar
1½ teaspoons salt
2 cakes compressed yeast
¼ cup lukewarm water
6 to 7 cups sifted bread flour
3 tablespoons melted shortening

Add sugar and salt to the scalded milk; cool to lukewarm. Crumble yeast cakes in a large mixing bowl; add the lukewarm water, stirring until dissolved; stir in the warm milk mixture.

Sift in 4 cups of the bread flour (also called all-purpose flour) in two installments, stirring to smoothness; add the melted shortening and 2 more cups of the flour.

Stir until the dough leaves the sides of the mixing bowl using a bit more flour if needed.

Turn upon a lightly floured board; knead until smooth, elastic and bubbled under the surface, using as little of the reserved flour as possible. The kneading time is five to eight minutes. Form the dough into a ball; place in a greased mixing bowl and brush over the top to prevent cracking. Cover with a dry cloth; put upon a rack over hot (not boiling) water; keep in a warm place till doubled in bulk and very light and fragrant. The time may vary from one and one-half to two hours with the temperature, draft and unforeseen conditions.

Cut down the dough; divide into two equal parts (it is always wise to weigh the dough); knead each one for a minute; shape into loaf form; brush with melted shortening; place in greased loaf pans. Again cover; place over hot water; let rise till very light and doubled in bulk. The time varies from forty to sixty minutes.

Place the loaves in a very hot oven (450° F.); in fifteen minutes reduce the heat to moderately hot; or, place in a steady moderate oven (350° F.), and bake until brown and shrunken from the sides of the pans. Remove from the pans to racks. When quite cold store in a fresh, well aired bread box.

IMPORTANT: If a soft crust is desired, brush the molded loaves with melted butter before setting them to rise; then brush the baked loaves with butter after removing them from the pans.

Smells delicious, looks delicious, is delicious!

(186) HOMEMADE COUNTRY BREAD

Makes 6 loaves. Oven temperature: 350° F.
Baking time: 45 minutes.
First rising time: 3 hours. Second rising time: 3 hours.
Third rising time: 1½ hours.

Because yeast mixtures require very different treatment from baking powder or soda bread, the beginner should read and study the recipe carefully before beginning the experiment. Yeast is a plant, requiring food, moisture and warmth for growth; too much heat kills it, while cold merely retards it. The optimum temperature lies between 80 and 82° F.

2 cups milk scalded, cooled
2 tablespoons sugar
4 cakes compressed yeast
4 cups (1 quart) bread flour, sifted
2½ teaspoons salt
1 cup shortening
⅓ cup granulated sugar
4 whole fresh eggs, well-beaten
6 cups (1½ quarts) bread flour, sifted
1 half-pound citron, chopped
1 lb. dates, pitted, chopped
1 lb. mixed nut meats

Stir the 2 tablespoons sugar into the scalded milk; let cool to lukewarm, then stir in the crumbled yeast cakes until dissolved. Add 4 cups of the flour, sifted and measured. Mix thoroughly. Cover; let rise over hot water until doubled in bulk. Cut down; again let rise until doubled in bulk. Stir in mixed salt, shortening, remaining sugar, and the beaten eggs, alternately with remaining flour. Mix thoroughly. Now, knead until dough is smooth, elastic and satiny. Then add the prepared fruits and nuts (any kinds, but in equal parts). Shape into six loaves, place in generously greased loaf pans; cover; let rise until light and doubled in bulk. Bake in a moderate oven as directed.

This bread, usually made around Christmas or New Years, makes a nice gift.

(187) HOMEMADE RAISIN NUT BREAD

YEAST METHOD

Makes 1 loaf. Oven temperature: 375°, then 325° F.
Baking time: 1¼ hours.

1 cup scalded milk, cooled	¼ cup lukewarm water
1¼ teaspoons salt	3 cups bread flour, sifted
1 tablespoon brown sugar	¼ cup seedless raisins
1 tablespoon butter	¼ cup currants
1 cake compressed yeast	½ cup cashew nut meats, chopped

To the scalded milk add salt, brown sugar and butter; stir well and when thoroughly blended and butter melted, cool to lukewarm and stir in the crumbled yeast cake which has been dissolved in warm water. Stir in half of the flour and beat until free from lumps. Then, stir in the remaining flour, previously sifted over mixed seedless raisins, currants and chopped cashew nuts. Mix thoroughly and knead until dough is elastic and satiny and bubbles form under surface (9 to 10 minutes). Shape into ball; brush with shortening; place in large greased mixing bowl; cover and set over hot water to rise to double in bulk. Place in greased loaf pan, brush top with softened butter and again let rise until doubled in bulk. Bake 10 minutes in moderately hot oven; lower temperature and continue baking as directed or until bread leaves sides of the pan. Let cool before slicing.

(188) HOMEMADE RYE BREAD

Makes 2 loaves. Oven temperature: 350° F.
Baking time: 55–60 minutes.

Use recipe for No. 185, substituting 3 cups rye flour for 3 cups bread flour. Proceed as indicated.

By way of variety, you may add raisins, currants, shaved almonds or nuts, or any two in combination, to the bread dough before the final folding. You can play games with any variety of fruits, too—blueberries, preserved pineapple, raisins with poppy seeds. The procedure is general: Roll out the dough, brush with melted butter, spread with the desired mixture, roll up tight, cut into slices of ¾ inch to an inch, place cut side down on greased pans; let rise until light and bake in a moderate oven as directed.

How about turning your bread dough into pecan or cinnamon rolls? Or spreading it with a layer of mincemeat over which brandy or rum has been poured and cinnamon and sugar sprinkled?

(189) HOMEMADE WHOLE WHEAT BREAD

Makes 2 loaves. Oven temperature: 350° F.
Baking time: 55–60 minutes.

Use recipe for No. 185, substituting 3 cups of *unsifted* whole wheat flour for 3 cups of bread flour. Bake as indicated.

(190) HOMEMADE WHOLE WHEAT HONEY BREAD

YEAST METHOD. NO SUGAR USED

Makes 2 loaves. Oven temperature: 350° F.
Baking time: 1 hour (about).

1 cup boiling water
4 tablespoons honey
½ cup lukewarm water
2 cakes compressed yeast
2 cups unsifted whole wheat flour
¾ cup lukewarm water
2¼ teaspoons salt
3 tablespoons shortening, melted
3½ cups *unsifted* whole wheat flour

Place the boiling water in large mixing bowl; stir in honey. Dissolve yeast cakes in the ½ cup lukewarm water, then add to water-honey mixture (which has been cooled to lukewarm) alternately with the 2 cups of whole wheat flour. Blend this sponge well. Cover and let rise to double its bulk over hot water. When raised, cut it down and add combined ¾ cup lukewarm water, salt and melted shortening, alternately with the remaining 3½ cups of flour. Blend thoroughly. Knead until smooth and elastic. Place in greased bowl; brush with melted shortening and let rise to double in bulk. Remove dough from the bowl; knead a few minutes, then let rise but not quite double in bulk this time. Divide into two equal parts; shape into loaves and brush with melted shortening. Place upon slightly greased baking sheet, and bake in a moderate oven as indicated. Let cool before slicing.

(191) HONEY BRAN BREAD

Makes 1 loaf. Oven temperature: 400° F.
Baking time: 1 hour (about).

½ cup bran flour
1 cup graham flour
1 cup bread flour, sifted
4 teaspoons baking powder
1 whole fresh egg, well-beaten
½ teaspoon salt
1 cup sweet milk
⅓ cup honey
½ cup chopped walnuts or raisins

Combine all dry ingredients and sift together over chopped nut meats or raisins. Blend thoroughly. Combine milk, honey and egg and beat briskly, then stir into dry mixture, blending well. Pour batter into greased loaf pan and bake in a hot oven as directed. Cool before slicing.

(192) HUSH PUPPIES

SOUTHERN CORN BREAD OR CORN PONES

Serves 6.

Embodied in the title of this bread recipe is a most interesting story. Years ago (in some sections it is still the custom) the Negroes of Tallahassee, Florida, that quaint southern capital, would congregate on warm fall evenings for cane grindings. Some of them would feed the sugar cane to a one-mule treadmill while others poured the juice into a large kettle where it was boiled to sugar. After their work was completed they would gather around an open fire over which was suspended an iron pot in which fish and corn pones were cooked in fat.

The Negroes were said to have a certain way of making these corn pones which were unusually delicious and appetizing. While the food was sizzling in the pot the Negroes would engage in rather weird conversations, spell-binding each other with "tall" stories of panther and bear hunts. On the outer edge of the circle of light reflected by the fire would sit their hounds, their ears pricked for strange sounds and their noses raised to catch a whiff of the savory odor of the frying fish and pones. If the talking ceased for a moment a low whine of hunger from the dogs would attract the attention of the men and subconsciously a hand would reach for some of the corn pone which had been placed on a slab of bark to cool. The donor would break off a piece of the pone and toss it to a hungry dog, with the command, "Hush, puppy!"

The effect of this gesture on the hounds was always instantaneous and the Negroes attributed the result to the remarkable flavor of what eventually became known as "The Tallahassee Hush Puppy."

2 cups fine corn meal, sifted	1½ cups milk
2 teaspoons baking powder	½ cup water
1 teaspoon salt	1 extra large onion, chopped fine

Sift the first three ingredients together. Combine milk and water and stir in, alternately with the onion. Add more corn meal (sifted) as may be necessary to form a soft but workable dough. With the hands dipped in flour, mold pieces of dough into pones (oblong cakes, about 5 inches long, 3 inches wide and ¾ of an inch thick). Fry in deep hot fat or oil until well browned on all sides. Serve hot.

(193) INDIVIDUAL SHIRRED SPOON BREAD

SOUTHERN METHOD

Serves 6. Oven temperature: 375° F.
Baking time: 20 minutes (about).

2 cups corn meal	3 cups buttermilk
1½ cups (about) boiling water	1 teaspoon baking soda
1½ tablespoons butter or margarine	1 egg yolk, well-beaten
1¾ teaspoons salt	2 whole fresh eggs, well-beaten

Add enough boiling water to the corn meal to make it the consistency of thick mush. Then stir in the butter or margarine and salt, alternately with combined buttermilk, soda, egg yolk and whole eggs. Fill 6 generously greased individual, shirred-egg dishes and bake in a moderately hot oven as directed. Serve hot. A fine bread for breakfast or luncheon, formal or informal.

(194) IRISH RAISIN BREAD

CALLED ALSO "IRISH SODA BREAD"

Makes 1 small round loaf. Oven temperature: 350° F.
Baking time: 40 minutes.

This quick bread, sweetened with raisins or currants and flavored with caraway seeds if desired, takes its name from the soda used with buttermilk or sour milk as the leavening agent. Most recipes for the small round loaf call for ½ teaspoon of baking soda to neutralize the acidity of one cup of buttermilk; but when the milk is *rather sour,* the addition of a little baking powder gives a lighter loaf.

2 cups bread flour, sifted
1½ teaspoons baking powder
½ generous teaspoon salt
¼ teaspoon baking soda
½ cup seedless raisins (or currants), cut
1 tablespoon caraway seeds
1 cup buttermilk (about)

Combine the flour, baking powder, salt and soda, and sift together over the washed, dried, cut raisins (or currants) and caraway seeds. Blend thoroughly. Stir in enough buttermilk to make a soft dough. Turn dough upon a scantily floured board and knead lightly until smooth and not sticky (about a minute). Shape the dough into a round loaf; place in a greased round pan. With a knife cut a cross on the top and bake in a moderate oven as indicated or until loaf is brown and shrinks from sides of pan. Should the loaf be very thick in the center, bake a few minutes longer. Let cool before cutting. The bread should sound hollow when tapped with the knuckles and may be rolled loosely in a clean cloth and tilted on end to cool.

(195) ITALIAN CORN MEAL, ONION AND GARLIC BREAD

Serves 6 generously. Oven temperature: 350° F.
Baking time: 30 minutes (about).

If baked in muffin tins, this makes a dozen little muffins which are very appropriate with green or fruit salad.

½ cup olive or other cooking oil
1 medium-sized onion, minced
1 clove of garlic, minced
1 quart (4 cups) hot water
1 scant tablespoon salt
⅛ teaspoon white pepper
1 lb. yellow corn meal
½ cup grated Parmesan or other cheese
1 cup seedless raisins, parboiled
½ cup pine nuts
½ cup chopped walnut meats

Brown the onion and garlic in oil; add hot water, salt and white pepper; bring to a quick boil; then scatter in corn meal, stirring it until smooth and thickened. Remove from the fire and stir in grated Parmesan or other hard cheese, mixed with seedless raisins (parboiled, drained and dried), pine nuts and walnut meats. Mix thoroughly; then pour into a well-greased baking dish and bake in a moderate oven as directed. Serve as hot as possible.

(196) JEWISH TWISTED BREAD

OVERNIGHT RISING BREAD

Makes 2 twists. Oven temperature: 350° F.
Baking time: 45–50 minutes.

½ cake compressed yeast
1 cup lukewarm water
2 teaspoons salt
1 tablespoon granulated sugar
8 cups (2 quarts) bread flour, sifted
1 cup sweet milk, lukewarm

Crumble half yeast cake into lukewarm water and add salt and sugar. Sift flour into a large deep bowl; make a depression in the center of the flour and pour in the yeast mixture mixed with the milk. Stir with a wooden spoon to make a dough; turn out on a lightly floured board and knead until smooth and velvety. Return to greased bowl; brush top with melted butter or oil, cover the bowl and let stand in a place free from draughts until morning. Then divide the dough in half (I advise weighing it) and shape into two twisted loaves. Allow to rise for about 40 minutes, or until almost doubled in bulk, and bake in a moderate oven as directed.

(197) JEWISH MATSOS CRIMSEL

Serves 6. Frying time: until delicately brown all over in deep fat.

3 matsos, soaked in cold water
12 tablespoons (6 ozs.) sugar
3 well beaten whole fresh eggs
¼ cup grated blanched almonds
1 teaspoon grated lemon rind
1 tablespoon goose fat
1 cup apples (or prunes) chopped

Press the soaked matsos until quite dry. Cream together sugar and eggs, then add the soaked pressed matsos, alternately with remaining ingredients, except the chopped fruit. Roll this dough out into circular pieces about the size of a tea cup saucer. Spread the chopped fruit on the dough, covering with another piece of dough. Pinch the edges firmly after brushing with water. Roll in matsos meal; and fry in deep hot fat until delicately browned all over. Serve warm, sprinkled with sugar mixed with cinnamon.

The true orthodox Jewish cookery reflects centuries of Jewish culture. It is based on the rituals of the religion itself. Jewish cookery is noteworthy not only because of its strict adherence to the Mosaic laws, but because its development through the ages has produced many tasty and interesting dishes. In the orthodox kitchen, only animals that have been killed in the Kosher way can be used. Blood as well as pork is prohibited and in the Kosher method of slaughtering, the animal is bled almost entirely. To make sure that no blood remains, all meat is soaked in cold water for one-half hour and in salted water for one hour before it is prepared as food.

(198) MINCEMEAT BREAD

VERY APPROPRIATE BREAD FOR THE HOLIDAYS

Makes 1 loaf. Oven temperature: 350° F.
Baking time: 70 minutes (about).

1 nine-ounce package mincemeat
½ cup cold water
¼ cup shortening
½ cup sugar
1 whole fresh egg, well-beaten
½ cup chopped walnuts
2½ cups bread flour, sifted
1 tablespoon baking powder
½ teaspoon salt
½ cup sweet milk (cold)

Break up the package of mincemeat into small pieces; place with cold water in a small saucepan and stir over low flame until mixture becomes smooth; then boil until almost dry, stirring constantly from the bottom of the saucepan. Cool thoroughly. Cream shortening; add sugar and continue creaming until smooth, adding while going along the beaten egg. Now stir into the butter mixture the cold, smooth mincemeat, alternately with chopped walnuts (or any other nuts). To the flour, add baking powder and salt, sift once, measure, and resift. Gradually add this to the first mixture, blending well, alternately with the cold milk. Pour dough into greased loaf pan with the sides higher than the center. Bake in a moderate oven as directed until a cake tester comes away clean. Remove from the oven; let stand 5 minutes or so, then invert on rack; carefully lift the pan and let stand until cold. Serve sliced very thin. Very good with cream cheese.

(199) MINCEMEAT BROWN BREAD

USING BAKING SODA AND MOLASSES

Makes 1 loaf. Oven temperature: 350° F.
Baking time: 1 hour (about).

1 nine-ounce package mincemeat
½ cup cold water
1 cup corn meal, sifted
1 cup bread flour, sifted
1 cup graham flour
1½ teaspoons baking soda
½ teaspoon salt
¼ cup molasses
1¾ cups (about) cold sweet milk

Break packaged mincemeat into a small saucepan and add the cold water. Place over medium flame and stir until lumps are thoroughly broken up; then bring to a brisk boil and continue boiling (about 3 minutes) until mixture is almost dry. Cool. Combine the flours, sift once and measure, then add soda and salt and sift together again. Stir into cooled mincemeat thoroughly. Mix molasses and milk well and gradually stir into the first mixture, blending thoroughly. Pour batter into greased loaf pan and let stand 15 or 20 minutes to mellow and ripen. Then bake in a moderate oven as directed. Let cool before slicing very thin.

(200) MIXED NUT BREAD

Makes 2 loaves. Oven temperature: 350° F.
Baking time: 1 hour (about).

Nuts are a very concentrated food and are better used as an integral part of the menu rather than as a supplement to an already adequate meal. Most nuts are extremely rich in fat. The starchy chestnut is the one exception. The pecan contains over 70 per cent of fat; the Brazil nut, butternut, filbert, hickory nut, and Persian (English) walnut, over 60 per cent. The eastern black walnut, almond, beechnut, and pistache have over 50 per cent; and the cashew, pine (Pignolia) and peanut have over 40 per cent. Fresh coconut contains about 35 per cent fat.

In protein value the different nuts range from less than 5 per cent to over 30 per cent. Although nut proteins are of good quality, the condensed form makes them unsatisfactory as a substitute for meat for most people, though they can be supplemented by bulky vegetables, whole grains, etc. Nuts make a useful contribution to the diet, but under most circumstances it is better to consider them as sources of fat rather than of protein. Their vitamin and mineral content is also worthy of note. For all-round nutrition the humble peanut probably leads and its flavor is intriguing.

The total carbohydrate in nuts is less than 25 per cent except in the chestnut. The fresh chestnut contains about 42 per cent of carbohydrate, chiefly in the form of starch, whereas the proportion in the dried nut amounts to about 80 per cent. Most nuts are good sources of phosphorus and fair sources of calcium. Some nuts, such as the unblanched almond and hazelnut, walnut, pecan, and hickory nut, are fair sources of iron. The pecan and walnut have a little vitamin A. The peanut, pecan, chestnut, almond, Persian (English) walnut, filbert and Brazil nut are good sources of vitamin B—the leading nut vitamin.

RECIPE

Sift 4 cups (one quart) bread flour once; measure; then add 4 teaspoons baking powder, 1 teaspoon salt, 1 scant cup sugar and sift together into large mixing bowl. Beat 1 egg; combine with 1½ cups of rich sweet cold milk, and stir into the dry mixture alternately with ¼ cup each of finely chopped black walnuts, pecans, cashew nuts and blanched almonds. Blend thoroughly. Pour mixture into 2 well-buttered loaf pans, and allow to stand in a warm place for about 25 minutes to mellow and ripen. Bake in a moderate oven as directed. When cold, slice very thin and serve either for afternoon tea or for tidbits, *canapés,* etc.

(201) MIXED NUT BREAD

VERY CRUNCHY

Makes 2 loaves. Oven temperature: 350° F.
Baking time: 1 hour.

4 cups bread flour, sifted
4 teaspoons baking powder
1 teaspoon salt
¾ generous cup granulated sugar
1 whole fresh egg, well-beaten
1½ cups milk
¼ cup chopped walnuts
¼ cup chopped pecans
¼ cup chopped almonds
¼ cup chopped Brazil nuts

Combine flour with baking powder, salt and sugar and sift together. Add beaten egg to milk, mix thoroughly and gradually add to flour mixture. Combine nut meats and shake with a little flour, then stir into batter, blending thoroughly. Divide batter between two greased loaf pans and bake in a moderate oven as directed. Slice the next day.

(202) MOLASSES BRAN FRUIT BREAD

VERY RICH

Makes 1 loaf. Oven temperature: 350° F.
Baking time: 1 hour.

- 2 cups bread flour, sifted
- ½ generous teaspoon salt
- 2 teaspoons baking powder
- ½ teaspoon baking soda
- ½ cup pitted dates, chopped
- ½ cup dried figs, chopped
- ½ cup seedless raisins, parboiled, dried
- ½ cup walnut meats, chopped
- 1 whole fresh egg, well-beaten
- ⅔ cup molasses
- 1 cup buttermilk
- 1½ cups bran flour

To the bread flour add salt, baking powder and soda and sift together over mixed fruit and nut meats. Blend well. Combine beaten egg, molasses and buttermilk and mix thoroughly, then stir well into flour-fruit-nut mixture, alternately with bran flour. Turn dough into greased loaf pan, and bake in a moderate oven as directed. Let cool before slicing. Keeps moist 2 or 3 days.

(203) MOLASSES OLIVE BREAD

Makes 1 loaf. Oven temperature: 350° F.
Baking time: 1 hour.

- 1½ cups bread flour, sifted
- 1½ cups graham flour
- 2 teaspoons baking powder
- ¾ scant teaspoon salt
- 1 cup ripe olives, chopped fine
- ½ cup molasses
- ½ teaspoon baking soda
- 1½ to 1¾ cups milk

Combine the flours with baking powder and salt and sift together over olives, chopped, then gently pressed in a dry towel. Mix well. Combine molasses, soda and milk and mix thoroughly, then stir into flour mixture. Turn dough into well-greased loaf pan and bake in a moderate oven as directed.

(204) MOLASSES ORANGE RAISIN BREAD

VERY FLAVORFUL AND NUTRITIOUS

Makes 1 loaf. Oven temperature: 350° F.
Baking time: 50 minutes.

- ½ cup unstrained orange juice
- 3 tablespoons unstrained lemon juice
- 1 cup seedless raisins, whole
- 1 tablespoon grated orange rind
- ½ cup molasses
- ¼ cup sugar
- 1 egg, well beaten
- 1¾ cups bread flour, sifted
- 1 teaspoon baking powder
- ¾ teaspoon baking soda
- ½ scant teaspoon salt
- 2 tablespoons melted butter

Mix fruit juices in a small pan and bring to the boiling point. Immediately pour over the washed raisins. Let cool. The raisins will be plump and the flavor will be enhanced. When cold, add orange rind, molasses, sugar and beaten egg. Beat slightly until well blended. Combine the flour, baking powder, soda and salt and sift together; then add to the first mixture gradually, stirring only until flour is dampened. Add last the melted butter. Turn dough into greased loaf pan and bake in a moderate oven as directed. Let cool before slicing.

(205) MOLASSES YEAST BREAD—BELGIUM METHOD

Makes 2 loaves. Oven temperature: 400–350° F.
Baking time: 1 hour (about).

- 2 cakes compressed yeast
- ¼ cup lukewarm water
- 2½ cups milk, lukewarm
- ¾ cup molasses
- 3 tablespoons butter or margarine
- 2¾ teaspoons salt
- 6 cups (1½ quarts) bread flour, sifted
- 1 cup additional bread flour, sifted
- 1 cup whole wheat flour (about), unsifted
- 1 tablespoon melted butter
- 1 tablespoon cold milk

Crumble yeast cakes in lukewarm water. Combine milk (which has been scalded and cooled to lukewarm) with molasses, butter or margarine and salt. Mix well and stir in the yeast mixture. Now stir in 3 cups of the six cups of bread flour and mix until smooth. Cover, place over hot water and let stand about 2 hours or until sponge is doubled in bulk. Cut down the sponge, take ⅓ of it and mix with whole wheat flour. Toss upon lightly floured board and knead until smooth with no stickiness. Brush with the melted butter and place in a buttered bowl.

Knead the remaining dough, adding the additional flour, sifted with the remaining 3 cups of bread flour, and knead until dough is elastic and stickiness has disappeared. Brush with a little butter and place over the whole wheat dough in the bowl. Cover and allow to rise for 30 minutes or so.

Divide the whole wheat dough into 6 parts. Cut the white dough into halves. Mold into loaves, using some of the whole wheat with the white dough to form a marbled effect. Place loaves in buttered loaf pans (you may make 3 smaller loaves, if desired), brush with melted butter; cover and allow to rise to double its bulk (about two hours) over hot water. Lastly brush loaves with cold milk. Bake 15 minutes in a hot oven, reduce temperature to moderate and continue baking for 45 minutes longer as directed above, or until loaves are well browned and give a hollow sound upon tapping. Cool before slicing.

(206) MONTGOMERY CORN BREAD

Serves 6 generously. Oven temperature: 350° F.
Baking time: 15 minutes or so.

Beat 4 whole fresh eggs briskly; stir in 1½ teaspoons salt and 1 teaspoon sugar. Then add 1 quart of sour milk with 2 level teaspoons of baking soda (*or,* 1 quart fresh milk with 2 level teaspoons of baking powder, *or,* 1 quart of sour cream, and 1 level tablespoon baking soda). Now add ½ cup bread flour, sifted with 1 pound of water-ground corn meal. Stir well. Add ½ cup melted butter. (If sour cream is used no fat is necessary.) Pour batter into hot greased pan and bake as directed. The finished product will bring great happiness to the breakfast, luncheon or dinner table of people accustomed to the best. You better make 2 pans! *i.e.* double the recipe!

(207) NEW ORLEANS CORN BREAD

Serves 6. Oven temperature: 400° F.
Baking time: 20–25 minutes (about).

2 cups yellow corn meal
1 cup boiling water
2 tablespoons of bacon drippings
¾ generous teaspoon salt
2 whole fresh eggs, well-beaten
1 tablespoon granulated sugar
2 teaspoons baking powder
½ cup cold milk

Combine corn meal, boiling water, bacon drippings and salt and stir briskly to make a rather stiff mush. Beat in the egg mixed with sugar and baking powder alternately with the milk. Turn batter into a hot greased shallow pan and bake in a hot oven as directed. Serve as hot as possible with plenty of butter.

(208) NORWEGIAN AFTERNOON TEA BREAD

VERY RICH FRUIT BREAD

Makes 3 loaves. Oven temperature: 375–300° F.
Baking time: 50–60 minutes.

- 2 cups milk, scalded
- 1 cup butter (no other shortening used)
- 1 cup sugar
- 1 teaspoon salt
- 1 cake compressed yeast
- 4 cups (1 quart) bread flour, sifted
- 5 additional cups bread flour, sifted
- 2 teaspoons ground cardamom
- ½ cup citron, chopped fine
- ½ cup seedless raisins, parboiled
- Melted butter (additional)

To the scalded milk add the butter, sugar and salt. Stir until thoroughly blended. Cool to lukewarm, then crumble in the yeast cake and stir until yeast is dissolved. Turn mixture into a large buttered bowl and stir in, beating and stirring alternately, the 4 cups of flour. Place the bowl over hot water, cover and let rise until sponge doubles its bulk (about 2½ hours). Cut down the sponge, then stir in the additional flour, gradually, beating well after each addition. Turn dough onto a lightly floured board and knead for about 10 minutes, or until dough is elastic and does not stick. Add, while kneading, the mixed ground cardamom, citron and parboiled, dried raisins. Return to the buttered bowl; cover; place over hot water and allow to rise again to double its bulk. Again turn out upon floured board and knead for about ½ minute. Divide dough into three equal portions; shape in loaves; place in buttered loaf pans; cover and stand again over hot water to double in bulk (about 30 minutes). Slash top of each loaf three times across and brush with melted butter. Bake in a moderately hot oven for about 10 minutes to set the bread, then reduce temperature to low and continue baking about 40 minutes longer. Allow to cool thoroughly before slicing.

(209) NORWEGIAN CHRISTMAS BREAD

Makes 2 loaves. Oven temperature: 375° F.
Baking time: 55–60 minutes.

2 cups rich milk, scalded
2 tablespoons granulated sugar
2 cakes compressed yeast
2 quarts (8 cups) bread flour, sifted
1¼ teaspoons salt
½ cup good butter, melted
2 egg yolks, well-beaten with
2 tablespoons granulated sugar
1 teaspoon grated lemon or orange rind

Into scalded milk stir the 2 tablespoons sugar. Allow to cool to lukewarm, then crumble in the yeast cakes and stir in 3 cups of the flour. Beat briskly until smooth, cover this sponge, place over hot water and allow to rise until double in bulk (about 2½ hours). Cut down the sponge then add gradually the remaining flour, re-sifted with the salt, alternate with the combined butter and egg yolks, beating well after each addition. Beat briskly for a minute or so adding the grated lemon or orange rind. Add more flour if dough is not stiff enough to handle easily. Turn upon lightly floured board and knead for about 10 minutes, or until dough is elastic and does not stick. Place in a greased mixing bowl; cover; set over hot water and allow to rise to double in bulk (about 30–35 minutes). Toss upon floured board, knead for a half a minute, shape into loaves; place in buttered loaf pans and let rise again until double in bulk. Bake in a moderate oven as directed. Cool before slicing.

In Norway, hospitality is simple but lavish. There is no time when a Norwegian does not seem able to eat. It is the result of the climate and the tremendous amount of exercise they take. They make, you know, almost a cult of physical culture. There in Norway you step out your front door, put on your skis and off you go. That is the kind of life that produces hearty appetites. To the Norwegians bread is truly the staff of life. It is not strange, therefore, that much thought is given to its preparation.

(210) NORWEGIAN FLAT BREAD

FLATBRØD

Makes about 1 dozen. Griddle temperature: moderate.
Baking time: until brown on both sides.

In some parts of Norway this hard bread is made with hot mashed potatoes, while in others water is used instead. But both are delicious little round breads. The following recipe is distinctive because of the mashed potatoes.

Into 2 rounded cups of hot mashed potatoes, seasoned with salt to taste, beat 2 tablespoons of butter and gradually work in 3 to 3½ cups of either white, rye, or rolled oatmeal flour, enough to make a stiff dough. Let the dough stand for 30 minutes then roll out on lightly floured board after kneading it for about 5 minutes. Shape into a long roll; cut into about 12 uniform pieces and roll each piece out into a paper-thin round 10 to 12 inches in diameter. Bake exactly as you would griddle cakes, turning with spatula when blistered on top. When done, stack in a covered container.

You may fry these disks in a frying pan with a little fat. No yeast or baking powder is used. To eat, break off small pieces as you would bread.

In olden times English housewives scratched a cross in a loaf of bread before baking so it wouldn't be bewitched and "turn out heavy."

(211) NORWEGIAN KLING BREAD

Use the same recipe as for No. 210. When the round disks are baked and dry, place between moist cloths and let stand from ½ to ¾ of an hour, or until softened, but not too much, stacking them one upon another. Then spread one disk at a time with creamed butter then with a thin slice of Mysost, a soft, deep yellow, cylindrical cheese made from whey and wrapped in tin foil. In Danish it is also known as "Primost cheese." Or you may spread brown sugar over the butter. Fold in thirds and cut crosswise in 2-inch strips, or in triangles. These "Kling" breads are also called "Lefse" breads. They are served with afternoon tea or coffee.

(212) NUT BREAD I

WITH BREAD FLOUR

Makes 1 loaf. Oven temperature: 350° F.
Baking time: 1¼ hours (about).

A generous loaf of nut bread, light in texture and rich in flavor, helps the homemaker to face unexpected Sunday guests. Buttered nutbread fingers are quite festive with afternoon tea or coffee, especially when spread with cream cheese or jam. They are also a favorite with fruit salad or for sandwiches. There are several methods for making them.

3 cups bread flour, sifted
1 tablespoon baking powder
¾ teaspoon salt
¾ cup sugar
1 cup walnut meats, chopped
2 whole fresh eggs, well beaten
1¼ cups sweet, cold milk
¼ cup melted butter

To the flour add baking powder, salt and sugar, and sift together over chopped walnut meats. Mix well. Blend eggs and milk and stir into flour mixture until smooth, adding as you go along the melted butter. Turn dough into greased loaf pan and bake in a moderate oven as directed. Cool before slicing.

(213) NUT BREAD II

WITH BREAD AND RYE FLOURS

Makes 1 loaf. Oven temperature: 350° F.
Baking time: 1 hour (about).

2 cups bread flour, sifted twice
1 cup rye flour, sifted twice
1 scant teaspoon salt
1 tablespoon baking powder
1 whole fresh egg, well-beaten
½ cup molasses
¼ teaspoon baking soda
1 cup cold sweet milk
1 cup nut meats (any kind chopped)

Mix flours together in sifter; add salt and baking powder and sift over chopped nut meats. Combine beaten egg, molasses and soda and mix thoroughly. Gradually add to the flour-nut mixture, stirring well. Turn mixture into a greased loaf pan and bake in a moderate oven as directed.

(214) NUT BREAD III

WITH BREAD AND WHOLE WHEAT FLOURS

Makes 1 loaf. Oven temperature: 350° F
Baking time: 1¼ hours (about).

¾ cup bread flour, sifted
1½ cups whole wheat flour, unsifted
2½ teaspoons baking powder
1 teaspoon soda
¾ teaspoon salt
1 cup chopped nut meats (any kind)
¾ cup brown sugar
1½ cups buttermilk or sour milk

Combine flour, baking powder, salt and soda and sift together. Mix with whole wheat flour combined with chopped nut meats.

Blend thoroughly. Combine brown sugar and buttermilk or sour milk, mixing well, and gradually add to the flour mixture, beating enough to dampen it. Turn dough into greased loaf pan, and bake in a moderate oven as directed. Cool before slicing.

(215) NUT BREAD IV

WITH WHOLE WHEAT FLOUR AND PECANS

Makes 1 large loaf. Oven temperature: 300° F.
Baking time: 1¼ hours (about).

The flavor of this bread made with molasses, brown sugar and cinnamon is very delicious when to it is added the subtle flavor of pecan meats.

- 3 cups whole wheat flour
- 1 tablespoon baking powder
- 1 teaspoon baking soda
- 1 teaspoon ground cinnamon
- 1¾ teaspoons salt
- ⅓ cup brown sugar
- ½ cup molasses
- 1 cup sweet milk
- ½ cup cold water
- 1 cup pecan meats, chopped fine
- 2 tablespoons butter, melted somewhat

To the flour add baking powder, soda, salt and ground cinnamon and sift twice over rolled brown sugar. Mix lightly. Combine molasses, sweet milk and water and mix thoroughly. Add this liquid to the dry mixture, stirring until moistened. Now stir in the pecan meats alternately with melted butter and beat briskly. Turn batter into a large greased loaf pan lined with heavy paper. Let stand about 15 minutes before baking in a slow oven as directed, or until top is brown and bread slightly shrunken from sides of pan. Cool before slicing very thin. You may divide the batter between two small loaf pans. In such case bake only one hour.

(216) NUT PRUNE BREAD

Makes 1 loaf. Oven temperature: 350° F.
Baking time: 60–70 minutes.

- 5 tablespoons butter or other shortening
- ¾ cup dark brown sugar, well packed
- 1 whole fresh egg, well beaten
- 1 cup shredded, pitted cooked prunes
- ⅓ cup milk
- 2 cups bread flour, sifted
- 1 tablespoon baking powder
- ½ generous teaspoon salt
- ¼ teaspoon baking soda
- ⅓ cup blanched almonds, chopped

Cream shortening with brown sugar; add beaten egg and beat briskly. To the flour add baking powder, salt and soda, and sift together over the shredded cooked prunes. Mix thoroughly, adding while going along the cold milk, alternately with lightly floured almonds. Turn batter into a greased loaf pan and bake in a moderate oven as directed, or until loaf is brown and slightly shrunken from the pan. Cool before slicing thin.

(217) NUT RAISIN BREAD I

WITH BREAD FLOUR

Makes 1 loaf. Oven temperature: 300° F.
Baking time: 1¼ hours (about).

3½ cups bread flour, sifted
¾ teaspoon salt
4 teaspoons baking powder
¾ cup fine granulated sugar
1 whole fresh egg, well-beaten
1 cup sweet milk, cold
1 cup seedless raisins, parboiled
¾ cup finely chopped walnut meats

Combine flour with salt, baking powder and sugar and sift over raisins (washed, parboiled, thoroughly drained and dried) mixed with finely chopped walnut meats. Mix thoroughly. Combine beaten egg with cold milk; beat well, and gradually stir into the flour-raisin-nut mixture, stirring just enough to moisten the dry ingredients. Turn into a greased loaf pan, lined with waxed paper, and bake in a slow oven as directed, or until bread is brown and slightly shrunken from the pan. Cool and slice very thin.

(218) NUT RAISIN BREAD II

WITH BREAD AND WHOLE WHEAT FLOURS

Makes 1 loaf. Oven temperature: 350° F.
Baking time: 60–70 minutes.

1½ cups bread flour, sifted
2 cups unsifted whole wheat flour
¾ teaspoon baking soda
½ generous teaspoon salt
1 scant tablespoon baking powder
⅓ cup fine granulated sugar
½ cup molasses
1½ cups buttermilk or sour milk
½ cup seedless raisins, parboiled, drained
½ cup white raisins, parboiled, drained
½ cup blanched almonds, chopped fine
½ cup walnut meats, chopped fine

Combine bread flour, soda, salt, baking powder and sugar and sift over whole wheat flour. Blend thoroughly. Sprinkle a little of the flour mixture over mixed raisins and nuts. Combine molasses and buttermilk (or sour milk) mixing well, and gradually stir into the dry mixture. Beat briskly. Bake in a moderate oven as directed. Cool before slicing. This bread may be steamed like Boston Brown Bread, if desired.

(219) OATMEAL BREAD—SCOTCH METHOD

YEAST METHOD

Makes 2 loaves. Oven temperature: 425–375° F.
Baking time: 45–50 minutes.

2 cups boiling water
1¾ teaspoons salt
1 cup rolled oats
1 tablespoon butter
1 cake compressed yeast
2 teaspoons granulated sugar
¼ cup lukewarm water
½ cup brown sugar
½ cup lukewarm water
5 cups twice-sifted bread flour

To the boiling water add salt and rolled oats. Mix well; then stir in the butter. Allow to stand until lukewarm, crumble in the yeast cake and add white sugar and the ¼ cup of lukewarm water. Blend thoroughly and allow to stand for about one hour, or until sponge is almost doubled in bulk. Combine the ½ cup lukewarm water and brown sugar and stir until dissolved; add to the sponge and blend well, adding gradually 2½ cups of the bread flour, alternately with rolled oat mixture, beating until smooth. Now add remaining 2½ cups of flour and mix well. Turn dough out on a lightly floured board and knead until smooth with no stickiness. Place in a greased mixing bowl; cover; place over hot water and let rise until doubled in bulk. Cut down the dough. Turn upon floured board and divide into two equal portions. Cover with a dry cloth and let stand on the floured board for 20 minutes. Then, shape into loaves; place in greased loaf pans; let rise until doubled in bulk and bake 15 minutes in a very hot oven to set the bread; reduce temperature to moderate and continue baking for 25 minutes longer, or until top is brown and bread has shrunk from side of pans. Cool before slicing.

"A baker's dozen of rolls must weigh a fixed amount. If it does not, the baker will be beheaded." So decreed Henry VII. His bakers took no chances. To insure themselves against the loss of their heads they began adding an extra roll. So the term "baker's dozen" came into being.

(220) ORANGE ALMOND BREAD

Makes 1 loaf. Oven temperature: 350° F.
Baking time: 45 minutes.

3 cups bread flour, sifted
1/3 teaspoon salt
4 teaspoons baking powder
1/2 cup granulated sugar
2 tablespoons melted butter or lard
1/3 cup chopped blanched almonds
Grated rind medium-sized orange
1 whole fresh egg, well-beaten
1 cup cold sweet milk
Melted butter for top

To the flour add salt, baking powder and granulated sugar and sift together over mixed almonds and grated orange rind. Blend thoroughly. Beat whole egg with melted butter or lard and add to cold milk. Gradually stir liquid into dry ingredients, just enough to dampen flour mixture. Toss gently a few seconds over lightly floured board, shape in loaf, and place in greased loaf pan. Let stand 10 minutes. Brush top with melted butter and bake in a moderate oven as directed. Allow to cool before slicing.

(221) ORANGE BANANA MARBLE BREAD

Makes 2 loaves. Oven temperature: 350° F.
Baking time: 1 hour.

This delicious bread, created by Sister Mary Bernardine of the Convent of the Sacred Heart, requires two distinct operations.

First Operation:

2 1/4 cups bread flour, sifted
4 teaspoons baking powder
3/4 teaspoon salt
1/2 cup fine granulated sugar
5 tablespoons shortening
3/4 cup cold sweet milk
1/4 cup unstrained orange juice
1 whole fresh egg, well-beaten
Grated rind of one medium-sized orange

To the flour add baking powder, salt and fine granulated sugar and sift together over grated orange rind. Mix thoroughly; then blend in shortening. Combine milk, orange juice and beaten egg and mix well. Set aside while preparing the other mixture.

Second Operation:

2 cups bread flour, sifted
2 teaspoons baking powder
½ teaspoon baking soda
½ teaspoon salt
½ teaspoon ground cinnamon
½ cup granulated sugar
½ teaspoon ground nutmeg
½ cup bran flour, unsifted
¼ cup shortening
2 whole eggs, well beaten
2 tablespoons honey
2 tablespoons sour cream
4 bananas, mashed (medium-sized)
Melted butter for tops

Add baking powder, soda, salt, cinnamon, sugar and nutmeg to flour and sift together over unsifted bran. Blend thoroughly. Combine shortening, beaten eggs, honey and sour cream, and beat briskly, adding while going along the mashed bananas, blending well. Add this to the flour mixture, a little at a time, beating well after each addition until smooth. Grease 2 loaf pans; line them with waxed paper; divide batter between the loaf pans; brush tops with melted butter and bake in a moderate oven as directed or until tops are brown and bread shrunken from sides of pans. Cool before slicing.

(222) ORANGE BREAD I

YEAST METHOD

Makes 2 loaves. Oven temperature: 350° F.
Baking time: 1 hour.

1 cake compressed yeast
1 cup lukewarm water
1 cup orange juice (unstrained)
Grated rind of 2 medium-sized oranges
2 tablespoons butter, melted
1 teaspoon salt
2 tablespoons granulated sugar
1 egg yolk, well-beaten
4 cups bread flour, sifted twice
Melted butter for tops

Crumble yeast cake into lukewarm water; mix well then stir in orange juice and grated rind, salt, sugar and beaten egg yolk. Beat briskly until well blended. Gradually stir in the flour, mixing thoroughly after each addition. Place upon lightly floured board and knead for one minute. Turn the dough into a greased mixing bowl; cover; and let rise to double its bulk, over hot water. Now cut down the dough and knead a half minute. Divide dough into two equal parts; shape into loaves; place in greased lined loaf pans and allow to rise to double in bulk. Brush tops with melted butter and bake in a moderate oven as directed. Serve warm and thinly sliced.

(223)

ORANGE BREAD II

BAKING POWDER METHOD

The syrup

Cut rinds of two large oranges; place in small saucepan, cover with cold water, and simmer for 10 minutes. Drain; cover again with cold water, bring to the boiling point, and let simmer slowly for 10 minutes longer, or about 20 minutes. Drain and put rind through food chopper, using the finest blade. Return to a small saucepan; add ½ cup sugar and ½ cup cold water. Stir until sugar is dissolved; then bring to the boiling point and simmer slowly until a thick syrup is formed and chopped rinds become semi-transparent. Remove from the fire, and let cool.

The dough

2½ cups bread flour, sifted
1 tablespoon baking powder
½ generous teaspoon salt
½ cup fine granulated sugar
2 whole fresh eggs, well-beaten
½ cup unstrained orange juice
1 teaspoon unstrained lemon juice
3 tablespoons melted butter or lard
The orange rind syrup, well-cooled
Melted butter for top

To the flour add baking powder, salt, sugar, and sift together. Combine beaten eggs, unstrained orange and lemon juice, melted butter or lard (or any other desired shortening) and last the orange rind syrup. Blend thoroughly, using a rotary beater. Skim off the foam; then add gradually to the flour mixture, blending thoroughly after each addition. Let stand 10 minutes before turning into greased loaf pan; brush with melted butter and bake one hour in a moderate oven (350° F.). Allow to cool before slicing.

I would not strain orange or lemon juice used in pastry, bread or cookies. To do so means that only the water-soluble material of the orange or lemon is used and there is nutrient value, notably vitamin A and iron, in the suspended particles of pulp which are discarded. In fact, the decrease in the use of whole fruit as a result of the greater convenience of orange juice represents to my mind and to that of dietitians some loss of nutritive value.

(224) ORANGE BREAD III

QUICK METHOD WITH CANDIED ORANGE PEEL AND BAKING POWDER

Makes 1 small loaf. Oven temperature: 350° F.
Baking time: 55 to 60 minutes.

3 tablespoons butter or margarine
¼ cup granulated sugar
1 whole fresh egg, well-beaten
1 cup sweet milk
½ generous teaspoon salt
2¼ cups bread flour, sifted over
½ cup candied orange peel put through food chopper
2 teaspoons baking powder

Cream butter; gradually add sugar, creaming until fluffy. Then add combined milk and egg and beat into butter-sugar mixture. To the flour add salt and baking powder and sift over ground candied orange peel. Blend well; then stir into the flour mixture the well-beaten first mixture. Turn batter into a greased loaf pan, and bake in a moderate oven as directed. Let cool before slicing.

It probably is a good thing that people live far apart in Labrador —else little work would be accomplished, for it is considered a breach of etiquette to pass a neighbor's house without stopping for some bread and tea.

(225) ORANGE HONEY BREAD IV

EXCELLENT TEA LOAF

Makes 1 loaf. Oven temperature: 325° F.
Baking time: 1¼ hours (about).

2 tablespoons butter or margarine
1 cup honey
1 whole egg, well-beaten
1½ tablespoons grated orange rind
1½ teaspoons ground citron
2½ cups bread flour, sifted
2½ teaspoons baking powder
½ teaspoon baking soda
½ teaspoon salt
¾ cup unstrained orange juice
¼ cup chopped blanched almonds
½ cup Brazil nuts, chopped fine

Cream butter and honey together until thoroughly blended; add beaten egg, alternately with mixed grated orange rind and citron. To the flour add baking powder, soda and salt and sift together. Gradually add dry mixture to the creamed mixture, alternately with combined nuts and orange juice, mixing thoroughly. Turn batter into buttered loaf pan, brush top with a little melted butter and bake in a moderately slow oven as directed or until bread is brown on top and has shrunk from sides of loaf pan. Let cool before slicing very thin.

It has been said that the amount of vitamin C—the vitamin for which orange juice is famous—is reduced if it is allowed to stand overnight. Consequently it is not recommended that, as a general practice, orange juice be prepared the night before for breakfast in the morning. If container is tightly covered, the loss is not great.

(226) ORANGE MARMALADE NUT BREAD V

Makes 1 loaf. Oven temperature: 350° F.
Baking time: 1 hour (about).

1 cup walnut meats, chopped
½ cup orange marmalade
2½ cups bread flour, sifted
1 tablespoon baking powder
1 teaspoon salt
1 cup sweet milk
2 whole eggs, well-beaten
2 tablespoons butter or other fat

To the flour add baking powder and salt and sift together over chopped walnut meats, blending well. Combine milk with beaten eggs, mix well, then stir in the melted fat and orange marmalade. Gradually add liquid to dry ingredients, mixing well; pour batter into a generously greased loaf pan, and bake in a moderate oven as directed or until lightly browned. Cool before slicing. The addition of 1 teaspoon grated orange rind improves the flavor.

(227) ORANGE MOLASSES NUT BREAD VI

Makes 1 large loaf. Oven temperature: 350° F.
Baking time: 1 hour (about).

Shred the rind of one orange thinly, or use ¾ cup of thinly shredded rind. Cover with cold water, bring to a slow boil, and cook for 20 minutes; then drain. Make a syrup of ½ cup granulated sugar (or ¼ cup each of white and brown sugars) and ¼ cup cold water. Cool, add the rind and cook with very little stirring until about 2 tablespoons of syrup are left. Cool before adding to the bread mixture.

You may divide the following dough in two equal portions and bake as usual.

4 cups bread flour, sifted
5 teaspoons baking powder
1 teaspoon salt
½ cup granulated sugar, or
¼ cup each granulated and brown sugars
The cooled orange rind syrup
2 whole eggs, well-beaten
1 cup sweet cold milk
¾ cup molasses
¼ cup orange juice, unstrained
2 tablespoons melted butter
1 cup sliced nut meats (any kind)

To the flour add baking powder, salt and sugar and sift together over sliced nut meats. Mix well. Combine orange rind syrup, beaten eggs, milk, molasses, orange juice and melted butter, blending well, and gradually add to flour mixture, stirring thoroughly. Turn batter into a long loaf pan or into 2 small pans, well-greased, and bake in a moderate oven as directed. Let stand 24 hours before slicing.

(228) ORANGE MOLASSES RYE BREAD—NORWEGIAN METHOD VII

Makes 5 small long loaves. Oven temperature: 350–400° F. Baking time: 30 minutes.

Orange peels

Cook the very thinly pared, shredded orange peels of 7 large oranges in enough water to cover until soft, white lining should be removed (about 5 or 6 minutes). Drain and add the peels to 2 cups of molasses, slightly warmed.

Dough

Pour one quart sour milk (scalded, then cooled to lukewarm) over 10 cups (2½ quarts) of rye flour, mixed with 2 cups sifted bread flour with 1 tablespoon salt, and ½ generous teaspoon baking soda; stir to make a very soft dough. Add 2 cakes of compressed yeast, crumbled into ⅓ cup of lukewarm water to which has been added 2 tablespoons granulated sugar, and stir briskly until well blended. Turn into a generously greased mixing bowl; cover with a dry cloth; place over hot (not boiling) water to rise to double its bulk (about 2½ hours).

Cut down the sponge, then add the prepared orange peels and molasses, and enough sifted bread flour to make a stiff dough. Toss on lightly floured board, and knead for 5 or 6 minutes, or until dough is elastic, smooth and free from stickiness. Return dough to greased mixing bowl; brush with melted lard or butter; cover with a cloth and set over hot water to rise to double its bulk (about 1½ hours). Turn dough onto lightly floured board, cut it down, then knead 1 short minute. Now, divide dough into 5 equal parts and shape into long narrow loaves; place these on a well-floured cloth, separating them with the folds and let rise to double in bulk. Carefully remove the loaves to a greased baking sheet; brush with warm water or milk and bake in a moderate oven for 15–20 minutes; then raise temperature as directed and bake 10 to 15 minutes longer, or until crusts are brown. Quickly brush again with hot water or milk and place in cloth to keep the crusts soft.

(229) ORANGE RYE BREAD—RUSSIAN METHOD VIII

YEAST METHOD WITH ONLY TWO RISINGS

Makes 3 small loaves. Oven temperature: 350° F.
Baking time: 50–55 minutes.

2 cups scalded sweet milk	1 cake compressed yeast
2 teaspoons salt	⅓ cup water, lukewarm
4 tablespoons granulated sugar	4 cups (1 quart) unsifted rye flour
2 tablespoons shortening	4 cups bread flour, sifted
2½ tablespoons grated orange rind	1 cup seeded or seedless raisins
1½ tablespoons anise seeds	Melted butter

To the scalded milk add salt, sugar and shortening. Blend well and when cooled to lukewarm, stir in the crumbled yeast cake which has been dissolved in the ⅓ cup lukewarm water. Gradually add the rye flour, alternately with the bread flour sifted again over seeded or seedless raisins (parboiled, dried and mixed with grated orange rind and anise seeds). Blend thoroughly. Knead upon lightly floured board until dough is smooth and does not stick to the hands. Let rise 3½ hours, or until double in bulk, in greased bowl, covered and placed over hot (not boiling) water. Cut down the dough and knead a half minute, then shape into three small loaves. Place loaves in greased loaf pans, and let rise 1½ hours, covered, or until light. Brush with butter (you may sprinkle a few anise seeds over butter) and bake in a moderate oven as directed or until tops are brown and bread leaves sides of pans. Allow to cool before slicing.

(230) PEANUT BUTTER SHORTBREAD SLICES

Makes 25 slices (about). Oven temperature: 325° F.
Baking time: 18–20 minutes.

Double the amount of ingredients and shape in 1½-inch rolls, which may be stored in refrigerator, tightly wrapped in waxed paper, to slice and bake as needed.

¾ cup bread flour, sifted twice
¼ cup granulated sugar
⅓ teaspoon salt
4 tablespoons peanut butter
1 tablespoon light corn syrup

To the flour add sugar and salt and sift together. Cut in peanut butter with pastry blender or two knives until mixture looks like coarse meal. Add light corn syrup and mix thoroughly. Cut into ¼-inch slices and bake on greased baking sheets in a moderate oven as directed until light brown. Serve hot or cold.

(231) PECAN BREAD—TEXAS METHOD

Makes 1 loaf. Oven temperature: 350° F.
Baking time: 1 hour (about).

2¾ cups bread flour, sifted
1 cup fine granulated sugar
1 teaspoon salt
2 teaspoons baking powder
1 whole egg, well-beaten
1 cup sweet milk
2 cups finely chopped pecan meats
Melted butter for top

To the flour add sugar, salt and baking powder and sift together over finely chopped pecan meats. Combine beaten egg and milk, blend well and gradually stir into the flour mixture. Beat well, turn dough into generously buttered loaf pan; brush with melted butter and let stand about 20 minutes covered with a light cloth. Bake in a moderate oven as directed. Cool before slicing very thin.

(232) PECAN CORN BREAD

Makes enough to serve 6 generously. Oven temperature: 400° F.
Baking time: 30–35 minutes.

1 cup rich milk, scalded
1 cup white or yellow corn meal
1 rounded tablespoon butter
2 egg yolks, well-beaten
½ cup bread flour, sifted
2¼ teaspoons baking powder
½ generous teaspoon salt
¾ cup chopped pecan meats
2 egg whites, stiffly beaten

Pour scalded milk over corn meal slowly, at the same time adding butter and stirring constantly until smooth and thoroughly blended. Beat in the egg yolks. Combine flour, baking powder and salt and sift together over chopped pecan meats. Blend well and stir into corn meal mixture. Lastly fold in the beaten egg whites and spread mixture in a greased, shallow baking pan. Bake in a hot oven as directed or until bread is delicately brown. Serve as hot as possible with plenty of butter.

Graham bread takes its name from Sylvester Graham, born in Suffield, Connecticut, a temperance lecturer who preached vegetarianism as well as temperance in the early eighteenth century.

(233) PERSIAN BREAD

"SESAME BREAD"

Serves 6 generously. Oven temperature: 400° F.
Baking time: 35 minutes (about).

Sesame is an annual plant which is native to Eastern countries, and for many centuries found invaluable for abundance of oil in the seed. Sesame is also called *benne* or *bene* from the Malay word, meaning "grain" or "seed."

Practically everyone will say, "Sesame? Do you mean the Open, Sesame kind?" And sure enough, it is the very same ancient and honorable grain. We may have first heard of sesame through John Ruskin's great essay, *Sesame and Lilies,* in which he makes *sesame* the secret word that will unlock the treasures to be found in books. Most of us as children enjoyed the old story of Ali Baba's brother, locked in the robber's cave and forgetting the "Open, Sesame!" which would have released him. Many will recall similar folk tales in which various magic flowers or plants were used to unlock treasures, the primrose in Germany, the Rasrivtrava in Russia, the fern, the mistletoe or the witch hazel branch which tells well-diggers where to look for water. The East Indians, also, have faith in the magic powers of sesame to open secret places and gave it the name of *Vajrapushpa,* meaning "thunderbolt." Offerings of the seed are made to the god of death.

Sesame in classic times was an herb of magic, always associated with Hecate, queen of the witches, and with Medea and Circe, her daughters. It was much used for its medicinal virtues by the Greek Hippocrates, great physician of the fifth century B.C. and by all who followed him. The Great Mogul of India in the sixteenth century was passionately fond of perfumes and had all the flowers of a sweet scent in his garden steeped in the oil of sesame seed, because it held the odor so well. The thick liquid was then used as a fragrant bath oil and as a dressing for his royal hair. Many and varied are the uses of the seed and oil. The sticks of India ink, Chinese ink, are made from the soot obtained by burning the oil.

The Greek writer Theophrastus, third century B.C., highly praised sesame seeds for their flavor. In the satires of the Roman Petronius, first century A.D., well-turned phrases are spoken of as being "sprinkled with Poppy and Sesamum." The oil, the first kind to be developed on a large scale, was and still is used much more than olive oil in Egypt, probably because of the fact that it doesn't readily become rancid. The flavor is delightful, like delicate tasting nuts. A most delicious confection is made by fixing sesame seeds with enough syrup to hold them together, molded into a form like a popcorn bar.

We read of the seeds sprinkled on Sicilian bread, but in America we use them for the most part in cake and cookies. Try some cookies and you will hear loud clamors for more. To the recipe given, add 2 good tablespoons of the seed slightly toasted to bring out the nutty flavor. Here is the famous recipe for Persian Bread, also called Sesame Bread:

3 cups bread flour, sifted twice with
1 tablespoon baking powder
¾ teaspoon salt
4 tablespoons butter or lard
⅔ cup very cold sweet milk
1 whole fresh egg, slightly beaten
2 (or more) tablespoons sesame seeds, toasted

To the flour add baking powder and salt, and sift twice together over mixing bowl. Cut butter or lard into flour mixture with pastry blender. With a knife blade stir in the milk, adding nearly all of it at once and stirring back and forth quickly to dampen the flour but not to make a smooth dough. Add enough milk to make a dough sticky to the touch. Turn onto well floured board, sprinkle lightly with flour and quickly and lightly knead the dough for not over a half minute. Now pat *(do not roll)* dough into a fairly deep, buttered layer cake tin, without shaping the dough into biscuits; sprinkle top with toasted sesame seeds, and bake in a hot oven as directed. Cut into wedges when cold.

(234) PINEAPPLE BREAD

"FRUIT BREAD"

Makes 1 loaf. Oven temperature: 325° F.
Baking time: 1 hour.

1 cup canned unsweetened pineapple juice
1 cup chopped, pitted dates
¼ cup honey
2 tablespoons butter or other shortening
1 whole fresh egg, well beaten
1½ cups bread flour, sifted (about)
¼ generous teaspoon salt
1 cup chopped mixed nut meats
2 teaspoons baking powder
¼ teaspoon baking soda
Melted butter for top

Heat pineapple juice slowly; add chopped dates and cook over a low flame, stirring almost constantly until mixture is thick. Cool. Cream honey and butter; gradually beat in the egg and add to cooled date mixture. Blend thoroughly. To the flour add salt, baking powder and baking soda and sift over mixed nut meats, using 3 or 4 kinds in equal parts; mix well, then stir into the first mixture. Pour batter into a generously greased loaf pan, the bottom of which is lined with waxed paper and bake in moderately slow oven as directed. Use next day thinly sliced. A fine bread for afternoon tea or coffee.

(235) PINEAPPLE BRAN BREAD

Makes 1 loaf. Oven temperature: 350° F.
Baking time: 1¼ hours (about).

1 cup honey
2 tablespoons butter
2¼ cups bread flour, sifted
1 tablespoon baking powder
½ generous teaspoon salt
1 scant cup of all-bran
1 cup chopped nut meats
1 whole fresh egg, well-beaten
1 cup unsweetened pineapple juice

Blend butter with honey thoroughly; add egg and beat in well. To the flour add baking powder and salt and sift together over all-bran. Blend well with chopped nut meats (any kind). Combine honey mixture and flour mixture, adding slowly the cold pineapple juice. Turn dough into a greased loaf pan, the bottom of which has been lined with waxed paper and bake in a moderate oven as directed. Let cool before slicing.

(236) PISTACHIO COCOA BREAKFAST BREAD

Makes 1 loaf. Oven temperature: 350° F.
Baking time: 40–45 minutes.

Breakfast is an important meal and morning, to some poetically minded individuals, is the time of day when there may be an eye-filling sunrise or a dew-pearled garden on view. To the majority, however, morning is more prosaically associated with the insistent jangle of an alarm clock. Every morning brings to the woman who looks after the diet of the family a challenging problem, the breakfast bread, which must be adequate and tempting. She must see to it that the family eats with pleasure and to this end she varies her breads constantly. Here is a bread which will disappear as soon as put on the table:

- 1/4 cup cocoa powder, unsweetened, sifted
- 2 1/3 cups bread flour, sifted twice
- 1 tablespoon baking powder
- 1/4 cup brown sugar, rolled, sifted
- 1/4 cup granulated sugar
- 3/4 cup blanched pistachio nuts, chopped
- 1 whole fresh egg, well-beaten
- 1 cup very cold sweet milk
- 2 tablespoons melted butter
- 1 teaspoon anise seeds, warmed

Melted butter for top

Combine cocoa with flour and sift together; add baking powder, salt and combined sugars and sift again over nuts mixed with anise seeds slightly warmed to enhance the flavor. Combine egg, milk and melted butter and stir into the flour mixture. Blend thoroughly. Turn batter into a buttered (not greased) loaf pan and bake in a moderate oven as directed. Use the next day, thinly sliced.

(237) PRUNE BRAN MOLASSES BREAD I

USING UNCOOKED PITTED, CHOPPED PRUNES

Makes 1 cylindrical loaf. Steaming time: 3 hours (about) in hot water.

To steam-bake means to place a pan or container of food in another pan of hot water and then bake. This method is used for cooking such breads as Boston Brown Bread and also for soufflés, timbales and other dishes requiring slow cooking, but in these cases the water container is usually a shallow one. The following bread is steamed (after being covered tightly) in a deep pan containing hot water up to lids of tins.

1 cup bran
1 cup sour milk, very cold
½ cup prunes, uncooked, but soaked overnight, drained then chopped
1 tablespoon Grandma's molasses
½ cup fine granulated sugar, sifted
1 cup bread flour, sifted
½ teaspoon baking soda
1 teaspoon baking powder
⅓ teaspoon salt

Combine bran, milk, prunes and molasses and blend thoroughly. Combine sugar, flour, soda, baking powder and salt and sift together. Gradually stir flour mixture into the bran mixture, blending well after each addition. Fill a generously greased coffee or baking powder can (or several) with the batter; cover tightly and steam for three hours. Cool before slicing. Twenty-four hours standing in a cool, dry place improves the flavor.

The following recipe requires baking and no steaming and individual loaves may be made in baking powder or similar tins, as above.

(238) PRUNE GRAHAM BREAD II

Makes 2 small loaves. Oven temperature: 325° F.
Baking time: 1½–1¾ hours.

1 cup granulated sugar
1 whole egg, slightly beaten
2 tablespoons shortening, melted
1 cup stewed prunes, chopped fine
1 cup nut meats, chopped fine
1 teaspoon baking soda
¾ cup sour milk or buttermilk
1 cup prune juice
1½ cups bread flour, sifted
1 cup unsifted graham flour
½ teaspoon baking powder
½ teaspoon salt

Beat granulated sugar and salt with egg until sugar is dissolved then add shortening, nuts and prunes. Blend thoroughly. Beat baking soda into sour milk, and stir into the first mixture alternately with prune juice (blending well). Combine flour with baking powder and sift over graham flour. Blend well and add flour mixture to the first mixture. Now beat all together briskly for a minute or two and turn into greased loaf pans. Bake as directed in a moderate oven. Let cool before slicing.

Another quick method is as follows:

(239) PRUNE WHOLE WHEAT BREAD III

Makes 2 loaves. Oven temperature: 350° F.
Baking time: 1 hour (about).

1½ cups bread flour, sifted
½ teaspoon baking soda
2 teaspoons baking powder
¾ teaspoon salt
¾ cup (generous) fine granulated sugar
1 cup whole wheat flour, unsifted
½ cup prune juice
1 whole egg, well-beaten
1 cup sour milk or buttermilk
2 tablespoons butter, melted

Combine flour, soda, baking powder, salt and sugar and sift over whole wheat flour. Blend thoroughly. Combine prune juice, beaten egg and sour milk; mix well, then stir into the first mixture. Lastly beat in the melted butter. Now beat briskly for almost a minute; turn batter into two well-greased loaf pans, and bake in a moderate oven as directed or until top is brown and bread has shrunken from sides of pans. Let cool before using. You may add 1 cup of nut meats (any kind) to the mixture. In that case sift the flour over mixed whole wheat and nut meats.

Shortening is added to bread to improve the flavor, make the dough tender and help to keep the loaf moist. But an excess of shortening may keep the dough from rising.

(240) RAISIN BREAD

YEAST METHOD

Makes 1 loaf. Oven temperature: 400° F.
Baking time: 45 minutes (about).
First rising: 50 minutes. Second rising: 2½ hours.
Third rising: 1 hour.

1 cup sweet milk, scalded, cooled
1 cake compressed yeast
1 tablespoon granulated sugar
1¼ cups bread flour, sifted
2 tablespoons shortening
⅓ cup dark brown sugar, sifted
¾ generous teaspoon salt
1 whole fresh egg, well-beaten
1 cup chopped seedless raisins
2 cups whole wheat flour

Scald milk and cool to lukewarm. Crumble yeast cake into a little lukewarm water, and stir into lukewarm milk, alternately with sugar. Add bread flour gradually and beat hard until very smooth. Cover the sponge; set over a pan containing hot water, and let rise for fifty minutes, or until light with large bubbles on the surface.

Cream shortening and brown sugar well, add beaten egg and salt and beat until smooth, then stir in the light yeast mixture called a sponge. Beat well until smooth, then stir in the whole wheat flour, mixed with raisins. Turn dough out upon a lightly floured board and knead until all stickiness disappears and the dough is elastic, using a little more whole wheat flour if needed. Place dough in a large greased bowl; cover; set in a warm place or over a pan of hot water and let rise again (second rising) until doubled in bulk. Mold quickly into one long, or two short, loaves; place in a well greased loaf pan (or two smaller pans); cover; let rise again (third rising) in a warm place or over hot water until doubled in bulk. Bake in a hot oven as directed or until brown on top and the loaf, tapped on the bottom, gives forth a hollow sound. Cool, uncovered, before slicing. If you bake in two loaf pans, bake for about 40 minutes.

(241) RICE CORN BREAD

Serves 6 generously. Oven temperature: 400° F.
Baking time: 35–40 minutes.

1 cup corn meal, sifted
2½ teaspoons baking powder
¾ scant teaspoon salt
1 cup cooked, well-drained rice
1 whole fresh egg, well-beaten
1 cup cold sweet milk
¼ cup melted butter

Combine sifted corn meal, baking powder and salt and sift together over the cold cooked rice. Mix well with the meal mixture using a fork, separating rice kernels as much as possible. Combine beaten egg and milk and stir into the corn meal mixture, alternately with half of the melted butter. Melt the remaining 2 tablespoons in baking pan and pour mixture into the pan, stirring well to blend thoroughly. Bake in a hot oven as directed or until brown on top and sides. Serve hot, cut into wedges, with plenty of butter.

(242) RICE SKILLET CHEESE BREAD

Serves 6. Oven temperature: 350° F.
Baking time: 35 minutes (about).

1 cup cooked rice, cold
¾ cup white corn meal
½ cup bread flour, sifted with
1 scant teaspoon baking powder
½ scant teaspoon salt
1 whole fresh egg, separated
½ to ¾ cup cold sweet milk
2 tablespoons butter, melted
1 scant cup shredded American cheese

Mix thoroughly the cold rice, corn meal and flour mixture (flour with baking powder and salt). Gradually stir in the beaten egg yolk mixed with milk, alternately with melted butter, mixing well. Then fold in the stiffly beaten egg white. Turn mixture into a generously buttered hot skillet; sprinkle top with American cheese (any other hard cheese may be used) and bake in a moderate oven as directed or until delicately brown on top. Serve as hot as possible.

(243) RICE YEAST BREAD

TWO RISINGS

Makes 2 loaves. Oven temperature: 350° F.
Baking time: 1 hour (about).

½ cup sweet milk, scalded
6 tablespoons butter or margarine
6 tablespoons granulated sugar
1 teaspoon salt
7 cups cold cooked rice
½ cake compressed yeast
¼ cup sweet milk, lukewarm
8 cups (2 quarts) bread flour, sifted twice
Melted butter for top

To the milk add shortening and sugar and stir until both are melted, then stir in the salt. Let cool to lukewarm and blend in the cold cooked rice, alternately with the yeast softened in lukewarm sweet milk. Gradually stir in the flour, blending well after each addition, adding more flour if needed to make a rather stiff dough. Knead on a lightly floured board until dough is smooth, elastic and not sticky. Place in a large, greased mixing bowl, cover and set over hot water. Let stand until doubled in bulk. Then cut it down and knead a half minute. Divide dough into two equal portions; shape in loaves; place in generously greased pans and allow to rise, covered, until light and almost doubled in bulk. Rub melted butter over the tops and bake in a moderate oven as directed. Let cool before slicing.

(244) ROLLED OATS MOLASSES BREAD

YEAST METHOD—TWO RISINGS

Makes 2 loaves. Oven temperature: 375° F.
Baking time: 55–60 minutes.

2 cups rolled oats
1¾ teaspoons salt
⅓ cup Grandma's molasses
1 tablespoon butter
2 cups boiling water
1 cake compressed yeast
¼ cup lukewarm water
4¼ cups bread flour, sifted
Melted butter for tops

Over combined rolled oats, salt, molasses and butter pour the rapidly boiling water. Mix thoroughly; then let cool to lukewarm. Soften crumbled yeast cake in lukewarm water and stir into the rolled oats mixture. Blend well. Gradually stir in the flour, beating well after each addition, until smooth and free from lumps. Cover; set over a pan of hot water and let rise to double its bulk, then cut down the dough. Turn upon a lightly floured board and knead a short minute; divide into two equal portions and shape into loaves. Place in two greased loaf pans; cover and allow to rise to double its bulk in a warm place. Brush tops with melted butter and bake in a moderately hot oven as directed or until tops are brown and bread shrunk from sides of pan. Let stand 24 hours before slicing.

(245) ROMANIAN EASTER BREAD OR PASKHA

Serve well-chilled.

Serves about 6. No cooking or baking needed.

Geographically, Romania forms a direct route to and from the Near East. So many travelers pass through Romania each year, that the capital, Bucharest, is most cosmopolitan. Almost all the European languages besides Romanian may be heard here: French, German, Greek, Hungarian, Bulgarian, Turkish, Russian and so on; and the many nationalities that pass through the Romanian cities are represented by restaurants that cater to the peculiarities of each country. Indeed, the kitchen of Romania is an international one. The Russian type of eating place is similar to the Romanian. The Russian appetizer, Sakuska, is served in both Russian and Romanian restaurants.

While the city-bred Romanians are generally connoisseurs of good food, the people of the rural districts eat very simply but substantially. And although most Romanian dishes show the effect of foreign influence, there are some that belong peculiarly to the Romanian kitchen, such as the following bread. Although it is more a dish than a bread, it is nevertheless called bread. It is made as follows:

1½ cups sieved cottage cheese
6 tablespoons butter
3 tablespoons powdered sugar
2 egg yolks, hard cooked and sieved
¾ cup blanched chopped almonds
Crackers

If the cottage cheese is too dry, moisten with one or two tablespoons of heavy cream. Cream butter well; gradually add powdered sugar alternating with sieved egg yolks and cream until fluffy and thoroughly blended. Mix well with the cottage cheese, alternately adding the almonds. Divide mixture between six small bowls, cover with a round of waxed paper and place a weight over each bowl. Chill thoroughly overnight and serve with crackers.

(246) RUSSIAN EASTER BREAD

CALLED "KOOLICH," "KOULITCHI" OR "KOOLITCH"

Serves about 10–12 persons. Oven temperature: 325° F.
Baking time: 1 hour.

Russian cooking is predominantly French and German, the dishes of these countries having been incorporated into the Russian language after becoming popular with the Russian people. Before the first World War, Russia was the home of various dishes celebrated for their peculiarity of flavor and their excellence, food then being both inexpensive and plentiful. There are few of the old, high-class restaurants remaining today. The important part of the meal is the *zhskaya* or *zakouska* corresponding to the French *hors d'oeuvre* or appetizers in America, and the famous Easter bread, which in reality is more a cake than a bread, is made in sizes ranging from six inches to nearly two feet tall. It is sliced horizontally from the top for serving, and is usually frosted and profusely decorated. It is made as follows:

Sponge

4 cakes (2 ounces) compressed yeast
1½ cups scalded milk, cooled to lukewarm
1 lb. bread flour (3¾ cups) sifted twice

Crumble yeast cakes into milk and when dissolved, stir in the flour. When smooth, place the large mixing bowl over hot water, cover with a clean, light, dry cloth and allow to rise until doubled in bulk and bubbling on top. Then cut it down with a few strokes of a wooden spoon and add:

Dough

7½ cups bread flour, sifted twice
1 lb. sweet butter, lukewarm (not hot)
2½ cups scalded milk, cooled to lukewarm
14 fresh egg yolks, well-beaten
2½ cups granulated sugar
3 tablespoons vanilla extract
10 egg whites, slightly beaten

Into the sponge beat the flour, alternately with the melted butter mixed with the lukewarm milk, which has been sweetened with the sugar and flavored with the vanilla extract. Beat briskly for a minute or so, then fold in the egg whites. Cover with a light, clean dry towel; set the pan over hot water, and let rise to twice its bulk (about one hour). Butter generously a round fluted or tall tube cake pan and sprinkle the pan with a mixture of equal parts of very dry bread crumbs (macaroon or cake crumbs may be used) and blanched almonds, coarsely ground. Fill half the tube pan with the cake batter; cover and allow to stand for 15 to 20 minutes in a warm place. Bake in a moderately hot oven as directed. Let cool 5 minutes in the pan before unmolding over a cake rack and when cold, cover with the following frosting:

Frosting

Make a meringue in the usual way from 3 egg whites, stiffly beaten and 3/4 cup or more of powdered sugar, sifted and measured; spread all over the *koulitch* or Easter bread and decorate according to fancy with almonds, bits of citron or pieces of candied fruits, such as apricots, cherries, pineapple, etc.

Divide the batter between two buttered molds if preferred.

The Russians also have their own Paskha, made as follows:

(247) RUSSIAN EASTER BREAD OR PASKHA

Serves 10–12. No cooking or baking. Serve thoroughly chilled.

Force 3 lbs. of cottage cheese through a fine sieve (the drier it is the better—the bread then unmolds without breaking). Stir in 1 1/4 lbs. butter and 1 1/2 lbs. powdered sugar until creamy and fluffy. Then add 8 hard-cooked egg yolks, sieved, a little at a time, beating briskly after each addition, adding while going along 1 1/2 to 2 teaspoons of salt to taste. Now combine a generous 1/2 cup of sultana raisins, seeded and chopped, with an equal amount of crystallized or candied fruits, mixed in equal parts (such as citron, orange peel, apricots and cherries), marinated in 4 tablespoons of brandy, for 30 minutes; press in a dry cloth and blend with the cheese mixture. Divide mixture between 10 or 12 individual decorative bowls; cover with a round of waxed paper and place a weight over each bowl. Chill thoroughly overnight, the longer the better. Unmold upon chilled individual plates and decorate each *pascha* with candied cherries and tiny pieces of candied fruit.

If the *pascha* is made in one large piece, candles may be stuck on it before serving. The letters *X.B.*, meaning *Krisstos Voskresseh* or "Christ is risen," are often designed on the large *pascha* as an additional decoration.

(248) RYE BREAD—SWISS METHOD

Makes 2 large loaves. Oven temperature: 325° F.
Baking time: 1½ hours.

This delicious bread should stand 24 hours before slicing. You may make your own ferment or sour dough, called in Switzerland *sauerteig,* one or two days in advance as follows: Crumble ½ cake compressed yeast into ¼ cup lukewarm water; when soft, stir in 1 cup of bread flour, sifted. Set this sponge in a warm place and within a day or so it will have reached the sour-dough stage necessary for raising two loaves of nearly three pounds each. This measurement includes water necessary for the leavening. If kept in a tin box, tightly covered, or in covered crock, this bread will keep fresh for a whole week.

5 pounds pure white rye flour
1¼ quarts lukewarm water
1 tablespoon salt
1½ tablespoons granulated sugar
1 generous tablespoon caraway seeds
2 cakes compressed yeast, or
1 cup of ferment

NOTE: "Ferment" is a piece of raw dough kept over from a previous baking or procured at a baker's shop; this, well mixed with the flour and lukewarm water and left to rise overnight, has the power to raise the dough to double its bulk and produce a sour but pleasant smelling sponge.

Stir half the amount of rye flour into the lukewarm water and add either the ferment or the yeast cakes, crumbled in a small part of the lukewarm water. Let stand, covered, in a warm place overnight. Next morning add the remaining flour mixed with salt and caraway seeds. Blend well, then toss upon a lightly floured board and knead until smooth, elastic and not sticky. Place in a large, greased mixing bowl; cover; set over a pan containing hot, but not boiling water, or in a warm place such as the back of the range or stove and let rise to double its bulk. Cut the dough down with a few strokes of a spatula or wooden spoon. Knead a minute or so then form into two large loaves. Cover and allow to rise again to double in bulk, over hot water. Bake in a moderately slow oven as directed. Let stand overnight before slicing.

The cookery of Switzerland may be divided into three distinct groups. Italy, France and Austria are represented in the Swiss kitchen. The dishes of these countries are served in the parts of Switzerland adjoining them. In the restaurants the French cuisine predominates.

(249) SAFFRON FRUIT BREAD

Makes 3 loaves. Oven temperature: 350° F.
Baking time: 1 hour (about).

This delicious English bread with its unusual color is much relished by the Cornish folks and is made also in this country, especially in the Middle West, as follows:

Make a sponge with the following ingredients:

- 4 cups scalded sweet milk
- 2 cups lukewarm water
- 1 tablespoon of salt
- 1 cup melted butter
- 1 cup pure lard
- 2 cups granulated sugar
- 4 cups bread flour, sifted
- 2 tablespoons Spanish saffron (more or less according to taste)

Place saffron in a small bowl, cover with ½ cup of boiling water and steep for 30 minutes. Scald the milk and let cool to lukewarm. Crumble the yeast cakes in remaining lukewarm water (1½ cups); stir well, then add salt, butter, lard, sugar and flour. Stir well, then beat in the saffron, liquid and all. Cover and set over a pan containing hot water to rise until bubbles form on top. Cut the sponge down with a wooden spoon, then beat in the following ingredients with 3 or 4 tablespoons flour sifted over them:

- 1 lb. currants, chopped
- 1 lb. small seedless raisins
- ¼ lb. lemon peel (candied, chopped)
- ¼ lb. orange peel, candied, chopped
- ¾ cup blanched, chopped almonds
- ½ lb. chopped citron

Beat briskly and vigorously. Toss dough upon lightly floured board and knead until smooth, elastic and not sticky. Return to the greased mixing bowl, brush with melted butter, and let rise to double its bulk. Toss once or twice upon floured board; divide the dough into two equal portions; shape and place in large greased loaf pans, lined with waxed paper, and allow to rise to double its bulk. Bake in moderate oven as directed. Do not cut before cooled; still better let stand overnight before slicing.

(250) SALLY LUNN BREAD I

YEAST METHOD

Makes 2 loaves. Oven temperature: 350° F.
Baking time: 50 minutes (about).

4 cups bread flour, sifted
1 teaspoon salt
1 cup milk, scalded, cooled to lukewarm
½ cup lukewarm water
2 whole fresh eggs, beaten slightly
1 cake compressed yeast
2 tablespoons granulated sugar

To the flour add salt and sift together. To the lukewarm milk add eggs and blend well. Crumble yeast cake into the lukewarm water and let stand 4 or 5 minutes, then stir into the milk mixture, gradually, with the flour and salt mixed with sugar. Beat vigorously for a few minutes. Cover; set the bowl over hot water and allow to rise to double its bulk. Cut down the dough, toss upon lightly floured board and knead until smooth, elastic and not sticky to the hands. Shape into two loaves; brush with melted butter, place in greased, floured loaf pans and let rise to double in bulk. Bake in a moderate oven as directed. Serve hot, cut into squares or slices, with plenty of butter.

(251) SALLY LUNN BREAD II

BAKING POWDER METHOD

Makes about 24 squares. Oven temperature: 400° F.
Baking time: 30 minutes.

This bread needs to be baked in a quick oven after being poured into a shallow baking pan which has been generously buttered. When the bread is done, it is cut into small squares and served very hot with plenty of fresh butter.

2 cups bread flour, sifted
1 tablespoon baking powder
½ teaspoon salt
3 tablespoons fine granulated sugar
¾ cup sweet cold milk
½ cup melted butter
2 whole fresh eggs, well-beaten

Combine flour with baking powder, salt and sugar and sift into mixing bowl. Make a well in center of sifted dry ingredients and pour in the combined milk, melted butter and beaten eggs, well mixed. Lift and fold mixture just enough to blend ingredients. Do not beat. Pour mixture into a shallow, greased oblong pan and bake in a hot oven as directed. Cut into squares and serve as hot as possible with plenty of butter.

(252) SALT-RISING BREAD

Makes 2 loaves. Oven temperature: 375° F. for ten minutes, then 350° F. for 25 minutes. Total time: 35 minutes.

Here is a real old-time family recipe for "salt-risin' bread"—the kind that many Americans remember from their childhood.

The sponge and dough require a higher temperature (115° F.) than yeast mixtures. The "starter" should be kept at a constant temperature for an active mixture. The home-made salt-rising bread is not so light as yeast bread; it is moist and crumbly.

1 cup sweet milk, scalded	1½ teaspoons salt
1 tablespoon granulated sugar	¼ cup white corn meal

Scald milk; remove from heat and stir in sugar, salt and white corn meal; turn into 2-quart jar or pitcher, cover and set in pan of water, hot to the hand (110 to 115° F.).

Let stand in a warm place 6 to 7 hours, or until it ferments; when gas escapes freely, stir in, in order named:

1 cup lukewarm water (100° F.)	2 tablespoons shortening
1 tablespoon granulated sugar	2¼ cups bread flour, sifted

Beat thoroughly. Return jar to hot water bath (115° F.) and let rise until sponge is very light and full of bubbles. Turn sponge into warm, greased large mixing bowl, and gradually stir in 2¼ cups bread flour, sifted, or just enough to make a stiff dough, or until smooth after kneading a few minutes.

Divide in half, shape into loaves, place in generously greased loaf pans. Brush with melted butter; cover and let rise in warm place until two and one-half times its original bulk. Bake in moderately hot oven to set the dough, then at moderate heat as directed. Let cool before slicing.

(253) SCOTCH OAT BREAD

BAKING POWDER METHOD

Serves about 6. Oven temperature: 350° F.
Baking time: until quite hard—25 minutes (about).

1 cup bread flour, sifted
1 teaspoon baking powder
½ teaspoon salt
1 cup oatmeal, uncooked
1 tablespoon butter
Enough very cold water to make a dry, stiff dough

Combine the flour, sifted with salt and baking powder, with oatmeal. Work in the butter and into this pour enough ice-cold water to make a stiff dough, as dry as possible just as though you were making a pie crust. Spread on lightly floured board by hand pressure, keeping edges from parting by the support of one hand while you spread with the other. Now pass the rolling pin, slightly floured, over the dough to smooth the surface, no more. The dough should be about ¼-inch in thickness. Cut in small squares; place on greased baking sheet and bake in a moderate oven as directed until bread is quite hard.

(254) SCOTCH SHORTBREAD I

ORIGINAL RECIPE

NOTE: It is very difficult to give any exact time for baking this delicious bread, but the baking is very slow and for 3 hours or more. The oven temperature should be as low as possible (flame only high enough to prevent its going out). The longer the baking, the better —it may even take 4 hours. The pan should be placed on the top shelf of oven because the shortbread becomes easily too brown on the bottom when the top is still almost white. The shortbread is done when it becomes crisp all through. You may turn it out of the pan to see that the bottom is not getting too brown. Scotch Shortbread should be a creamy color when done.

½ of a large whole fresh egg
1 cup fine granulated sugar
1 cup butter, or ½ butter and ½ lard
3 cups bread flour, sifted
3 tablespoons white corn meal, sifted
1 teaspoon baking powder
½ teaspoon salt

Sift half of the sugar with the flour, corn meal and salt. Work in the butter or shortening mixture until flour looks like coarse meal.

Make a well in this and into it sift the remaining sugar. Beat the half egg into the sugar in center of well and with a wooden spoon start to stir. When the egg has picked up the sugar and flour mixture, work with the hands, kneading thoroughly. Turn the dough upon a large piece of waxed paper or cloth and shape, pressing into a square or round pan to about ¾ inch in thickness. Now stab the dough with a knife, once in center and four times about 1½ inches from the outside edge. The stabs should go through the dough. Turn over into another pan of the same size; remove the paper, pressing the dough around the edge, making, if desired a scalloped border. Again stab through and through the dough with the tines of a fork so the entire dough, except fancy scalloped edge, is covered with little holes.

Place the pan upon the top shelf in a very slow oven (about 200° F.) and bake for 3 hours or more. If you can get the oven lower, the baking will take about 4 hours. Serve hot; cut as you would corn bread, either in wedges or squares, with plenty of sweet butter.

Following is a short method—a poor imitation of the real Scotch Shortbread:

(255) SCOTCH SHORTBREAD II

4 cups bread flour, sifted
½ cup granulated sugar
¾ teaspoon salt
1 cup butter

Cream butter well, add sugar and cream until mixture is fluffy. Gradually work in flour, re-sifted with salt. When mixture is too stiff to mix with spoon, turn on lightly floured board and rub in the rest of flour mixture. Roll out to ¾ inch thick with lightly floured rolling pin. Spread in generously greased shallow baking pan and bake 5 minutes in a hot oven (400° F.); reduce heat to moderate (350° F.) and continue baking about 25 minutes longer. It should be very pale brown. Cut in wedges and serve hot with jam or butter.

There is also a variation of this very popular bread which consists in adding 1 or more tablespoons of caraway seed to the dough before rolling out. You may also cut the dough with a round cutter, divide circles into fan shapes, pinch and flute the edges, prick all over with a fork and bake in a moderate oven (350° F.) for 15 minutes or until delicately brown.

(256) SOUFFLÉ SPOON BREAD

SOUTHERN METHOD

Serves 6 generously. Oven temperature: 475° F.
Baking time: 30–35 minutes.

This kind of bread needs plenty of baking powder and should be served at once from the baking dish.

2 cups rapidly boiling water
1 cup farina
1 tablespoon butter
1½ teaspoons salt
4 whole eggs, separated
½ cup milk
½ cup bread flour, sifted
2 tablespoons sugar
2 tablespoons baking powder

Sprinkle farina on top of boiling water; stir in butter and salt and cook for five minutes, stirring constantly until mixture is thick. Turn into a large mixing bowl and beat in the egg yolks, one at a time, alternately with the milk, beating well after each addition. Combine flour, sugar and baking powder and sift together, then beat into the mixture. Lastly fold in the stiffly beaten egg whites; turn into a generously buttered baking dish and bake in a very hot oven as directed. Serve hot with plenty of butter.

(257) SOUR CREAM CORN BREAD

Serves about 8. Oven temperature: 425° F.
Baking time: 25 minutes (about).

IMPORTANT: Sour milk, sour cream and buttermilk are two other forms of milk important in low cost food. Substitute sour milk for sweet milk, cup for cup, in butter cakes and in all quick-breads except popovers. For every cup of really sour milk use ½ teaspoon of soda. For milk just beginning to turn sour, use ¼ teaspoon for every cup.

Baking soda furnishes leavening power equal to four times its measure of baking powder. If more leavening power than that is needed in the recipe, make up the remainder with baking powder.

It is better to use *too little soda than too much,* because too much gives your baked product bad flavor, bad odor and a yellow color. Mix soda with the dry ingredients, not with the milk.

1 cup bread flour, sifted
4 tablespoons granulated sugar
2 teaspoons baking powder
½ teaspoon baking soda
1 scant teaspoon salt
¾ cup yellow corn meal
1 whole fresh egg, well-beaten
½ cup sweet milk
1 cup heavy sour cream
2 tablespoons melted butter or margarine

To the flour add sugar, baking powder, soda and salt, mixed with yellow corn meal, and sift together. Combine egg, milk, heavy sour cream and shortening. Mix well and gradually pour into the flour mixture, beating briskly until blended. Pour batter into a hot greased shallow pan (8 × 12 inches), and bake in a very hot oven as directed or until firm and brown. Serve very hot with plenty of butter.

(258) SOUR CREAM YEAST BREAD

Makes 2 small loaves. Oven temperature: 400° F.
Baking time: 30–35 minutes.

This special bread should be baked for a short time in a hot oven and not be cut until the next day.

1½ cakes compressed yeast
¼ cup lukewarm water
½ cup sweet milk
1 cup heavy sour cream
1 generous tablespoon granulated sugar
1½ teaspoons salt
1 generous tablespoon butter, melted
4½ cups bread flour, sifted twice
Melted butter for tops

Into the lukewarm water crumble yeast cakes and mix until dissolved. To sweet milk add sour cream, sugar, salt and melted butter, or other shortening, and beat into dissolved yeast until well blended. Gradually add the flour, beating well after each addition, until smooth. Cover and allow to rise until doubled in bulk. Turn onto a lightly floured board and knead down until smooth, elastic and not sticky. Return to a large greased mixing bowl, cover after brushing with melted shortening and again let rise until doubled in bulk. Knead down for a minute, working in a little flour if necessary. Divide dough into 2 equal portions; shape in loaves; place in greased 8 × 4 × 3 loaf pans; brush with butter and allow to rise for the third time until doubled in bulk. Brush again with butter and bake in a hot oven as directed. Let stand 24 hours before slicing.

(259) SOUTHERN FRUIT BREAD

YEAST METHOD

Makes 2 small loaves. Oven temperature: 375° F.
Baking time: 1 hour.

2 cups sweet milk, scalded
2 tablespoons brown sugar
2 tablespoons granulated sugar
1¼ teaspoons salt
¼ cup butter
3 cups bread flour, sifted
2 yeast cakes
¼ cup lukewarm water
3 egg yolks, well beaten
2 cups bread flour, sifted
¼ cup chopped walnut meats
¼ cup chopped candied orange peel
¼ cup chopped citron
¼ cup chopped seedless raisins
1 unbeaten egg white for tops

To the scalded milk add the sugars, salt and butter and blend well. Stir in the 3 cups of flour and when slightly cooled, stir in the yeast cakes, crumbled into the lukewarm water and dissolved. Cover; place over hot water and let rise till doubled in bulk. Then work down with spatula and mix in the beaten egg yolks, alternately with remaining 2 cups of bread flour mixed with combined nut meats and fruit. Blend thoroughly. Cover and let rise again for the second time, over hot water (not boiling), until doubled in bulk. Knead upon lightly floured board about a minute; shape into two equal loaves; place in greased loaf pans, brush with butter and allow to rise, covered, until double in bulk (third time). Bake in a moderate oven as directed. Ten minutes before breads are done brush with unbeaten egg white to glaze. Let cool before slicing.

(260) SOUTHERN PLANTATION BREAD

Makes 2 large loaves. Oven temperature: 10 minutes at 425° F., then 40 minutes at 350° F. Total baking time: 50 minutes (about).

2 yeast cakes
1 cup sugar (fine granulated)
2 tablespoons cold water
1¼ cups sweet milk
1½ teaspoons salt
8½ to 9 cups bread flour, sifted
¾ cup melted lard
½ cup strained honey
3 whole fresh eggs, well beaten
1 12-ounce can or 4 3-ounce packages mixed candied fruit peels
1 cup white raisins (seedless)
⅔ cup chopped nut meats (any kind)
2 generous teaspoons of cinnamon
Extra milk for tops

Mix crumbled yeast cakes with ½ cup of the sugar and the water. Scald milk and cool to lukewarm. Add yeast mixture, salt and 3 cups of the flour, and beat well; cover and let stand in a warm place or over hot water (not boiling) until sponge is full of bubbles. Add ½ cup lard, eggs, honey and remaining flour; mix thoroughly. Knead on lightly floured board until smooth and elastic. Put into large greased bowl; cover and let rise until doubled in bulk. Cut down; sprinkle with fruit and nuts; knead well. Divide dough in halves; pat to oblongs about 9 inches wide and ½ inch thick. Brush with remaining lard and sprinkle with cinnamon mixed with remaining sugar. Roll and place in greased loaf pans (9½ × 5½ × 2¾ inches) or shape into braids. Cover and let rise until doubled in bulk. Brush top with a little milk. Bake as directed. Cool thoroughly before slicing the next day.

(261) SPICED MUSTARD BREAD

NO BAKING POWDER USED

Makes 1 loaf. Oven temperature: 350° F.
Baking time: 45 minutes (about).

½ cup butter or margarine
½ cup granulated sugar
1 whole fresh egg, well-beaten
2½ cups bread flour, sifted
1½ teaspoons baking soda
¼ teaspoon ground ginger
1 scant teaspoon ground cinnamon
1 scant teaspoon dry mustard
½ teaspoon ground cloves
½ generous teaspoon salt
1 cup molasses
1 cup hot water

Cream butter or margarine until fluffy; gradually add sugar and cream until mixture is thoroughly blended, adding while going along the beaten egg. Combine flour with baking soda, ginger, cinnamon, dry mustard, cloves and salt and sift twice. Add dry ingredients to creamed mixture, alternately with combined molasses and hot water, beating briskly after each addition until smooth. Turn batter into a large, greased loaf pan, and bake in a moderate oven as directed. Let cool before slicing.

(262) SPIDER CORN BREAD

Serves 6 generously. Oven temperature: 425° F.
Baking time: 20 minutes.

2 cups corn meal (yellow or white)
1 teaspoon salt
1 teaspoon baking soda
2 cups sour milk or buttermilk
2 whole fresh eggs, well-beaten
2½ tablespoons butter or margarine

Combine corn meal, salt and baking powder and mix thoroughly. Gradually stir in combined sour milk or buttermilk and beaten eggs. Heat spider very hot and add the butter, rolling pan to spread it. Pour batter all at once into the spider and bake in a quick oven as directed until brown. Turn out upon a hot round platter and serve as hot as possible with plenty of butter.

(263) SPOON BREAD

If you like to think of the U.S.A. as one united country, you had better not go into the question of corn meal and how the natives of different sections feel about it. To say that the tastes of citizens of one state differ from those of another in the matter of corn bread is to put it mildly. If you have had any truck with Southerners in this matter, and have come up against their preference for white meal and little or no sugar, you will be inclined to hand over to them the prize for intolerance in this contest of prejudices. Such an award, however, will be ill advised before you have investigated how the Rhode Islanders feel about their gray meal and its use in their famous johnny cakes. Or until you have learned what Missourians have to say about their own corn muffins, or what any down-Easterner will tell you about New England gems (muffins to you) made of yellow corn meal and as sweet as cake.

Even after your bread is baked, however, the corn meal question is far from being settled. What to eat with corn bread is equally a sectional issue. Georgia looks on with shocked amazement as the Green Mountain boys and girls pour syrup on their fried mush; Missourians shake their heads over the report that spoon bread is an accompaniment for soft herring roes; and Bostonians learn with pain that there are poor souls to the South of them who never have the honey passed with their corn muffins.

It is my opinion—and not advanced with any hope of convincing other embattled corn bread fanciers—that it is Southern cooks who have worked out the most satisfactory combinations along this line. Crisp corn sticks with a thick summer time vegetable soup rich with corn and okra and tomatoes; hoe cake with boiled bacon and greens, and corn muffins with a fine Virginia ham all seem, to any Southerner's palate, to complement each other with complete perfection, while undoubtedly molasses or maple syrup on hasty pudding is to New Englanders their *raison d'être*.

Whether coarse or fine, white or yellow, corn meal has many uses. Scrapple, made of corn meal batter and chopped cooked pork, is an appetizing meal in itself; it is popular with the Pennsylvania Dutch. Hot cakes, a combination of corn meal, water, chopped suet and plenty of red pepper, are a favorite of the Zuni Indians. The oddly named "Stamp and Go" is a salt fish, lard and corn meal mixture often served by the natives of Jamaica. Delicately brown, fried corn meal mush blocks are a common accessory to Southern fried chicken, and corn meal codfish balls cooked in deep fat are a variation of New England potato fish balls. As for the delicious and easily made corn pone, it no doubt tasted as good to the King and Queen of England when they dined at the White House as it did to the Pilgrims when they were introduced to it by the Indians in Massachusetts.

When the South was going through the dark days of the Civil War, many a mistress of a once prosperous plantation rolled up her sleeves and invaded the kitchen to help the cook prepare a meal from handy supplies. Thus, born of necessity, there emerged spoon bread, a glorified corn bread and a descendant of the old time "corn pone." So good did it taste that its popularity soon spread throughout the South and now it has become traditional. Epicures of Southern cooking like it especially when dining on fried chicken or baked ham. There are various ways of preparing spoon bread, and here are a few (spoon bread is always served with a spoon):

(264) SPOON BREAD I

LOUISIANA METHOD

Serves 6 generously. Oven temperature: 400° F.
Baking time: 20–25 minutes.

2 cups sweet milk
1 cup white corn meal, sifted
1 tablespoon brown sugar
1 teaspoon salt
½ lb. butter
6 egg yolks, well-beaten
6 egg whites, stiffly beaten

Heat sweet milk to the scalding point; gradually and very slowly stir in the corn meal with brown sugar and salt and stir briskly from the bottom of the pan, gradually adding the butter. After cooling, add beaten egg yolks a little at a time, beating vigorously the while; then fold in the stiffly beaten egg whites. Turn into a generously buttered soufflé dish or light earthenware casserole and bake in a hot oven as directed. Serve sizzling hot.

(265) SPOON BREAD II

ALABAMA METHOD

Serves 6 generously. Oven temperature: 350° F.
Baking time: 45 minutes (about).

1 cup boiling water
¾ cup yellow corn meal
1 teaspoon salt
¼ cup butter
1 cup sweet milk, lukewarm
2 whole fresh eggs, well-beaten
2 teaspoons baking powder

To the rapidly boiling water add yellow corn meal, salt and butter gradually, stirring briskly to prevent lumping, then beat vigorously a few minutes to blend thoroughly, adding, while beating, the combined beaten eggs, warm milk and baking powder. Mix well; turn into greased casserole and bake in a moderate oven as directed. Serve hot.

(266) SPOON BREAD III

GEORGIA METHOD

Serves about 6. Oven temperature: 375° F.
Baking time: 30 minutes (about).

2 cups boiling milk
¾ cup white corn meal
1 teaspoon salt
3 tablespoons butter
3 egg yolks, well-beaten
3 egg whites, stiffly beaten

Bring milk to a boil with salt; gradually scatter in the corn meal, stirring it briskly. Cook slowly until thick and smooth; remove from the fire and stir in butter. Let cool and beat in the egg yolks; then fold in the stiffly beaten egg whites. Turn mixture into generously buttered casserole and bake in a moderate oven as directed. Serve hot.

(267) SPOON BREAD IV

KENTUCKY METHOD

Serves 6 generously. Oven temperature: 375° F.
Baking time: 30 minutes (about).

1 cup yellow corn meal
¾ teaspoon salt
2 teaspoons baking powder
1 cup briskly boiling water
1 cup sweet milk, scalded
3 whole fresh eggs, unbeaten
½ cup butter

Mix yellow corn meal, salt and baking powder thoroughly and gradually sprinkle into rapidly boiling water, beating briskly. Gradually stir milk into the corn meal mixture; then add the eggs and beat briskly. Place baking dish containing half of the butter in the oven, stirring remaining half into the corn meal mixture. When butter is melted and baking dish is rather hot, pour in the corn meal mixture as evenly as possible and bake in a moderate oven as directed until delicately browned. Serve hot.

(268) SPOON BREAD V

VIRGINIA METHOD

Serves 6 generously. Oven temperature: 400° F.
Baking time: 30 minutes.

2 cups sweet milk, scalded
1 cup yellow or white corn meal
3 tablespoons butter
3 egg yolks, well-beaten
1 generous teaspoon salt
1 tablespoon granulated sugar
2 teaspoons baking powder
3 egg whites, stiffly beaten

Add the corn meal gradually to the scalded milk (stirring briskly to prevent lumping) alternately with butter. Blend until smooth. Gradually pour in the beaten egg yolks, beating vigorously while pouring. Now stir in combined salt, sugar and baking powder, blending well, and lastly fold in the stiffly beaten egg whites. Turn batter into a hot, generously buttered baking dish or casserole and bake in a hot oven as directed. Serve hot.

When the weather was warm enough to do so, eighteenth century Italians placed their bread on hot stones in the sunlight, toasting it slightly. This was supposed to improve the disposition of the consumer.

(269) SPOON BREAD VI

TENNESSEE METHOD

Serves 6 generously. Oven temperature: 400° F.
Baking time: 25 minutes.

2 cups cold water
2 cups yellow corn meal
2 cups sour milk (cold)
1 generous tablespoon butter
1 scant teaspoon baking soda
1 teaspoon salt
4 whole fresh eggs, well-beaten

Stir corn meal into cold water; bring slowly to the boiling point, stirring constantly, and cook for 5 minutes, stirring from the bottom of the pan. Gradually add the sour milk, mixed with butter, soda and salt, beating briskly. Turn batter into a hot, generously buttered casserole and bake in a hot oven as directed until a delicate brown. Serve hot.

(270) SPOON BREAD VII

CAROLINAS' METHOD

Same as above plus the addition of one tablespoon of brown sugar to the corn meal while cooking.

(271) SPOON BREAD VIII

Same as for Tennessee except that peanut butter is substituted for butter. Gravy, bacon or sausage fat, butter or jam are all good accompaniments. When baked, the bread should be crusty on top, but moist and soft inside.

(272) SPOON BREAD IX

CHARLESTON METHOD

Serves 6. Oven temperature: 375° F.
Baking time: 30–35 minutes.

2 cups sweet milk
3 whole fresh eggs, well beaten
⅓ cup cooked grits
¼ cup melted butter
1 cup yellow corn meal
½ generous teaspoon salt
2 teaspoons baking powder

Add eggs to the milk and beat briskly, adding the grits and melted butter while beating. Gradually stir in corn meal mixed with salt and baking powder sifted together. Beat briskly, then turn mixture into a generously buttered, hot baking dish and bake in a moderately hot oven as directed. Serve immediately, with a spoon.

(273) STEAMED HONEY CORN MEAL GRAHAM BREAD

Makes 3 small breads. Steaming time: 2½ hours.
Baking time: 20 minutes at 400° F.

4 cups (1 quart) sour milk
1½ cups honey
2 teaspoons baking soda
4 cups graham flour
4 cups corn meal (yellow or white), sifted
4 cups graham flour
1 teaspoon salt
¼ cup butter or margarine, melted

Mix thoroughly sour milk, honey and salt. Gradually stir in the combined soda, corn meal and graham flour, then beat briskly, adding while going along the melted fat. Pour batter into three greased molds; cover tightly, and steam for 2½ hours steadily, being sure to have constantly enough rapidly boiling water to cover the molds. Then remove lids from molds and bake in a hot oven as directed. Let cool before slicing. Do not fill molds more than two-thirds full. The addition of 1 generous cup of seedless raisins improves the bread.

(274) STEAMED MAPLE CORN MEAL BREAD

Makes 2 loaves. Steaming time: 3 long hours.

2 cups corn meal, sifted
1 teaspoon salt
2 teaspoons baking soda
1 cup bread flour, sifted
1 cup maple sugar
2 cups sour milk or buttermilk
1 scant cup seedless raisins (optional)

Combine corn meal, salt, soda, flour and maple sugar and sift together over raisins (if used). Gradually beat in the buttermilk or sour milk until well blended. Turn dough into two greased molds, filling them two-thirds full, and steam steadily as directed. Unmold and let cool overnight before slicing.

(275) STEAMED ROLLED OATS BROWN BREAD

DUTCH METHOD

Makes 4 small loaves. Steaming time: about 2 hours in steadily boiling water.

1 cup rolled oats
1 cup corn meal, sifted
1 cup whole wheat flour, unsifted
1 cup soft bread crumbs
1 cup coarsely chopped nut meats (any kind)
1½ cups sweet milk
½ cup molasses
1 generous teaspoon salt
2 teaspoons baking soda
¾ cup water

Combine rolled oats, corn meal and whole wheat flour and mix with nut meats. Soak crumbs in milk and when soft rub through a strainer; add molasses, salt and soda. Blend well, then combine with cold water. Gradually stir in the combined oats, meal, flour and nuts. Blend thoroughly. Fill 4 generously greased small molds, such as baking powder cans with a cover, a scant two-thirds full; adjust the cover tightly; place the filled cans on a trivet; cover with briskly boiling water and steam steadily for 2 hours or more, replenishing the water as needed to keep cans constantly covered. Unmold carefully and allow to cool before slicing. Delicious! Raisins may be used instead of nuts, or both, using ½ cup of each. May be dried out in oven for 15 minutes.

(276) STEAMED RUSSIAN FRUITED BROWN BREAD

MUSCOVITE METHOD

Makes 1 loaf. Steaming time: 3 hours or more. Eaten very hot and sliced.

½ cup whole wheat flour, unsifted
½ cup bread flour, sifted
½ cup yellow corn meal, sifted
1 teaspoon baking soda
¾ teaspoon salt
3 tablespoons each of raisins and candied lemon peel
⅓ cup of dark molasses
⅔ cup buttermilk

Combine sifted flours with baking soda and salt and sift over whole wheat flour mixed with fruit. Toss to insure a thorough blending. Combine molasses and buttermilk and pour into dry ingredients, mixing only enough to dampen them. The batter should be of pourable consistency. Pour batter into a greased mold (one quart size); cover with several thicknesses of waxed paper and secure with cord. Place mold on a trivet; cover with briskly boiling water and steam steadily for 3 hours or more, replenishing the water as needed to keep mold constantly covered. Unmold carefully upon a heated platter and cut in slices.

(277) SWEDISH LIMPE BREAD

CARAWAY BREAD

Makes 4 small loaves. Oven temperature: 350° F.
Baking time: 1 hour.

Like almost all Swedish yeast breads, this typical bread is started the night before it is to be baked. Requires only two risings.

Sponge

1 cake compressed yeast
1 cup water, lukewarm
1 cup (or more) sifted rye flour

Crumble yeast cake into lukewarm water; when dissolved, beat in enough rye flour to make a rather thick batter. Beat batter until smooth; cover with a clean, dry cloth, and let rise overnight, in a warm place.

In the morning add:

1 cup hot water
½ cup brown sugar
2 teaspoons salt
1 tablespoon lard or butter
1 tablespoon caraway seeds
6 cups or more of bread flour, sifted

Beat together hot water, brown sugar, salt, butter and caraway seeds till well mixed; cool to lukewarm and add gradually to the sponge, beating until thoroughly blended. Then beat in, a small amount at a time, enough flour, to make a soft dough which can be kneaded. Turn out onto a lightly floured board, allow to stand 10 minutes, then knead until smooth, elastic, and not sticky. Place in a large, greased mixing bowl and let rise to double in bulk. Now, cut down; shape into 4 small, equal loaves, place in greased loaf pans; let rise to double in bulk. Bake in a moderate oven as directed or until top is brown and bread leaves sides of the pans. Let cool before slicing.

In the eighteenth century it was the custom for a Bulgarian bride-

groom to carry a loaf of fresh bread with him to the altar as a token that he would provide well for his bride.

(278) SWEDISH COFFEE RINGS

Makes about 4 dozen rings. Oven temperature: 350° F. Baking time: 7 or 8 minutes.

These little coffee rings will keep indefinitely in a covered jar.

2 cups bread flour, sifted
⅓ cup fine granulated sugar
½ teaspoon salt
½ cup butter, creamed
1 whole fresh egg, well-beaten

Sift together the flour, fine granulated sugar (or equivalent of powdered sugar) and salt; add the butter creamed with beaten egg, and when well blended, turn onto a lightly floured board, shape into a long roll and cut off very small pieces. Roll each piece with the palm of the hand, lightly floured, into a pencil-like roll, about ⅛ inch in diameter. Cut off 5 or 6 inch lengths and shape into a circle. Place circles on a lightly greased baking sheet and bake in a moderate oven as directed or until delicately browned.

(279) SWEDISH CORN MEAL BRAN SWEET BREAD

Serves 6 generously. Oven temperature: 350–375° F. Baking time: 20 minutes.

¾ cup butter
¾ cup granulated sugar
3 whole fresh eggs, unbeaten
3 cups bran, unsifted
1 cup bread flour, sifted
½ cup yellow corn meal, sifted
2 teaspoons baking powder
½ generous teaspoon salt
1½ cups sweet cold milk
¾ cup seedless raisins, parboiled
¼ cup shredded blanched almonds

Cream butter; gradually add sugar and continue creaming until light and fluffy. Add eggs, one at a time (creaming well after each addition) alternately with bran. Combine yellow corn meal, baking powder and salt and sift together over drained raisins mixed with the almonds and beat into the creamed mixture, alternately with the milk. Spread batter in large, shallow, buttered baking pan to ⅓-inch thickness and bake in a moderate oven as directed. Let cool before cutting in wedges.

(280) VIENNA BREAD

YEAST METHOD

Makes 2 small loaves or several fancy shapes.
Oven temperature: 425° F.
Baking time: 25 to 30 minutes.

3¾ cups bread flour, sifted twice
1 generous teaspoon salt
2 tablespoons butter (no substitute)
1 cake compressed yeast
1 teaspoon granulated sugar
1 cup sweet milk, lukewarm
1 whole fresh egg, well beaten
Melted butter for tops

Add salt to flour and sift together. Cream yeast and sugar thoroughly, then add milk and beaten egg mixing well; then mix with flour mixture. The dough should be very smooth. Cover; place over a pan of hot (not boiling) water, and let rise one hour. Knead on lightly floured board until smooth, elastic and not sticky; shape into two small loaves or into several fancy shapes; place on generously buttered baking sheet; let rise 15 minutes and bake in a quick oven as directed. Brush tops with melted butter and let cool before slicing.

(281) WHEAT GERM CORN BREAD

Serves 6 generously. Oven temperature: 400° F.
Baking time: 35–40 minutes.

Imbedded deep in the heart of each small grain of wheat there is a golden spot—that tiny speck known as the germ of wheat—holding within its structure a rich storehouse of precious vitamins, minerals and protein, as well as fat.

Nature has been most generous to the germ of wheat, endowing it with an abundant supply of vitamins B, E, and G, and a little vitamin A.

The introduction of wheat germ into flour is a step which will do much to restore the somewhat threadbare reputation of white bread. Heretofore it was thought impossible to retain the wheat germ because of poor keeping qualities, but it's a *fait accompli.*

1 cup yellow corn meal, sifted
1 tablespoon fine granulated sugar
1½ teaspoons salt
1 scant tablespoon baking powder
1 cup wheat germ
1 whole fresh egg, well beaten
1½ cups sweet milk, cold
2 tablespoons butter, melted

To the corn meal sifted with sugar and salt add the wheat germ and blend well. Combine egg with milk and stir thoroughly into the flour mixture and lastly stir in the melted butter. Pour batter into a generously buttered shallow pan and bake in a hot oven as directed. Serve hot.

(282) WHEAT GERM SPOON BREAD

COOKED METHOD

Serves 6 generously. Boiling time: 15–20 minutes.
Oven temperature: 400–425° F.
Baking time: 45 long minutes.

1 cup yellow or white corn meal, sifted
1 scant teaspoon salt
1 cup wheat germ
2 cups briskly boiling water
1½ cups sweet cold milk
3 whole fresh eggs, well beaten
3 tablespoons butter, melted

To the briskly boiling, salted water gradually add combined corn meal and wheat germ, stirring briskly while pouring mixture into the water. Place in top of double boiler; cover, and cook for 15–20 minutes, stirring frequently to prevent lumping.

Remove from heat and cool to lukewarm, then stir in the combined milk and beaten egg, adding while going along the melted butter. Turn batter into a generously buttered shallow baking dish and bake for 35 minutes in a hot oven (400° F.). Then increase the temperature to a quick oven (425° F.) and continue baking 10 minutes longer to brown. Serve as hot as possible with plenty of butter.

(283) WHEAT GERM YEAST BREAD

Makes 1 large loaf. Oven temperature: 350° F.
Baking time: 35–40 minutes.

¾ cup sweet milk, scalded
1¼ teaspoons salt
1 scant tablespoon granulated sugar
1 tablespoon butter or lard
¼ cup sweet milk, lukewarm
1 cake compressed yeast
3 cups bread flour, sifted over
1 cup wheat germ (unsifted)
Melted butter for top

To the scalded milk add salt, sugar and butter and stir until blended. Cool to lukewarm. To the lukewarm ¼ cup of milk add the crumbled yeast and stir until yeast is dissolved. Combine the two mixtures thoroughly and add flour to wheat germ gradually, beating briskly after each addition, until a not too stiff dough results (use more bread flour if needed). Toss upon lightly floured board and knead until dough is smooth, elastic and not sticky. Place dough in a large, greased mixing bowl; cover, and let rise to double in bulk over hot water (not boiling) or in a warm place. Punch down and knead lightly for a short minute. Allow to rise again to double in bulk, covered and in a warm place. Shape into a large loaf; let rise again until doubled in bulk, and bake upon a greased baking sheet (or in a large greased loaf pan) in a moderately hot oven as directed. Brush with melted butter, when removed from oven and allow to cool before slicing. Serve with plenty of butter, jam or marmalade.

Good health is born of the earth and the sun and the cooking pot.

—French Proverb

(284) WHOLE KERNEL CORN BREAD

A VERY CRUNCHY AND DELICIOUS QUICK BREAD

Serves 6. Oven temperature: 400° F.
Baking time: 30 minutes (about).

1 cup bread flour, sifted
1 tablespoon sugar
1¼ teaspoons salt
2 teaspoons baking powder
1 whole fresh egg, well-beaten
¼ cup shortening
¼ cup sweet cold milk
2 cups canned whole kernel corn

To the flour add sugar, salt and baking powder and sift together. Combine beaten egg with milk and shortening and gradually add to the flour mixture, blending thoroughly. Then fold in the corn; pour batter into a generously greased, shallow pan and bake in a hot oven as directed. Serve hot with plenty of butter.

(285) WHOLE WHEAT FIG BREAD

Makes 1 loaf. Oven temperature: 350° F.
Baking time: 1 hour (about).

1 cup bread flour, sifted
1 teaspoon baking powder
1¼ teaspoons baking soda
1 teaspoon salt, and
⅓ cup granulated sugar
2 cups whole wheat flour, unsifted
1 cup chopped dried figs
2 cups sour milk or buttermilk
½ cup molasses
Melted butter for top

To the flour sifted again with soda and baking powder add the whole wheat flour mixed with chopped dried figs and blend thoroughly. Combine sour milk (or buttermilk) with molasses and gradually add to flour mixture, stirring lightly until mixed. Turn batter into a generously greased loaf pan, brush top with melted butter and bake in a moderate oven as directed. Let cool before slicing.

In Colonial Days it often took more than two days to make bread. Home-prepared yeast was made from malt, potatoes and hops. Dough was mixed in troughs and the loaves were baked in either indoor or outdoor brick ovens.

(286) WHOLE WHEAT FIG HONEY BREAD

A VERY RICH BREAD APPROPRIATE FOR AFTERNOON TEA

Makes 1 large loaf. Oven temperature: 325° F.
Baking time: 1½ hours (about).

1½ cups bread flour, sifted
¾ teaspoon baking soda
2 teaspoons baking powder
1 scant teaspoon salt
1½ cups whole wheat flour, unsifted
¼ cup light brown sugar
¼ cup chopped walnut meats
1 cup chopped dried figs
1 whole fresh egg, well beaten
1½ cups sweet cold milk
½ cup strained honey
¼ cup melted butter
Melted butter for top

To the flour add baking soda, baking powder, salt and sift together over combined whole wheat flour, brown sugar, walnut meats and chopped dried figs, blend thoroughly. Combine and mix well beaten egg, milk, honey and melted butter. Then stir into the first mixture. Pour into a buttered loaf pan, let stand 15 minutes, then bake as directed in a very moderate oven, after brushing top with melted butter. Cool before slicing.

(287) YEAST CHEESE BREAD

Makes 1 large loaf. Oven temperature: 400, then 350° F.
Baking time: 1 hour (about).

1 cup sweet milk, scalded
2 tablespoons granulated sugar
1 scant teaspoon salt
1 tablespoon butter
1 cake compressed yeast
¾ cup grated American cheese
1 cup bread flour, sifted
2 cups, more or less of bread flour, sifted
Melted butter for top

Scald milk and let cool to lukewarm, then add sugar, salt and butter. Blend well. Now add crumbled yeast and stir until dissolved.

Gradually add the first cup of flour and beat briskly until thoroughly mixed and smooth. Place the mixing bowl over a pan of hot water (not boiling), cover with a dry cloth and let rise until doubled in bulk; then beat in combined American cheese and remaining 2 cups (more or less) of flour to make a soft dough. Toss upon lightly floured board until smooth, elastic and velvety. Return to a greased mixing bowl; brush top with melted butter or lard; cover with a dry cloth and place over hot water (not boiling). Let rise until doubled in bulk. Turn out on lightly floured board and knead for a short minute. Let stand 5 minutes; shape into a loaf; place in generously greased pan; brush top with melted butter or lard; cover with a dry cloth and again let rise until doubled in bulk. Bake in a hot oven for 10 long minutes to set the bread; reduce heat to moderate, and continue baking for about 50 minutes until nicely browned. Let cool before slicing.

(288) YEAST CINNAMON BREAD ROLL

VERY APPROPRIATE FOR BREAKFAST OR AFTERNOON TEA OR SNACK

Makes 2 small rolls. Oven temperature: 375° F.
Baking time: 1 hour (about).

Crumble 1 yeast cake into ¼ cup lukewarm water and stir until yeast is dissolved. Stir in 1 cup lukewarm sweet milk, mixed with ⅓ cup granulated sugar, 1 teaspoon salt and 4 tablespoons of butter or lard, beaten with 1 whole fresh egg. Blend thoroughly, then beat in 2 cups of sifted bread flour until smooth. Cover; place over hot (not boiling) water and allow to rise until doubled in bulk. Punch down the sponge, then gradually beat in 2 cups of sifted bread flour, gradually, beating well after each addition. Cover again and let rise to double in bulk. Knead upon lightly floured board for a short minute then roll out to ¼ inch thick. Sprinkle with 2 generous teaspoons of ground cinnamon mixed with ⅔ cup of dark brown sugar; roll up as for jelly roll and fit into 2 small, well buttered or larded (no other shortening substituted) loaf pan. Allow to rise for 30 long minutes, then bake about one hour in a moderate oven as directed. Cool thoroughly before slicing.

(289) YEAST ONION BREAD

A REAL MEAL IN ITSELF

Makes 1 large loaf. Oven temperature: 375° F.
Baking time: about 30 minutes.

First operation:

1 cake compressed yeast
2 tablespoons lukewarm water
1 scant tablespoon granulated sugar
1 cup sweet milk, scalded
¼ cup lard
3 cups bread flour, sifted
¾ teaspoon salt

Crumble yeast cake into lukewarm water and stir until dissolved. To the scalded milk add sugar and lard and allow to cool to lukewarm. Then combine with yeast mixture and blend well. Gradually add the flour sifted together with salt, beating briskly until smooth. Place over a pan of hot water; cover with a dry cloth and allow to rise until doubled in bulk. Toss upon a lightly floured board and knead until smooth, elastic and not sticky. Place in a warm mixing bowl, generously greased (using lard); brush top with melted lard; cover with a dry cloth and allow to rise to double in bulk.

Second operation: Meanwhile simmer 6 medium-sized onions, sliced thin, in about 3 tablespoons of butter until tender, but not brown, stirring frequently with a wooden spoon. Let cool. Combine 2 well beaten fresh eggs with ¼ cup sour cream seasoned with ¼ teaspoon salt.

Third operation: Take dough from mixing pan; knead for 30 seconds; shape into a loaf and place in a generously larded loaf pan. Let rise until double in bulk; spread cooked onions on top of dough, then pour sour cream mixture over the onions; sprinkle with 3 finely chopped slices of raw bacon, then with a scant teaspoon of caraway seeds. Let rise until light and bake in a moderate oven as directed. Let cool to lukewarm before slicing.

(290) YEAST POTATO BREAD

Makes 3 loaves. Oven temperature: 350° F.
Baking time: 1 hour (about).

Boil 2 medium-sized peeled potatoes in 1 quart of water until they can be mashed into the water. This is the water to be used in the making of this bread which remains moist several days.

1 quart potato water
1 cup milk
$\frac{1}{4}$ cup lard or butter
8 to 10 cups bread flour, sifted
5 tablespoons granulated sugar
2 tablespoons salt
$2\frac{1}{2}$ cakes compressed yeast

To the mashed potato water, boiling briskly, add milk and lard or butter; then set where it will be lukewarm. Sift flour, sugar and salt together into large mixing bowl. Make hole in center and add potato water to which has been added the crumbled yeast cakes, soaked in $\frac{1}{2}$ scant cup lukewarm water. Mix just enough of the flour into the center to make a light sponge, beating it well to prevent lumping. Then stir in the rest of flour to the smooth stage. Brush top with lard or butter; cover and allow to rise until double in bulk. Knead down and when smooth, elastic and not sticky, return to the greased mixing bowl; brush with lard or butter and allow to rise to double in bulk. Cut down; knead a short minute; form into three loaves; place loaves in greased loaf pans and let rise again to double in bulk. Brush tops with melted shortening and bake in a moderate oven as directed or until brown and bread leaves sides of pans. Let cool before slicing.

(291) YEAST ROLLED WHEAT BREAD

Makes 2 loaves. Oven temperature: 400, then 375° F.
Baking time: 45 minutes.

2 cups scalded milk
1 cup rolled wheat
4 tablespoons dark brown sugar
2 teaspoons salt
$\frac{1}{2}$ teaspoon ground cinnamon (optional)
2 cakes compressed yeast
4 to $4\frac{1}{2}$ cups bread flour, sifted

To the scalded milk add rolled wheat, sugar and salt mixed. Allow to cool to lukewarm, then stir in the crumbled yeast cakes. Gradually add $2\frac{1}{2}$ cups of the sifted bread flour, beating well after each addition. Cover with a light, clean cloth and let rise over hot water until doubled in bulk. Cut down the sponge; then stir in the remaining flour, adding enough to make a stiff dough. Knead on lightly floured board; return to a greased mixing bowl; brush with melted shortening; cover with a clean cloth, and let rise again to double in bulk. Toss upon floured board and knead a short minute; divide dough into two equal portions; place in greased loaf pans; brush with melted shortening, cover and let rise for the third time to double in bulk. Bake 10 minutes in a hot oven to set the bread as directed; reduce temperature to moderate and continue baking for

35 minutes longer, or until bread is brown on top and leaves sides of pans. Cool thoroughly before slicing.

(292) YEAST WALNUT BREAD ROLL

Makes 2 rolls. Oven temperature: 350° F.
Baking time: 1½ hours (about).

Dough:

1 cake compressed yeast
2 cups sweet milk, scalded
¾ scant cup granulated sugar
2 whole eggs, well beaten
2 teaspoons salt
⅓ cup butter
6 cups (about) bread flour, sifted
1 teaspoon grated lemon rind

Crumble yeast cake into large mixing bowl and slowly add scalded milk, which has been cooled to lukewarm, stirring until yeast is dissolved. Stir in sugar (less may be added to taste), beaten eggs, salt and butter. Blend well, then gradually beat in half of the sifted bread flour, beating until smooth. Now, add remaining flour mixed with grated lemon or orange rind and mix well. Turn out on lightly floured board and knead until smooth, elastic and not sticky. Place dough in generously buttered bowl (no other grease used but butter); brush with melted butter, cover with a clean, dry towel and place the bowl on a cake cooler over a kettle of hot water. The water should be reheated when necessary, but should never be boiling. Allow to rise until double in bulk. Knead a short second in the mixing bowl, that is punch hard to break the air; toss upon a lightly floured board, or still better onto a floured cloth spread over a board. Roll dough as much as possible and then stretch it to ¼ inch thickness; trim edges neatly, and spread with—

Walnut filling:

Into a saucepan put 1½ cups sweet milk, ½ generous cup granulated sugar, 2 cups ground walnut meats, 2 tablespoons butter, ½ teaspoon salt and ¼ cup honey and bring to the boiling point, stirring constantly. Gradually stir in 2 whole eggs, beaten with 2 egg yolks, stirring briskly over a low flame and cook until thick.

Spread filling over the rolled dough as evenly as possible; roll up as for jelly roll; cut in two equal portions and twist into an oval shape. Place in a generously greased baking pan; cover with a light, clean cloth and allow to rise in a warm place or over hot water until light (about 1½ hours). Bake in a moderate oven as directed. Serve lukewarm or cold, thinly sliced.

Buns

. . . To take a seed, as countless men have done
And press it softly down amid the dark
Excitement of the soil; to call the sun
And bid it make dawn's chemic mark
Of light; this is the gift within my hand
That all may share and none may understand.
—*A. M. Sullivan*

BUNS

(293) BUN RECIPES

It is in the nature of things American that gates should be crashed and customs strained. Feminine spring fashions emerge in January, St. Patrick's shamrocks shrivel in February gales and hot cross buns are piled high in bakeshop windows a fortnight before Easter.

In one way and another history, tradition and popular usage have become tangled around the hot cross bun till its origin, growth and function have been obscured. Wherever and however it came into being, it's a tasty bit of pastry for breakfast or tea at any time, but a notion has spread over the land that it is properly to be associated with the traditions of Good Friday, whereas the most august authorities hold that the original, modern, hot cross buns in England were hospitably distributed in the churches on Easter Sunday for the sustenance of good country folk who had traveled long distances to break their lenten fast after early mass or morning prayer. At any rate, a feast of luscious sugar buns, rich with fruit and spices, is scarcely congruous on a holy day that finds altars stripped of ornament and celebrants in black vestments; but on a sunny Easter morn, with lilies perfuming the spring breeze, such cakes go right well with purple, pink and golden Easter eggs and if the sugar-bun season must be prolonged, why not keep it up through Whitsuntide?

None of our pious forebears of mother countries and fatherlands seems to have been particularly concerned with eatables for the lenten season or Holy Week, but on and after Easter there was relaxation from the rigors of discipline and the fat eating that ended on Shrove Tuesday was taken up again with hearty appetite. The historical *schiacciata* of Tuscany, served on Easter Sunday, are cakes that would pass most favorably as hot cross buns on any table, though they are somewhat richer than the latter. Our domestic buns have largely degenerated through the years into baking powder makeshifts, but the Tuscan buns are properly made with yeast and sugar and plenty of eggs, like brioche; fifteen to twenty eggs are not considered too many for a single pound of flour. Aniseed, coriander, rosewater and orange-flower water are prescribed in various recipes, and the *schiacciata* are glazed with sugar and egg yolk and baked to a golden brown.

The people of Prague are supposed to have been among the first Europeans to celebrate an Easter festival with good cheer and they distributed cakes at their feasts which are said to have been similar to the Czechoslovakian *kolace* of today. The *kolace* is made of yeast, warmed milk, eggs, butter and sugar, with white flour, like buns or brioche, and flavored with lemon and grated lemon peel, or kirsch. The dough is kneaded and molded into round cakes with a depression in the center of each and brushed with egg yolk. Then marmalade is put into the center, if lemon or orange flavoring was used, and preserved cherries are put in if the flavoring was of kirsch. The cakes are allowed to rise again and after careful baking they are brushed with butter and sprinkled with sifted sugar.

Of our thrifty bakers who expedite the sale of sugar buns by marking each one with a cross, probably few either know or care about the origin of the custom, but it is traceable, not to Christian sources, but to the early pagans. The Babylonians and the Egyptians made votive offerings to the moon goddess in the form of cakes crossed with the horns of the sacred bull. The Greeks tendered to Astarte in the temples cakes of meal and honey marked with crosses symbolic of the four quarters of the moon; in some of the Roman ruins small loaves of bread marked with crosses have been found, and it is known that such cross-bread was sold to worshippers in the porticos of the temples. St. Paul referred to it in I Corinthians, X, 27–28: "If any of them that believe not bid you to a feast, and ye be disposed to go, whatsoever is set before you, eat, asking no question for conscience's sake. But if any man say unto you, *this* is offered in sacrifice unto idols, eat not for his sake that shewed it, and for conscience's sake: for the earth is the Lord's, and the fullness thereof." Possibly the cross-bread traveled to Britain with Caesar's legions, but at any rate the Saxons in Britain offered cross buns to their goddess of light, and in the course of time Anglo-Saxon curates came to offer cross buns to their parishioners on Easter morn.

It was not cake, but a breakfast bun, that the reckless, frivolous madcap Marie Antoinette offered as a substitute for bread to the hungry populace of Paris. Cake it has been, in history and anecdote, but the words that may have hastened the progress of that royal head to the guillotine have been given by competent authority as: "*. . . Si le peuple n'a pas de pain, qu'il mange des brioches.*" And brioche is not cake, any more than Scottish scones, or English muffins and crumpets, or American tea biscuits are cake. With a few somewhat exaggerated exceptions of Danish, German and Austrian pastry cooks, the French brioche is the richest of breads.

(294) A FEW GOOD HINTS ABOUT BUNS

According to old custom, the Scottish bride is carried over the threshold of her new home. She is met on the other side by the groom's mother or some other female relative who breaks a currant bun over her head. A miss is considered an unlucky omen.

Buns are surprisingly simple to make. They are merely a variation of the standard yeast bread recipe. Like any yeast bread, these buns are most successful if the home baker will follow the rules for handling this type of bread. The most common mistake made by home bakers is permitting the dough to become hot. This results in killing the yeast plants and it follows that the dough will not be properly leavened.

A second point is to have a correct, even temperature for baking. Too low heat will give a product too light and porous in texture, while too high a temperature may result in uneven baking or burning of the buns. The correct temperature is about 400° to 425° F.

Towards the end of the eighteenth century in Bath, England, a young girl, Sally Lunn, sold her buns night and morning on the city streets. They were so delicious that they were named after her and the recipe came to America soon afterwards.

The American version of the hot cross bun probably comes from England. In the old days a hot cross bun was hung in the chimney place on Good Friday and left there throughout the year to bring good luck by preventing evil spirits from coming down the chimney to ruin bread baking and cause other domestic troubles. Today we do not think about good luck in connection with these delicious buns except perhaps to appreciate the good luck that lets us enjoy them!

There used to be an old English superstition (and maybe there still is) that on Easter Day the sun danced or leaped as it came up above the horizon, and our forefathers used to get up very early on Easter morning to catch him at it. Unfortunately the Devil always put a hill in the way, and so nobody ever got a chance to see the miracle. Of all the old legends there couldn't be one easier to believe, for if ever the sun were inclined to dance, it would undoubtedly be on an Easter morning, which is, beyond all question, the gayest holiday of the whole year. Naturally, it calls for the gayest fare.

Everybody whose grandmother came to these shores from Russia, or Ireland, or Italy, or Hungary, or France, or from most anywhere else, is going to enjoy the Easter lamb, or the Easter cakes, or the Easter loaf, or the Easter bun. All the same, one of these recipes may find a place on the Easter table, too.

(295) BRAN JELLY BUNS

BAKING POWDER METHOD

Makes about 1½ dozen buns. Oven temperature: 425° F. Baking time: 15 minutes.

- ⅔ cup sweet cold milk
- 1 cup whole bran shreds
- 1 cup bread flour, sifted
- 1 tablespoon baking powder
- ¾ teaspoon salt
- ¼ cup shortening
- Melted butter
- Jelly or jam

Pour milk over bran and let stand 5 minutes. To the flour add baking powder and salt and sift together. Cut in shortening, then add bran mixture and stir until a soft batter or dough is formed, adding more milk if needed. Turn out on slightly floured board and knead or punch a half minute or enough to shape. Roll out ½-inch thick and cut with floured biscuit cutter. Place on ungreased baking sheet; make a deep depression in center of each bun; brush with melted butter and fill with either jelly or jam. Bake in a hot oven as directed. Serve hot or cold.

(296)

BUNS

YEAST METHOD

Makes 1½ dozen buns. Oven temperature: 400° F.
Baking time: 12 to 15 minutes.

1 whole fresh egg, well-beaten
½ yeast cake
1¼ cups lukewarm water
3 tablespoons lard or other shortening
¾ teaspoon sugar
3 additional tablespoons sugar
1 teaspoon salt
3½ to 4 cups bread flour, sifted

Beat egg and add half of the water in which yeast and the ¾ teaspoon sugar have been dissolved. Let stand ½ hour. Mix together salt, lard or other shortening and remaining sugar and water and add to first mixture. Blend thoroughly. Put about half of the flour into the liquid mixture and beat thoroughly, then add more sifted bread flour until dough is stiff enough to be handled, keeping dough softer than bread dough. Brush dough with shortening; place it in a generously greased mixing bowl and let rise to double its bulk. Knead down and let rise again or make into buns after first rising. Cut with floured biscuit cutter, then press flat and lay on a generously greased pan at least 1 to 1½ inches apart according to size. Brush top and set in a warm place to rise. It will probably take 2 to 2½ hours. Bake in a hot oven as directed or until golden brown.

Bad planning as to the time table can be as disastrous as bad planning in the menu itself. Including in the same course a dish requiring a hot oven and another which takes slow cooking can produce a small panic in the kitchen when each begins to stalemate the other. A failing common to all disorganized cooks lies in planning such things as biscuits, buns or muffins to be served piping hot with some dish like egg timbales or chicken soufflé—the first needing a hot-as-blazes oven and the eggs and chicken dish taking very slow heat.

(297) BUTTERSCOTCH BUNS

BAKING POWDER METHOD

Makes 16 buns. Oven temperature: 425° F.
Baking time: 15 to 20 minutes.

First operation:
Mix one teaspoon white and one tablespoon of brown sugar in each of 16 muffin pans. Let stand while preparing the batter as follows:
Batter: You may use either cake or bread flour. If bread flour is used sift twice, measure, then sift again with dry ingredients. If cake flour is used sift once, measure and sift again with dry ingredients.

2½ cups bread flour, sifted twice	1½ cups milk
1 tablespoon baking powder	1 whole egg, well-beaten
1 scant teaspoon salt	2 tablespoons softened butter
½ cup butter or other shortening	¼ cup brown sugar

To the flour add baking powder and salt and sift together. (If buns are desired sweet, you may add to the flour 3 tablespoons also of sugar.) Cut in shortening until of consistency of corn meal. Combine cold milk and beaten egg and stir into flour mixture to produce quickly a soft dough. Roll out dough on a lightly floured board to ¼-inch thickness and spread with softened butter. Over butter sprinkle brown sugar and roll up like a jelly roll. Cut the roll in ¾-inch slices; set in the prepared muffin pans and bake in a hot oven as directed. Turn buns at once from pans and serve hot or warm.

(298) CINNAMON BUNS

YEAST METHOD

As cinnamon buns became more and more popular, home bakers as well as professionals experimented with the original recipes and changed them about a bit to conform to their own ideas and taste. As a result, today there are two schools of thought among cinnamon bun gourmets. One insists that the buns should be made with currants, following tradition; the other argues enthusiastically that seedless raisins give the buns a certain subtle flavor which is lacking when they are made with currants. The latter faction points out that since the cinnamon bun was not a creation, but rather a series of departures from a baked product that started out as something else, it is perfectly all right to improve it still further by using seedless raisins.

The conservative school, however, points to an old recipe for what many claim is the perfect cinnamon bun. Here it is:

½ cup shortening
1 cup scalded milk
1 teaspoon salt
¾ cup granulated sugar
2 yeast cakes
2 whole fresh eggs, well beaten
5 cups bread flour, sifted
½ cup melted butter
1 cup brown sugar
2 tablespoons of cold milk
1½ teaspoons cinnamon
½ cup currants

Add shortening to hot milk. Add salt and sugar and dissolve thoroughly. Cool to lukewarm, then crumble in the yeast cakes. When dissolved, stir in beaten eggs, then the flour. Knead till smooth and elastic and allow to rise until double in bulk. Combine ¼ cup of the butter, ½ cup of the brown sugar and the milk (2 tablespoons). Mix well and spread on bottom of pan. Roll dough to ¼-inch thick, and spread with remaining butter and sugar mixed with the cinnamon, and the currants which have been washed, then sponged dry. Roll as for jelly roll and cut in one-inch slices. Place cut side down in pan over the butter-brown-sugar and milk mixture and allow to rise to double in bulk; brush with melted butter and bake in a hot oven as directed.

While fanciers of the Philadelphia sticky cinnamon bun say that the buns have been popular "as long as they can remember" and the name of the chef who first thought of adding cinnamon to the other ingredients and giving it a distinctive taste is lost to culinary history, there are many theories as to how the bun originated in this country.

One of the most logical of these theories is advanced by the Department of Nutrition, American Institute of Baking, which believes that when the Dutch sailed into the New World they brought with them a recipe for spice cakes which was very popular in 1623 and which Philadelphians later changed to cinnamon buns. The old recipe reads as follows:

. . . *To make excellent spice cakes, take halfe a pecke of very fine Wheat-flower, take almost one pound of sweet butter, and some good milke and creame mixt together, set it on the fire, and put in your butter, and a good deale of sugare, and let it melt together; then straine Saffron into your milke a good quantity; then take seven or eight spoonful of good Ale barme, and eight egges with two yelkes and mixt them together, then put your milke to it when it is somewhat cold, and into your Wheat-flower put salt. Aniseedes bruised, Cloves and Mace, and a good deale of Cinamon; then worke all together good and stiffe, that you neede not worke in any Wheat-flower after; then put in a little rose water cold, then rub it well in the thing you knead it in, and worke it thoroughly; if it be not sweet enough, scrape in a little more sugar and pull it all in pieces, and hurle in a good quantity of Currants, and so worke all together againe, and bake your Cake as you see cause in a gentle warme oven. . . .*

When in a hurry, here is a quick bun which is really good if the directions are followed:

(299) CINNAMON NUT RAISIN BUNS

QUICK BAKING POWDER METHOD

Makes about 10 buns. Oven temperature: 475° F.
Baking time: 12 minutes (about).

Preliminary preparation for the pan:

½ cup brown sugar
½ cup butter
A pinch salt
½ cup broken pecans

Combine these ingredients and mix well; spread in bottom of shallow pan; then lay the cinnamon slices on top, cut side down.

Dough:

4 cups bread flour, sifted twice
2½ tablespoons baking powder
1½ teaspoons salt
8 tablespoons shortening
1½ cups sweet cold milk
4 tablespoons melted butter
½ cup seedless raisins, parboiled, sponged
½ cup chopped pecan meats
1½ teaspoons ground cinnamon
½ cup brown sugar

Add baking powder and salt to the flour (be sure to use 2½ tablespoons baking powder) and sift together in a mixing bowl; cut in shortening, then stir in the milk slowly and gradually, mixing well. Toss mixture upon a lightly floured board and roll out to ¼ inch thickness. Brush with melted butter. Combine well dried raisins, pecan meats, cinnamon and brown sugar and dust over flat dough; and roll it up like a jelly roll. Cut into 1¼ inch slices; lay them in prepared shallow pan, cut side down. Bake in a very hot oven as directed. Then ring the bell!

(300) CLOVER LEAF EASTER SUPPER BUNS

YEAST METHOD

First rising: 50 minutes. Second rising: 1½ hours.
Third rising: 1½ hours (about).
Makes 2 dozen buns. Oven temperature: 400° F.
Baking time: 15 minutes.

1 cup scalded milk cooled to lukewarm
1 cake compressed yeast
2 tablespoons granulated sugar
1½ cups bread flour, sifted twice
¼ cup granulated sugar
3 tablespoons melted butter
1 whole fresh egg, well beaten
1 teaspoon salt
½ teaspoon lemon extract

Crumble yeast cake into lukewarm milk in which the 2 tablespoons of sugar have been dissolved; stir well until yeast is dissolved. Then stir in the flour, beating until smooth. Cover with a clean, dry cloth and place the mixing bowl over hot (not boiling) water to rise for 50 minutes. Cut down and add remaining ingredients in order named, beating till smooth. Toss upon lightly floured board and knead until smooth, elastic and not sticky. Place in greased mixing bowl; brush with melted shortening; cover with clean, dry cloth and let rise (second time) over hot water until double in bulk (about 1½ hours). Turn on floured board and shape as clover leaf buns by forming three small portions into balls and fitting them into generously buttered muffin pans. Cover with a cloth; allow to rise to double in bulk (about 1½ hours), brush with melted butter and bake in a hot oven as directed.

The addition of ½ generous cup of parboiled, drained, seedless raisins adds to flavor. These buns are not sticky.

(301) CZECH BUNS

KOLACHKY—YEAST METHOD

The recipe for these delicious buns varies in the many homes in which they are made for some like a sweet dough while others prefer the bread-type. Each home either in the United States or in Czechoslovakia or in Bohemia has its own particular recipe, handed down through generations, but after the dough is prepared, it is shaped into the *Kolachky,* a standard shape. For fluffy *Kolachky* the dough should be a little on the soft side. See Recipe No. 147.

(302) ENGLISH BATH BUNS

YEAST METHOD

Makes about 24 buns. Oven temperature: 400° F.
Baking time: 25 minutes (about).

Crusted with brown sugar, chopped raisins and nuts these little buns made with yeast are really delicious. They may be served hot or warm, but never cold.

- 1 cup milk, scalded, then cooled to lukewarm
- 3 tablespoons granulated sugar
- 1 teaspoon salt
- 1 cake compressed yeast
- 4 cups (1 quart) about, of bread flour, sifted
- ½ cup softened butter
- 3 whole fresh eggs, unbeaten
- ½ cup brown sugar, rolled
- ½ cup mixed raisins and nut meats
- 3 tablespoons melted butter

To the milk add sugar, salt and crumbled yeast cake and stir until smooth. Add then half of the flour alternately with the softened butter and blend thoroughly, using a wooden spoon. Now add eggs, one at a time, beating well after each addition, alternately with the remaining flour (more or less). Knead in the mixing bowl for a half-minute; turn dough into a greased bowl; brush with butter; cover with a clean, light, dry towel and let rise over a pan containing hot (not boiling) water, until doubled in bulk (about 3 hours). Turn the dough upon a lightly floured board; flour your hands and pat gently; then shape into 2 dozen buns. Place buns upon a well-greased baking sheet; brush with melted butter; sprinkle with mixed brown sugar, seedless raisins and chopped nut meats (any kind). Cover with a clean, dry towel; let rise until light (about 30 minutes) and bake in a hot oven as directed until a delicate brown. Serve hot or warm with plenty of butter, jam or marmalade.

(303) HOT CROSS BUNS

Makes 2 dozen buns. Oven temperature: 425° F.
Baking time: 20 minutes.

- 1/4 cup shortening
- 1 cup boiling water
- 1/2 cup granulated sugar
- 1 teaspoon salt
- 1 cup sweet milk, scalded
- 1 1/2 cakes compressed yeast
- 1/4 cup lukewarm water
- 2 whole fresh eggs, unbeaten
- 1 cup seedless raisins or currants
- 1/4 cup shredded citron or orange peel
- 3/4 teaspoon ground cinnamon
- 4 cups bread flour, sifted twice

Put the shortening, boiling water, sugar, salt and scalded milk in large mixing bowl; stir well; then let cool to lukewarm. Add the yeast, which has been dissolved in the lukewarm water. Blend well. Add unbeaten whole eggs one at a time, beating well after each addition, alternately with mixed raisins and citron, and the flour, which was sifted, the last time over the fruit with the cinnamon. Blend thoroughly, then knead for a half minute on floured board, adding more sifted bread flour if necessary. When smooth, place dough in a greased bowl; cover and let rise to double in bulk over hot water. Cut down the dough; place on lightly floured board, cut off small pieces and form them into balls. Place balls on a greased baking sheet; allow to rise until double in bulk (about one hour or more) and bake in a very hot oven as directed until brown. Remove from oven; brush with melted butter and when cold mark a cross with white icing on the top.

For icing: To 1 tablespoon hot water add sifted confectioner's sugar until thick and flavor to taste with either vanilla, lemon or almond extract. Or, just before removing from the oven, brush with sugar and water and fill the cross with the above icing.

There may be doubts about how to entertain for Christmas and what sort of a party to give on New Year's and whether Thanksgiving dinner should be in the middle of the day or at night, but surely everybody will agree that Easter breakfast is the gayest and most completely satisfactory occasion imaginable.

Of course those righteous souls who rise early and go to church deserve an especially fine breakfast waiting their return, but even the lazy and the unregenerate can appreciate, although they may not merit, a perfectly grand meal with which to begin the day. Easter breakfast ought to be so good and so bountiful that no more food is needed till tea time.

The early Fathers of the Church undoubtedly knew how to work up to a dramatic climax—the lean, gray days of Lent and the emotions of Good Friday and Holy Saturday all leading up to the joy bells of Easter with a breakfast featuring Hot Cross Buns.

(304) LEMON YEAST BUNS

Makes about 3 dozen buns. Oven temperature: 400° F.
Baking time: 25 minutes.
First rising: 2 hours (about). Second rising: 1 hour.

½ cup granulated sugar
2 tablespoons butter
2 whole fresh eggs, well beaten
6 cups (1½ quarts) bread flour, sifted twice
2 cups lukewarm milk
½ teaspoon salt (generous)
1 cake compressed yeast
¼ cup lukewarm water
1 cup seedless raisins or currants
¼ teaspoon ground nutmeg
Grated rind of one lemon
Juice of half lemon
1 egg white and confectioner's sugar

Cream sugar and butter until fluffy; beat in the eggs and add 2 cups of flour, alternately with lukewarm milk. Sift remaining flour with salt and add to mixture, alternately with yeast dissolved in lukewarm water. Beat briskly for 15 minutes; cover; let rise over hot water until double in bulk (about 2 hours). Then cut down the dough and stir in the seedless raisins or currants, mixed with 2 tablespoons of flour, alternately with nutmeg, grated lemon rind and lemon juice mixed together. Blend well. Roll out upon a lightly floured board to one-half inch thick; cut with floured biscuit cutter (2-inch). Place half of the buns in greased biscuit pans, an inch apart; then place the remaining buns on top of those in the pan; let rise until double in bulk and bake in a hot oven as directed. Remove from the oven and brush tops with unbeaten egg white, then dust with confectioner's sugar. Serve hot or warm.

The ancient Greeks were the most skillful bakers of their day; they knew how to make at least 72 varieties of bread.

(305) MAPLE BUNS

QUICK METHOD USING PREPARED BISCUIT MIX

Makes about 1 dozen buns. Oven temperature: 400° F.
Baking time: 20 minutes.

Combine 2 cups of prepared biscuit mix and 3/4 cup rich milk (or half milk and half cream or use undiluted evaporated milk). In each section of small muffin pans place 1 1/2 teaspoons chopped nut meats (any kind desired), 2 teaspoons maple syrup and 1/4 teaspoon of butter. Fill 2/3 full with biscuit dough and bake in a hot oven as directed. Serve hot.

(306) STICKY BUNS

BAKING POWDER METHOD

Makes about 15 buns. Oven temperature: 400° F.
Baking time: 20–25 minutes.

Butter muffin pans generously and put into each one a tablespoon brown sugar and a few chopped walnuts.

Dough:

2 cups bread flour, sifted
4 teaspoons baking powder
1/2 teaspoon salt
1/3 cup butter
2/3 cup rich sweet milk, cold
Softened butter
1/2 cup seedless raisins, parboiled, drained
1 tablespoon brown sugar
1/2 teaspoon ground cinnamon

Add baking powder and salt to the flour and sift together into mixing bowl. Rub in butter and when blended mix to a soft dough with the milk. Turn out on a lightly floured board and roll the dough into a rectangle, a scant 1/8-inch thick. Spread with softened butter, then with seedless raisins (parboiled, drained and thoroughly dried) and a little brown sugar mixed with cinnamon. Roll up the dough like a jelly roll and cut down in inch slices. Place a slice in each muffin pan and bake in a hot oven as directed until delicately brown. Let stand 5 minutes after removing from the oven and then turn the pans upside down so that the sticky surface of the buns will be uppermost.

(307) STICKY BUNS—PENNSYLVANIA DUTCH METHOD I

BAKING POWDER METHOD

Makes 10 large buns. Oven temperature: 425° F.
Baking time: 25 minutes.

This method results in a cluster and should be turned out in one cake and separated as needed.

Preliminary preparation—skillet or baking pan:

Cream 4 tablespoons of butter and ½ cup brown sugar by stirring them together in a bowl until creamy and fluffy. Spread this all over the bottom and sides of skillet or baking pan.

Dough:

3 cups bread flour, sifted
6 teaspoons (2 tablespoons) baking powder
2 tablespoons granulated sugar
1 teaspoon salt
4 tablespoons butter
1 whole fresh egg, well beaten
¾ cup sweet cold milk

To the flour add baking powder, granulated sugar and salt and sift together. Stir to mix thoroughly. Add butter and cut it into small pieces with two knives or pastry blender. Then completely work in butter with lightly floured hands. Combine well-beaten whole egg with milk and pour slowly into the mixture, stirring with a large wooden spoon. There should be just enough liquid to make a dough. If a little more liquid is necessary, add a very little milk. Now knead slightly about ½ minute. Roll out on a lightly floured board into an oblong 20 inches by 9 inches wide, keeping corners as square as possible and edges of dough straight.

Spread:

3 tablespoons butter, softened
1 cup brown sugar
1 teaspoon ground cinnamon
¾ cup seedless raisins, parboiled, sponged

Spread butter over the dough. Over butter sprinkle combined brown sugar and ground cinnamon, then distribute prepared raisins as evenly as possible over the whole.

Now roll dough like a jelly roll. Cut with a sharp knife into pieces each about 2 inches long. Place the cut pieces of rolled dough in the prepared skillet or pan, cut side up and let stand 15 minutes, covered with a light, dry cloth. Bake in a hot oven as directed. Remove pan or skillet from oven and immediately turn the buns upside down on a large platter. Be careful in turning the buns out, because of the hot brown sugar.

(308) STICKY BUNS—PENNSYLVANIA DUTCH METHOD II

YEAST METHOD

Makes about 16 buns. Oven temperature: 425° F.
Baking time: 20–25 minutes.

This method results in a cluster and should be turned out in one cake and separated as needed.

Preliminary preparation: Same as for Recipe No. 307 above.

Dough:

2 cups scalded sweet milk
1½ teaspoons salt
¼ cup granulated sugar
1 cake compressed yeast
¼ cup lukewarm water
6 cups (about) bread flour, sifted twice

Cool scalded milk to lukewarm; add salt, granulated sugar and yeast cake which has been dissolved in the lukewarm water and blend well. Gradually add the flour, beating briskly after each addition, using enough flour to make a soft dough which can be handled easily. Knead dough until smooth, elastic and not sticky. Place dough in a generously greased mixing bowl; cover with a light, clean, dry towel and let rise over hot water until it trebles in bulk. Toss upon lightly floured board and roll into a sheet ¼ inch thick and spread with the following mixture:

Spread:

4 tablespoons butter, softened
1½ cups brown sugar
1¾ teaspoons ground cinnamon
1 generous cup seedless raisins

Spread softened butter over the dough. Over butter sprinkle combined brown sugar and cinnamon; then cover with raisins (or currants) which have been parboiled, drained and thoroughly dried between two towels.

Roll the dough as for jelly roll. Cut with a sharp knife into pieces about 2 inches long. Place the cut pieces of rolled dough in the prepared skillet or pan, cut side up and let stand, covered with a clean cloth, until light and almost double in bulk. Bake in a hot oven as directed until delicately brown. Remove pan or skillet from oven and immediately turn the buns upside down on a large platter. Be careful in turning the buns out because of the hot brown sugar.

The first dunker on record appears to be the Danish Lord of Fres who in A.D. *1160 commented on the tastiness of bread dipped in ale.*

(309) WASHINGTON'S STICKY APPLE BUNS

BAKING POWDER METHOD

Makes 1 dozen. Oven temperature: 425° F.
Baking time: 25–30 minutes.

This method results in a cluster and should be turned out in one cake and separated as needed.

Preliminary preparation: Same as for Recipe No. 307.

Dough: Same as for Recipe No. 307.

Filling:

3 tablespoons butter, softened
1 scant cup brown sugar
1 scant teaspoon grated lemon rind
1 teaspoon ground cinnamon
2 large apples, pared, cored, chopped
½ cup seedless raisins, parboiled

Spread dough with softened butter. Over butter sprinkle grated lemon rind, then the rolled brown sugar combined with cinnamon; next distribute the combined chopped apples and prepared raisins (thoroughly dried) over the whole as evenly as possible.

Roll up dough like a jelly roll. Cut with a sharp knife into pieces about 2 inches long. Place cut pieces of rolled dough in the prepared skillet or pan, cut side up and let stand 15 minutes, covered with a light, dry cloth. Bake in a hot oven as directed. Remove pan or skillet from oven and immediately turn the buns upside down on a large platter. Be careful in turning the buns out, because of the hot brown sugar.

NOTE: Cranberries, prunes, figs, dates, and in fact any kind of fruit, fresh or dried, may be substituted for apples, if desired, using the same proportion for each fruit as for apples. For breakfast, especially on Good Friday or Easter Day, you may serve these fruit buns with plain or whipped cream.

(310) YEAST MINCEMEAT BUNS

Makes about 16 buns. Oven temperature: 400° F.
Baking time: 20 minutes (about).

Preliminary preparation:

Break a half 9-oz. package dry mincemeat into pieces in a saucepan; add 3/4 cup cold water and 1 tablespoon granulated sugar; place over heat and stir until all lumps are thoroughly broken up. Bring to a brisk boil and continue the boiling for one minute. Let cool, then combine with 1/2 cup of pared, cored, chopped raw apple and 1 generous tablespoon of brandy.

Dough:

2 cups scalded sweet milk
1 1/2 teaspoons salt
1/4 cup granulated or brown sugar
1 cake compressed yeast
1/4 cup lukewarm water
6 cups (about) bread flour, sifted twice

Cool scalded milk to lukewarm; stir in the salt, sugar and yeast cake which has been crumbled into the lukewarm water. Blend well. Gradually add the flour, just enough to make a soft dough which can be handled easily. Turn dough upon lightly floured board and knead until smooth, elastic and not sticky. Place dough in a greased large mixing bowl; cover with a light, clean, dry towel and allow to rise to treble in bulk, over a pan of hot (not boiling) water. Turn upon lightly floured board; knead a half minute, then roll out into a sheet 1/4 inch thick and spread with the filling.

Filling:

4 tablespoons butter, softened
The prepared mincemeat
1 cup brown sugar, rolled and sifted with
1 1/2 teaspoons ground cinnamon

Spread softened butter over the rolled dough; over butter sprinkle combined brown sugar and cinnamon; then distribute mincemeat mixture as evenly as possible over the whole.

Roll up the bread dough as for jelly roll. Cut with a sharp knife, dipped in flour, into pieces about 2 inches long. Place the cut pieces in a generously greased pan about 2 inches apart; cover with a clean, light, dry cloth and let rise until light (about 30 minutes). Bake in a hot oven as directed. Serve hot or warm.

(311) YEAST STICKY MINCEMEAT BUNS

Proceed as indicated for recipe No. 310 above, placing the slices close together in a skillet or pan prepared as indicated in "Preliminary Preparation" for recipe No. 307.

(312) YEAST SWEET POTATO BUNS

Makes about 12 buns. Oven temperature: 400° F.
Baking time: 15–20 minutes.

1 medium-sized sweet potato
¾ teaspoon salt
2 tablespoons granulated sugar
2 tablespoons butter
1 cup sweet milk, scalded
2 cups (about) bread flour, sifted twice
1 cake compressed yeast

Peel sweet potato and boil in enough water to cover until tender. Drain, saving 2 tablespoons of the water in which boiled. Mash sweet potato at once and melt the butter in it as you mash, alternately with combined salt and granulated sugar. Dissolve yeast cake in the 2 reserved tablespoons of potato water cooled to lukewarm. Gradually add scalded milk, cooled to lukewarm, alternately with enough flour to make a fairly stiff dough. Turn onto a lightly floured board and knead until smooth and elastic and not sticky. Place in greased mixing bowl, brush with melted butter, cover with a clean, light, dry cloth and set to rise over hot water for 5½ to 6 hours, or until trebled in bulk. Turn onto floured board, punch once or twice, then roll out to about ¾-inch thickness. Cut out with biscuit cutter dipped in flour; place upon greased baking pan to rise until more than double in bulk. Bake as directed in a hot oven until delicately brown. Serve as hot as possible with plenty of butter.

Gems—Johnny Cakes—Muffins

"... Call for de doctor, an' de doctor said,
Feed dem darkies on short'nin' bread."
—*Old Plantation Song*

MUFFINS, GEMS AND JOHNNY CAKES

(313) JOHNNY CAKES

The jolly miller by the old mill stream, of poetry and song, is a *rara avis* in this scientific and mechanized age, but in the sometimes gentle, sometimes rude, irony of circumstance he comes into his own as a specialist and a purveyor of luxuries which still create their own demand and are not to be denied.

The old-time mill stones, hand wrought by patient stone cutters of primitive and more leisurely days, are rated among antiques now. Antiquaries buy them and set them up as monuments to the past. Mill stones with histories are set like huge jewels in the pavements of terraces and displayed in museums along with "one-hoss shays" and ancient hand-pump fire engines; but once in a while, here and there, some enterprising person, of knowledge and experience, restores the venerable stones to their former duties and supplies a limited but appreciative public with water-ground flours and meals for the johnny cakes and pones and breads such as great-grandmother used to make.

Most of the brisk and busy housewives of today think of corn bread or muffins, order some corn meal from the grocer's and let it go at that. And the steel-cut and highly refined product comes in sealed packages, with printed recipes and instructions for the cook; but when the johnny cake is made and served, some critical person of a reflective and nostalgic turn recalls that the Rhode Island johnny cake of his earliest recollections was somehow different and indubitably better; and one of the oldest inhabitants informs him that Rhode Island johnny cake and Virginia hoe cake were made from water-ground meal and "that's why."

One can always get water-ground meal, usually made from sweet white corn, at the best grocery shops at higher price than the regular commercial product. In fact, the price may be approximately three times the price of the regular granulated meal—but it's worth it. It can also be bought direct, by mail order, from a few specialized producers.

Monographs and essays have been written on Rhode Island johnny cake and it is so hedged about with legends and traditions that one must be bold and daring to offer a casual recipe. Every family descended from Roger Williams has its own recipes and they are cherished and guarded like the corn pone and spoon bread formulas of the Old Dominion and the Deep South.

In some homesteads of Washington and Newport counties you may eat johnny cake that has a superstructure of a peculiar creamy consistency which mingles with melted butter on your breakfast plate and becomes a luscious custard on a base of crisp but tender crust. Baking powder and other leavening agents rarely figure in the classic recipes for corn breads, either in New England or the South, and in some of the most famous ones there is nothing but meal, water and salt.

It is a long step from Colonial johnny cake to the corn breads of metropolitan hotels and restaurants, but do you happen to know why hotel corn bread is often more delicious and luscious than the modern home product? It is because most of the popular cook books recommend the use of baking powder or sour milk and soda, but the hotel chef habitually uses yeast for his corn breads and muffins, and his product is always moist, tender and delicate in flavor.

A FEW GOOD HINTS ABOUT MUFFINS, GEMS AND JOHNNY CAKES

Quick mixing of dry and liquid ingredients is the secret of obtaining light muffins. *Stir* only until all the flour is moistened. The batter may look lumpy, but it is ready for the pans.

A muffin is a gem and a gem is a muffin. The only difference is that old-time recipes used a heavy muffin pan, which was then, and still is, called a "gem pan." Otherwise the ingredients of muffins are the same as for gems.

Knobs or peaks on top of muffins and long narrow holes inside may indicate that the batter has been stirred too long.

When filling gem or muffin pans, leave one of the small sections empty and fill with water—the gems or muffins will never scorch.

All muffins or gems need a moderately hot oven and will take from twenty to twenty-five minutes to bake, depending on their size. If you like a crisp crust, use the old-fashioned iron gem pans for baking them.

Muffin or gem batter should *not be beaten.* The flour should be *stirred* with the liquid only enough to dampen the flour so that no dry flour is visible around edges of the bowl.

Muffins made partly with cooked cereal will not be heavy if the cereal is first worked into the flour by means of the finger tips.

Try buttermilk muffins. If you don't have buttermilk on hand, you can sour sweet milk by adding one tablespoon of vinegar to each cup of milk used.

Bread flour may be used to replace part of the corn meal called for in corn muffins; if more corn meal than flour is used, the finished muffin will resemble corn bread somewhat in texture and taste. When the amount of flour exceeds the meal, the product is more like regular muffins. Either white or yellow corn meal may be used according to preference; the use of sugar is also a matter of taste.

Use canned unsweetened pineapple juice instead of milk in making muffins. Top each muffin, before baking, with a small lump of sugar dipped in the fruit juice or with a cube of the canned fruit sprinkled with sugar.

Top the corn muffins, before baking them, with uncooked diced bacon. Bake for 15 minutes in a hot oven; then place the muffins under the flame of the broiling oven and let the bacon crisp. Fine for breakfast, luncheon, afternoon snacks and supper.

Drop a teaspoon of peanut butter in each muffin pan, over which pour batter. This gives muffins a delightful nutty flavor.

Speaking of peanut butter, try substituting ⅓ cup of peanut butter or one-half cup of grated cheese for the regular shortening.

Left-over biscuits and muffins make fine foundations for luncheon dishes. Scoop out the inside crumbs, brush generously with melted butter, then fill with a creamed vegetable, meat, fish or chicken mixture. Bake about 10 minutes in a moderately hot oven (350° F.).

Serve as hot as possible. Muffins not eaten at Sunday supper may be sliced, toasted and buttered for Monday breakfast.

Try glazing your muffins. First brush the muffins with slightly beaten egg white; then sprinkle with poppy seeds. Watch them disappear.

In graham muffins one-half graham flour replaces one-half the white flour.

A bran muffin is, at breakfast, a bran muffin—and very good too. Add a crushed banana to the mixture. Cake can't beat it.

For afternoon tea, little rice muffins may be neatly hollowed out and filled with some of your newly made strawberry or raspberry jam or marmalade. Have the muffins hot, of course.

For the simplest bran muffins, part of the flour may be replaced with bran, from 1/3 to 2/3 as a rule, and the amount of liquid increased to supply the additional moisture the bran makes necessary.

For date muffins, add 1/2 cup finely cut dates to dry ingredients.

Use odd bits of jelly, jam, peanut butter, apple butter and all the gamut of fruit butters by putting one teaspoonful into center of muffin after it is partly baked. It will not go to bottom nor make muffins or gems fall. Do not remove pan from oven. Work quickly.

(314) AFTERNOON CHOCOLATE MUFFINS

THESE ARE MORE CUP CAKES THAN MUFFINS

Makes about 1 dozen muffins. Oven temperature: 375° F.
Baking time: 20 minutes.

2 squares chocolate, unsweetened
1/2 cup sweet milk
2 egg yolks, well-beaten
1 cup granulated sugar
3 tablespoons butter
1/4 teaspoon vanilla extract
1/2 cup cold milk
1 scant teaspoon baking soda
1 1/4 cups bread flour, sifted twice
2 egg whites, stiffly beaten

Put broken chocolate in top of double boiler; add 1/2 cup milk and place over hot water. Stir until chocolate is dissolved and mixture is smooth; stir in the beaten egg yolks, a little at a time, beating well after each addition and stirring constantly until smooth. Remove from hot water, stir in sugar, butter and vanilla extract. Blend till sugar is dissolved; then gradually add second 1/2 cup of milk in which soda has been dissolved, adding alternately with the flour. Lastly fold in the stiffly beaten egg whites. Pour batter into greased muffin pans, and bake in a moderate oven as directed. Frost the muffins if desired.

(315) AFTERNOON CINNAMON MUFFINS

Makes 24 small muffins. Oven temperature: 400° F.
Baking time: 20–25 minutes.

1½ tablespoons butter
¼ cup brown sugar
¼ cup granulated sugar
1 whole fresh egg, well beaten
2 cups bread flour, sifted twice
½ teaspoon ground nutmeg
½ teaspoon salt
2 teaspoons baking powder
½ cup milk
Mixed sugar and cinnamon

Cream butter and combined sugars until fluffy; gradually add beaten egg and beat well. To the flour add nutmeg, salt and baking powder and sift together; add alternately with milk to the first mixture. Pour batter into small buttered muffin pans and bake in a hot oven 20 to 25 minutes, or until delicately brown. Remove from oven and while still very hot, dip each muffin top in melted butter. Roll in confectioner's sugar mixed with cinnamon to taste (about ½ teaspoon). Serve hot.

(316) AFTERNOON STRAWBERRY MUFFINS

Makes about 10 muffins. Oven temperature: 375° F.
Baking time: 20–25 minutes.

2 cups bread flour, sifted twice
2 tablespoons granulated sugar
4 teaspoons baking powder
½ teaspoon salt
1 whole egg, well beaten
¼ cup melted butter
1 cup crushed ripe strawberries

To the flour add sugar, baking powder and salt and sift together. Add egg to melted butter; blend well and add to crushed ripe strawberries. Combine with flour mixture, stirring only until it is moistened. Pour batter into buttered muffin pans, having them ⅔ full, and bake until brown and shrunken from the pans, in a moderate oven as directed. Serve hot with butter.

In medieval England, bread was both food and plates for all but the wealthy. Food was served in hollowed-out bread loaves. The juice-soaked loaves were the forerunner of "Bread and Gravy."

(317) AFTERNOON BREAD CRUMB AND DATE MUFFINS

Makes about 12 small muffins. Oven temperature: 375° F.
Baking time: 20–25 minutes.

In this recipe, the moisture is furnished by the eggs; no other liquid is added.

2 cups fine bread crumbs, sifted
1 teaspoon baking powder
⅓ teaspoon salt
1 cup chopped dates
1 cup chopped walnut meats
¼ cup granulated sugar
6 egg yolks, well-beaten, with
¼ teaspoon almond extract
6 egg whites, stiffly beaten with
⅓ teaspoon salt
Whipped cream

Add baking powder and salt to bread crumbs and sift together over mixed dates and nut meats, already mixed with granulated sugar. Blend well. Gradually stir in the beaten egg yolks with almond extract. Lastly fold in the stiffly beaten egg whites with remaining salt. Turn batter into greased muffin pans, having them ⅔ full, and bake in a moderate oven as directed. Serve with whipped cream.

(318) AFTERNOON JAM GEMS

Makes 1 dozen. Oven temperature: 375° F.
Baking time: 20–25 minutes.

⅓ cup butter
⅓ cup granulated sugar
1 whole fresh egg, well beaten
2 cups bread flour, sifted twice
4 teaspoons baking powder
½ teaspoon salt
1 cup sweet cold milk
Jam (any kind desired)

Cream butter until fluffy; gradually add sugar, alternately with beaten egg and beat well. Add baking powder and salt to flour and sift over first mixture; stir, alternately with cold milk into the mixture, stirring as little as possible to make batter look smooth. Drop by spoonfuls into generously buttered muffin pans and bake until puffed (about 7 or 8 minutes). Pull pan to front of oven but *do not remove.* With a teaspoon, working quickly, slip a teaspoon of your favorite jam, marmalade or jelly into center of half of the muffins. Swing pan around. Fill the rest of the muffins; push pan back quickly into oven to finish baking. Serve hot.

(319) AFTERNOON MINCEMEAT GEMS

Makes 1 dozen muffins. Oven temperature: 375° F.
Baking time: 20–25 minutes.

Proceed exactly as indicated for recipe No. 318, substituting prepared mincemeat for jam.

Fine breads, perhaps, are the best test of good cooking. They require quick, accurate workmanship and a dash of imagination to lift them from the commonplace. A superb cook goes about her mixing and baking with an endless zest. Such cooks are bold, creative artists, blending everyday staples into tender-textured or crisply-browned culinary masterpieces, with a skilled hand.

(320) APPLE AND BACON MUFFINS

Makes about 10 muffins. Oven temperature: 375° F.
Baking time: 25 minutes.

2 cups bread flour, sifted twice then measured
4 teaspoons baking powder
1 tablespoon sugar
3/4 teaspoon salt
1 whole fresh egg, well beaten
1 cup sweet milk
2 tablespoons melted shortening
3/4 cup sweet apple sauce
3 strips uncooked bacon, finely chopped

Add baking powder, sugar and salt to the flour and sift together. Combine egg, milk and melted shortening well and add into flour mixture, stirring just enough to make batter look smooth. Drop a spoonful of batter into generously buttered muffin pans; place 1 tablespoon sweetened apple sauce over batter, and cover with another tablespoonful of batter. Sprinkle top with finely chopped raw bacon and bake in a moderate oven as directed. Serve hot.

(321) APPLE CINNAMON MUFFINS

Makes 1 dozen muffins. Oven temperature: 400° F.
Baking time: 20–25 minutes.

2 cups bread flour, sifted twice
3/4 teaspoon salt
4 teaspoons baking powder
1/4 cup granulated sugar
2 tablespoons butter
1 cup pared, cored, finely chopped apple
1/2 cup sweet cold milk
2 whole eggs, well beaten
Cinnamon

Add salt, baking powder and one-half of the sugar to the flour and sift together. Cut in butter. Add chopped apples and mix well. Combine cold milk and beaten eggs; mix well and stir into first mixture. Fill generously buttered muffin pans with batter; place a thin slice of pared, cored apple on top of each muffin; sprinkle with remaining sugar and cinnamon to taste (about ½ generous teaspoon) and bake in a hot oven as directed. Serve hot.

(322) APPLE MUFFINS—DANISH METHOD

LAEKRE AEBLESKIVER

Makes 2 dozen muffins. Medium flame.
Frying time: 4–5 minutes each side (about).

2¼ cups bread flour, sifted twice
1 generous tablespoon baking powder
½ teaspoon salt
3 egg yolks, well beaten
⅔ cup melted butter
1 scant tablespoon granulated sugar
Grated rind of a small lemon
2 cups sweet cold milk
3 apples, pared, cored, sliced
3 egg whites, stiffly beaten

Add baking powder and salt to the flour and sift together. Blend beaten egg yolks, melted butter, sugar and grated lemon rind very well and add to flour mixture, alternately with cold milk, stirring just enough to moisten it. Now add apple slices alternately with stiffly beaten egg whites, folding in well. Drop by tablespoons into generously buttered rings on heavy iron skillet or griddle, and brown nicely 4 to 5 minutes on each side. Serve hot with your favorite fruit sauce or whipped cream.

(323) APPLE HONEY MUFFINS

USING PREPARED BISCUIT MIX

Makes about 1 dozen. Oven temperature: 375° F.
Baking time: 25 to 30 minutes.

5 medium-sized apples (about)
1 cup prepared biscuit mix
1 tablespoon sugar
A small pinch salt
1 whole fresh egg, well beaten
¾ cup sweet cold milk
½ teaspoon vanilla extract
⅔ cup honey (about)

Pare, core and halve 5 or 6 medium-sized apples. Sift biscuit mix with sugar and stir. Combine salt, egg, milk and vanilla extract and add to the biscuit mix, stirring until just blended. Pour batter into greased muffin pans, about an inch deep, and place an apple half in each, putting a tablespoon of honey in the center of each apple. Cover with remaining batter and bake until apples are tender in a moderate oven as directed. Serve with plain or whipped cream and very hot.

(324) APRICOT JOHNNY CAKE

Serves about 6. Oven temperature: 375° F.
Baking time: 25 minutes (about).

- 1½ cups bread flour, sifted
- 1 teaspoon salt
- 2 tablespoons granulated sugar
- 5 teaspoons baking powder
- 1¼ cups water ground (preferably) corn meal
- 2 whole fresh eggs, well beaten
- 1¼ cups sweet cold milk
- ¼ cup shortening, melted
- ¾ cup well-drained, cooked, sweetened dried apricots

Add salt, sugar and baking powder to flour and sift together, then combine with corn meal. Blend thoroughly. Combine beaten eggs, milk, melted shortening and apricots, whole or sieved; and stir into the flour mixture. Transfer batter to a shallow greased baking pan and bake in a moderate oven as directed. Serve hot with plenty of butter.

Lucius Quintius Cincinnatus, Roman Dictator in the fifth century B.C. *ordered that every person able to bear arms should eat two loaves of bread daily.*

(325) BACON MUFFINS

Makes about 12 muffins. Oven temperature: 400° F.
Baking time: 20–25 minutes.

- 2 cups bread flour, sifted
- 1 tablespoon baking powder
- 2 tablespoons granulated sugar
- 1 generous teaspoon salt
- 2 tablespoons melted (not too hot) bacon fat
- 1 whole fresh egg, well-beaten
- 1 cup cold milk
- 3 strips raw bacon, chopped very fine

Add baking powder, sugar and salt to flour and sift together. Combine melted bacon fat (lukewarm), beaten egg, cold milk and chopped fine bacon; blend well; then stir into dry ingredients. The batter should be somewhat lumpy in appearance. Fill well greased muffin pans ⅔ full and bake in a hot oven as directed. Serve as hot as possible.

(326) BAKED BEAN MUFFINS

Makes 1 dozen (about). Oven temperature: 375° F.
Baking time: 25–30 minutes.

These nourishing muffins are very good with pot roast and browned gravy.

- 2 whole fresh eggs, well beaten
- 1 cup sieved, drained baked beans
- ½ cup sweet cold milk
- ⅓ cup melted bacon drippings
- 2 cups bread flour, sifted with
- 2 teaspoons baking powder, and
- 1 scant teaspoon salt

Combine beaten eggs, sieved beans, milk and bacon drippings. Add baking powder and salt to flour and sift together over bean mixture; stir just enough to dampen the flour; pour into greased muffin pans ⅔ full; bake in a moderate oven as directed. Serve hot.

(327) BANANA BRAN MUFFINS

Makes 6 large or 12 small muffins. Oven temperature: 375° F.
Baking time: 30 minutes.

Someone has said that in the days of Alexander the Great bananas were called "The fruit of the wise men." That may or may not be a true statement. However, modern scientists are sure that bananas are a fine source of vitamins, essential minerals and energy-giving substances. And, furthermore, bananas are available the year round at low cost. They are always picked green and ripened off the tree. When partially ripe, they are yellow with green tips and at that stage may be classed as a vegetable, for they must be cooked to be really edible. When the green tip disappears, they may be eaten raw but do not yet have the sweetness and aromatic flavor that is distinctive. When brown flecked, they have reached eating perfection and are so digestible that they are often given to infants.

NOTE: This recipe calls for diced or sliced bananas. This makes a somewhat stiffer batter than usual for muffins.

- 1 cup bread flour, sifted
- ½ teaspoon salt
- ¾ teaspoon baking soda
- 2 tablespoons shortening
- ¼ cup granulated sugar
- 1 whole egg, well-beaten
- 1 cup unsifted bran
- 2 tablespoons buttermilk or sour milk
- 3 bananas (2 cups finely diced or very thinly sliced)

Add salt and baking soda to flour and sift together. Cream shortening and sugar well. Combine beaten egg, unsifted bran and buttermilk or sour milk well and stir in the bananas. Mix again; then add to combined flour mixture and creamed shortening, stirring only enough to dampen all the flour. Turn batter into generously greased muffin pans, ⅔ full, and bake in a moderate oven as directed. Serve hot with plenty of butter.

You may substitute one cup bread flour, whole wheat flour, or corn meal for bran, if desired.

(328) BLACKBERRY MUFFINS

Makes about 14 small muffins. Oven temperature: 400° F. Baking time: 20 minutes (about).

1½ cups bread flour, sifted
3½ teaspoons baking powder
¾ teaspoon salt
1 whole egg, well-beaten
¾ generous cup sweet cold milk
3 tablespoons melted butter
¾ cup carefully-washed, hulled, drained blackberries

Add baking powder and salt to the flour and sift together. Combine beaten egg with cold milk and melted butter and add to flour mixture, alternately with blackberries, stirring only enough to dampen the flour. Turn batter into greased muffin pans and bake in a hot oven as directed. Serve hot.

(329) BLUEBERRY BRAN MUFFINS

Makes 16 medium muffins. Oven temperature: 400° F. Baking time: 25 minutes.

The ease with which muffins can be mixed and dropped into greased pans for the oven recommends them to busy homemakers over biscuits that need rolling and cutting preparatory to baking. Also the standard muffin recipe permits wider variation for breakfast use than those for some other hot breads. Part of the flour may be replaced by whole wheat flour, oatmeal, bran or corn meal, for example. Something may be added, such as fresh berries, raisins, dates or nuts.

1 cup bran, unsifted
1 cup sweet cold milk
2 tablespoons shortening
¼ cup granulated sugar
1 whole fresh egg, well-beaten
1 cup bread flour, sifted twice
3 teaspoons baking powder
½ scant teaspoon salt
½ generous cup fresh blueberries, washed, sponged

Pour cold milk over the unsifted bran, let stand 5 minutes to soak and absorb almost all the milk. Cream shortening and sugar; beat in the egg; then stir in the bran mixture alternately with flour mixed with salt and baking powder and sifted over the blueberries. Stir just enough to dampen the flour mixture or until it disappears. Turn into greased muffin pans ⅔ full and bake in a hot oven as directed, until muffins are brown and slightly shrunken from sides of pans. Serve very hot with plenty of butter.

Blueberry gems are made in the same manner, except that the batter is turned into heavy iron muffin pans.

(330) BLUEBERRY GRIDDLE JOHNNY CAKES

Serves 6 generously. Very hot griddle.
Time: until crisp and brown.

2 cups white corn meal
1 scant teaspoon salt
1½ cups (about) boiling water
¾ cup washed fresh blueberries
1 tablespoon melted bacon drippings

Combine the above ingredients in order named. The batter should have the consistency of pancake batter. Drop by spoonfuls onto greased hot griddle; flatten each cake slightly and cook until crisp and brown on both sides. Serve very hot with butter and honey, maple syrup or molasses.

(331) BLUEBERRY MUFFINS

MASTER RECIPE

Makes 1 dozen muffins. Oven temperature: 375° F.
Baking time: 20–25 minutes.

2 cups bread flour, sifted twice
2 tablespoons granulated sugar
1 tablespoon baking powder
½ teaspoon salt
2 tablespoons melted butter
1 whole egg, well beaten
½ cup sweet cold milk
1 cup washed, sponged blueberries

Mix ½ cup of the flour lightly with the blueberries, let stand 10 minutes. Add sugar, baking powder and salt to remaining flour and sift three times. Combine egg and milk and add to flour mixture alternately with floured blueberries. Turn batter into generously buttered muffin pans and bake in a moderate oven as directed until tops are brown and muffins shrunk from edges of pans. Serve very hot and with plenty of butter.

(332) BLUEBERRY SALLY LUNN

Serves 6. Oven temperature: 350° F.
Baking time: 45–50 minutes.

There are few things that become as monotonous as planning and preparing meals and yet that same task offers many possibilities of interest. Perhaps like so many other jobs, what we get out of it depends upon what we put into it. Approaching the subject with an active and ambitious mind and a desire to turn out interesting foods helps a lot.

½ cup butter
½ cup granulated sugar
2 whole fresh eggs, well beaten
¾ cup sweet cold milk (about)
1¾ cups bread flour, sifted twice
1 tablespoon baking powder
½ teaspoon salt
⅔ cup washed, sponged blueberries

Cream butter with sugar until lemon-colored and fluffy; gradually beat in the beaten eggs. Add flour to baking powder and salt and sift a little over the blueberries; then sift the remaining flour mixture over milk, which has been combined with the creamed butter-sugar-egg mixture. Stir just enough to dampen the flour, adding as you go along the floured blueberries. Turn batter into a generously buttered pan 8 × 8 × 2 inches; sprinkle with the following mixture:

Topping: Roll ¼ cup of brown sugar and sift with ½ generous teaspoon of ground cinnamon. Bake in a moderate oven as directed and serve hot, cut into squares, with plain or whipped cream.

(333) BRAN DATE MOLASSES MUFFINS

Makes 10 muffins. Oven temperature: 375° F.
Baking time: 25–30 minutes.

½ cup bread flour, sifted
½ generous teaspoon salt
½ generous teaspoon baking soda
1 teaspoon baking powder
¾ cup pitted, chopped dates
1 cup bran
1 egg, well beaten
½ cup buttermilk or sour milk
3 tablespoons molasses
1 tablespoon melted butter

Add salt, baking soda and baking powder to flour and sift over mixed chopped dates and bran. Combine egg, sour milk, molasses and melted butter and add into the first mixture, stirring just enough to dampen the dry ingredients. Turn batter into generously buttered muffin pans, ⅔ full, and bake in a moderate oven as directed. Serve hot.

(334) BRAN MOLASSES MUFFINS

MASTER RECIPE

Makes 1½ dozen muffins. Oven temperature: 375° F.
Baking time: 25 minutes.

1 cup bread flour, sifted twice
1 scant teaspoon salt
1 teaspoon baking soda
1 cup buttermilk or sour milk
½ cup molasses
2 tablespoons cold water
1 whole fresh egg, well-beaten
2 cups all-bran

To the bread flour add salt and soda and sift together over all-bran. Blend thoroughly. Combine buttermilk or sour milk (for richer muffins use sour cream), molasses, cold water and beaten egg. Mix well and pour all at once over flour mixture, stirring just enough to dampen flour. Pour batter into generously buttered muffin pans and bake in a moderate oven as directed until muffins leave sides of pans and are delicately brown. Serve as hot as possible with plenty of butter.

Should you desire to omit molasses and consequently baking soda and sour milk, here is another master recipe:

(335) BRAN MUFFINS

MASTER RECIPE

Makes 8 large or 12 small muffins. Oven temperature: 400° F.
Baking time: 25–30 minutes.

2 tablespoons butter
¼ cup granulated sugar
1 whole fresh egg, well beaten
1 cup bran
¾ cup sweet cold milk
1 cup bread flour, sifted with
2½ teaspoons baking powder, and
½ generous teaspoon salt

Cream butter and sugar; gradually add egg, then beat briskly until mixture is fluffy. Stir in bran, dampened with milk, and let stand 5 minutes, or until moisture is taken up, then add combined flour, baking powder and salt, sifted together, and stir until flour is dampened, no more, no less. Turn batter into generously buttered muffin pans and bake until muffins are brown and leave sides of pans, in a hot oven as directed. Serve as hot as possible.

(336) BRAN RAISIN MUFFINS

Makes 10 large muffins. Oven temperature: 375° F.
Baking time: 25 minutes.

For the simplest bran muffins, part of the flour in the recipe is replaced with bran (from 1/3 to 2/3, as a rule) and the amount of liquid increased to supply the additional moisture the bran makes necessary. Brown sugar or molasses is preferred to white sugar as the sweetening agent.

1 cup sweet milk
1 cup bran
2 tablespoons shortening
1/4 cup dark brown sugar
1 whole fresh egg, well beaten
3/4 cup seedless raisins, parboiled, sponged
1 cup bread flour, sifted with
1 tablespoon baking powder, and
1/3 teaspoon salt

Pour milk over bran and let stand 5 minutes. Cream shortening and brown sugar; then add the egg, beating briskly until thoroughly blended. Add bran-milk mixture, mixed with seedless raisins which have been parboiled, drained and well sponged. Over this sift combined bread flour, baking powder and salt and blend just enough to moisten flour. Mixture will look lumpy, but do not attempt to stir out the lumps. Fill generously buttered muffin pans 2/3 full; bake in a moderately hot oven as directed or until firm, brown and shrunken slightly from the pans. Serve hot with plenty of butter.

(337) BROWN BREAD CRUMBS MUFFINS

Makes 1 dozen large muffins. Oven temperature: 375° F.
Baking time: 25–30 minutes.

1/4 cup granulated sugar
1 whole fresh egg
1/4 cup Grandma's molasses
1/2 teaspoon baking soda
1/2 teaspoon salt
1 cup bread crumbs
1 cup bran
1 cup bread flour, sifted
1 cup buttermilk or sour milk
1/4 cup sour heavy cream

Beat together sugar, egg, molasses, baking soda and salt thoroughly; gradually add bread crumbs alternately with bran. Blend well. Sift flour over mixture; then stir in combined buttermilk and heavy sour cream. Disregard lumps. Pour batter into generously greased muffin pans (2/3 full) and bake in a moderate oven as directed until muffins are brown and have shrunk from sides of pans. Serve very hot with plenty of butter or jam.

(338) BUTTERMILK MUFFINS

Makes about 1½ dozen muffins. Oven temperature: 400° F.
Baking time: 20 minutes.

4 cups bread flour, sifted twice
3 tablespoons corn meal
1 tablespoon salt
1 scant teaspoon baking soda
2 whole fresh eggs, well beaten
1 tablespoon brown sugar
3 to 3½ cups buttermilk

Add corn meal, salt and soda to flour. Beat eggs with brown sugar into buttermilk, then add to dry ingredients, gradually, stirring just enough to dampen flour mixture. Pour batter into generously greased muffin pans and bake in a hot oven as directed until muffins are brown and leave sides of pans. Serve very hot with plenty of butter, jam or marmalade.

"Breakfast," states a certain author of good cheer, "is a very serious subject. The first meal of the day has exercised more influence over history than many people are aware of. It is not easy to preserve a clear mind or keep a stiff upper lip upon an empty stomach."

Breakfast should always be a warming, cheering event and not just a hurried, sketchy affair or orange juice, toast and coffee. The morning meal offers a homemaker her first chance to start the day right for her family—to stage a real culinary triumph with chilled fruit or a hot cereal, with griddle cakes or hot muffins, such as these:

(339) CARAMEL CINNAMON MUFFINS

Makes 12 small muffins. Oven temperature: 350° F.
Baking time: 20–25 minutes.

Preliminary operation: Butter 12 muffin pans liberally with butter and drop 1 generous (rounded) teaspoon of brown sugar in the bottom of each pan. Set aside.

Batter:

2 cups bread flour, sifted with
1 tablespoon baking powder, and
½ teaspoon salt, and
1 teaspoon ground cinnamon
1 whole fresh egg, well beaten with
1 cup sweet cold milk, and
¼ cup brown sugar, and
2 tablespoons melted butter

To the flour mixture add, all at once, the liquid mixture and stir just enough to dampen the flour, disregarding the lumps. Turn batter into prepared muffin pans and bake until muffins are brown and have shrunk from the sides of the pans, in a moderate oven as directed. Serve upside down on a sizzling hot platter with plenty of butter and your favorite jam, marmalade or jelly. The family or guests will certainly okay these delicious muffins.

(340) CASHEW NUT MUFFINS

Makes 2 dozen small muffins. Oven temperature: 400° F. Baking time: 25–30 minutes.

It may surprise you to learn that the cashew nut is among the favorite nuts in America and second in popularity only to the peanut. We have considerable sympathy with the point of view of the school child who began an essay with the sentence: "The cashew are a funny nut." And no small contribution to the world's descriptive humor was made by a hurried metropolitan commuter who was commanded by his wife to bring home a pound of cashews. He had forgotten the name of the nut and was about to give up in despair when, catching sight of some shelled peanuts, he said to the clerk: "The nut I want looks like a peanut with the 'bends'."

Both the school child and the commuter would have outdone themselves had they seen the cashew growing on its native heath, for the nut hangs from a quince-like cashew "apple" exactly like an earring. It has over 40 per cent fat, a distinctive flavor and is rich and crumbly in texture.

- 2 cups bread flour, sifted twice
- 1 tablespoon baking powder
- 2 tablespoons granulated sugar
- ½ scant teaspoon salt
- ¾ cup toasted, cooled, chopped cashew nuts
- 1 whole egg, well beaten
- 1 cup sweet cold milk
- ¼ scant cup melted butter

Add baking powder, sugar and salt to the flour and sift over prepared cashew nuts. Combine egg, milk and melted butter; blend well and pour all at once over flour-nut mixture. Blend just enough to dampen flour. Bake in a hot oven as directed. Serve hot with butter.

(341) CHERRY MUFFINS

Makes 1 dozen muffins. Oven temperature: 400° F.
Baking time: 25 minutes.

2 cups bread flour, sifted
4 teaspoons baking powder
½ teaspoon salt
2 tablespoons granulated sugar
1 whole egg, well beaten
1 cup sweet milk
¼ cup butter, melted
1 cup canned unsweetened, drained cherries

Add flour to baking powder, salt and granulated sugar and sift over cherries. Blend well. Combine egg, milk and melted butter, and pour all at once over flour-cherry mixture, stirring just enough to dampen the flour. Pour batter into liberally buttered muffin pans, ⅔ full, and bake as directed until muffins are brown and slightly shrunken from edges of pans. Serve hot with plain or whipped cream.

(342) CINNAMON MUFFINS

Makes about 12 small muffins. Oven temperature: 375° F.
Baking time: 25 minutes.

¼ cup butter
½ cup granulated sugar
1 egg, well beaten
½ cup sweet cold milk
1½ cups bread flour, sifted twice
2 teaspoons baking powder
½ teaspoon salt

Cream butter and sugar until fluffy; gradually add egg and continue beating and creaming alternately, until mixture is smooth; then beat in the milk until thoroughly blended. Add baking powder and salt to the flour and sift together over the first mixture. Stir only enough to dampen it. Turn batter into generously buttered muffin pans, ⅔ full, brush top of each muffin with melted butter and bake in a moderately hot oven as directed until muffins are brown and shrunk from edges of pans. Remove from oven and immediately spread generously with a mixture of 2 teaspoons granulated sugar and ¾ teaspoon ground cinnamon. Serve at once with jam.

(343) COOKED MEAT MUFFINS

Makes about 8 muffins. Oven temperature: 375° F.
Baking time: 15 minutes.

The problem of utilizing left-overs to avoid waste is one that bothers many homemakers. It is, of course, almost impossible when planning meals to calculate so closely that no odds and ends are left over and personally the writer rather counts on them!

It may not sound logical, but the end of a good roast always seems to taste better than the first slice. Perhaps it is because those tasty bits of brown outside that fall off in slicing and those juicy bits that one has to dig out from around the bones are actually the choicest part of the meat.

Cut all the bits of meat from the bones just as soon as the roast is taken from the dinner table. Don't let the meat dry out. Place the cut meat in a bowl and cover it. The bones go into the soup kettle.

The secret of making a delicious dish from the tasty end-of-roast pieces is to keep them moist. Too often a reheated piece of meat is overcooked and distinctly dry. If it goes into a hot dish, protect the meat from overcooking with a layer of mashed potatoes, turnips, or other mashed vegetables; spaghetti, noodles, macaroni, a cream sauce or a barbecue sauce may be used. Cook it long enough to reheat the meat. Meat pies, turnovers, croquettes, meat patties, loaves, casserole dishes and muffins are all grand concoctions from the end of the roast.

2 cups bread flour, sifted
1 tablespoon baking powder
3/4 teaspoon salt, or more
3 to 4 tablespoons shortening
3/4 cup sweet cold milk (about)
1 whole fresh egg, well beaten
1 cup ground cooked meat (any kind)

Add baking powder and salt to the bread flour and sift together into a bowl; cut in shortening, then add the milk combined with beaten egg, stirring just enough to moisten the flour. Roll out on lightly floured board to 1/4-inch thick. Brush with melted butter and spread with ground, cooked, seasoned meat (any kind). Roll up as for jelly roll and cut in one-inch slices. Place slices in buttered muffin pans and bake as directed until brown. You may serve with left-over reheated gravy or with a quickly made brown gravy.

(344) CORN KERNEL MUFFINS

Makes about 1 dozen muffins. Oven temperature: 375° F.
Baking time: 25 minutes.

1 whole fresh egg, well beaten
1¼ cups sweet cold milk
3 tablespoons shortening, melted
1 cup whole kernel canned corn, drained
1½ cups bread flour, sifted
3½ teaspoons baking powder
1 scant teaspoon salt
3 tablespoons sugar
1 cup yellow corn meal, sifted

Combine egg, milk, melted shortening and corn and mix thoroughly. Add baking powder, salt, sugar (more or less, according to taste) and yellow corn meal to the flour and sift together over liquid mixture. Stir just enough to moisten the flour; turn batter into buttered muffin pans, and bake in a moderate oven as directed until muffins are brown and have shrunk from sides of pans. Serve as hot as possible. Very crunchy.

(345) CORN MUFFINS

MASTER RECIPE

Makes 1 dozen muffins. Oven temperature: 375° F.
Baking time: 25–30 minutes.

2 cups bread flour, sifted twice
2 tablespoons granulated sugar
1 tablespoon baking powder
1 cup corn meal (white or yellow)
½ teaspoon salt
1 cup sweet milk (about)
1 whole fresh egg, well beaten
4 tablespoons melted shortening

Add sugar, baking powder and salt to flour and sift into a warm bowl containing the corn meal and mix well. Combine milk, egg and melted shortening, blend well and pour over flour mixture all at once, then stir just enough to dampen flour. Fill greased muffin pans ⅔ full and bake as directed or until muffins are brown and have shrunk from sides of pans. Serve hot with butter, jam or marmalade.

(346) CORN MEAL BRAN MUFFINS

Makes 1 dozen large muffins. Oven temperature: 400° F. Baking time: 20 minutes.

4 tablespoons butter or margarine
1 tablespoon granulated sugar
1 tablespoon dark brown sugar
2 whole eggs, unbeaten
2/3 cup sweet cold milk (about)
2/3 cup bread flour, sifted
2/3 cup yellow corn meal, sifted
4 teaspoons baking powder
3/4 teaspoon salt
1 cup unsifted bran

Combine butter or margarine, granulated and brown sugars, unbeaten eggs and milk and mix well. Add flour to sifted corn meal, baking powder and salt and sift over unsifted bran. Blend thoroughly. Pour liquid mixture over flour mixture and stir just enough to dampen it. Turn batter into generously buttered muffin pans and bake until muffins are brown and have shrunk from sides of pans, in a hot oven as directed. Serve hot with butter.

(347) CRANBERRY BRAN MUFFINS

Makes 10 large muffins. Oven temperature: 400° F. Baking time: 25–30 minutes.

2 whole fresh eggs, well beaten
3/4 cup sweet cold milk
1/2 cup bran flakes
1 1/2 cups bread flour, sifted twice
1 tablespoon baking powder
3 tablespoons granulated sugar
1/2 generous teaspoon salt
1/3 cup canned cranberry sauce
4 tablespoons butter, melted

Beat eggs until thick and lemon-colored. Stir in milk alternately with bran flakes and let stand 5 minutes. Add baking powder, sugar and salt to the flour and sift together. Melt butter in muffin pans; spread over pans and turn excess melted butter into milk mixture alternately with cranberry sauce; blend well and pour liquid over flour mixture. Stir only enough to dampen flour; turn batter into buttered, hot muffin pans, 2/3 full and bake in a hot oven as directed. Serve hot.

(348) CRANBERRY CORN MUFFINS

Makes 8 muffins. Oven temperature: 400° F.
Baking time: 25 minutes.

1 cup bread flour, sifted with
¾ cup yellow corn meal, and
1 tablespoon baking powder, and
1 tablespoon granulated sugar, and
½ generous teaspoon salt
1 generous tablespoon melted butter
¾ cup sweet cold milk
1 whole egg, well beaten
Firm cranberry sauce

To the sifted dry ingredients add combined melted butter, milk and beaten egg, stirring only just enough to dampen the dry mixture. Cut firm cranberry sauce into ⅛-inch cubes. Alternate layers of batter and cranberry cubes in generously buttered muffin pans, slightly heated, making the first and last layer of batter, and having pans filled ⅔ full. Bake in a hot oven as directed until muffins are brown and have shrunk from sides of pans. Serve sizzling hot with plenty of butter.

(349) CRUSHED PINEAPPLE BRAN MUFFINS

Makes 1 dozen large muffins. Oven temperature: 375° F.
Baking time: 30 minutes.

¼ cup shortening, softened
2 tablespoons brown sugar
1 whole fresh egg, well beaten
⅓ cup strained honey
1 cup all-bran
2 cups bread flour, sifted
½ teaspoon salt
1½ teaspoons baking powder
¼ teaspoon baking soda
¾ cup sweet cold milk
½ cup canned, drained, crushed pineapple

Place softened butter or shortening in a mixing bowl with brown sugar, egg and honey and use a rotary beater and beat until mixture is creamy; stir in the bran, alternately with well-drained, pineapple, mixing well. Then stir in sweet milk. To the flour add salt, baking powder and soda, and sift together over first mixture. Stir just enough to dampen flour. Turn batter into warm, greased muffin pans and bake in a moderately hot oven as directed. Serve hot with plenty of butter.

(350) CURRANT JELLY MUFFINS

Makes about 10 large muffins. Oven temperature: 400° F. Baking time: 25–30 minutes.

Drop a scant teaspoon of currant jelly into each buttered, warm muffin pan.
Batter: Use Recipe No. 345 and bake as indicated.

(351) DATE BRAN MUFFINS

Makes 10 muffins. Oven temperature: 400° F. Baking time: 30 minutes (about).

Dates have a high caloric (energy unit) content in relation to weight, running about 1430 calories to the pound.

2 tablespoons butter or margarine
2 tablespoons brown sugar
2 tablespoons granulated sugar
1 whole fresh egg, well beaten
1 cup bran, unsifted
¾ cup (about) sweet cold milk
1 cup bread flour, sifted
1 scant tablespoon baking powder
½ teaspoon salt
½ cup pitted, chopped, or thinly sliced dates

Cream butter or margarine and combined sugars thoroughly (you may use all brown or all granulated sugar if desired). Add egg and beat briskly until thoroughly blended. Combine milk and bran and add to creamed mixture. Let stand until most of the moisture is taken up, then add sifted bread flour, mixed with baking powder and salt, sifted over prepared dates and well mixed. Stir, do not beat, until flour mixture is dampened. Turn batter into warm, greased muffin pans, and bake in a hot oven as directed until muffins are delicately brown and have shrunk from edges of pans. Serve hot.

(352) DATE MUFFINS

Makes 1 dozen muffins. Oven temperature: 375° F. Baking time: 25–30 minutes.

These date muffins are unusually light and flavorsome.

2 cups bread flour, sifted twice
1 tablespoon baking powder
½ teaspoon salt
2 generous tablespoons granulated sugar
¼ cup butter, melted
2 whole fresh eggs, well beaten
1 cup milk (sweet and cold)
1 cup pitted, chopped dates

Add baking powder, salt and sugar to flour, sift once, measure, and resift over chopped dates. Blend well. Combine melted butter, beaten eggs and milk and beat with rotary beater; then pour all at once over flour mixture and stir just enough to dampen flour. Turn batter into buttered muffin pans, slightly warmed, and bake until muffins are brown and have shrunk from edges of pans, in a moderate oven as directed. Serve hot with butter and jam, marmalade or jelly.

(353) DATE AND OATMEAL MUFFINS

FOR BREAKFAST SERVE THESE MUFFINS WITH CREAMED DRIED BEEF

NO SIFTING NEEDED

Makes 1 dozen large muffins. Oven temperature: 400° F.
Baking time: 25–30 minutes.

1 cup whole wheat flour
1 cup rolled oats
1 cup yellow corn meal
1 teaspoon salt
1 teaspoon baking powder
1 teaspoon baking soda
¼ cup strained honey
¾ cup pitted, chopped dates
1 whole fresh egg, well beaten
2 tablespoons melted butter
1½ cups buttermilk or sour milk

Put whole wheat flour, rolled oats, corn meal (yellow), salt, baking powder and soda into a large mixing bowl and stir until mixture is thoroughly blended; then stir in prepared dates. Combine remaining ingredients, beat till well mixed, and pour all at once over flour-date mixture. Stir just enough to dampen dry ingredients; pour batter into warm, buttered muffin pans and bake until muffins are brown and have left sides of pans, in a hot oven as directed. Serve as hot as possible with plenty of butter.

(354) DATE, ORANGE AND MOLASSES MUFFINS

Makes 1 dozen muffins. Oven temperature: 400° F.
Baking time: 20–25 minutes.

For these delicious afternoon tea muffins, the muffin pans must be hot. Do not sift whole wheat flour.

½ cup bread flour, sifted twice
2 teaspoons baking powder
½ generous teaspoon salt
1 tablespoon brown sugar
1 cup dates, pitted, chopped
Grated rind of a small orange
1 scant teaspoon grated lemon rind
1½ cups unsifted whole wheat flour
¼ cup molasses
1 whole fresh egg, well beaten
1 cup sweet cold milk
¼ cup butter, melted

Add baking powder, salt and sugar to the flour and sift over combined dates and grated orange and lemon rinds, mixed with whole wheat flour. Blend thoroughly. Combine molasses, beaten egg, cold sweet milk and melted butter; beat with rotary beater and pour all at once over first mixture, stirring just enough to dampen it. Pour batter into greased *warm* muffin pans and bake in a hot oven as directed until muffins are brown and have shrunk from sides of muffin pans. Serve very hot.

(355) DRIED APRICOT BRAN MUFFINS

USING UNCOOKED DRIED APRICOTS

Makes 16 muffins. Oven temperature: 400° F.
Baking time: 25–30 minutes.

1 cup uncooked dried apricots
Boiling water (enough to cover fruit)
3 tablespoons shortening
4 tablespoons granulated sugar
2 tablespoons Grandma's molasses
2 whole fresh eggs, well beaten
1¼ cups sweet cold milk
1½ cups all-bran
1½ cups bread flour, sifted
½ teaspoon salt
4 teaspoons baking powder
⅛ teaspoon baking soda

Cover washed apricots with boiling water and let stand five minutes; drain thoroughly and chop coarsely. Cream shortening with sugar; then blend with molasses; stir in the coarsely chopped apricots and eggs. Pour sweet milk over bran and let stand 5 short minutes, or until moisture is absorbed, then add to fruit mixture and beat briskly to blend thoroughly. Add baking powder, salt and soda to flour and sift together over bran mixture. Stir just enough to dampen flour; turn batter into warm, greased baking pans and bake in a hot oven as directed until muffins are brown and have shrunk from sides of pans. Serve hot with plenty of butter.

(356) DRIED FIG BRAN MUFFINS

Proceed as indicated for recipe No. 355, substituting ¾ cup dried figs, chopped fine, for the apricots. Bake as indicated.

Figs have a rich history merged in a mythical background. Pliny stated that in his time the fig tree under which Romulus and Remus were reared was pointed out as a sacred object. Xerxes of ancient Persia had the famous figs of Attica brought to him daily as a reminder that some day he must conquer the country that grew such a fine fruit.

Franciscan Fathers brought the black fig, which is now known as the Mission or Black Mission, to California in the eighteenth century. It is thought that they got it from Mexico where it was introduced by the Spanish missionaries who followed the Conquistadores. For almost a hundred years no other fig grew in the monastery gardens or on the Spanish ranches of California. Immigrants from Europe and Asiatic lands brought cuttings of other varieties to this country. The first cutting of the Smyrna fig arrived in 1880. The result of its culture is the Calimyrna fig, meaning the Smyrna grown in California.

French settlers brought cuttings from France to Louisiana. The most famous of these is the light green Celeste. So we find a large number of varieties grown throughout the southern and Gulf states. California is the chief producing area for Calimyrna, Adriatic and Mission varieties.

There is one strange thing about fig trees: they never have blossoms on their branches. The flowers are inside the fruit; that is why figs are so full of seeds.

(357) DRIED FIG MUFFINS

Makes 12 large muffins. Oven temperature: 400° F.
Baking time: 25–30 minutes.

Preliminary preparation: Pour boiling water over figs, cover, and let stand 10 minutes; drain, clip the stems and chop fine.

2 cups bread flour, sifted
1 tablespoon baking powder
½ teaspoon salt
2 tablespoons granulated sugar
¾ cup figs, chopped fine
1 cup sweet cold milk
¼ cup shortening, melted
1 whole egg beaten

Add baking powder, salt and sugar to flour and sift together over chopped figs. Combine milk, melted shortening and beaten egg, beat well and pour all at once over flour-fig mixture, which has been well mixed. Stir just enough to moisten flour, then pour batter into warm, greased muffin pans and bake in a hot oven as directed until muffins are delicately brown and leave edges of pans. Serve very hot with plenty of butter.

You may combine equal parts of dried figs and prunes, or use ¼ cup each of chopped figs, chopped prunes or apricots, or dates and chopped nut meats.

Who does not like hot breads for breakfast, luncheon or supper? It's always practical to have a full jar of plain or fruit muffin mix on hand, which will provide hot muffins for several meals. Here is a recipe which will keep a whole week in a good refrigerator:

(358) DRY MUFFIN MIX

NOTE: Store in covered jar in refrigerator until wanted; use part of it and return the remainder to refrigerator for later use.

The following mix will make six dozen 2-inch muffins (about 14 cups).

- 12 cups (3 quarts) bread flour, sifted twice
- 5 tablespoons baking powder
- 1 tablespoon salt
- 1½ cups shortening

Add baking powder and salt to flour and sift into a large mixing bowl; cut in shortening as you would for a pie, using a pastry blender or two knives, until mixture resembles meal. Store in a covered jar in refrigerator.

All you have to do when using is to add milk and egg as for plain muffins (*see* Recipe No. 345). Or you may substitute corn meal for bread flour; or add any kind of fruit or nut meats, following the recipes given.

(359) EGGLESS CORN MUFFINS

Makes 1 dozen muffins. Oven temperature: 375° F.
Baking time: 30 minutes.

- 1½ cups corn meal, sifted
- ¾ cup bread flour, sifted twice
- ¼ cup granulated sugar
- ¾ teaspoon salt
- 1 tablespoon baking powder
- 1 cup sweet cold milk
- 3 tablespoons melted butter

Combine corn meal, flour, sugar, salt and baking powder, and sift into a large mixing bowl. Mix milk and melted butter well and pour all at once over flour mixture. Stir just enough to dampen it and pour batter into warm, buttered muffin pans. Bake in a moderate oven as directed until muffins are brown and leave sides of pans. Serve sizzling hot with butter, jam, marmalade or jelly.

"*. . . May dons the apple blossoms pink and June, the roses red. July in faded overalls, picks cherries for his bread. . . .*"—Old Song

(360) EGGLESS RYE MUFFINS

Makes about 1 dozen muffins. Oven temperature: 400° F.
Baking time: 20–25 minutes.

2¼ cups rye flour, sifted
4 teaspoons baking powder
½ generous teaspoon salt
¼ cup brown or granulated sugar
1 cup sweet cold milk
1½ tablespoons melted butter

Combine the first four ingredients and sift into a large mixing bowl. Mix milk and melted butter well and pour all at once over the flour mixture. Stir just enough to moisten it and pour batter into warm, greased muffin pans. Bake in a hot oven as directed until muffins are brown and leave sides of pans. Serve hot with butter, jam, marmalade, preserves or jelly.

(361) ENGLISH MUFFINS

YEAST METHOD

Makes about 10 muffins. Hot greased griddle.
Baking time: 15 minutes (about).

1 cup scalded milk
2 tablespoons butter
½ generous teaspoon salt
1 teaspoon granulated sugar
¼ cup milk, lukewarm
1 yeast cake
3½ to 4 cups bread flour, sifted

To the scalded milk add butter, salt and sugar. Stir well and let cool to lukewarm. Crumble yeast cake into lukewarm milk, stir until dissolved, then stir into first mixture. Gradually stir in flour (enough to make a thick batter). Turn batter into a greased mixing bowl; brush top with melted shortening; cover and allow to rise over hot (not boiling) water until doubled in bulk. Knead a half minute over lightly floured board; roll batter into ¾-inch thickness; let rise on board, covered with a dry towel, until doubled in bulk and cut into 3-inch rounds. Bake on a hot, greased griddle about 15 minutes, turning often. When cool, split, toast and butter generously. Serve as hot as possible.

(362) FIG, RAISIN AND MOLASSES BRAN MUFFINS

Makes 1 dozen muffins. Oven temperature: 400° F.
Baking time: 25 minutes (about).

2 cups bran
½ cup corn meal
½ cup sifted bread flour
½ generous teaspoon salt
¼ cup brown sugar
2 teaspoons baking powder
½ teaspoon baking soda
¼ cup seedless raisins, parboiled
¼ cup chopped figs, parboiled
1 whole egg, well-beaten
2 tablespoons melted butter or margarine
1 cup sweet cold milk
⅓ cup molasses

Parboil seedless raisins and figs, drain, chop figs and mix well with raisins. Mix bran, corn meal, flour, salt, brown sugar and soda thoroughly, and combine with fruit mixture, tossing well so as to flour every particle of fruit. Mix egg, melted butter or margarine, cold milk and molasses thoroughly and pour all at once over flour-fruit mixture. Stir just enough to dampen it; then pour batter into warm, greased muffin pans. Bake in a hot oven as directed until muffins are brown and leave sides of pans. Serve very hot with plenty of butter.

(363) FLUFFY FRENCH MUFFINS

AFTERNOON TEA MUFFINS

Makes 1 dozen muffins. Oven temperature: 400° F.
Baking time: 20 minutes.

3 tablespoons butter
¼ cup granulated sugar
3 egg yolks, well-beaten
1 cup sweet, rich cold milk
2 cups bread flour, sifted twice
1 tablespoon baking powder
1 scant teaspoon salt
3 egg whites, stiffly beaten

Cream butter until fluffy and lemon-colored; gradually add sugar and cream until well blended, adding alternately the beaten egg yolks; then beat in milk. Add baking powder and salt to flour and sift twice. Turn flour mixture all at once over first mixture and stir (do not beat) gently, folding in the stiffly beaten egg whites gradually. Pour batter into heated, buttered muffin pans and bake in a hot oven as directed until muffins are light and brown and have left sides of pans. Serve very hot with butter, jam, marmalade, jelly, honey or preserves.

Bread was introduced in England by the early Phoenicians who traded it for tin. Rye, however, was used in place of wheat and continued to be the common bread flour in England until the eighteenth century.

(364) FRESH PLUM MUFFINS

Makes 8 large or 12 small muffins. Oven temperature: 400° F. Baking time: 25 minutes.

Preliminary preparation: Wash and cook 4 large plums in boiling water, to which has been added 1 teaspoon lemon juice, for about 10 minutes; drain, cool, remove pits and cut into small pieces. Add to batter at the very last, after flouring them lightly.

Batter:

4 tablespoons melted butter	2¼ cups bread flour, sifted twice
3 tablespoons brown sugar	4 teaspoons baking powder
1¼ cups sweet, warm milk	½ generous teaspoon salt
1 whole egg, well-beaten	Prepared plums

Combine the first four ingredients and blend thoroughly. Add baking powder and salt to the flour, sift together and sift again over the liquid mixture. Stir just enough to moisten flour; then lightly stir in prepared plums. Turn batter into hot, generously buttered muffin pans and bake until muffins are delicately brown and leave sides of pans, in a hot oven as directed. Serve very hot with butter, jam, marmalade, jelly or preserves.

Any kind of plums may be used; but if using green gage plums, have at least half a cup of prepared fruit. You may substitute an equal amount of corn meal (white) for flour.

(365) GINGERBREAD MUFFINS

Makes 1 dozen large muffins. Oven temperature: 350° F. Baking time: 25 minutes.

½ cup each butter and lard mixed	1½ teaspoons baking soda
¼ cup brown sugar	1 teaspoon cinnamon
¼ cup granulated sugar	1 teaspoon ginger
1 whole fresh egg	¾ teaspoon salt
1 cup molasses	1 cup hot water
3 cups bread flour, sifted twice	½ teaspoon ground cloves

Cream thoroughly butter and lard with brown and granulated sugars. Blend in the beaten egg alternately with the molasses. To the flour add baking soda, cinnamon, ginger, salt and ground cloves and sift together over first mixture. Stir in alternately with just enough hot water to dampen the dry mixture. Turn batter into warm, buttered muffin pans (2/3 full) and bake until muffins are brown and leave sides of pans, in a moderately hot oven as directed. Serve very hot with plenty of butter. For afternoon tea, bake in small muffin pans which will yield 1 1/2 dozen muffins.

(366) GINGER CHEESE MOLASSES MUFFINS

VERY APPROPRIATE FOR AFTERNOON TEA OR COFFEE

Makes 1 dozen small muffins. Oven temperature: 375° F.
Baking time: 25–30 minutes.

2 cups Dry Muffin Mix No. 358
1 teaspoon ground ginger
1/2 cup grated *soft* American cheese
1 whole egg, well-beaten
2/3 cup molasses

Add ground ginger, well-mixed with grated soft American cheese, to Dry Muffin Mix and blend thoroughly. Mix well beaten egg and molasses and pour all at once over the dry muffin mix; stir just enough to blend, disregarding the lumps, and fill hot, greased muffin pans 2/3 full. Bake in a moderate oven as directed until brown and muffins leave sides of pans. Serve very hot.

(367) GRAHAM CRACKER RAISIN MUFFINS

Makes about 12 small muffins. Oven temperature: 425° F.
Baking time: 20–25 minutes.

16 graham crackers
2 tablespoons granulated sugar
1/2 scant teaspoon salt
2 tablespoons butter, melted
1/2 cup sweet hot milk
1 whole fresh egg, well-beaten
2 teaspoons baking powder
1/2 cup seedless raisins, parboiled
1/4 cup blanched, shredded almonds

Crumble crackers and add sugar, salt and melted butter. Blend thoroughly and add to hot milk. Blend well. Combine egg, baking powder, seedless raisins (parboiled, drained and dried) and almonds. When cracker mixture is cold, stir egg-fruit combination into it as gently as possible, disregarding the lumps. Turn batter into hot, buttered muffin pans and bake until muffins are brown and leave sides of pans, in a very hot oven as directed. Serve very hot with plenty of butter.

Hospitality, the generous sharing of one's home with friends and the gracious art of entertaining others, has always included the sharing of one's culinary masterpieces with guests. Our mothers and grandmothers knew how to prepare and to serve attractive and appropriate foods, including hot breads of any denomination.

Today the young homemaker is confronted with the problem of serving delicious party dishes on a very restricted budget and in a kitchen no larger than the jam cupboard that used to intrigue her mother and grandmother. The following recipe is very economical:

(368) GRAHAM MOLASSES MUFFINS

Makes 2 dozen small muffins. Oven temperature: 400° F. Baking time: 20–25 minutes.

1 whole fresh egg, well-beaten
¼ cup granulated sugar
½ cup molasses
1 teaspoon salt
½ cup melted shortening
2 cups bread flour, sifted
1 cup unsifted graham flour
1¾ cups sweet cold milk
1 teaspoon baking soda dissolved in
1 tablespoon cold water
½ cup currants or seedless raisins, chopped

Add sugar to the beaten egg and mix gradually with combined molasses, salt and melted shortening, beating well. Add graham flour to bread flour and sift together over molasses mixture; add, while stirring lightly, the combined milk, soda dissolved in cold water and the lightly, floured currants or raisins. Do not beat, but stir gently. Pour batter into hot, greased muffin pans, and bake, until muffins are brown and leave sides of pans, in a hot oven as directed. Serve hot with butter, jam, marmalade, jelly, honey or preserves.

(369) GRAPEFRUIT NUT MUFFINS

Makes 1½ dozen small muffins. Oven temperature: 375° F. Baking time: 25–30 minutes.

Preliminary preparation: Separate sections of medium-sized grapefruit; remove seeds and white membrane as carefully as possible; place in a shallow dish and sprinkle with ¼ cup of granulated sugar. Let stand for 25 minutes in a cool place.

Batter:

- ½ cup butter or margarine
- ¼ cup brown sugar
- ¼ cup granulated sugar
- 2 whole fresh eggs, well-beaten
- 1 cup sweet cold milk
- 3 cups bread flour, sifted twice
- 2 teaspoons baking powder
- 1 scant teaspoon salt
- 1 cup prepared grapefruit sections
- ¼ teaspoon baking soda
- 1 scant cup of chopped nut meats (any kind)

Cream butter or margarine with combined brown and granulated sugars until fluffy alternately with well-beaten eggs. Stir in cold milk; then beat briskly until mixture is thoroughly blended and smooth. Add baking powder and salt to the flour and sift over grapefruit sections sprinkled with soda and lightly floured nut meats. Add all at once to the liquid mixture. Stir just enough to dampen the flour, disregarding the lumps, and pour batter into hot, buttered muffin pans. Bake until muffins are brown and leave sides of pans, in a moderate oven as directed. Serve hot with plenty of butter.

(370) HAM MUFFINS

DELICIOUS AND QUITE SUFFICIENT FOR A LIGHT LUNCHEON

Makes 1 dozen muffins. Oven temperature: 400° F.
Baking time: 25–30 minutes.

NOTE: If ham is salty, reduce salt in recipe.

- 2 cups bread flour, sifted twice
- 4 teaspoons baking powder
- ½ teaspoon (about) salt
- 2 tablespoons sugar
- 1 egg, well-beaten
- 1 cup warm milk
- ¼ cup shortening (preferably ham fat)
- 1½ cups finely chopped cooked ham (lean)

Add baking powder, salt and sugar to the flour and sift together. Combine egg with warm milk, shortening and one cup of the ham. Blend thoroughly and add all at once to the flour mixture. Stir just enough to dampen flour mixture; pour batter into hot, greased muffin pans, and bake in a hot oven as directed until muffins are brown and leave sides of pans. Remove from oven; brush with melted butter and quickly sprinkle the remaining half cup of ham over the muffins. Serve at once.

(371) HONEY NUT BRAN MUFFINS

Makes 16 small muffins. Oven temperature: 400° F.
Baking time: 20–25 minutes.

Preliminary preparation: Place 1 teaspoon strained honey in each muffin pan; add 3 or 4 pieces of nut meats (any kind desired). Set aside.

1¼ cups unsifted all-bran
1 cup scalded sweet milk
1 whole fresh egg, well-beaten
3 tablespoons melted butter
¾ cup bread flour, sifted
1 tablespoon baking powder
2 tablespoons granulated sugar
½ teaspoon salt

Pour scalded milk over unsifted all-bran, stir well and let stand until moisture is almost all absorbed, then stir in beaten egg alternately with melted butter. Add baking powder, granulated sugar and salt to the flour and sift over first mixture. Stir just enough to dampen the flour; then fill prepared muffin pans ⅔ full with batter. Bake until muffins are brown and leave sides of pans, in a hot oven as directed. Remove from oven; let stand a few minutes to cool and set and turn upside down upon a hot platter, removing the pans carefully, so as not to disturb the nuts. The hot honey will drip down the muffins, giving a kind of shadow glaze.

(372) HONEY MUFFINS

Makes 16 small muffins. Oven temperature: 400° F.
Baking time: 20–25 minutes.

The variety of ways in which honey is used in the American home has grown far beyond those known to the ancients, who made use of it in both food and beverage.

1 cup sweet cold milk
½ cup strained honey
½ cup granulated sugar
3 cups bread flour, sifted twice
1½ tablespoons baking powder
¾ teaspoon salt
3 whole fresh eggs, well-beaten
¼ cup melted butter

Combine cold milk, honey and sugar in a mixing bowl and blend thoroughly. Gradually add beaten eggs and beat well. Add baking powder and salt to flour and sift over first mixture. Stir just enough to dampen flour mixture and lastly stir in the melted butter. Pour batter into hot, buttered muffin pans, ⅔ full; and bake in a hot oven as directed until muffins are golden brown and leave sides of pans. Serve sizzling hot with plenty of butter.

(373) HONEY BRAN NUT MUFFINS

Makes 1 dozen large muffins. Oven temperature: 400° F. Baking time: 25–30 minutes.

2 cups bread flour, sifted twice
4 teaspoons baking powder
1 scant teaspoon salt
2 cups all-bran, unsifted
¾ cup broken nut meats (any kind)
1 whole fresh egg, well-beaten
½ cup strained honey
1¼ cups rich sweet milk, cold
1 tablespoon melted butter, cooled

Add baking powder and salt to flour and sift together over mixed all-bran and broken nut meats. Blend thoroughly. Combine egg, strained honey, milk and melted butter; mix well, and pour all at once over dry ingredients. Stir just enough to dampen flour, about 25–30 strokes. Pour batter into hot, buttered muffin pans, ⅔ full, and bake until muffins are brown and separate from sides of pans, in a hot oven as directed. Serve immediately with plenty of butter, jam, jelly, marmalade or preserves.

Bake or buy different breads, serve different breads from meal to meal, put two or three kinds of bread in the same basket, and watch your family sit up and take notice. Thousands of homemakers have, without realizing it, fallen into the "one bread" habit. It is an easy habit to break. Frequent change and a variety of breads heighten appetite and interest in the whole meal.

(374) JOHNNY CAKES I

AMERICAN ORIGINAL RECIPE

Makes about 2 dozen cakes. Oven temperature: 375° F. Baking time: 15–20 minutes.

"Johnny Cake" is said to come from "Journey Cake," so-called because in the days of Daniel Boone no man left the settlements without his sack of corn meal, the prime ingredient of "Johnny Cake."

This is a sophisticated recipe; but for the authentic Johnny Cake a griddle is used and cakes are baked until browned on both sides and eaten with an abundance of sweet butter.

Rich Johnny Cakes baked in buttered iron skillet:

2 cups water-ground white corn meal
1 teaspoon salt
Boiling water
Cold sweet milk
2 whole fresh eggs, well-beaten
2 tablespoons butter

Combine white corn meal with salt, mixing well; pour onto it rapidly boiling water to make a thick paste and when slightly cooled, thin with enough milk beaten with the eggs to give a smooth, soft pancake consistency. Lastly stir in melted, cooled butter. Pour batter into a very hot, well greased skillet all at once and bake in a moderate oven as directed until brown on top. Bubbles form similarly to those appearing on pancakes made on a hot griddle.

To serve: Turn the big cake upside down upon a hot, round platter, spread generously with butter and serve in wedges at once.

For the original recipe, bake upon a hot, generously greased griddle until brown on both sides. You may omit the eggs, but cakes will be less tender. Down South the batter is dropped upon a greased baking sheet by spoonfuls and baked in a hot oven (400° F.) for about 15 to 20 minutes, until brown.

Another method in great favor in the Middle West is the following:

(375) JOHNNY CAKES II

Serves 12. Oven temperature: 425° F.
Baking time: 25 minutes.

1 cup water-ground white corn meal
¼ cup bread flour, sifted
1½ teaspoons baking powder
½ teaspoon salt
2 whole eggs, well-beaten
½ cup sweet milk
4 tablespoons melted butter

Mix and sift dry ingredients. Combine beaten eggs and milk and pour over dry ingredients; stir until smooth and lastly stir in melted butter. Pour batter into a well greased baking pan, about ¾ of an inch in thickness, and bake in a hot oven as directed. Serve hot, cut in wedges, with plenty of butter.

(376) LEMON JUICE MUFFINS

Makes about 10 small muffins. Oven temperature: 375° F.
Baking time: 20 minutes.

½ cup shortening
½ cup granulated sugar
2 egg yolks, lightly beaten
¼ cup lemon juice, unstrained
Grated rind of half lemon
1 cup bread flour, sifted
1 teaspoon baking powder
½ teaspoon salt
2 egg whites, stiffly beaten

Cream shortening and sugar; add beaten egg yolks and beat briskly until smooth and fluffy, adding while going along the lemon juice. Add baking powder and salt to flour and sift over the first mixture; stir lightly; fold in egg whites stiffly beaten with grated lemon rind. Turn batter into hot, greased small muffin pans, ½ to ⅔ full, and bake as directed until muffins puff up brown and slightly leave sides of muffin pans. Serve very hot with butter.

(377) LOGANBERRY MUFFINS

Makes 10 small muffins. Oven temperature: 400° F.
Baking time: 20–25 minutes.

You may use loganberries, strawberries, raspberries or anv kind of berries, fresh or canned.

2 tablespoons butter
5 tablespoons granulated sugar
1 whole egg, well beaten
½ cup sweet milk
1¼ cups bread flour, sifted twice
2 teaspoons baking powder
¾ cup canned or fresh loganberries
½ teaspoon salt

Cream butter and granulated sugar until smooth and fluffy; add well-beaten egg and beat briskly until well blended. Add baking powder and salt to flour and sift over washed (if fresh) or drained (if canned) loganberries. Blend well and pour all at once over the first mixture, stirring just enough to dampen flour. Fill greased small muffin pans ⅔ full and bake in a hot oven as directed. Serve hot with plenty of butter.

"Alas, what things I dearly love—Pies, fresh breads, puddings and preserves."—Eugene Field

(378) MAPLE SYRUP MUFFINS

Makes 1 dozen small muffins. Oven temperature: 400° F.
Baking time: 20 minutes.

2 cups bread flour, sifted twice
4 teaspoons baking powder
½ teaspoon salt
1 whole fresh egg, well-beaten
½ cup sweet cold milk
½ cup maple syrup
¼ cup melted butter

Sift the flour, baking powder and salt together into mixing bowl. Combine egg, cold milk and maple syrup and beat well. Pour liquid mixture over flour and stir just enough to dampen it. Lastly stir in melted butter. Fill hot, greased, small muffin pans ⅔ full and bake in a hot oven as directed until muffins are brown and leave sides of pans. Serve hot with plenty of butter, jam, jelly, marmalade or preserves.

(379) MARMALADE CORN MEAL MUFFINS

APPROPRIATE FOR BREAKFAST, LUNCHEON, DINNER OR SUPPER

Makes 2 dozen small muffins. Oven temperature: 400° F.
Baking time: about 25 minutes.

Any kind of marmalade may be used, so long as it is not too dry. The marmalade provides the sweetening in the recipe so that no sugar is necessary.

1½ cups bread flour, sifted twice
2½ teaspoons baking powder
1 scant teaspoon salt
⅔ cup yellow corn meal (unsifted)
2 whole fresh eggs, well-beaten
1 cup any marmalade
5 tablespoons melted butter

Add baking powder and salt to the flour and sift into a mixing bowl, in which is the unsifted yellow corn meal. Blend thoroughly. Combine eggs and marmalade, blend thoroughly and pour all at once over flour mixture. Stir just enough to dampen evenly and lastly stir in the melted butter. Pour batter into small greased, hot muffin pans, ⅔ full, and bake in a hot oven as directed until muffins are brown and leave sides of pans. Serve hot with butter.

Half the battle in successful catering to the family is the realization that the eye as well as the tongue must be considered. The secret of happy, successful budget making is to spend for those things you want and need most; and stop leaks for the things that you don't particularly need or like. Delicious, well-balanced meals can be served regularly at small cost if you know your brands and values. How money is spent for food, rather than how much, is the important thing in assuring adequate diets.

Speaking of budgets, this English word comes from the old French *bougette* meaning "a wallet." So if you want to take care of your wallet, follow these *don'ts:*

Don't be bashful about asking the price per pound and the weight.

Don't accept a six-ounce package for a half-pound. Remember there are sixteen ounces in a pound.

Don't fail to read price signs carefully. Some dealers have a quaint habit of marking a price sign in large letters and then putting a small "three-quarters" down in the corner.

Don't permit a merchant to put his hand on the scale or "steady" it with a knife.

Don't permit the weigher to take the merchandise from the scale until the pointer has come to a full stop.

Don't neglect to look in the pan before your merchandise is placed on the scale. Dishonest dealers often allow an inconspicuous bit of weighted matter to remain in the pan.

Don't chase after bargains offered at a ridiculously low price. You can't expect an honest merchant to sell below cost.

Your budget is one of the paths to your goal of financial security. Be faithful and conscientious in keeping within your budget and you'll have no regrets.

If you want to make muffins and have no milk, no eggs and no butter, here is a recipe that will fill the bill:

(380) MILKLESS, EGGLESS, BUTTERLESS MUFFINS

Makes 2 dozen small muffins. Oven temperature: 400° F.
Baking time: 45 minutes.

4 cups bread flour, sifted twice
2 tablespoons baking powder
1 scant tablespoon granulated sugar
¾ teaspoon salt
1 generous teaspoon caraway seeds
2½ cups cold water

Add baking powder, sugar and salt to the flour and sift into a mixing bowl; stir in slightly toasted caraway seeds. Pour in the cold water all at once and stir just enough to dampen the flour. Spoon batter into hot, oiled muffin pans up to 2/3 full and bake in a hot oven as directed, until muffins are brown and leave sides of pans. Serve hot with jam, jelly, marmalade or preserves.

(381) MISSOURI PUMPKIN MUFFINS

Makes about 1 dozen muffins. Oven temperature: 400° F.
Baking time: 25–30 minutes.

1 cup bread flour, sifted
1 tablespoon baking powder
3/4 teaspoon salt
1/2 teaspoon baking soda
1 cup corn meal (yellow)
1/2 cup canned or cooked pumpkin, sieved
1 whole fresh egg, well-beaten
1/2 cup molasses
1 cup sour milk or buttermilk
1/2 cup lard, melted, cooled

Add baking powder, salt and baking soda to flour and sift together over yellow corn meal; mix well. Combine pumpkin, beaten egg, molasses and sour milk and pour all at once over flour mixture; then stir just enough to dampen it evenly, adding the lard while stirring. Pour batter into hot, greased muffin pans to 2/3 full and bake in a hot oven as directed until muffins are brown and leave sides of pans. Serve hot with plenty of butter.

(382) MOLASSES CHEESE MUFFINS

Makes 2 dozen small or 15 large muffins. Oven temperature: 400° F.
Baking time: 25 minutes.

The advantage of these muffins is that they may be eaten hot or cold. They afford a nourishing afternoon snack or an after theater bite.

1/2 cup yellow corn meal, sifted
3/4 cup bread flour, sifted
2 1/2 teaspoons baking powder
1/2 generous teaspoon salt
1 cup grated American cheese
1 teaspoon chopped green pepper
1 whole fresh egg, well-beaten
1/2 tablespoon molasses
2 tablespoons butter, melted
1 teaspoon chopped parsley
1 teaspoon chopped chives
3/4 teaspoon grated onion
3/4 cup sweet cold milk

Combine the first four ingredients and sift into a large mixing bowl; stir in cheese, blending well. Combine green pepper, egg, molasses, butter, parsley, chives, grated onion and milk and mix thoroughly. Pour all at once over flour mixture, stirring just enough to dampen it, disregarding lumps. Pour batter into hot, greased muffin pans, up to 2/3 full, and bake in a hot oven as directed until muffins are brown and leave sides of pans. If eaten hot, serve with plenty of butter; if cold, serve with jam, jelly, marmalade, honey or preserves.

(383) NEW ORLEANS SASSAFRAS MUFFINS

Makes 1 dozen large muffins. Oven temperature: 400° F. Baking time: 25 minutes.

- 4 tablespoons granulated sugar
- 3 tablespoons butter
- 1 whole fresh egg, well-beaten
- 1/2 cup thin cream
- 1/2 cup sassafras tea, cold
- 1 cup bread flour, sifted twice
- 1 cup whole wheat flour, unsifted
- 4 teaspoons baking powder
- 1/2 teaspoon salt
- 1/4 cup chopped pecan nuts

Cream butter; gradually add sugar and cream until mixture is smooth and fluffy. Add egg, creaming and beating alternately until mixture is smooth and well blended. Combine thin cream (undiluted, evaporated milk may be used) and strong sassafras tea and blend well; then beat into creamed mixture until smooth. Add baking powder and salt to sifted bread flour and sift over mixed whole wheat and chopped pecan meats. Add flour mixture to liquid mixture and stir just enough to dampen it. Pour batter into large, hot, greased muffin pans and bake in a hot oven as directed until muffins are brown and leave sides of pans. Serve hot with plenty of butter, jam, jelly, marmalade, honey, maple syrup or preserves.

NOTE: Substitute chopped parboiled figs, dates, raisins, or any kind of dried fruit for nuts if desired, or combine equal parts of nut meats and any kind of dried fruit.

(384) OATMEAL MUFFINS I

Makes 9 large muffins. Oven temperature: 400° F. Baking time: 25 minutes.

The difference between regular oats and quick cooking oats or oatmeal is very little. Both are made from the same grain. The latter variety differs from the larger, or "regular" flakes only in size, thickness and cooking time required. The flakes in the regular style are rolled from whole kernels, while the quick cooking flakes are made from kernels which are first steel-cut, then rolled, and sometimes pre-cooked or oven-toasted.

½ cup, cold cooked oatmeal	1¼ cups bread flour, sifted
1 cup cold sweet milk	1 teaspoon granulated sugar
1 whole fresh egg, well-beaten	½ teaspoon salt
¼ cup melted shortening	1 tablespoon baking powder

9 pecan halves

Mix cooked oatmeal with cold milk, stirring until free from lumps. Add egg, alternately with melted shortening and stir. Add granulated sugar, salt and baking powder to flour and sift over liquid mixture. Stir just enough to dampen the flour. Pour batter into large, hot, greased muffin pans, press a pecan half into center of each muffin. Bake in a hot oven as directed until muffins are delicately brown and leave sides of pans.

(385) OATMEAL MUFFINS II

Makes 1½ dozen small 2-inch muffins. Oven temperature: 400° F. Baking time: 25 minutes (about).

1 cup quick cooking oatmeal	1 teaspoon salt
1 cup sweet milk, heated	¼ cup brown sugar, packed solid
2 cups bread flour, sifted	1 whole egg, well-beaten
4 teaspoons baking powder	¼ cup melted shortening

1 cup lukewarm milk (about)

Pour first cup of milk over oatmeal, let stand ten minutes. Brush 18 muffin pans (2 inches in diameter at top) with melted shortening. Add baking powder and salt to flour and sift together into mixing bowl; stir in the brown sugar thoroughly. Combine egg, melted shortening and ¾ of remaining cup of lukewarm milk and beat briskly to blend. Reserve remaining ¼ cup of milk to use if needed. Pour liquid mixture over flour mixture, alternately adding the oatmeal mixture. Stir only until flour is dampened. Spoon batter into greased muffin pans to ⅔ full, working quickly, and bake in a hot oven as directed until muffins are brown. It may be necessary to add the remaining ¼ cup lukewarm milk to batter, if too thick.

(386) OATMEAL MUFFINS III

OVERNIGHT METHOD

Makes 1 dozen large muffins. Oven temperature: 400° F. Baking time: 25–30 minutes.

1⅓ cups sour milk
2 cups rolled oats
1 cup bread flour, sifted
¾ teaspoon salt
1 scant teaspoon baking soda
2 tablespoons granulated sugar
¼ cup shortening, melted
1 whole fresh egg, well-beaten

Pour sour milk over rolled oats and let stand overnight.

Next day when ready to bake sift flour once; add baking soda, sugar and salt, and sift together into mixing bowl. Stir in melted shortening, alternately with beaten egg and prepared rolled oats, stirring just enough to dampen it evenly. Turn batter into greased muffin pans and bake in a hot oven as directed or until muffins are delicately brown. Serve hot with jam, jelly, marmalade, honey, maple syrup or molasses.

(387) ORANGE JUICE BRAN MUFFINS

Makes 1 dozen muffins. Oven temperature: 400° F. Baking time: 25 long minutes.

1¼ cups bread flour, sifted twice
2 teaspoons baking powder
¼ teaspoon baking soda
½ generous teaspoon salt
⅓ cup fine granulated sugar
1 whole fresh egg, well beaten with
6 tablespoons unstrained orange juice, and
1 tablespoon grated orange rind, and
¼ teaspoon grated lemon rind, and
6 tablespoons unsifted all-bran, and
3 tablespoons sweet milk

To the flour add baking powder, baking soda, salt and fine granulated sugar (or equal parts each of granulated and brown sugar) and sift into mixing bowl. Add the remaining ingredients, thoroughly mixed, and stir just enough to dampen flour mixture, disregarding lumps, if any. Turn batter into hot, buttered muffin pans, up to ⅔ full, and bake in a hot oven as directed until muffins are delicately brown and have left sides of pans. Serve hot with plenty of butter and your favorite jam, jelly, marmalade or preserves.

(388) ORANGE JUICE CORN MEAL MUFFINS

Makes 1½ dozen small tea muffins. Oven temperature: 400° F.
Baking time: 25 minutes.

¼ cup butter
½ cup granulated sugar
1 whole fresh egg, well-beaten
Grated rind of a small orange
½ generous teaspoon grated lemon rind
1 cup canned or fresh orange juice, unstrained
1 cup unsifted corn meal (yellow)
1 cup bread flour, sifted
2 teaspoons baking powder
¼ teaspoon baking soda
½ generous teaspoon salt

Cream butter and sugar until fluffy and smooth and beat in the egg until light; mix well the orange, lemon rind and orange juice and stir it into the corn meal. Add to creamed mixture. To the flour add baking powder, baking soda and salt and sift together over the first mixture. Stir just enough to dampen flour. Pour batter into hot, buttered muffin pans and bake in a hot oven as directed until delicately brown and muffins leave sides of muffin pans. Serve very hot with plenty of butter and your favorite marmalade.

(389) ORANGE MARMALADE MUFFINS

Makes 1 dozen muffins. Oven temperature: 400° F.
Baking time: 25–30 minutes.

2 cups bread flour, sifted
1 tablespoon baking powder
½ teaspoon salt (generous)
4 tablespoons granulated sugar
1 whole fresh egg, well-beaten with
½ teaspoon grated lemon rind
1 cup sweet cold milk
5 tablespoons butter, melted
Orange marmalade

Add baking powder, salt and granulated sugar to flour and sift into mixing bowl. Combine the remaining ingredients, except marmalade, and pour all at once over flour mixture. Stir just enough to dampen it evenly. Pour batter into hot, buttered muffin pans, filling half full; place a teaspoon of orange marmalade on top of batter then add enough batter to fill pans ⅔ full. Bake in a hot oven as directed until muffins are delicately browned. Serve hot with plenty of butter.

Have you ever thought of dropping a bright blob of jelly on top of your muffins just before you popped the pan into the oven? Better still, you might add a sprinkling of grated cheese over the tops of the muffins first, then place a teaspoonful of clear currant jelly very lightly in the center of the batter. After the muffins have baked in a hot oven as directed, the jelly will have seeped gently down into the centers, leaving just a bright crusting of color to sparkle on top. Try it sometime!

Digging in the ruins of an Indian kiva near Glorietta, New Mexico, scientists recently discovered corn meal believed to be five centuries old.

(390) ORANGE ALMOND FLUFFY TEA MUFFINS

Makes 1 dozen muffins. Oven temperature: 400° F.
Baking time: 20–25 minutes.

- 1/3 cup butter
- 2/3 cup granulated sugar
- 3/4 teaspoon grated orange rind
- 1/3 teaspoon grated lemon rind
- 2 egg yolks, unbeaten
- 1 3/4 cups bread flour, sifted twice
- 1 tablespoon baking powder
- 1/2 generous teaspoon salt
- 4 tablespoons unstrained orange juice
- 2 egg whites, stiffly beaten
- 1/3 cup blanched, toasted, cooled almonds, shredded

Cream butter until fluffy and smooth; gradually add sugar and continue creaming, adding egg yolks, one at a time, beating and creaming alternately until thoroughly blended. While going along, add the combined grated orange and lemon rinds. To the flour add baking powder and salt and sift over creamed mixture. Stir just enough to dampen flour, adding while stirring the unstrained orange juice. Lastly fold in the stiffly beaten egg whites. Spoon batter into hot, buttered muffin pans, filling half-full; spread a scant half-teaspoon of prepared almonds over each muffin and cover with more batter, filling pans 2/3 full. Bake in a hot oven as directed until muffins are uniformly brown and leave sides of muffin pans. Serve hot with your favorite jam, jelly, marmalade, honey or preserves. No additional butter is needed on account of the richness of these tea muffins.

You may serve them cold after icing with your favorite frosting.

(391) ORANGE PECAN WHOLE WHEAT MUFFINS

Makes 1 dozen large muffins. Oven temperature: 375° F.
Baking time: 20 minutes.

- 1/2 cup butter or other shortening
- 3/4 scant cup granulated sugar
- 2 egg yolks, well-beaten
- 1 cup bread flour, sifted twice
- 3/4 cup unsifted whole wheat flour
- 1 tablespoon baking powder
- 3/4 teaspoon salt
- 1/4 cup sweet cold milk
- 1/2 cup unstrained orange juice
- 1/2 teaspoon grated orange rind
- 1/4 teaspoon grated lemon rind
- 2 egg whites, stiffly beaten
- 3/4 cup chopped pecan meats

Cream butter and blend in sugar thoroughly. Add beaten egg yolks, stirring until well blended. To the flour add baking powder and salt and sift over unsifted whole wheat flour. Mix thoroughly. Combine milk and orange juice with grated orange and lemon rinds and blend well. Pour liquid mixture over dry mixture, to which has been added the chopped pecans and stir just enough to dampen flour, gradually folding in the stiffly beaten egg whites. Pour batter into hot, buttered muffin pans, up to 2/3 full and bake in a moderate oven as directed until muffins are brown and separate from pans. Serve very hot with butter.

(392) ORANGE RAISIN MUFFINS

Makes 1 dozen muffins. Oven temperature: 400° F.
Baking time: 25 minutes.

- 2 cups bread flour, sifted twice
- 3/4 teaspoon baking soda
- 1/2 teaspoon salt
- 1/3 cup granulated sugar
- 1/2 cup seedless raisins, parboiled, dried, chopped
- 1 whole fresh egg, well-beaten
- 1/3 cup unstrained orange juice
- 1/2 teaspoon grated orange rind
- 1/4 teaspoon grated lemon rind
- 2/3 cup buttermilk or sour milk
- 1/3 cup melted shortening

Add baking soda, salt and granulated sugar to the flour and sift over prepared raisins. Mix well. Combine egg, orange juice, grated rinds and buttermilk or sour milk and beat until well blended. Pour liquid mixture over flour mixture and stir just enough to moisten evenly, adding meantime the melted shortening. Pour batter into hot, greased muffin pans and bake in a hot oven as directed until muffins are delicately brown. Serve hot with butter.

(393) OZARK MOUNTAINS SWEET POTATO MUFFINS

YEAST METHOD

Makes 2 dozen muffins. Oven temperature: 375° F.
Baking time: 20–25 minutes.

2 cups cooked mashed sweet potatoes
2 tablespoons brown sugar
1 teaspoon salt
¼ teaspoon cinnamon
⅓ cup lard
A generous pinch of powdered thyme
1 whole fresh egg, well beaten
1 yeast cake
½ cup warm water
3½ cups bread flour, sifted (about)

Mix cold potato with brown sugar, salt, spices and lard, then stir in the egg. Dissolve yeast in warm water and add to potato mixture. Gradually stir in flour until dough is stiff enough to be kneaded. Turn onto a lightly floured board; knead until smooth, satiny and does not stick, working in more flour if needed. Place dough into a greased bowl, brush top with lard lightly, cover with a clean, dry, light cloth and let rise over hot water (not boiling) until doubled in bulk. Punch down, and drop by spoonfuls into generously greased (using lard) muffin pans. Brush tops with melted lard, cover and let rise until doubled in bulk (second rising), and bake in a moderate oven as directed until muffins are delicately brown and have left sides of pans. Serve hot with butter, jam, jelly, marmalade, preserves, honey, maple syrup or molasses.

(394) PARSLEY MUFFINS

Makes 16 small muffins. Oven temperature: 400° F.
Baking time: 25–30 minutes.

In the following recipe you may substitute one cup of bran, corn meal or whole wheat for one cup of bread flour, if desired.

2 cups bread flour, sifted twice
1 tablespoon baking powder
½ teaspoon salt
2 tablespoons finely minced parsley
1 whole fresh egg, well-beaten
1 cup sweet cold milk
3 tablespoons melted butter

To the flour add baking powder and salt and sift into mixing bowl; stir in the finely chopped parsley. Pour over the flour mixture, all at once, the combined egg, milk and melted shortening. Pour batter into hot greased muffin pans up to ⅔ full and bake in a hot oven as directed until muffins are brown and leave edges of pans. Serve very hot with plenty of butter.

(395) PEANUT BUTTER MUFFINS

Makes 1 dozen muffins. Oven temperature: 400° F.
Baking time: 20 to 25 minutes.

⅓ cup peanut butter
¼ cup granulated sugar
1 whole fresh egg, well-beaten
1 cup sweet tepid milk
1 cup unsifted all-bran
1 cup bread flour, sifted
1 tablespoon baking powder
½ teaspoon salt

Cream peanut butter and granulated sugar together until smooth and fluffy; beat in the egg and milk. When thoroughly mixed, stir in the all-bran. Let stand until moisture is almost taken up. Add all at once the flour sifted with baking powder and salt, and mix well. Turn batter into hot, greased muffin pans up to ⅔ full, and bake in a hot oven as directed until muffins leave sides of pans. Serve hot with butter, jam, jelly, marmalade, honey, maple syrup or molasses.

(396) PEANUT BUTTER DATE MUFFINS

Makes 12 small muffins. Oven temperature: 400° F.
Baking time: 25 minutes.

¼ cup peanut butter
1 tablespoon butter
¼ cup granulated sugar
1 whole fresh egg, well-beaten
1 cup sweet milk, tepid
1¾ cups bread flour, sifted twice
2 teaspoons baking powder
¼ teaspoon baking soda
½ teaspoon salt
¾ cup pitted, chopped dates

Cream peanut butter and butter together until well blended; gradually add sugar and beat until smooth and fluffy. Now beat in the egg mixed with tepid milk until smooth. To the flour add baking powder, baking soda and salt and sift over prepared dates. Mix well and add all at once to liquid mixture, stirring just enough to moisten flour. Pour batter into hot, greased muffin pans, up to ⅔ full, and bake in a hot oven as directed. Serve hot with jam, jelly, marmalade or preserves.

Some of the dried fruits of the date palm have a natural sugar content as high as 80 per cent, combined with other carbohydrates, proteins and fats, and they figure as one of the world's most important staple foods; yet we know them best as an occasional treat for the children and the practical confectioner, with unconscious irony, dresses them up in jackets of sugar—quite literally "sweets to the sweet."

Eat your dates "as is" from the clean, tidy packages or put them into many good dishes from appetizer to dessert.

Superior date culture is responsible for these delicacies. In March and April, pollen is taken from the male palm and dusted by hand onto the female bloom. Later the bunches are thinned to provide greater growth in the remaining fruit. The great bunches of ripening dates are covered with bags as a protection from birds and rain. As the dates mellow, they are picked one by one. Each is a selected date, thoroughly cleaned before packing.

(397) PECAN WHOLE WHEAT MUFFINS

Makes 1 dozen medium muffins. Oven temperature: 400° F. Baking time: 25 minutes.

- 1 cup unsifted whole wheat flour
- 1 cup bread flour, sifted
- 4 teaspoons baking powder
- ¾ teaspoon salt
- 1 whole fresh egg, well-beaten
- 3 tablespoons brown sugar
- 1 cup tepid sweet milk
- ¼ cup shortening, melted, slightly cooled
- ½ cup chopped pecan meats

Combine flour, baking powder and salt; sift over unsifted whole wheat flour and blend well with pecan meats. Mix egg, brown sugar, tepid sweet milk and melted shortening, beating well, and pour all at once over flour mixture, stirring just enough to dampen it. Then pour batter into hot, greased muffin pans to ⅔ full and bake in a hot oven as directed. Serve hot with butter.

(398) PINEAPPLE JUICE BRAN MUFFINS

Makes 1 dozen muffins. Oven temperature: 400° F. Baking time: 25 minutes.

- 1 cup bread flour, sifted twice
- 1 teaspoon baking soda
- ¾ teaspoon salt
- 1 cup graham flour, unsifted
- 1 cup all-bran, unsifted
- ½ cup molasses
- 1 cup canned unsweetened pineapple juice
- 2 tablespoons melted shortening
- ¼ cup sweet milk

Combine flour, soda, salt and sift over mixed graham and all-bran; mix thoroughly. Combine all the remaining ingredients and beat briskly until blended and smooth. Pour all at once over flour mixture stirring just enough to dampen it; fill hot, greased muffin pans to 2/3 full and bake in a hot oven as directed until delicately brown. Serve hot with plenty of butter, jam, jelly, marmalade or preserves.

(399) POTATO FLOUR MUFFINS

ENGLISH METHOD

Makes about 10 muffins. Oven temperature: 400° F.
Baking time: 20 minutes (about).

In this fine recipe only potato flour is used, and enough additional moisture is furnished by a very little cold water and strictly fresh eggs.

- 3 egg yolks, beaten until creamy
- 1/2 scant teaspoon salt
- 1 tablespoon granulated sugar
- 1/2 generous cup potato flour, sifted
- 1 generous teaspoon baking powder
- 3 egg whites, stiffly beaten

Combine creamed egg yolks, salt, sugar and cold water and beat briskly. Add baking powder to potato flour and sift over first mixture. Stir just enough to dampen evenly, gradually folding in the stiffly beaten egg whites (about 25 strokes). Pour batter into hot, buttered muffin pans and bake in a hot oven as directed until muffins are brown and leave sides of pans. Serve hot with plenty of butter, jam, jelly, marmalade, honey, maple syrup, molasses or preserves.

(400) PRUNE MUFFINS

Makes 18 small muffins. Oven temperature: 400° F.
Baking time: 20–25 minutes.

During the winter season, it's good to make the most of the dried fruits. Apricots, prunes, peaches, pears, whole figs and the apples may bolster up a sagging menu-plan with real deliciousness and economy. All of these products are now greatly improved, being more tender and flavorful than in years past.

Indeed one of the first things which the average homemaker must do is to cast aside her ideas that dried fruits, dried prunes in particular, must be soaked overnight or for several hours. Nothing is further from the truth. The newer packs are so tenderized in their process of manufacture that any long soaking is out, and this holds for apricots, peaches and pears as well. They do need to be carefully washed, however, since the light fruits especially are usually sulphured.

Quick cooking is the key-word in preparing these fruits, which may be eaten directly out of the box, or "out of hand" as they say, like confections. In the first place they are tender and since they are wrapped in waxed paper, in closed containers, they come to the pantry shelf with that all-important attribute of cleanliness and freshness. Quite different, indeed, from the old days when a large box of dried fruit stood on the grocer's shelf, open to dust and exposed to air which daily dried it more.

How shall these tender, dried fruits be prepared? Wash, immerse in boiling water and boil gently for 5 to 10 minutes—never longer—depending on the use to which they are to be put. Nor is dried fruit confined to the breakfast table. Too long has the "boarding-house prune" been a stock joke.

3 cups bread flour, sifted
4 teaspoons baking powder
¼ teaspoon nutmeg
¼ generous teaspoon salt
½ cup lard
1 scant cup brown sugar
2 whole fresh eggs, well beaten
1¾ cups sweet cold milk
1½ cups cooked prunes, cut into small pieces

Add baking powder, salt and nutmeg to flour and sift together. Cream lard until fluffy; gradually add brown sugar and cream until thoroughly blended; beat in the eggs alternately with milk. Pour liquid mixture over dry mixture all at once and stir just enough to dampen evenly. Add prunes last. Turn batter into hot, greased muffin pans (if large ones there will be 9 muffins); fill them ⅔ full and bake in a hot oven as directed. Serve with plenty of butter and very hot.

Prunes are a good source of iron and they also provide some calcium—two minerals that you have to check carefully in planning your meals each day.

Prunes also contribute some vitamin B_1 and some vitamin A to the diet; they are low-cost fruit, full of flavor and easy to keep on hand. Yes, it is safe to eat uncooked prunes and other dried fruit. It's safe but foolish. Cooking renders them more palatable and relieves the digestive organs of a good deal of work.

(401) PRUNE MUFFINS

BUTTERMILK METHOD

Makes 18 small muffins. Oven temperature: 400° F.
Baking time: 25 minutes.

1 cup uncooked tenderized prunes
5 tablespoons shortening
3 tablespoons granulated sugar
½ teaspoon salt
¼ teaspoon nutmeg
2 whole fresh eggs, well-beaten
1 cup buttermilk or sour milk (tepid)
½ teaspoon baking soda
3 cups bread flour, sifted
1 tablespoon baking powder

Scald prunes and let stand 5 minutes in boiling water. Drain and chop fine. Cream shortening until fluffy; add sugar gradually and cream until well blended, adding while going along the beaten eggs. Beat in the tepid buttermilk or sour milk until smooth. Add baking powder and baking soda to flour and sift over cut prunes. Mix well; then pour all at once over liquid mixture. Stir just enough to dampen flour. Spoon batter into hot, greased muffin pans, filling them ⅔ full, and bake in a hot oven as directed until muffins are leaving sides of muffin pans. Serve hot with butter.

(402) PUMPKIN CORN MEAL MOLASSES MUFFINS

Makes 18 small muffins. Oven temperature: 400° F.
Baking time: 25–30 minutes.

2 cups bread flour, sifted twice
2 tablespoons baking powder
1¾ teaspoons salt
¾ teaspoon baking soda
2 cups yellow corn meal, unsifted
1 cup sieved, canned or cooked pumpkin
2 whole fresh eggs, well-beaten
1 cup molasses
2 cups buttermilk or sour milk
¾ cup melted shortening

To the flour add baking powder, salt and soda and sift yellow corn meal. Blend thoroughly. Combine sieved pumpkin, beaten eggs, molasses and buttermilk and beat well. Pour all at once over flour mixture and stir just enough to dampen it evenly, adding while stirring the melted shortening. Fill hot, greased muffin pans ⅔ full, and bake in a hot oven as directed until muffins are brown and separate from sides of pans. Serve hot with butter.

(403) RICE MUFFINS

Makes 1 dozen muffins. Oven temperature: 400° F.
Baking time: 25 minutes.

1 cup cold boiled rice
1 cup sweet cold milk
2 whole fresh eggs, well-beaten
5 tablespoons shortening, melted
1½ cups bread flour, sifted
2 teaspoons granulated sugar
¼ scant teaspoon nutmeg
½ teaspoon salt
1 tablespoon baking powder

Combine rice, milk, eggs and melted shortening and blend well. Add sugar, nutmeg, salt and baking powder and sift over liquid mixture. Stir just enough to dampen flour evenly. Fill hot, greased muffin pans ⅔ full and bake in a hot oven as directed until muffins are brown and leave sides of pans. Serve hot with butter.

Children are taught never to leave bread beside their plates at the end of a meal. Finishing one's bread is an important requisite of the French table. Under no circumstances is bread thrown away like a common thing. To toss a crust into the gutter would be a sacrilege. You have never seen bread in French waste pans. It is either crumbled, fed to chickens or to birds, or it may, if unfit to be eaten, be burned as you would burn an ancient flag.

(404) RICE RYE MUFFINS

Makes 1 dozen muffins. Oven temperature: 400° F.
Baking time: 25 minutes.

In the following recipe water is used instead of milk, and rice flour instead of boiled rice. The quantity of baking powder is not a misprint; the large amount is required to prevent sogginess of the bread. No egg is used.

1⅓ cups rye flour, sifted
⅔ cup rice flour, sifted
2 tablespoons baking powder
½ cup granulated sugar
½ teaspoon salt
1⅓ cups cold water
2 tablespoons melted butter

Combine dry ingredients and sift into cold water. Stir just enough to dampen flour mixture, adding melted butter while stirring. Fill hot, greased muffin pans, ⅔ full, and bake in a hot oven as directed until muffins are brown and separate from sides of pans. Serve hot or cold.

(405) RICE WHOLE WHEAT MUFFINS

Makes 1 dozen muffins. Oven temperature: 400° F.
Baking time: 20–25 minutes.

1 cup boiled rice, cold
1 cup sweet cold milk
2 whole fresh eggs, well-beaten
⅓ scant cup melted butter
1 cup unsifted whole wheat flour
1 cup bread flour, sifted
2 tablespoons granulated sugar
1 tablespoon baking powder
½ teaspoon salt

Combine the first four ingredients in order named and beat briskly. Add sugar, baking powder and salt to flour and sift over unsifted whole wheat flour. Blend well and add all at once to liquid mixture. Stir just enough to dampen flour evenly. Fill hot, buttered muffin pans ⅔ full and bake in a hot oven as directed until muffins are brown and leave sides of pans. Serve hot with butter.

(406) SALLY LUNN MUFFINS

Makes 18 small muffins. Oven temperature: 400° F.
Baking time: 25–30 minutes.

Toward the end of the eighteenth century in Bath, England, a young girl, Sally Lunn, sold her buns, muffins and home-made breads night and morning on the city streets. They were so delicious that they were named after her and the recipe came to America soon afterwards.

½ cup lard or butter or half and half
½ cup granulated sugar
3 whole fresh eggs, well-beaten
1 cup rich sweet milk, cold
2 cups bread flour, sifted twice
4 teaspoons baking powder
½ generous teaspoon salt

Cream shortening until smooth and fluffy. Gradually add sugar and cream until thoroughly blended. Combine eggs with milk and beat gradually into creamed mixture. To the flour add baking powder and salt and sift over first mixture; stir just enough to dampen evenly. Fill hot, buttered *(not greased)* muffin pans ⅔ full, and bake in a hot oven as directed until muffins are delicately brown and separate easily from sides of pans. Serve at once with butter, jam, jelly, marmalade or preserves.

(407) SALLY LUNN SAUSAGE MUFFINS

Proceed as indicated above (No. 406). Fill muffin pans ⅔ full; stand up in the center of each muffin half a small partly cooked pork sausage and bake as directed. A fine winter afternoon snack, or may be used for buffet, Sunday supper, etc., instead of sandwiches.

(408) SOUR CREAM, DATE, WHOLE WHEAT MUFFINS

Makes 18 small muffins. Oven temperature: 400° F.
Baking time: 25–30 minutes.

2 whole fresh eggs, well-beaten with
2 tablespoons sweet milk
1 cup heavy sour cream
⅓ cup dark brown sugar
1 cup bread flour, sifted twice
2½ teaspoons baking powder
¼ teaspoon baking soda
¾ teaspoon salt
1 cup unsifted whole wheat flour
1 cup pitted, chopped dates

Combine the first four ingredients and beat briskly to blend and dissolve brown sugar. To the flour add baking powder, soda and salt and sift over mixed whole wheat and chopped dates. Mix thoroughly and pour all at once over the first mixture. Stir just enough to dampen evenly; spoon the batter into hot, greased muffin pans, up to ⅔ full, and bake as directed until muffins are firm and brown and easily leave sides of pans. Serve hot with plenty of butter, jam, jelly, marmalade or preserves.

Dried apricots, figs or any other kind of dried fruit may be substituted for dates if desired.

(409) SPICED BREAD CRUMB MOLASSES MUFFINS

Makes 1 dozen medium-sized muffins. Oven temperature: 425° F.
Baking time: 30–35 minutes.

½ cup dried, sieved bread crumbs
1 cup sweet cold milk
1 whole fresh egg, slightly beaten
½ cup molasses
2 tablespoons lard
1½ cups bread flour, sifted
½ teaspoon salt
½ teaspoon baking soda
½ teaspoon cinnamon
½ scant teaspoon nutmeg
2 teaspoons baking soda
½ scant teaspoon cloves

Add crumbs to cold milk and allow to stand 3 minutes. Add slightly beaten egg, molasses and melted lard. Mix and sift dry ingredients and add all at once to first mixture, stirring just enough to dampen evenly; spoon the batter into hot, greased muffin pans, up to 2/3 full, and bake in a hot oven as directed until muffins are firm and brown and easily leave sides of pans. Serve hot with plenty of butter, jam, jelly, marmalade or preserves.

(410) SPICED BRAN MOLASSES MUFFINS

Makes 12 large muffins. Oven temperature: 375° F.
Baking time: 25–30 minutes.

3/4 cup sweet milk, scalded
3/4 cup unsifted all-bran
1/2 cup dark molasses
1 whole fresh egg, well-beaten
2 tablespoons melted lard
1 1/2 cups bread flour, sifted twice
1 tablespoon (3 teasp.) baking powder
1/2 scant teaspoon salt
1/2 scant teaspoon baking soda
1/2 teaspoon cinnamon
1/2 teaspoon nutmeg
1/2 teaspoon cloves
1/3 cup seedless raisins, parboiled, drained, chopped

Pour scalded milk over unsifted all-bran and let stand 5 minutes, then beat in molasses, egg and melted lard. Combine all remaining ingredients, except raisins and sift over milk mixture, reserving a little to flour raisins. Stir just enough to dampen evenly, adding floured raisins. Fill large muffin pans 2/3 full and bake in a moderate oven as directed until muffins are firm and brown on top and separate easily from sides of pans. Serve hot with butter, jam, jelly, marmalade, preserves, honey, maple syrup or molasses.

Should you desire small muffins, fill 18 pans and bake 20 minutes at same temperature. These muffins are very appropriate for luncheon with a bland creamed fish, meat or poultry. Dates, figs or any kind of tenderized dried fruit may be substituted for raisins and whole wheat flour (unsifted) may be used instead of all-bran.

That Cinderella of the garden patch, the herb, blossoms as the belle of the culinary ball—for there is a definite herb and spice revival under way in the land and the modern hostess who wishes to keep her table on a par with that of her neighbors will do well to abandon the "sin" of forgetting to season and learn the uses of a few simple herbs and spices.

What is good food?—good bread? The touch-stone of good food among all nationalities is *flavor*. But when to natural flavor and to hidden flavors we add a third type, namely, herbs and spices proportioned by the hand of the skilled cook, then we have that perfect blend which we call "sophisticated flavor."

It is a known fact that Creole cooking takes more time than money. Most Creole recipes follow the French trait for economy. Nothing in the kitchen goes to waste. The seasonings used—spices, herbs and so on—are on every cupboard shelf. Economy lies in the perfect blending of a number of well-cooked simple ingredients producing such hearty dishes as Okra Gumbo, a meal in itself.

Addicted as Americans are to hot breads—whether for breakfast, luncheon or dinner—they must surely introduce guests from over the ocean and from below the Rio Grande way down to Argentina to the "rollicking bun" or the gay "Sally Lunn." But perhaps more typical of American food are Indian gems or muffins, concocted of the yellow corn meal and molasses. A newcomer is the muffin flavored with spices and tomato juice. Here's how:

(411) SPICED TOMATO JUICE MUFFINS

CREOLE METHOD

Makes about 2 dozen small muffins. Oven temperature: 400° F. Baking time: 20–25 minutes.

3 tablespoons melted lard
¾ cup granulated sugar
1 whole fresh egg, well beaten
1 can of tomato juice, tepid
1¾ cups bread flour, sifted twice
½ scant teaspoon nutmeg
2 teaspoons baking powder
½ scant teaspoon baking soda
½ scant teaspoon salt
¾ teaspoon cinnamon
¼ teaspoon cloves

Mix lard, sugar, egg and tomato juice and beat briskly until well blended. To the flour add all the remaining ingredients and sift twice to insure a thorough blending; the last time sift over the first mixture. Stir just enough to moisten evenly. Pour batter into hot buttered muffin pans and bake in a hot oven as directed until muffins are firm and brown on top and separate from sides of pans. Serve hot with almost any hot or cold dish.

Any kind of canned or bottled fruit or soup may be used in this manner. If sweet fruit juice is used, the sweetening ingredient should be reduced accordingly. If desired, substitute half all-bran (unsifted) for half bread flour, or use 1 cup of bread flour, sifted of course, and ¾ cup unsifted whole wheat flour; or 1 cup of bread flour and ¾ cup corn meal, yellow or white.

Tomatoes seem to have originated in Central or South America. The name itself comes from an Aztec word, *Zitomate.* The plant was grown by Indians in Mexico and Peru long before the time of Columbus. It was taken from Peru to Italy, where it met with favor. There it was called "golden apple" and "love apple," but by 1695 the name "tomato" had come into general use. When the cultivation of the plant first started in northern Europe, the fruit was considered poisonous and was grown more for curiosity and ornament than for use for food. The English herbalist Gerard wrote in 1597 that "love apples" were eaten abroad, prepared and boiled with pepper, salt, and oil and also a sauce, but he reported that they "yield very little nourishment to the bodie, and the same naught and corrupt. . . ."

(412) SPICY CAKE CRUMB MOLASSES MUFFINS

Proceed exactly as directed for No. 409, substituting cake crumbs for dried, sieved bread crumbs, and using only ⅓ cup of molasses instead of ½ cup. Bake as directed.

Like England's rich plum pudding, famous grown,
The muffin reigns in realms beyond his own,
Through foreign latitudes his power extends,
And only terminates where eating ends.

—*Old Christmas Plum Pudding Song*

SPINACH

References to spinach date back to the fourteenth century. Apparently it was first cultivated by the Arabs, by whom it was introduced into North Africa and thence taken to Spain by the Moors. During the Middle Ages it was grown in monastic gardens and eaten by monks on fast days. It is curious that its name is nearly the same in many languages. In French it is *épinard,* in German, *spinat,* in Italian, *spinace,* in Spanish, *espinaca,* in Arabic, *hispane.*

The first mention of the cultivation of spinach in America was in 1806, but it has become in recent years the most widely grown pot-herb in the country. Its importance as a food is reflected by the increase in commercial acreage since people have become vitamin and mineral conscious. No product in the food world—certainly no vegetable—has received more publicity than spinach. It has been praised for its food value and maligned for its flavor by those who happen to dislike it. It has achieved real fame by being made the subject of cartoons and vaudeville jokes.

To all goddesses of the kitchen I bequeath with pleasure this successful attempt at the rescue of spinach—the ill-fated vegetable so long held in contempt by men, children and ex-children, in various zones where it has been growing, apparently without irrigation, since the dawn of time. Spinach muffins, once introduced into American homes, will quell the anti-spinach bloc now so active throughout the entire nation.

Canned or freshly cooked spinach may be used.

(413) SPINACH NUTMEG MUFFINS

Makes 1 dozen muffins. Oven temperature: 425° F.
Baking time: 15 minutes.

1 lb. canned or cooked fresh spinach drained, and put through food chopper
2 egg yolks, well-beaten
½ teaspoon nutmeg
4 tablespoons melted butter
1 teaspoon baking powder
A pinch baking soda
½ scant teaspoon salt
¾ cup bread flour, sifted twice
2 egg whites, stiffly beaten

Combine spinach, egg yolks beaten with nutmeg, and melted butter and blend thoroughly. Return to food chopper to insure thorough blending. Add baking powder, baking soda and salt to flour and sift over spinach mixture. Stir just enough to dampen evenly, folding in the stiffly beaten egg whites. Spoon batter into hot, buttered muffin pans up to ⅔ full to allow for expansion, and bake in a very hot oven as directed until tops are brown and firm and muffins separate easily from pans. Serve very hot with almost any kind of fish, meat, poultry or vegetables, especially the creamed ones; or for luncheon serve topped with a rich tomato, mushroom or cheese sauce.

(414) SUNDAY BREAKFAST TOASTED BREAD MUFFINS

Makes 1 dozen muffins. Oven temperature: 400° F.
Baking time: 25 minutes.

2 cups broken toasted bread
2 cups scalded sweet milk
1 generous tablespoon melted butter
2 egg yolks, well-beaten
½ generous teaspoon cinnamon
1½ cups bread flour, sifted twice
¾ teaspoon salt
2 teaspoons baking powder
2 egg whites, stiffly beaten
12 pecan halves, toasted, cooled

Pour scalded milk over broken toast and allow to stand for 25 minutes or until cold, stirring occasionally. Stir in melted butter, alternately with egg yolks re-beaten with cinnamon. To the flour add salt and baking powder and sift over toast-bread mixture; stirring just enough to moisten evenly. Lastly fold in the stiffly beaten egg whites. Spoon batter into hot, buttered muffin pans, ⅔ full; bump muffin pans on the table to settle; press a pecan half in center of each one, and bake in a hot oven as directed until muffins are firm and brown and easily separate from pans. Serve very hot with plenty of butter. Also appropriate for afternoon tea or supper.

(415) SUNDAY TEA MUFFINETTES

VERY RICH AND SWEET

Makes 18 small muffins. Oven temperature: 400° F.
Baking time: 20–25 minutes.

2 cups bread flour, sifted twice
4 tablespoons granulated sugar
¾ teaspoon salt
4 teaspoons baking powder
1 whole fresh egg, well-beaten
1 cup sweet milk, tepid
4 tablespoons melted butter

Mix and sift together flour, granulated sugar, salt and baking powder. Combine egg, tepid milk and melted butter and beat briskly until thoroughly blended. Pour all at once over flour mixture and stir just enough to dampen flour evenly. Fill hot, buttered muffin pans half full; press into each muffin the following ingredients:

½ teaspoon of your favorite jam or marmalade
A bit of peanut butter
1 steamed, cooled, pitted date
½ preserved fig or prune

Cover filling with more batter, up to ⅔, and bake in a hot oven as directed until muffins are firm and brown and separate easily from pans. Serve hot or warm without any butter.

You may, if desired, substitute cooked ham, chicken, tongue, chicken livers, etc.. for fruit and marmalade, operating exactly as directed above.

(416) SWEET CINNAMON HONEY MUFFINS

Makes 9 large or 15 small muffins. Oven temperature: 400° F. Baking time: 25–30 minutes.

1 whole fresh egg, well-beaten
1 cup sour milk, tepid
4 tablespoons butter, melted
2 cups bread flour, sifted twice
1 teaspoon baking powder
½ teaspoon baking soda
½ teaspoon salt
3 tablespoons granulated sugar
1 generous tablespoon cinnamon
Strained honey

Mix beaten egg, milk and butter and beat well. Combine flour and all remaining ingredients, except honey, and sift over egg-milk-butter mixture. Stir just enough to dampen evenly. Fill hot, buttered muffin pans ⅔ full and bake in a hot oven as directed until muffins are brown and firm and separate easily from pans. Remove from oven, place muffins on a hot platter and pour over each hot muffin a generous tablespoon of strained honey. Serve hot.

You may omit honey and serve with plenty of butter, jam, jelly, marmalade or preserves.

(417) SWEET POTATO CLOVER LEAF MUFFINS

YEAST METHOD

Makes about 2 dozen muffins. Oven temperature: 350–375° F. Baking time: 25 minutes.

1½ cups scalded milk
2 tablespoons granulated sugar
1½ tablespoons butter
2 cakes compressed yeast
1 teaspoon salt
4½ cups (about) bread flour, sifted
1 cup mashed sweet potatoes
3 tablespoons lukewarm water
Butter for brushing, melted

Add granulated sugar, butter, salt and mashed sweet potatoes to scalded milk, and stir until smooth. Dissolve yeast cakes in lukewarm water and add to first mixture. Gradually beat in flour, adding just enough to make a soft dough. Knead until smooth, elastic and not sticky. Place dough in large, well-greased mixing bowl; brush top with melted butter, cover and set over hot water in a warm place to rise until double in bulk. Punch dough down, toss upon a lightly floured board; shape dough into marble-shaped balls. Place three, scarcely touching, in greased muffin pans; cover and allow to rise over hot water until almost double in bulk, then bake in a moderately hot oven as directed, brushing tops with butter after 10 minutes of baking. This brushing operation should be done very quickly. When taken from oven, brush again with butter and serve hot with plenty of butter.

(418) WALNUT BRAN MUFFINS

Proceed as indicated for No. 335, adding ½ cup floured chopped walnut meats to the sifted flour and mixing well before stirring into bran mixture. Serve very hot with butter.

(419) WHOLE WHEAT MOLASSES MUFFINS

Proceed as indicated for No. 368, substituting one cup whole wheat (unsifted) for graham flour.

During many of the Saint Days in Yugoslavia, house guests are served as a good luck token a raw wheat or barley called "zhito."

Gingerbread

. . . If odours, or if taste worke satisfaction, they are both so soveraigne in plants, and so comfortable, that no confection of the Apothecaries can equall their excellent vertue. But these delights are in the outwards senses: the principall delight is in the minde, singularly enriched with the knowledge of the visible things, setting foorth to us the invisible workmanship of Almightie God. . . .

—*Gerard, Preface to the "Herball" (1597)*

GINGERBREAD

(420) GINGER

Ginger is regarded as the mystery plant by the Sherlock Holmeses of the botanical world, for none of them can tell for a certainty just where this important spice plant had its origin. Some say Asia, some say Brazil, but however indefinite its background, its popularity as a seasoner has been known from prehistoric times. Today, in a cold, thirst-quenching drink such as ginger ale or in appetizing and aromatic gingerbread, this spice is among the most useful and widely employed seasoners. *To ginger* means to put spirit into and that is exactly what the ginger root does to anything with which it comes in contact, be it candy or preserves. Wise old kings of the Orient nibbled ginger properly boiled in honey. Great-grandmama kept a little stone jar of candied ginger on the pantry shelf. Today we are losing track of the fine practice of "gingering" our food.

Add a few snips of candied or preserved ginger to a fruit cocktail, to a salad—zingo! Every taste bud snaps into strict attention. Like that little cup of black coffee, the morning eye-opener, ginger has the power to waken you. Put the bite of ginger into a soufflé, either the ground ginger or preserved, and the dish begins to sing.

Marco Polo, that adventurous Venetian traveler, is said to be the first Westerner who actually saw a ginger plant. Both he and a long line of his ancestors were familiar with its pungent flavor for ginger was featured in Roman, Greek and Arabian cooking even in the ages when its source of supply was kept a secret by the crafty traders. During the Middle Ages ginger was second only to pepper in general culinary and medicinal use and ran pepper a close second, too, in value.

Ginger is made from the roots of a tuberous plant, now known to flourish in many countries, and belongs to the iris family. It is found in such widely separated countries as China and our own neighbor-island of Jamaica in the West Indies. The roots grow into a shape that roughly resembles the palm and fingers and are therefore commonly referred to as "hands." When the roots are dug up, they are placed in baskets and when enough baskets are ready, the handles are looped through ropes held by two men, one on each end. They yank the ropes, something like a tug-of-war, for two hours a day for two days. This shakes up the roots and removes scales and other adhering matters. Then the ginger roots are sun-dried for eight days, after which they get another good shaking and another two-day drying. By this time they are ready for export.

For culinary use, ginger is cracked into small pieces and put through a refining process that reduces it to powder. Small cracked pieces are also used in making the assortments of spices used for pickling. Preserved ginger (in syrup) and crystallized ginger are classified as confections and have achieved a degree of popularity in this country. They are highly prized in the Orient, especially in China, whence so much of the ginger root comes. Chinese and Indian curry powders nearly always contain ground ginger root. Native doctors still use ginger in several forms for many ailments. They recommend chewing a piece of the root to relieve a toothache, a ginger plaster to dull a headache and as a tea to stimulate the gastro-intestinal tract.

The "Gingerbread Man" is a veritable Methuselah, for gingerbread is perhaps the oldest of all sweet cakes, tracing its lineage to those dim and distant ages when men were learning to "live to eat instead of eating to live." Egypt knew it when the Pyramids were young, but it really was a Greek of the island of Rhodes, who discovered it, and that was about the time, 2800 B.C., when, according to authorities, Sgen-Nung, Chinese Emperor, was compiling his huge cookery book.

In fact Rhodes became so famous for its "melitates," as they called their gingerbread—perhaps because of its golden color—that all the countries around the Mediterranean, and even those beyond the Pillars of Hercules, were crowding the port for their supplies of the delicious cakes. Besides their gingerbread, of flour, honey (honey of Hymettus, perhaps) and of course ginger, the Rhodians invented nougat, which they made of dried currants and almonds, a confection that, like the "melitate," has enjoyed undying popularity.

In England, even before the Norman Conquest, it was, as already said, next to pepper, the most common of all spices. By the thirteenth century gingerbread was a well-established food. Chaucer, who gives us many pointers upon the foods and feasts of his day, tells us that "they sette hym Roiall spicerye and Gyngerbreed. . . ."

Old English spelling was elastic; apparently any spelling sufficed, it was the gingerbread that was important. So it appears as gingibretum . . . gensbrede . . . gengerbread, and also as gynberbrede. Strange as it may seem, it often was made without any ginger at all. According to a recipe from an old Harleian manuscript:

Take a quart of hony and seethe yt and skeme yt clene; take Saffroun, poudir Pepir, and throw ther-on; take grated Brede and make yt so styff that yt wol be cut into strips; then take poudir Cinnamon and strew ther-on y-now; then make yt square, lyke as thou wolt slyce yt; then when thou slycest hyt, caste Box leaves above, y-styked ther-on Cloves, and if thou wyll have yt Red, coloure yt with Saunderys y-now (Saunderys was red Sandalwood).

It was about this time that people began making gingerbread into fanciful shapes—men, birds, animals, and the letters of the alphabet. Sometimes these were given a coating of gilt; hence the expression: "Take the gilt off the gingerbread." All through the sixteenth and well into the eighteenth century it was a common article of food, much favored as a gift of honor by workmen to their patrons and also by youngsters to their elders, as a symbol of their love and respect.

If it was to be a gingerbread of "honor," then it frequently measured as much as three feet across and weighed more than 150 pounds, according to the nature of the occasion being celebrated, whether a birth, baptism, wedding, anniversary, or even a funeral feast; each had its own individual and characteristic gingerbread pattern. But it was in Russia they really "went to town" in the matter of the "honor" gingerbreads. It is said that at the time of the birth of Peter the Great, the Czar, his father, was presented with more than 120 loaves, the largest being the arms of the City of Moscow. Two, of a hundred pounds each, represented the double Imperial Eagle; while another reproduced the Kremlin with all its turrets, surrounded by many horsemen. Besides, there were dozens of ducks,

GINGERBREAD RECIPES

(421) AFTERNOON TEA (OR DESSERT) GINGERBREAD

Serves 6 generously. Oven temperature: 350° F.
Baking time: 35 long minutes.

½ cup butter	1 teaspoon cinnamon
1 cup brown sugar	½ generous teaspoon ginger
½ cup molasses	¼ teaspoon allspice
1 cup sweet milk	¼ teaspoon cloves
1 whole fresh egg, well beaten	¼ teaspoon salt (generous)
2½ cups bread flour, sifted	1 teaspoon baking powder

1 teaspoon baking soda

Cream butter until fluffy; gradually add brown sugar and continue creaming until thoroughly blended. Stir in molasses mixed with sweet milk and beaten egg until thoroughly blended. To the flour add all the remaining ingredients and sift twice, the last time over the first mixture. Beat all together for three or four minutes until smooth. Pour into a generously greased, shallow, square pan and bake in a moderate oven as directed. Serve with whipped cream or chocolate sauce for dessert; or hot with butter for afternoon tea.

(422) APPLE SAUCE GINGERBREAD

Serves 6 generously. Oven temperature: 350° F.
Baking time: 40–45 minutes.

6 tablespoons butter or lard	1 teaspoon baking soda
⅓ cup light brown sugar	¼ teaspoon cloves
1 whole fresh egg, well beaten	1 teaspoon cinnamon
½ cup molasses	½ teaspoon ginger
1¾ cups bread flour, sifted	½ scant teaspoon salt

⅔ cup strained thick apple sauce

Cream butter or lard until fluffy; gradually add light brown sugar and continue creaming until mixture is light and creamy. Combine egg and molasses and add to creamed mixture. To the flour add the remaining dry ingredients and sift twice, the last time over creamed mixture. Beat briskly, gradually adding the apple sauce. Mixture should be very smooth and thoroughly blended. Turn into a greased square, shallow pan, and bake in a moderate oven as directed. Serve warm. Top may be spread with softened cream cheese.

(423) CHOCOLATE GINGERBREAD

Serves 6 generously. Oven temperature: 350° F.
Baking time: 40 minutes.

½ cup shortening	1 generous teaspoon baking soda
½ cup light brown sugar	½ teaspoon baking powder
1 whole egg, well beaten	½ teaspoon salt
2½ squares melted chocolate	¾ teaspoon cinnamon
1 cup molasses	1 generous teaspoon ginger
2½ cups bread flour, sifted	⅓ teaspoon cloves

¾ cup hot water

Cream shortening until fluffy; gradually add brown sugar, alternately with beaten egg, and beat until light. Blend together melted chocolate and molasses and add to first mixture, stirring well. To the flour add all the remaining dry ingredients and sift twice, the last time over the first mixture. Blend well, adding gradually the hot water and beating rather briskly for a minute or so. Pour into a shallow, greased, square pan and bake in a moderate oven as directed, until firm in center. Serve warm or cold.

(424) CROWN OF GINGERBREAD

Serves 6 generously. Oven temperature: 350° F.
Baking time: 35–40 minutes.

A fine de luxe afternoon tea or dessert. The center may be filled with cut-up fruit, whipped cream, or almost any kind of soft, creamy dessert.

Add 2 well-beaten whole eggs to ¾ cup of brown sugar, stirred into ¾ cup of dark molasses and beat briskly for one long minute. Then stir in ¾ cup of melted lard. Blend well. Sift 2½ cups of bread flour, measure, add 2 teaspoons baking powder, 2 teaspoons ginger, 1½ teaspoons cinnamon, ½ teaspoon cloves, ½ teaspoon nutmeg, ½ generous teaspoon baking soda and ½ teaspoon salt and sift three times, the last time over the first mixture, alternately with 1 cup of boiling water. Beat to a smooth batter. Pour batter into a greased ring mold and bake in a moderate oven as directed until firm in center. Serve either warm or cold, depending on filling in center. This gingerbread is spicy, very rich and delicious.

It is known that George Washington was very fond of molasses, and that a great deal of the fine cookery in his Mount Vernon kitchen was effected with the aid of this most delightful sweetening. There is still extant a letter from Washington in which he requests a captain of a sloop in the West Indies to "Bring me—one HHD. of best molasses, one ditto of best rum, one barrel of lymes if good and cheap —two small ditto of mixed sweetmeats, about 5 lbs. each. . . ." Evidently the Father of this Country had a notable "sweet tooth."

(425) GINGERBREAD FARMER METHOD

Serves 6 generously. Oven temperature: 350° F.
Baking time: 25 minutes (about).

2⅓ cups bread flour, sifted twice
½ generous teaspoon salt
2 teaspoons ginger
¼ teaspoon cinnamon
¼ teaspoon nutmeg
1 cup rich sweet milk
1 tablespoon mild vinegar
1½ teaspoons baking soda
1 cup molasses
¼ cup melted butter

To the flour add salt, ginger, cinnamon and nutmeg and sift together. Combine milk, vinegar, baking soda, molasses and melted butter and blend well. Combine dry ingredients and liquid ingredients and beat briskly until smooth and free from lumps. Pour batter into a generously greased shallow pan and bake in a moderate oven as directed until firm in center. Serve warm or cold.

(426) GINGERBREAD CUP CAKES

Makes 8 cakes. Oven temperature: 350° F.
Baking time: 35 minutes.

This recipe makes light, fluffy, gingerbread cup cakes which may be frosted with vanilla or chocolate icing. Very appropriate for afternoon tea or dessert.

2 whole fresh eggs, well beaten
¾ cup brown sugar
¾ cup molasses
¾ cup melted shortening
2½ cups bread flour, sifted twice
2 teaspoons baking powder
2 teaspoons ginger
1½ teaspoons ground cinnamon
½ teaspoon cloves
½ teaspoon nutmeg
½ teaspoon baking soda
½ generous teaspoon salt
1 cup boiling water

Combine eggs, sugar, molasses and melted shortening and blend thoroughly. To the flour add the remaining dry ingredients; sift over the first mixture and beat briskly, adding the boiling water gradually. Fill greased muffin pans ⅔ full and bake in a moderate oven as directed until center is firm. Cool before icing.

(427) HONEY NUT GINGERBREAD

Serves 6 generously. Oven temperature: 350° F.
Baking time: 45 minutes.

⅓ cup shortening
1 cup honey
2 whole fresh eggs, well beaten
1 cup lukewarm water
2 cups bread flour, sifted
½ teaspoon baking soda
1 teaspoon ground ginger
1 teaspoon ground cinnamon
½ generous teaspoon salt
1 cup chopped nut meats
2 teaspoons baking powder

Combine shortening, honey and cream until thoroughly blended; then beat in eggs and gradually add lukewarm water. To the flour add baking powder, soda, ginger, cinnamon and salt and sift over chopped nut meats. Mix well and add to the first mixture, stirring again. (You may add equal parts of nut meats and seedless raisins. In such case, plump the raisins, that is parboil them until puffed and drain thoroughly.) Pour batter into a greased, floured, square, shallow pan and bake in a moderate oven as directed until firm in center. Serve immediately.

Important: You may substitute strained fruit juice for water. In such case, reduce the amount of honey or whatever kind of sugar is used.

(428) HOOSIER GINGERBREAD

ALSO CALLED "DATE GINGERBREAD"

Serves 6 generously. Oven temperature: 350° F.
Baking time: 25 minutes.

1 cup granulated sugar
½ cup boiling orange juice
2½ cups bread flour, sifted twice
1 teaspoon baking soda
1½ teaspoons ground ginger
½ teaspoon ground nutmeg
½ teaspoon salt
½ generous cup chopped, pitted dates
¼ cup melted lard

Combine sugar and boiling orange juice and blend thoroughly. To the flour add soda, ginger, nutmeg and salt and sift twice, the last sifting over chopped dates. Mix well and add to first mixture alternately with melted lard (or ½ lard and ½ butter). Beat briskly until smooth, pour batter into a shallow, greased, square pan, and bake in a moderate oven as directed until firm in center. Serve warm or cold. Boiling water may be substituted for boiling orange juice.

It is in France that gingerbread comes to its peak perfection under the name of *pain d'épices,* "spiced bread." Dijon, in Burgundy is the center of its making, in almost any shape; animals and human shapes vie with each other around Christmas to provide the grotesque figures which in the oven will puff, huff and stretch out their legs or their tails and wings.

(429) LOAF GINGERBREAD

Makes 2 loaves. Oven temperature: 350° F.
Baking time: 50–55 minutes.

4 cups bread flour, sifted twice
2 teaspoons baking soda
1½ teaspoons ground ginger
¾ teaspoon salt
1½ teaspoons ground cinnamon
½ teaspoon ground cloves
¼ teaspoon nutmeg
1 cup melted butter or other shortening
1 cup buttermilk or sour milk
1 cup molasses
1 cup honey
4 whole fresh eggs, well-beaten

To the flour add the next 6 ingredients listed and sift together. Combine butter, buttermilk or sour milk, molasses, honey and eggs and beat briskly until thoroughly blended. Add this liquid mixture to the dry mixture gradually, beating well so that there are no lumps.

Pour batter into 2 generously greased bread pans and bake in a moderate oven as directed until center is firm. Cool before slicing.

Christmas Loaf Gingerbread is made in the same way, plus 1/4 cup each of chopped nut meats, seedless raisins and mixed chopped candied fruit, added to the flour mixture.

(430) OLD-FASHIONED GINGERBREAD

CALLED ALSO "HOT WATER GINGERBREAD"

Serves 6 generously. Oven temperature: 350° F.
Baking time: 35 minutes.

- 1/2 cup brown sugar
- 1/4 cup butter
- 1/4 cup lard
- 1 egg, well-beaten
- 1 cup New Orleans molasses
- 2 1/2 cups bread flour, sifted
- 1 1/2 teaspoons baking soda
- 1 generous teaspoon ginger
- 1 teaspoon cinnamon
- 1/2 teaspoon salt
- 1/2 teaspoon cloves
- 1 cup hot water

Cream sugar and mixed fats together until fluffy; add egg and beat briskly to blend thoroughly. Gradually add molasses, mixing well. To the flour add all the remaining ingredients, except hot water, and sift together over first mixture. Mix thoroughly, adding the hot water gradually. Then beat for 1 or 2 minutes or until batter is smooth and free from lumps. Turn batter into a square, shallow, greased pan, and bake in a moderate oven as directed until firm in center. Cut into squares and serve warm or cold.

(431) ORANGE GINGERBREAD

Serves 10 generously. Oven temperature: 350° F.
Baking time: 30 minutes.

If this gingerbread is served as a dessert for afternoon tea or on special occasions, you may frost it with orange icing; but if served for breakfast or for an afternoon snack for the children, it is rich enough plain.

- 1 cup butter, melted
- 1 cup molasses
- 1 cup brown sugar
- 2 whole fresh eggs, well-beaten
- 1 cup orange juice
- 1 teaspoon grated orange rind
- 1/4 generous teaspoon grated lemon rind
- 4 cups bread flour, sifted twice
- 1 teaspoon baking soda
- 1/2 teaspoon nutmeg
- 1/2 teaspoon cinnamon
- 1 generous teaspoon ginger
- 1/4 teaspoon cloves
- 1/2 teaspoon salt (generous)

Into top of double boiler put the first seven ingredients; place over hot water and heat well. *Do not let it boil.* To the flour add all the remaining ingredients and sift together. Combine liquid and dry ingredients and beat briskly until thoroughly blended and free from lumps. Turn batter into a greased, paper-lined, large pan (or two pans), and bake in a moderate oven as directed until center is firm. If icing is used, let bread cool thoroughly before spreading it. If not iced, cut into squares and serve either warm or cold.

Should you desire a hard, crunchy gingerbread, spread any gingerbread batter very thin in the greased pan and bake as usual. Cut while very hot and let cool.

(432) PINEAPPLE UPSIDE-DOWN GINGERBREAD

Serves 8 generously. Oven temperature: 350° F.
Baking time: 40–45 minutes.

First operation:

Grease an oblong cake pan, about 2 inches deep, using 3 tablespoons of butter; then sprinkle with brown sugar. Now line the bottom of the pan with drained pineapple sticks or halved pineapple slices. Set aside.

Second operation:

2/3 cup hot pineapple juice
2/3 cup molasses
3 tablespoons brown sugar
1 whole egg, well beaten
1/3 cup butter or lard, melted
2 1/2 cups bread flour, sifted twice
1 1/2 teaspoons baking powder
1 teaspoon baking soda
3/4 teaspoon salt
1 teaspoon powdered cinnamon
1 generous teaspoon powdered ginger
1/2 teaspoon powdered cloves

Combine the first five ingredients and blend thoroughly. To the flour add the remaining ingredients and sift twice, the last sifting over the first mixture. Mix well; then beat vigorously to obtain a smooth batter. Pour very carefully over the prepared pineapple in the pan. Bake in a moderate oven as directed until firm to the touch. Remove from oven, turn bread upside down to cool, let stand a few minutes before lifting the pan and serve warm with plain whipped cream.

Any kind of fruit may be used in this way.

In some sections of Bulgaria, bread-making is much too social a task to be conducted in the privacy of the home kitchen. Instead, the homemakers set their ovens up on the streets where they may talk.

Popovers

THE GOAL

. . . For this, I nightly touch my toes,
And roll with vigor on the floor,
And turn a most disdainful nose
At every cake and candy store,
And gallop daily for the train
Like Johnstown of the famous races . . .
That some day I'll be slim as rain
Yet bulge in all the proper places. . . .
—*Frances M. Miller*

POPOVERS

(433) A FEW GOOD HINTS

Popovers, feather light, are a treat whenever served, for breakfast, luncheon, dinner, afternoon tea or evening party. And they are versatile, too.

From a standard recipe can be made many variations. But popovers, even more than biscuits and muffins, must be so hot that they burn your fingers when you break them open. They must be baked long enough to have a deep brown crust and be thick enough to prevent falling when they are removed from the pans. The inside, however, should not be too dry lest the flavor be entirely lost.

Those are the standards for real popovers. The question is how to meet them. First of all, follow the recipe and *sift your flour before measuring.* After the batter is mixed, make sure that it is about the consistency of heavy cream. Not all eggs are of the same size; if they are small, your batter may be a little too thick. In this case add a little more milk.

Heavy iron muffin pans are best for popovers and gem pans are very handy. In order to promote the rising of the batter, the pans should be heated before they are generously greased. The full time for baking given in the recipe should be allowed and it will *not hurt* the popovers to stand in the closed oven for five or even 10 minutes after it is turned off.

A very hot oven is required at the start; then when the batter is set, the temperature is lowered and the baking continued for an average of 40–45 minutes all together.

For large popovers to be used as patty shells and filled with a creamed mixture, it's better to use individual custard cups.

Next to iron pans and gem pans, earthenware pans, custard cups or glass pans are better than agate or tin for baking popovers. The use of earthenware or glass pans gives the bottom of popovers a glazed appearance.

Popovers will always double when baked; so when pouring batter, fill only ⅔ full *or less.*

Although popovers have a reputation for trickiness, they are the easiest of hot breads to make and bake. The heat of the oven has a great deal to do with success or failure. It must be hot enough to generate the steam that leavens the batter. Once the popovers have risen and popped, the heat is reduced (unless otherwise indicated) to moderate to drive out all moisture and bake the little breads until they hold their shape.

The reason why the cold batter is poured into sizzling hot iron, custard cups or glass cups is to provide more steam than cold cups. No baking powder or soda is needed in any popover recipe; steam is the raising agent.

Never cover hot baked popovers with a napkin lest they become soggy.

Yorkshire pudding is made from the same mixture. Always make a slit in each popover to allow steam to escape.

POPOVER RECIPES

(434) CHEESE POPOVERS I

Makes 8 popovers. Oven temperature: 450–475° then 350° F.
Baking time: 40–45 minutes.

1 cup bread flour, sifted twice
½ scant teaspoon salt
1 whole fresh egg, well-beaten
1 cup sweet milk
1 cup grated cheese
A few grains of cayenne pepper

Make pans very hot; then grease or butter generously. Sift salt with flour. Combine egg with milk, mix well and gradually add to the flour mixture, beating briskly until smooth. Add cayenne pepper. Into each greased hot pan, spoon 1 tablespoon of batter, then 1 teaspoon grated cheese, then 1 tablespoon of batter, and again cheese, repeating until pans are ⅔ full. Set in a very hot oven as directed and bake 30 minutes; reduce oven temperature to moderate and continue baking 10 to 15 minutes longer until popovers have risen and are delicately brown. Serve very hot.

Handkerchiefs inscribed with recipes for bread and cake baking were carried by fashionable belles of seventeenth-century England.

(435) CHEESE POPOVERS II

Makes about 8 popovers. Oven temperature: 450–475° F.
Baking time: 40–45 minutes.

1 whole fresh egg, well-beaten
1 cup sweet milk
4 tablespoons grated cheese
1 cup bread flour, sifted twice
½ scant teaspoon salt
⅛ teaspoon paprika

Pre-heat pans for 10 long minutes then grease or butter generously. To the flour add salt and paprika and sift over thoroughly mixed egg, milk and grated cheese and beat briskly until smooth. (Note that cheese is mixed into batter.) Turn batter into the hot pans and bake in a hot oven as directed until popovers have risen and are delicately brown. Serve very hot. Fine with applesauce, jam, jelly, marmalade, honey, maple syrup or molasses.

The American Indians ate "Wuttahimneash," a bread made of strawberries and corn meal.

(436) CRABMEAT POPOVERS

Makes 8 popovers. Oven temperature: 450° F.
Baking time: 35 minutes (about).

1 cup hot milk
1 whole fresh egg, well beaten
¼ cup flaked crabmeat (canned) chopped
1 cup bread flour, sifted twice
½ scant teaspoon salt
A pinch of cayenne pepper
A pinch of dry mustard

Heat pans for 10 minutes; then brush generously with butter. To the flour add salt, cayenne pepper and dry mustard and sift twice, the last sifting over combined hot milk, well-beaten egg and finely chopped crabmeat. Blend thoroughly and pour into prepared pans. Bake in a hot oven as directed until muffins are puffed and brown. Serve at once.

Shrimps and lobster may be used in the same way.

(437) GRAHAM POPOVERS

Makes 8 popovers. Oven temperature: 450° F., then 350° F.
Baking time: 40–45 minutes.

⅓ cup bread flour, sifted
½ scant teaspoon salt
⅔ cup graham flour, unsifted
1 scant cup sweet milk
1 whole egg, well beaten
½ teaspoon melted butter

Add sifted bread flour to the graham flour and mix well. Combine remaining ingredients and add to the dry mixture. Beat 2 minutes with rotary beater and pour into hissing hot, greased pans. Bake in a very hot oven as directed; reduce to moderate and continue baking 10 minutes longer until popovers are puffed and brown. Serve sizzling hot.

At the height of a bread shortage in Sicily during the seventeenth century, bread was actually used for currency.

(438) NUT POPOVERS

THE FAVORITE BREAD OF THEODORE ROOSEVELT

Makes 8 large popovers. Oven temperature: 450–350° F.
Baking time: 40–45 minutes.

2 whole fresh eggs, well-beaten
1 cup cold sweet milk
1 cup bread flour, sifted twice
½ scant teaspoon salt
⅓ cup ground blanched almonds

Break eggs into mixing bowl and beat until light, adding milk gradually, while beating briskly with rotary beater. To the flour add salt and sift together over almonds (other nuts may be used) and blend well. Add flour mixture all at once to milk-egg mixture and continue beating until it is smooth and as thick as heavy cream. Bake in hissing hot, iron muffin pans or glass or earthenware custard cups (cups filled ⅔ full) in a very hot oven. Then reduce heat to moderate and continue baking 10 or 15 minutes, according to size. Remove from oven, make a slit on top for escape of steam, and serve at once on a napkin with plenty of butter, jam, jelly, marmalade, preserves, honey, maple syrup or molasses.

(439) RICE POPOVERS

MILKLESS

Makes 16 small popovers. Oven temperature: 425° F.
Baking time: 15–20 minutes.

This emergency recipe requires only short baking; so it is very handy for breakfast. There is no baking powder in real popovers, but in this one baking powder is used as well as separated eggs.

2 cups cold cooked rice, sieved or mashed
2 egg yolks, well-beaten
2 egg whites, stiffly beaten
2 cups bread flour, sifted
2 teaspoons baking powder
2 tablespoons granulated sugar
1 scant teaspoon salt

Into the rice beat the light egg yolks and fold in the stiffly beaten egg whites. To the flour add baking powder, salt and sugar, and sift twice, the last time over the rice mixture. Turn batter into hot, buttered popover pans and bake in a hot oven as directed. Serve very hot with butter, jam, jelly, marmalade, preserves or honey.

Greek and Roman entertainers, welcomed at the tables of rich men in return for their flattering remarks, were called "parasitos," from Greek "para" (beside) and "sitos" (food). Hence our "parasite"—any organism or person living at the expense of another.

(440) RICH POPOVERS I

Makes 8 large popovers. Oven temperature: 450–350° F.
Baking time: 40–45 minutes.

3 whole fresh eggs, well beaten	1 cup bread flour, sifted twice
½ cup of sweet milk	½ generous teaspoon salt
½ cup thin cream	A generous pinch of nutmeg

2 tablespoons melted butter

Combine well-beaten eggs with milk and cream (you may use undiluted evaporated milk instead of thin cream) and beat with rotary beater until thoroughly blended. Add salt and nutmeg to flour and sift over egg-milk mixture. Beat until smooth and as thick as heavy cream, adding the melted butter while beating. Fill sizzling hot generously buttered custard cups up to ⅔ full and bake in a hot oven and then in a moderate oven as directed until popovers are almost double in size and delicately browned. Immediately make a slit in each and serve at once with butter, jam, jelly, marmalade, preserves, etc.; or split in two and use as patty shell for creamed fish, meat, poultry or vegetables.

The famous monument called the "Uneven Dozen," in Sucre, Bolivia, was built with money collected from bakers who were fined for not selling a "baker's dozen" (13 pieces to the dozen).

(441) RICH POPOVERS II

APPROPRIATE FOR AFTERNOON TEA WHEN FILLED WITH FRUITS, BERRIES, ETC.

Makes 8 large popovers. Oven temperature: 425–350° F.
Baking time: about 40 minutes.

Break 6 fresh eggs into mixing bowl; add ¾ teaspoon salt and ¼ teaspoon almond extract and beat well. Sift a cup of flour, measure and sift again over egg mixture; then pour in 1 cup of sweet rich milk and beat 2 minutes with rotary beater. Turn mixture into sizzling hot custard cups, generously buttered and sprinkled with granulated sugar. Bake 25 minutes in a hot oven as directed; reduce heat to moderate and continue baking for 10 to 15 minutes. Shut off the heat and let the popovers remain in the oven for 5 long minutes. Make a slit at once in top, or remove the entire top and fill with either a macédoine (mixture of fruits, fresh or frozen berries) or mixed fruit with whipped cream. Very rich.

(442) RYE MEAL POPOVERS

Makes 8 popovers. Oven temperature: 425–350° F.
Baking time: 40–45 minutes.

- 1/3 cup bread flour, sifted
- 1/2 scant teaspoon salt
- 2/3 cup rye meal, unsifted
- 1 cup sweet milk
- 2 whole eggs, well-beaten

Add salt to the flour and sift over rye meal. Blend thoroughly. Combine milk and well-beaten eggs and beat with rotary beater until well mixed. Pour all at once over flour mixture and beat briskly for 2 or 3 minutes, or until smooth and free from lumps. Fill hissing hot, buttered, iron gem pans or custard cups 2/3 full and bake 20 to 25 minutes in a very hot oven as directed, reducing heat to moderate and continue baking about 15 to 20 minutes longer until popovers are puffed and brown. Immediately make a slit in top for escape of steam and serve at once with plenty of butter, jam, jelly, marmalade or preserves.

(443) STRAWBERRY POPOVERS

A BREAKFAST BREAD, AN AFTERNOON TEA SNACK OR A DESSERT

Makes 8 popovers. Oven temperature: 425–350° F.
Baking time: 40–45 minutes.

- 2 whole fresh eggs, well-beaten
- 1 generous cup bread flour, sifted twice
- 1 generous cup rich milk
- 1/2 teaspoon salt
- Strawberry filling

Combine eggs with milk and beat with rotary beater until well blended. To the flour add salt and sift over egg-milk mixture. Stir briskly, adding the milk mixture gradually, until smooth. Fill buttered, sizzling hot, iron gem pans or custard cups 2/3 full and bake 20 minutes in a very hot oven; reduce heat to moderate and continue baking about 20 minutes longer until crisp, puffed and browned. Immediately cut a slit in the top of each popover; fill with 1 cup of crushed strawberries mixed with 1/4 cup powdered sugar and 3/4 cup of whipped cream. You may decorate each popover with whipped cream forced through a pastry bag with a fancy tube and top with a whole strawberry. Serve immediately.

The "bone box" was a sixteenth-century English institution. It was kept beneath the table and well-mannered diners tossed bones into it when meat was served.

(444) SUNDAY POPOVERS

A SUNDAY BREAKFAST DISH

Makes 8 popovers. Oven temperature: 450–350° F. Baking time: 40–45 minutes.

The thoughtful homemaker with an eye to good nutrition and her mind on the food budget will serve eggs in some form regularly, and winter meals are in particular need of a "lift." She may serve eggs either coddled, scrambled, in omelets or poached for her breakfast menu, but here is a delicious and tempting way to serve this concentrated food—for after milk and meat, it's eggs!

Make your favorite popover recipe. As soon as baked, cut an opening in the top of each popover and fill with scrambled eggs, either plain or country method (that is, scrambled with canned tomato). Serve at once topped with one or two crisp slices of bacon. You may omit the bacon and replace the top of popover. Serve steaming hot, bearing in mind that the best scrambled eggs must be rather moist.

(445) WHOLE WHEAT POPOVERS

Makes 8 popovers. Oven temperature: 450–350° F. Baking time: 40–45 minutes.

½ cup bread flour, sifted
½ teaspoon salt
½ cup unsifted whole wheat flour
2 whole fresh eggs, well-beaten
1 cup rich milk
2 teaspoons melted butter

Add salt to sifted flour and sift over unsifted whole wheat flour. Blend thoroughly. Combine eggs, milk and melted butter and beat until thoroughly blended. Pour all at once over flour mixture and beat with rotary beater until smooth. Pour batter into hissing hot custard cups and bake 25 minutes in a very hot oven as directed; reduce heat to moderate and continue baking about 15 minutes longer until popovers are puffed and delicately browned. Make a slit in top for escape of steam and serve at once with plenty of butter, jam, jelly, marmalade, honey, maple syrup or molasses.

Homemakers of Reykjavik, the Iceland capital which is named for its hot springs, often use the hot flowing earth near-by for baking their bread.

Rolls

. . . Foods may be likened to the pipes of an organ—the homemaker to the organist. Press whatever keys you like and something results—either bodily harmony or inharmony according to the skill and intelligence applied. . . .

—*Dr. Irving S. Cutter*

ROLLS

(446) A FEW GOOD HINTS

Browning once wrote: "Now we shall arbitrate? Ten men love what I hate, shun what I follow, slight what I receive; ten who in ears and eyes match me: we all surmise, they this thing, and I that; whom shall my soul believe?" And his appeal may be applied quite as well to the problems of bread-making, appetite and taste as to those of philosophy, ethics, or morals. *Chacun à son goût!*—the pot should think twice before calling the kettle black.

As there is no one article of food that enters so largely into our daily fare as bread, no degree of skill in preparing other articles can compensate for lack of knowledge in the art of making good, palatable and nutritious bread, rolls, etc.

The first thing required for making wholesome bread, rolls, etc., is the utmost cleanliness; the next is the soundness and sweetness of all the ingredients used; and in addition there must be attention and care through the whole process.

An almost certain way of spoiling dough is to leave it half-made and allow it to become cold before it is finished.

Never allow the bread to remain in the pan, or on a pine table to absorb the odor of wood.

When any recipe calls for baking powder and you do not have it, you can use one level teaspoonful of soda to two of cream of tartar. When making rolls either with baking powder or soda and cream of tartar (cream of tartar is a wholesome fruit product made from fine, ripe grapes—it has been known for generations as the finest baking-powder ingredient), the oven should be prepared first; the dough handled quickly and put into the oven immediately.

The flavor of rolls is influenced considerably by the shaping and baking. A small roll with a large proportion of crust, like a finger roll, will taste altogether different from a product made from the same dough into large rolls baked close together in a pan and so having little crust.

Various flavorings may be added to rolls by using poppy seeds, anise, caraway seeds, crystal salt and so on.

Sweet rolls are similar to plain, but they are richer, having more shortening, eggs and usually more sugar and flavoring.

To freshen stale rolls or biscuits, put them into a steamer for ten minutes, then dry off in a hot oven (425–450° F.); or dip each roll for an instant in cold water and heat them crisp in the oven. You also may use a double boiler for steaming rolls or biscuits. Reheated rolls or biscuits should always be served immediately.

Yeast dough, stored in the refrigerator, keeps well several days and permits the baking of hot rolls at will. Because the dough may develop an off-flavor, it should not be stored longer than three days before being baked. Stirring down the dough daily helps to drive off the gas and slow up yeast growth. When wanted, the dough is taken from the refrigerator, kneaded and shaped into rolls of the desired size and kind; they are allowed to rise until double in bulk before being baked in a very hot oven. The remaining dough is greased on top, placed in a smaller bowl, covered with waxed paper and returned to the refrigerator.

The choice of a tested simple recipe with concise, easy-to-follow directions is the initial step for a beginner; next comes careful reading and study of the recipe to gain a clear understanding of the process from first to last. Then practice will make perfect.

When decorating the rolls with poppy seeds, spread just a little unbeaten white of egg on top of the rolls before sprinkling on the seeds. After baking, the seeds will remain on the rolls.

For most rolls, a moderately hot oven (400° F.) should be used. The time of baking will be from 15 to 20 minutes, depending upon the size of the rolls.

You can make cinnamon rolls from light bread dough. After letting them rise, just before putting them in the oven, pour an uncooked filling of one cup brown sugar and ½ cup cream over them. It really makes them delicious.

In Elizabethan days every Englishman carried a knife in his belt for cutting his bread and meat in case the host failed to provide one.

ROLL RECIPES

(447) AFTERNOON COFFEE ORANGE ROLLS

YEAST METHOD

Makes 2 dozen rolls. Oven temperature: 450–350° F.
Baking time: 20–25 minutes (about).

1 cake compressed yeast
¼ cup lukewarm water
½ cup milk, scalded, cooled to lukewarm
¼ cup shortening
1 scant tablespoon granulated sugar
½ teaspoon salt
2 to 2½ cups bread flour, sifted twice
2 whole fresh eggs, unbeaten

Filling:

Wash one large orange or 2 medium-sized ones. Peel, removing white membrane. Add enough water to cover and cook until tender. Pour off water; then run peel through food chopper. To the peel add same amount of brown sugar, mix well and use at once.

NOTE: The peel should be finely ground; if coarse blade of grinder is used, run through twice.

Soften yeast cake in lukewarm water. Scald milk and add the shortening, sugar and salt. Blend well, then cool to lukewarm. Gradually add flour, beating well after each addition, and combine with softened yeast cake. Now add the unbeaten eggs, one at a time, beating well after each addition until mixture is smooth. Cover and let rise until dough doubles in bulk (about one hour), placing the pan over hot water or in a warm place. Stir down and toss upon lightly floured board. Butter your hands and take off enough to pull out to make an oval, half an inch thick and as large as you can pat and pull it, keeping it ½ inch thick. Spread with melted butter and then with the ground orange filling. Roll up as for cinnamon rolls, cut into slices with the kitchen scissors instead of a knife. (This pressure from both sides at once keeps filling intact.) Repeat with other half of dough.

Dip both sides in melted butter, place in greased muffin tins, let raise 45 minutes to one hour in a warm but not hot place. Keep covered with a light, dry, clean towel to prevent crusting. Preheat oven to 450° F. Bake 10 to 12 minutes. Reduce heat and finish baking at about 350° F. Total baking time 25 minutes (about).

(448) ALMOND YEAST ROLLS

Makes 2 dozen rolls. Oven temperature: 375° F.
Baking time: 15–20 minutes.

Proceed as indicated for No. 447. When dough has raised to double its bulk (about an hour), stir down and add ½ generous cup blanched, shredded almonds. Fill greased muffin pans one-half full. Sprinkle with another half-cup of the almonds, mixed with ¼ cup of granulated sugar. Cover and let rise until doubled in bulk (about 30 minutes). Bake in a moderate oven as directed.

(449) AMERICAN CRESCENT ROLLS

YEAST METHOD

Makes about 2 dozen crescents. Oven temperature: 400° F.
Baking time: 15 minutes.

- 1 cake yeast
- 2 tablespoons lukewarm water
- ¼ cup granulated sugar
- ¼ cup butter
- ½ generous teaspoon salt
- ½ cup milk, scalded
- 1 whole fresh egg, slightly beaten
- 2 cups bread flour, sifted twice
- Melted butter

Dissolve yeast in lukewarm water. Combine sugar, butter, salt and milk. When lukewarm add egg, mix thoroughly and add to yeast mixture. Gradually stir in flour, beating well after each addition. Turn mixture into greased bowl, cover with a light, clean, dry cloth and place over hot water to double in bulk (about one hour). Turn dough onto slightly floured board; knead for a short minute, or until smooth and not sticky. Roll dough to a very thin sheet (about ⅛-inch thick). Cut into 4-inch squares, cut each square diagonally into 2 triangles; brush with melted butter; roll triangles, beginning on diagonal; shape in horseshoe or crescent form. Place on greased baking sheet; let rise until light (about 30 minutes), and bake in a hot oven as directed above. Serve warm for breakfast, luncheon or afternoon tea or coffee.

(450) BAKING POWDER ROLLS

MOCK PARKER HOUSE ROLLS—QUICK METHOD

Makes 2 dozen rolls. Oven temperature: 400° F.
Baking time: 18–20 minutes.

2½ cups bread flour, sifted twice
½ generous teaspoon salt
2 teaspoons granulated sugar
3½ teaspoons baking powder
6 tablespoons butter or shortening
1 whole egg, lightly beaten
1 scant cup rich milk or thin cream
Melted butter for tops

Combine flour, salt, granulated sugar and baking powder, and sift together into mixing bowl. Work in the shortening with tips of fingers or two forks. Moisten with egg in a measuring cup, the cup being then filled with milk, cream, or undiluted evaporated milk. Toss out on a lightly-floured board; roll about ¼-inch thick; cut in rounds with floured cutter; brush with melted butter and crease each round with the back of a knife, dipped in flour. Fold over as for Parker House rolls and bake in a hot oven as directed.

Peter the Great, wandering about Moscow, saw a man hawking pies, cakes and rolls. Afterward this man became a renowned pastry cook and baker. Peter sought him out and made him his prime minister. As Prince Menshkoff, he wielded tremendous power and became the richest subject in Europe.

(451) BAKING POWDER RYE DINNER ROLLS

QUICK METHOD

Makes 1½ dozen rolls. Oven temperature: 400° F.
Baking time: 25–30 minutes.

1½ cups milk, lukewarm
1½ tablespoons butter or shortening
4 cups rye flour, sifted
4 teaspoons baking powder
1 teaspoon salt
2 tablespoons caraway seeds
1 egg yolk, slightly beaten

Combine milk and shortening and mix thoroughly. To the rye flour add baking powder and salt and sift into mixing bowl. Add half of caraway seeds to flour mixture, mix well, then stir in the milk mixture. Turn out on lightly floured board and knead lightly for about 2 minutes, or until mixture is glossy and smooth. Roll out to ½ scant inch thickness and cut into rounds with floured cutter; or pinch off pieces of the dough 3 inches long. Place on greased baking sheet and allow to stand 15 long minutes, covered with a light, dry, clean towel. Brush with egg yolk and sprinkle with remaining caraway seeds and a little coarse salt. Bake in a hot oven as directed.

(452) BOW KNOT TEA ROLLS

BAKING POWDER METHOD

Makes 1½ dozen rolls. Oven temperature: 425° F.
Baking time: 20 minutes (about).

2 cups bread flour, sifted twice
2 teaspoons baking powder
⅔ cup milk
1 tablespoon butter
½ teaspoon salt
Melted butter

To the flour add baking powder and salt and sift into mixing bowl; work in butter; gradually add milk to make a soft dough. Turn out on lightly floured board and knead for about 2 minutes, or until dough is glossy and not sticky. Roll to ¼-inch thickness; cut into pieces 6 inches long and ½ inch wide. Tie each in loose knot, similar to pretzel; place on baking sheet; brush generously with melted butter and allow to stand for 20 minutes in a warm place (not hot); brush again with melted butter. Bake in a hot oven for 10 minutes; brush again with melted butter and continue baking 10 minutes longer until golden brown on top. Serve at once.

(453) BRAN MOLASSES ROLLS

YEAST METHOD

Makes 3 dozen rolls. Oven temperature: 375° F.
Baking time: 20 minutes (about).

These rolls are so delicious that you should not hesitate to make 3 dozen of them and watch them disappear. The left-overs may be reheated the next day and used for luncheon, the school lunch box, or even dinner. For smaller baking, reduce amount of ingredients one-half.

3 cups milk, scalded
2 tablespoons brown sugar
2 tablespoons butter, melted
2 tablespoons molasses
1 scant tablespoon salt
2 cakes compressed yeast
¼ cup lukewarm water
1½ cups unsifted graham flour
2½ cups unsifted bran meal
½ teaspoon baking soda
3 to 3¾ cups bread flour, sifted

Scald milk; add sugar, butter, molasses and salt and blend thoroughly. When lukewarm, stir in dissolved yeast cakes, softened in lukewarm water. Stir briskly. Combine graham flour, bran and soda and add to the mixture, then stiffen with bread flour. Turn dough into generously greased mixing bowl; cover with a light, dry clean towel, set the bowl into or over a pan containing hot (not boiling) water, and let rise until doubled in volume. Cut the dough down and let rise to about the same volume again. Roll out on lightly floured board to ½-inch thickness; cut with biscuit cutter, dipped in flour; brush with melted butter; fold so that upper edge overlaps the under one like a pocket book; let rise again for 40 to 45 minutes, covered, and over hot water or in a warm place free from draft; then bake in a moderate oven as directed. Remove from oven; quickly brush again with melted butter and serve as hot as possible. Really delicious!

(454) BREAKFAST CINNAMON ROLLS

BAKING POWDER METHOD

Makes about 1½ dozen rolls. Oven temperature: 400° F.
Baking time: 12–15 minutes.

Follow No. 36. Roll the dough out on a lightly-floured board; spread with melted butter; sprinkle with ½ cup granulated or brown sugar mixed with a generous teaspoon powdered cinnamon; roll up, like jelly roll; cut in crosswise slices and bake on a greased baking sheet, in a hot oven as directed. Serve warm or hot.

(455) BUTTER FLAKE ROLLS

YEAST METHOD

Makes about 3 dozen rolls. Oven temperature: 400° F.
Baking time: 18–20 minutes.

- 2 cakes compressed yeast
- 2 tablespoons granulated sugar
- 2 tablespoons dark brown sugar
- 1½ cups sour milk or buttermilk, lukewarm
- 1 teaspoon salt
- ½ cup butter, melted, not hot
- 5 cups (about) bread flour, sifted twice
- ½ teaspoon baking soda

Crumble yeast cake into mixing bowl; add both sugars; mix well, then pour sour milk or buttermilk over mixture. Blend and let stand 15 minutes. Then add salt and melted butter. Add soda to the flour and sift over first mixture. Beat briskly until smooth and free from lumps. Turn into greased mixing bowl; brush top with butter; cover with a dry cloth and set the bowl over hot water. Let rise until very light (about 40 minutes). Empty the bowl onto lightly floured board and roll out as thin as possible with floured rolling pin. With a brush, spread a thin coat of flour over the thin sheet of dough and cut into strips 2 inches wide. Cut strips into squares; brush with melted butter, and set in a warm place, covered with a dry towel to rise until very light (10–12 minutes). Bake in a hot oven as directed. Rolls separate in layers easily and require no butter. Serve warm or cold.

Today we use two varieties of wheat from among the more than 30,000 that are known. To be usable, the kernels must be ground to powder. Hence the development of the millstone, operated by water. When the roller process came into vogue, the embryo was completely removed and almost all of the bran to make white flour. Furthermore, various bleaching agents were utilized to banish all traces of carotene—a source of vitamin A. . . . Have we lost anything through refinements? Yes. The crude product possessed higher nutritive value. When flour is highly milled, there is a notable deficiency in calcium, iron, phosphorus, vitamin B and carotene, and there is less protein. In a well-balanced, liberal and varied diet it is possible to make up for the abstracted ingredients, but at much greater cost.

(456) BUTTER ROLLS—FRENCH METHOD

YEAST METHOD

Makes 24 rolls. Oven temperature: 400° F.
Baking time: 20 minutes.

2 cakes compressed yeast
1 tablespoon granulated sugar
¼ cup milk, lukewarm
1 scant teaspoon vanilla extract
3 egg yolks, well-beaten
1½ cups bread flour, sifted twice
½ scant cup butter
½ scant cup granulated sugar
¼ cup finely chopped nut meats (any kind)

Dissolve yeast cakes and sugar (the tablespoon) in lukewarm milk which has been scalded and cooled. Add vanilla and beaten egg yolks and blend thoroughly. Cut flour into butter and combine with the first mixture. Form into a ball; place the ball in a cheesecloth and put in pan of cold water. Let stand from ¾ to 1 hour. Remove from the cloth. Shape into balls, the size of an egg and roll in mixed sugar and finely chopped nut meats. Twist. Place on greased baking sheet and allow to rise for 20 minutes. Then bake in a hot oven as directed. Serve cold.

In the fifteenth century, Diaprun or Diaprunum, a concoction of Damson plums, violet seeds, grated ivory (yes ivory), sandalwood and other odd ingredients, was a favorite afternoon bread which was eaten with wine, also sweetened with odd ingredients. It must have been hard on stomach linings!

(457) BUTTERMILK POPPY SEED DINNER ROLLS

YEAST METHOD

Makes 2 dozen rolls. Oven temperature: 400° F.
Baking time: about 20 minutes.

2 yeast cakes
¼ cup granulated sugar
1½ cups buttermilk, lukewarm
½ cup melted butter, not hot
5 cups bread flour, sifted twice
1 scant teaspoon baking soda
Melted butter
1 scant teaspoon salt
¼ cup poppy seeds

Crumble yeast cakes into mixing bowl; add granulated sugar and buttermilk; stir until dissolved, adding while stirring the melted (not hot) butter. To the flour add salt and soda and sift over liquid mixture. Stir well until smooth, adding while stirring half of the poppy seeds. Place in greased mixing bowl; cover with a light, clean, dry cheesecloth, and let rise to double its bulk (about 30 minutes). Cut down; shape into balls the size of a small egg; brush with melted butter; sprinkle with remaining poppy seeds and let rise again until double in bulk (about 15 minutes), on greased pan. Bake in a hot oven as directed. Serve warm or cold. (You may omit poppy seeds.)

(458) BUTTERMILK ROLLS—CANADIAN METHOD

YEAST METHOD

Makes 2 dozen rolls. Oven temperature: 400° F.
Baking time: 20 minutes.

1 cake compressed yeast
½ cup lukewarm buttermilk
2 tablespoons granulated sugar
1 teaspoon (scant) salt
¼ teaspoon baking soda
1½ cups lukewarm buttermilk
4 cups (1 quart) bread flour, sifted twice
2 tablespoons melted shortening

Crumble yeast cake into the ½ cup of lukewarm buttermilk; add sugar, salt and soda to the 1½ cups lukewarm buttermilk; mix well and combine with crumbled, dissolved yeast. Let cool. Then add half of the flour and beat briskly until smooth and free from lumps, adding while going along the melted shortening, then the remaining flour. *Do not let rise to double its bulk,* but turn onto lightly floured board and knead until smooth, elastic, and not sticky. Roll out about ½-inch thick; cut with floured cutter; put on a greased baking sheet, brush with butter, cover with a dry cheesecloth, and only then let rise for one hour. Bake in a hot oven as directed. Serve warm with plenty of butter.

(459) BUTTERSCOTCH SPICE ROLLS

BAKING POWDER METHOD

Makes about 2 dozen. Oven temperature: 400° F.
Baking time: 12 minutes (about).

- 2 cups bread flour, sifted twice
- 4 teaspoons baking powder
- ½ teaspoon salt
- ¼ cup shortening
- ⅔ cup sweet milk (about)
- Cinnamon mixed with sugar

To the flour add baking powder and salt and sift into mixing bowl; cut in the shortening and add enough milk to make a soft dough. Roll out upon lightly floured board to about ¼-inch thick; spread with additional softened butter; sprinkle with mixed cinnamon and sugar (¼ cup sugar and 1½ teaspoons of powdered cinnamon) and roll up as for jelly roll. Cut into 1-inch slices and place them, cut side down, on a greased cookie sheet. Bake in a hot oven as directed until delicately browned. Serve warm. Fine for afternoon coffee or tea. You may sift ¼ teaspoon each of nutmeg and ginger with flour.

(460) BUTTERY ROLLS—SOUTHERN METHOD

YEAST METHOD

Makes 60 buttery rolls. Oven temperature: 400° F.
Baking time: 20 minutes (about).

This recipe will serve about 25 persons.

- 1 cup rich milk or thin cream, scalded, cooled
- 2 tablespoons granulated sugar
- 1 teaspoon salt
- ¼ cup butter, melted
- 1 cake compressed yeast
- 1 cup pastry flour, sifted once, or
- 1 cup bread flour, sifted thrice
- 1 whole fresh egg, well-beaten
- 2 additional cups either flour
- Additional sweet butter

To the milk add granulated sugar, salt and melted butter (no other shortening should be used). Blend thoroughly, then crumble in the yeast cake and stir until dissolved. Add one cup flour (either one) and beat briskly until smooth; after brushing top with melted butter, cover and let stand in a warm place until bubbly (about 30 minutes). Then add egg and the remaining 2 cups of either flour. Blend thoroughly. Turn out on very slightly floured board and knead lightly until dough is smooth. Place in a buttered mixing bowl; brush with melted butter; then cover with a cloth wrung out in warm water. Let rise until light. Roll out to 1/8-inch thick; cut into 1-inch rounds; in center of each round place 1/4 scant teaspoon butter and cover with another round, pinching edges together. Place close together, pinched edges down, in buttered (not greased, but buttered) shallow pan and let rise, covered and in a warm place, until doubled in bulk. Bake in a hot oven as directed. Serve hot.

(461) POPPY SEED CRESCENT ROLLS

BAKING POWDER METHOD

Makes about 20 crescents. Oven temperature: 400° F.
Baking time: 18–20 minutes.

This recipe is very appropriate for afternoon tea, dinner or buffet supper.

2 cups bread flour, sifted thrice
3 teaspoons baking powder
1/2 teaspoon salt
1/4 cup shortening
2/3 cup sweet milk
Melted butter
Poppy seeds, or equal parts of poppy and caraway seeds

To the flour add baking powder and salt; cut in shortening; pour on the milk all at once and stir until all the flour is dampened and mixture forms a soft dough that follows the spoon around the bowl. Turn out on a lightly floured board and knead lightly for about 2 minutes or until smooth. Cut into crescents with floured cutter; brush tops with melted butter and sprinkle with seeds. Place upon generously greased baking sheets; cover with a dry, clean cheesecloth and let stand 20 minutes in a warm place, away from any draft. Then bake in a hot oven 10 minutes. Again brush tops with melted butter and continue baking 8 to 10 minutes longer. Remove from oven and quickly add melted butter from teaspoon as before. Serve as hot as possible.

(462) CHEESE ROLLS

YEAST METHOD

Makes 25 small rolls. Oven temperature: 450° F.
Baking time: 7 to 8 minutes.

1/4 cup granulated sugar	1/2 yeast cake
1 1/4 teaspoons salt	3 tablespoons lukewarm water
1/4 cup butter	2 3/4 cups bread flour, sifted twice
1 cup sweet milk, scalded	Melted butter and grated cheese

Dissolve sugar, salt and butter in scalded milk. Cool to lukewarm after blending thoroughly. Add yeast dissolved in lukewarm water and beat vigorously. Stir in enough flour slowly to form a soft ball that can be handled easily. Put in a greased mixing bowl; cover with a light, clean, dry cloth and keep in a warm place to raise until doubled in bulk. Toss lightly onto floured board and roll out 1/3-inch thick. Butter generously, then sprinkle with 1/4 inch grated cheese after dividing dough in two equal parts. Roll out each half in rounds like pie crust, until 1/4 scant inch thick. Spread with a little cold butter then cut each round like a pie into 4 pieces. Roll each piece from the center, forming rolls about 3 inches long, pointed at one end and large at the other. Arrange far apart on generously greased baking sheet and brush with beaten egg yolk. Let rise until double in bulk and bake in a hot oven as directed. Serve hot.

In the early eighteenth century little strips of salted hard cheese were sold to New York City theater audiences who could eat them or throw them at the actors. They did both.

(463) CINNAMON ROLLS

BAKING POWDER METHOD

These little rolls look like muffins, but are called rolls in restaurants.

Make baking powder biscuits by Recipe No. 36. Roll out and cut one small biscuit, the size of the bottom of a muffin pan, place in bottom of generously buttered muffin pan; shape with fingers to resemble a small bottom pie crust. Brush generously with butter, then sprinkle with cinnamon to taste. Fill hollow with a little strained honey; top with a bit of butter, and place another small biscuit on top. Spread second biscuit with softened butter, then with cinnamon and bake in a hot oven as directed. When removed from muffin pans, each little roll will be in one well-formed piece, extra tender and light.

For variations you may add chopped almonds, nut meats, seedless raisins, chopped figs or dates. You may brush tops with cold milk, egg yolk or cream before baking.

(464) CLOVER LEAF ROLLS I

WALDORF METHOD

This is a combination of yeast and baking powder method. The dough will keep in refrigerator for several days.

½ cup cooked hot potatoes, riced	4 cups bread flour, sifted twice (about)
½ cup lard	1 teaspoon baking powder
2 cups sweet milk, scalded	½ teaspoon baking soda
½ cake compressed yeast	1 teaspoon salt
½ cup granulated sugar	

Cook potatoes until tender and rice them. Add lard while potatoes are warm. Heat milk, cool to lukewarm and crumble in the yeast, stirring until dissolved; add to potato mixture. To the flour add baking powder, soda, salt and sugar and sift together; gradually add to liquid mixture; turn dough into greased mixing bowl; brush with lard; cover with a light, clean, dry cloth and let rise until doubled in bulk (about one hour) in a warm place or over hot (not boiling) water. Cut dough down, add more flour if needed to make a stiff dough; brush top with melted lard to prevent a crust from forming.

Place in refrigerator and keep overnight. When used, knead for a minute or so on lightly floured board; shape into small rolls and bake in moderate oven as directed. Serve hot or cold.

Everyone knows that an artistic presentation can turn a drab, everyday affair—whether it be a movie or a meal—into a delightful experience. One intangible ingredient in such artistry is "highlighting." Following is a second method for a quick and easy recipe for "highlighting" menus with the ever popular Clover Leaf Rolls.

(465) CLOVER LEAF ROLLS II

YEAST METHOD—HOME MANNER

Makes about 15 rolls. Oven temperature: 375° F.
Baking time: 20 minutes (about).

- 1 cake compressed yeast
- 2 tablespoons granulated sugar
- 1 cup sweet milk, scalded, cooled to warm
- 1 cup bread flour, sifted twice
- ¾ teaspoon salt
- 1 tablespoon butter, melted
- 1 whole fresh egg, well-beaten
- 2 cups bread flour (about) sifted twice
- Additional melted butter

Crumble yeast cake, mix with sugar and set aside for 10 minutes. Then stir in warm milk, alternately with the first cup of flour. Beat vigorously; cover with a light, clean, dry cloth, after brushing with melted butter, and set over hot water (not boiling) to rise until almost doubled in bulk (about 30 minutes). Then cut down. Add salt and melted butter to egg and add to yeast mixture. Blend thoroughly and add remaining two cups of flour, a little at a time, beating well after each addition, until dough is smooth and elastic, adding more flour if dough seems sticky when touched lightly.

Set covered dough over a pan of hot water to rise. When doubled in bulk, shape into rolls. Place upon lightly greased baking sheet; let rise until triple in bulk and brush with melted butter. Bake in a moderate oven as directed until rolls are delicately brown. Serve warm.

(466) CRUSTY ROLLS

YEAST METHOD

Makes about 2 dozen rolls. Oven temperature: 400° F.
Baking time: 18–20 minutes.

- 1 cake compressed yeast
- ½ scant cup lukewarm water
- ½ cup milk, scalded
- 2 tablespoons lard
- ¾ scant teaspoon salt
- 1 teaspoon granulated sugar
- 1½ cups bread flour, sifted twice
- 2½ cups (about) additional bread flour, sifted twice
- Ice cold water

Crumble yeast cake into lukewarm water and stir until dissolved. Scald milk; add lard, salt and sugar, stir and let cool until lukewarm. Add dissolved yeast mixture, then stir in the 1½ cups flour and beat briskly to a smooth batter; cover; place over hot water (not boiling) and let rise for about 45 minutes or until very light and doubled in bulk. Toss a minute or so, then add enough of the additional flour to make a soft dough. Turn out on a lightly floured board and knead for 2 or 3 minutes until smooth, elastic, and not sticky. Brush with lard; cover and let rise again until doubled in bulk (about 1½ hours). Turn out on lightly floured board, knead very lightly, cut off pieces the size of an egg and shape into flat rounds about ⅓-inch thick. Crease each one through the center with the back of a knife. Place on a generously greased baking sheet, let rise for 40 minutes, sprinkle with a little ice water and bake in a hot oven as directed until well browned and crusty. Serve warm or cold.

In 1909 French explorers in Senegal discovered that the fruit of the baobab tree tastes very good. They dubbed it "monkey-bread."

(467) DINNER ROLLS I

YEAST METHOD—REFRIGERATOR

Makes 2½ dozen rolls (about). Oven temperature: 400° F.
Baking time: 18–20 minutes.

2 cups sweet milk, scalded
¼ scant cup granulated sugar
¾ teaspoon salt
1 generous tablespoon shortening
1 cake compressed yeast
2 tablespoons lukewarm water
1 whole fresh egg, well-beaten
3½ cups bread flour, sifted twice
Ice water for tops

Scald milk; combine with sugar, salt and shortening. Cool to lukewarm. Meanwhile crumble yeast cake in lukewarm water, adding 1 generous teaspoon of the sugar; stir well until dissolved and add to lukewarm milk mixture. Add egg and stir in half of the flour. Beat thoroughly until smooth, then beat in the remaining flour, and as much more as can be stirred in *without kneading*. Brush surface with melted shortening. Set in refrigerator covered tightly. When ready to bake, turn out on a lightly floured board and invert so that both sides are covered with flour. Take off small pieces the size of an egg and roll out to the thickness to make the type of roll desired, *i.e.:* Parker House, Clover Leaf, etc. When rolls have been shaped, place them on a greased baking sheet, let rise until *very light* (refrigerator rolls take a longer time for rising than those which have not been chilled to 45° F. or lower). Sprinkle with a little ice water and bake in a hot oven as directed. Serve warm or cold.

(468) DINNER ROLLS II

YEAST METHOD

Makes 1½ to 2 dozen rolls. Oven temperature: 400° F. Baking time: 18–20 minutes.

1 cup sweet milk, scalded, cooled to lukewarm
1 yeast cake
3 tablespoons granulated sugar
1 scant teaspoon salt
1 whole fresh egg, well-beaten
2 tablespoons melted shortening
4 cups bread flour, sifted twice
1½ tablespoons melted butter

Scald milk; let cool to lukewarm and crumble in the yeast cake, stirring well until yeast is dissolved. Stir in sugar, salt, beaten egg and melted shortening. Mix well, then add half of the flour. Beat until smooth. Add remaining flour, then melted butter and blend well. Knead on lightly floured board until dough is smooth, elastic and not sticky. Place dough in a well greased bowl; brush with melted butter or lard; cover with a light, clean, dry cloth; set in a warm place, or still better over a pan containing hot water (not boiling) and let rise until doubled in bulk. Punch dough once or twice; form into desired shapes; arrange on greased baking sheet and brush with melted butter, or sprinkle with ice water. Bake in a hot oven as directed. Serve warm or cold.

Established in 1678, the Brotherhood of Chefs was a culinary society which every chef in China eagerly tried to join. Its culinary tests were so difficult that only one in thirty passed.

(469) DINNER ROLLS III

SWEET—YEAST METHOD

Makes 18 rolls (about). Oven temperature: 400° F. Baking time: 18–20 minutes.

NOTE: These rolls are sweet and very rich. They are called also "Two-Hour Rolls."

1½ cups sweet milk, scalded
1 cup granulated sugar
2 cakes compressed yeast
3 cups bread flour, sifted twice
4 whole fresh eggs, well-beaten
¾ teaspoon salt
1 cup butter, melted
3 additional cups bread flour, sifted twice
Melted butter for tops

Pour scalded milk over sugar and let stand until lukewarm, stirring occasionally to dissolve sugar. Crumble in the yeast cakes and stir until dissolved. Add the first 3 cups of bread flour and beat well. Place over a pan containing hot water (not boiling), cover with a light, clean dry towel and let rise until light and full of bubbles. Then add eggs, beaten with salt and melted butter and beat briskly. Gradually add the additional cups of bread flour, beating well after each addition. Cover; let rise until light and doubled in bulk; punch dough once or twice then shape as desired. Place upon buttered baking sheet; brush tops with melted butter and allow to rise until light or doubled in bulk. Bake in a hot oven as directed. Serve warm or cold.

(470) DINNER ROLLS IV

FRENCH MANNER—YEAST METHOD

Makes about 18 rolls. Oven temperature: 400° F.
Baking time: 18–20 minutes.

2½ cups bread flour, sifted twice
1 tablespoon granulated sugar
1 scant teaspoon salt
3 tablespoons cold butter
1 cake compressed yeast
⅓ cup lukewarm water
Melted butter for tops
½ cup sweet milk, lukewarm

To the flour add sugar and salt and sift into a mixing bowl. Work in cold butter as for pie. Crumble yeast cake into water, mixed with milk and stir until yeast is dissolved, then combine with flour mixture and beat briskly until dough is smooth. Brush top with butter or lard, cover with a light, clean dry cloth and let rise until dough is doubled in bulk. Turn out on lightly floured board; knead one short minute, then roll out gently about ⅓-inch thick. Cut in rounds with floured cutter; brush half of each round with melted butter; fold over, pocket-book fashion, buttered-side-up; place close together on greased baking sheet; let rise until very light, almost triple in bulk, then bake in a hot oven as directed. Serve warm or cold.

To ensure and assure authentic foreign bread-making and cooking, Count Albard de Resnek of Sweden engaged a skilled chef from each European country (1651).

(471) EMERGENCY CINNAMON RAISIN ROLLS

BAKING POWDER METHOD

Makes about 1 dozen rolls. Oven temperature: 350° F.
Baking time: 20–25 minutes.

2 cups bread flour, sifted twice
½ generous teaspoon salt
1 tablespoon granulated sugar, or
1 tablespoon dark brown sugar, rolled
¾ teaspoon cinnamon
4 teaspoons baking powder
⅓ cup shortening
1 whole fresh egg, well-beaten
⅓ cup sweet cold milk
1 generous tablespoon softened butter
2 tablespoons sifted brown sugar
1 teaspoon cinnamon
½ generous cup parboiled, sponged seedless raisins

To the flour add salt, sugar, the ¾ teaspoon cinnamon and baking powder and sift into mixing bowl. Rub in shortening as for pie with a fork or pastry cutter. Combine egg and milk and stir into flour mixture to make a soft dough. Turn dough out on a lightly floured board and roll out into an oblong sheet a scant ½ of an inch thick.

Spread quickly and lightly with softened butter; then sprinkle with sifted brown sugar mixed with remaining powdered cinnamon and prepared raisins. Roll dough up like a jelly roll from the long side of the oblong. Cut down in slices ½ inch thick and place cut side down and *close together* on greased baking sheet. Bake in a moderate oven as directed. Serve warm or cold.

You may brush one side with a thin sugar icing as soon as removed from oven. Warm slices are much more delicate than cold ones. May be reheated in a covered pan in a hot oven (400° F.) for 5 minutes, if not iced.

(472) FINGER ROLLS

BAKING POWDER METHOD

Makes about 30 medium rolls. Oven temperature: 425° F.
Baking time: 15–18 minutes.

One-half of the recipe may be made.

2 cups bread flour, sifted twice
1 scant tablespoon baking powder
½ teaspoon salt
1 tablespoon cold butter
⅔ cup sweet milk
Plenty of butter for tops, melted

Add baking powder and salt to flour and sift into mixing bowl. Cut in shortening as for pie; add milk all at once and stir carefully until all flour is dampened. Then stir briskly until mixture forms a soft ball and follows wooden spoon around bowl. Turn onto generously floured board and knead lightly 2 minutes. Shape dough into balls; then pat out with floured hand. Place on greased baking sheet; brush tops with melted butter; cover with a light, clean cheesecloth and leave in a warm place for about 20 minutes, to mellow, ripen and rise slightly. Bake in a very hot oven for 6 or 7 minutes. Again brush tops with melted butter and continue baking 7 or 8 minutes longer. Remove from oven and brush again with melted butter. Serve warm.

(473) FRENCH FRIED ROLLS

YEAST METHOD

Makes about 8 dozen rolls. Deep fat temperature: 350° F. Frying time: until brown.

This method of frying little pellets of dough makes them particularly light and airy and it takes a heap to fill you up; so you better make plenty when you serve them to the family or guests. There is no waiting for dough to rise. Properly fried foods have a savor and delicacy which no other form of cooking can develop, and if fried in the right way they have a strong appetite-appeal. However, it is advisable to strain fat used for deep fat frying each time. This removes any little particles of food which are likely to be in the fat.

1 cup rapidly boiling water
¼ cup butter or lard
½ cup granulated sugar
1 generous teaspoon salt
1 cup undiluted evaporated milk
1 cake compressed yeast
½ scant cup lukewarm water
2 whole fresh eggs, well-beaten
7 cups bread flour, sifted (about)

Pour boiling water over butter or lard; add granulated sugar and salt with evaporated milk; stir thoroughly to melt, dissolve and blend ingredients; let cool to lukewarm; stir well and blend in the dissolved, crumbled yeast cake in lukewarm water. Stir in the eggs alternately with flour, and beat hard and briskly, adding more flour if necessary to make a soft dough. Knead dough lightly for about 5 minutes or until smooth, elastic, and not sticky. Flour your hands; pull off small pieces of dough, the size of a large walnut; roll between palms of hands and press out flat, about ¼-inch thick. Drop a few at a time into hot, deep fat and fry until brown on both sides (about 5 to 6 minutes). Serve as hot as possible with plenty of butter, jam, jelly, marmalade or preserves.

"Deacon Porter's hat" is a bread pudding shaped like a hat and since 1837 it has been very popular as a dessert in New England's oldest family.

(474) GRAHAM ROLLS

YEAST METHOD—REFRIGERATOR

Makes about 1½ dozen rolls. Oven temperature: 400° F. Baking time: 18–20 minutes.

1 cup milk, scalded
¼ cup granulated sugar
2 tablespoons butter or lard
1 generous teaspoon salt
1 cake compressed yeast
¼ scant cup lukewarm water
1 whole fresh egg, well-beaten
2½ cups bread flour, sifted
1 cup unsifted graham flour

Pour scalded milk over sugar, fat and salt in large mixing bowl; stir; let cool to lukewarm. Crumble yeast cake into lukewarm water and stir until dissolved; add to milk mixture and stir well, adding the egg while stirring. Turn in 1½ cups of the bread flour and beat briskly until smooth; then gradually add remaining bread flour mixed with unsifted graham flour, beating well after each addition. Turn dough into greased bowl; brush with melted butter or lard; cover tightly and place in refrigerator overnight or until ready to use. Roll with floured rolling pin to the desired thickness to make the type of roll desired, *i.e.*, Parker House, Clover Leaf (three small balls of dough in each greased muffin pan), etc. When rolls have been shaped, place them on a greased baking sheet and let rise until very light (refrigerator rolls take a longer time for rising than those which have not been chilled to 45° F. or lower); sprinkle with a little milk, then with a little granulated sugar and bake in a hot oven as directed. Serve hot or cold.

(475) HONEY CLOVER LEAF ROLLS

YEAST METHOD—REFRIGERATOR

Makes about 2 dozen rolls. Oven temperature: 400° F. Baking time: 18–20 minutes.

A typical group of bee-colonies in a New England farm backyard rises like a series of tall, narrow, white-painted chests of drawers beneath a protective roof, with the bottom drawer as the standard hive proper and each ascending drawer a "super." About ten wooden frames are placed vertically in each of the compartments and it is upon these that the worker bees build their cells, one row on each side of the frame.

Standing a respectful distance from the hive, the onlooker may watch as many as 100,000 bees intent on their flight to or from the hive. Armored with a bee-mask, one may look into the private lives of the hardy French or the more gentle Italian bees common in America. There are the patient workers going about their task of storing honey in the comb cells and finally sealing the cells with wax. There are the queen and her male consorts, supported in lazy luxury by the workers. And there are the young bees who will come to the opening of the hive to execute their "bee-dance" when they are ready to test their wings.

2 cakes compressed yeast
½ cup (scant) lukewarm water
⅓ cup sweet milk, scalded
⅔ cup shortening
⅔ cup strained honey
1 cup cooked, mashed potatoes
1 teaspoon (scant) salt
2 whole fresh eggs, well-beaten
6 to 7 cups bread flour, sifted twice

Crumble yeast in lukewarm water and stir until dissolved. Scald milk; add shortening, strained honey, mashed potatoes and salt and mix thoroughly. Let cool to lukewarm and add eggs. Combine with dissolved yeast cakes. Add enough flour to make a soft dough that will not stick to the hands or bowl. Knead for about 8 to 10 minutes; wrap in waxed paper or put in thickly covered mixing bowl; store in refrigerator and use as needed. This dough will keep several days.

When ready to use, form dough into small balls that will fill a muffin pan about one-half full or place three smaller balls of dough in each greased pan. Let rise until very light, in a warm place. Brush tops with melted butter, and bake in a hot oven as directed. Serve warm.

(476) HONEYED AFTERNOON TEA ROLLS

BAKING POWDER METHOD

Makes about 18 slices. Oven temperature: 425–350° F.
Baking time: 25 minutes.

NOTE: These delicious sweet rolls are very appropriate for Sunday breakfast or supper.

Initial preparation:

1 cup dark brown sugar
½ cup strained honey
½ cup butter or shortening

Combine the above ingredients in a small pan and set over a low flame to blend while rolls are prepared.

Dough:

2½ cups bread flour, sifted twice
1 scant teaspoon salt
4 teaspoons baking powder
½ cup butter or shortening
1 cup cold sweet milk

Add baking powder and salt to flour and sift into a mixing bowl; cut in shortening as for pie then stir in the milk. Turn out on lightly floured board and knead for 3 or 4 minutes. Roll out into a rectangular shape and sprinkle with a rounded teaspoon powdered cinnamon; then roll up beginning from the long side. Cut in slices about ¾-inch thick.

Stir the ingredients of the initial preparation well; spread in a shallow baking pan, covering the entire surface, and place the slices of dough on top of the mixture. Bake in a hot oven as directed; reducing heat to moderate after 15 minutes and baking 10 minutes longer. Remove pan from oven; let stand 3 or 4 minutes, and invert on a hot platter. Serve immediately.

You may use unsulphured old-fashioned molasses instead of honey, in which case add ¼ generous teaspoon baking soda to the milk before stirring into dry ingredients. Or sprinkle half a cup of finely ground nut meats over the honey or molasses.

(477) LEMON CLOVER LEAF ROLLS

Makes about 1½ dozen small rolls. Oven temperature: 425° F.
Baking time: 20 minutes.

In the following recipe, orange, lime or pineapple juice may be substituted for lemon juice.

2 cups bread flour, sifted
½ teaspoon salt
¼ cup fine granulated sugar
⅓ cup shortening
¾ teaspoon baking soda
½ cup cold sweet milk
3½ tablespoons unstrained lemon juice

Add sugar, soda and salt to the flour and sift into a mixing bowl; cut in shortening as for pie; combine milk with unstrained lemon juice and stir into flour mixture to form a stiff dough. Turn onto a lightly floured board and knead slightly. Flour your hands, take off pieces the size of a small walnut and form into balls; place 3 balls in each muffin pan; sprinkle with sugar and bake in a hot oven as directed until rolls are delicately browned. Serve warm on a folded napkin.

In 1487, it was unlawful to purchase flour in Holland except by physician's prescription.

(478) MAPLE NUT ROLLS

Makes about 1 dozen rolls. Oven temperature: 400° F.
Baking time: 15–18 minutes.

2 cups bread flour, sifted
1 scant tablespoon baking powder
½ teaspoon salt
¼ cup shortening
¾ cup cold sweet milk (about)
Softened butter for spreading
½ cup maple sugar mixed with ½ cup chopped nut meats

Add baking powder and salt to flour and sift into a mixing bowl; cut in shortening as for pie; gradually add milk, stirring until a soft dough is formed. Turn onto lightly floured board, knead a half minute and roll into an oblong piece about ¼-inch thick. Spread with softened butter then sprinkle with maple sugar mixed with nut meats. Roll up as for jelly roll and cut in scant inch slices. Place slices on greased baking sheet or in muffin tins; spread tops with butter and bake in a hot oven as directed until delicately brown. Serve warm.

MAPLE SYRUP

Maple syrup, America's favorite on pancakes, is mainly drawn from the trunks of maple trees, chiefly in northern New England where the industry accounts for about 42 per cent of the nation's production of the syrup and 52 per cent of the country's maple sugar.

The United States annually produces an average of 1,050,000 pounds of maple sugar and an average of 2,360,000 gallons of maple syrup (Department of Agriculture's statistics). While highly prized on the breakfast table, much crude maple syrup is bought up by the tobacco companies who use it to cure and season tobacco.

Methods of securing maple sap and reducing it to syrup and sugar vary little today from the methods the early New England settlers learned from the Indians. A hole is driven into the trunk of the tree, a drain is inserted and a bucket suspended where it will catch the fall. The sap is then run through an evaporating process which draws off the water content until a syrup remains. Maple sugar is made by heating the syrup and, when it has reached the proper temperature, quickly cooling it. The resultant mass is broken up and pulverized into grains which are still considerably larger than granulated sugar.

Sugar parties are a popular pastime in the north woods of Vermont. After the syrup has been boiled to the proper temperature, it is poured very thin on snow or cracked ice and permitted to harden. The result is delicious, but rather hard on the teeth!

About thirty-three gallons of maple tree sap are required to make one gallon of maple syrup.

(479) ORANGE MARMALADE TEA ROLLS

BAKING POWDER METHOD

Makes about 1½ dozen rolls. Oven temperature: 425° F.
Baking time: 15–18 minutes.

2 cups bread flour, sifted twice
1 tablespoon baking powder
½ teaspoon salt
¼ cup butter or shortening
1 whole fresh egg, well-beaten
¼ cup cold sweet milk
⅓ cup orange marmalade

Add baking powder and salt to the flour and sift into mixing bowl; cut in butter or other shortening as for pie. Combine beaten egg, milk and orange marmalade and mix well; then add to flour mixture gradually and mix to a soft dough. Turn onto a lightly floured board and knead 2 minutes; roll out to ½-inch thick and cut with floured cutter. Butter half of each circle, fold, place on greased baking sheet; brush top with additional melted butter and allow to stand in a warm place for about 15 minutes. Bake in a hot oven as directed. Again brush tops with additional melted butter and bake for 3 to 5 minutes more or until rolls are delicately browned. Serve warm.

You may substitute any other jam for orange marmalade, if desired.

(480) ORANGE RIND DINNER ROLLS

YEAST METHOD

Makes about 2 dozen rolls. Oven temperature: 375° F.
Baking time: 15–18 minutes.

NOTE: You may substitute grapefruit, lime or lemon for orange rind, and granulated sugar may be replaced by brown or maple sugar.

2 cakes compressed yeast
1/3 cup granulated sugar
1 cup scalded milk, cooled to lukewarm
3 whole fresh eggs, well-beaten
1/4 cup melted shortening
1 teaspoon salt
1 rounded teaspoon grated orange rind
4 cups bread flour, sifted twice

Crumble yeast cake and mix with sugar; let stand for 5 minutes. Add half of the lukewarm milk and stir until yeast is dissolved. Combine remaining lukewarm milk, eggs, shortening, salt and orange rind; mix well, and add to yeast mixture, blending thoroughly. Then, gradually add the flour, beating vigorously after each addition, until light and thoroughly blended. Brush top of dough with melted shortening; cover, set mixing bowl over hot water and allow to rise until doubled in bulk (about 2 1/2 hours). Place 1 teaspoon melted butter, 1 pecan half, and 1/2 teaspoon brown sugar in each greased muffin pan. Spoon dough into pans to half-full. Allow to rise until doubled in bulk (about 1 1/2 hours); then bake in a moderately hot oven as directed. A slow baking is much better than a quick baking for this kind of rolls. Serve warm.

(481) ORANGE JUICE AND RIND ROLLS I

YEAST METHOD

Makes about 4 dozen rolls. Oven temperature: 400° F.
Baking time: 15–18 minutes.

For 2 dozen rolls, cut down amount of ingredients one-half. These rolls are very light and of average size.

1 cake compressed yeast
1/4 cup lukewarm water
1 1/2 cups sweet milk, scalded, cooled to lukewarm
1 cup cooked, sieved potatoes
4 cups (1 quart) bread flour, sifted
1/2 scant cup granulated sugar
1 generous teaspoon salt
2 whole fresh eggs, well-beaten
1/4 cup melted butter
Juice of 2 medium-sized oranges, unstrained
Rind of two oranges
3 1/2 cups bread flour, sifted

Crumble yeast cake into lukewarm water, and stir until dissolved; stir in milk mixed with potatoes. Blend well and gradually stir into this the 4 cups of flour, beating vigorously after each addition until sponge is smooth. Cover with a dry cloth and set over a pan of hot water (not boiling) to rise until doubled in bulk (3½ to 4 hours).

Combine sugar, salt, eggs, butter, orange juice and grated rind and blend thoroughly. To this, gradually add the remaining 3½ cups of flour, beating well until smooth and bubbling. Then stir this into the raised sponge, beating briskly until smooth. Turn dough onto lightly floured board and knead until it is smooth, elastic and not sticky. Return to the mixing bowl; brush with melted shortening; cover with a cloth; set over hot water; let rise again until doubled in bulk. Turn dough again onto lightly floured board; knead a minute or so lightly and form into rolls of desired shape and size. Place on greased baking sheet and allow to rise for the third time until light (1½ to 2 hours). Bake in a hot oven as directed. Immediately after removing from the oven, brush with melted butter and serve warm or cold. You may substitute grapefruit, lemon or lime juice for orange and grated rind, if desired.

It was in 1671 that a whimsical Paris baker made the first five-foot-long French bread, thus making culinary history.

(482) ORANGE JUICE AND RIND ROLLS II

QUICK BAKING POWDER METHOD

Makes about 1½ dozen rolls. Oven temperature: 425° F.
Baking time: 15 minutes.

2 cups bread flour, sifted twice
2 tablespoons granulated sugar
1 tablespoon baking powder
1 scant teaspoon salt
¼ cup shortening
½ cup unsieved orange juice
1 scant teaspoon grated orange rind
Melted butter for tops
1 whole fresh egg, well-beaten

To the flour add baking powder and salt and sift into a mixing bowl. Rub in shortening as for pie. Combine well beaten egg, orange juice and grated rind and stir into flour mixture until dampened. Turn out dough on slightly floured board; knead gently for a half minute; roll out into a rectangular sheet ¼-inch thick; brush with melted butter; roll up like a jelly roll and cut into 1-inch slices. Place slices in greased muffin pans and bake in a very hot oven as directed. Serve as hot as possible.

(483) ORANGE JUICE PARKER HOUSE CHEESE ROLLS

YEAST METHOD

Makes about 1½ dozen rolls. Oven temperature: 400° F.
Baking time: 12 to 15 minutes.

1 cup boiling orange juice
½ lb. grated cheese (any kind)
1 cake compressed yeast
¾ cup lukewarm milk
½ generous teaspoon salt
1 scant tablespoon granulated sugar
2¾ cups (about) bread flour, sifted twice
½ teaspoon baking soda

Add grated cheese to boiling orange juice and beat until thoroughly blended and smooth. Dissolve crumbled yeast cake in lukewarm milk with salt and sugar and add to first mixture, mixing well. To the flour add soda and sift over liquid mixture, beating vigorously until mixture is smooth, adding more sifted bread flour, if necessary, to make a fairly stiff dough. Turn out on a lightly-floured board and knead until smooth, spongy and not sticky. Place dough in a greased bowl; brush top with melted shortening; cover with a light, clean, dry cloth and place the bowl over a pan containing hot (not boiling) water; let rise until dough is very, very light (about 3 hours). Knead a minute or so lightly; return to the greased bowl and allow to rise 45 minutes. Knead again and allow to rise 15 minutes. Now, turn out on lightly-floured board; shape, brush lower half of each "pocketbook" with melted butter before folding over. Press edges together. Place on greased baking sheet about an inch apart. Cover with a dry cloth and let rise until light (about 25 minutes). Bake in a hot oven as directed until delicately browned. Serve warm.

(484) PARKER HOUSE ROLLS

Makes 2 dozen small rolls. Oven temperature: 450° F.
Baking time: 12 to 14 minutes.

1 cup sweet milk, scalded
¼ cup granulated sugar
1½ scant teaspoons salt
¼ cup butter
½ cake compressed yeast
¼ cup lukewarm water
2¾ cups bread flour, sifted
Melted butter for tops

Dissolve sugar, salt and butter in scalded milk. Cool to lukewarm. Add crumbled yeast dissolved in lukewarm water and beat vigorously. Add flour slowly and only just enough to make a ball that can be handled easily. Put in a greased bowl, cover and keep in a warm place to rise until it doubles in bulk. Toss lightly on slightly floured board and roll to the thickness of 1/3 inch. Cut the dough in rounds with a biscuit cutter. Brush one-half of each round with melted butter, dip knife handle in flour and make a deep crease across the middle of each roll. Fold over and place in a row in a generously greased baking pan. Brush with melted butter and let rise until double their bulk. Bake in a very hot oven as directed until delicately brown. Serve warm.

In 1626 Louis XIII of France became so fond of gingerbread that his courtiers carried it around for him in ornamental cases.

(485) PARKER HOUSE ORANGE ROLLS

YEAST METHOD

Makes about 2 dozen small rolls. Oven temperature: 450° F.
Baking time: 12 to 14 minutes.

NOTE: These Parker House rolls, weighing each 1½ ounces, may be sugar or orange iced.

¼ cup granulated sugar
¼ cup butter
1½ scant teaspoons salt
½ cup boiling water
½ cup orange juice, lukewarm
½ cake compressed yeast
¼ cup lukewarm water
2 egg yolks, well-beaten
1 scant teaspoon grated orange rind
2¾ cups twice-sifted bread flour
Melted butter for brushing
24 peeled sections seedless oranges or tangerines freed from white membrane

Dissolve sugar, butter and salt in boiling water. Stir well; cool to lukewarm. Stir in orange juice and the half yeast cake, dissolved in water, mixed with well-beaten egg yolks and grated orange rind. Beat vigorously until smooth. Gradually add the flour and beat and stir alternately, until a soft ball is formed and dough can be handled easily. Turn dough into a greased mixing bowl; cover with a light, clean, dry cloth and place over a pan containing hot water to rise until it doubles in bulk. Toss lightly on slightly floured board and roll out to the thickness of 1/3 inch. Cut the dough in rounds with a biscuit cutter. Brush one-half of each round with melted butter, dip handle of a knife in flour and make a deep crease across the middle of each roll; place a prepared section of orange in the crease; fold over, pocketbook-like, and place in generously greased baking pans. Brush with melted butter and let rise until doubled in bulk. Bake in a very hot oven as directed or until rolls are delicately brown. Serve warm.

(486) PARKER HOUSE VINEGAR ROLLS

YEAST METHOD

Makes about 3 dozen rolls. Oven temperature: 450° F. Baking time: 12–14 minutes.

½ cup lukewarm water
1 cake compressed yeast
½ cup shortening (preferably butter)
¾ cup granulated sugar
1 whole fresh egg, well-beaten
1½ scant teaspoons salt
1 tablespoon mild vinegar
½ teaspoon powdered nutmeg
½ teaspoon grated lemon rind
8 cups bread flour, sifted twice
Melted butter for tops

Dissolve crumbled yeast cake in the water. Cream shortening and sugar until light; add beaten egg and beat vigorously; combine salt, vinegar and nutmeg and add to creamed shortening; combine this with dissolved yeast mixture. Beat briskly until smooth; then gradually add flour enough to make a rather stiff dough, which will recede when poked with finger. Grease a large mixing bowl and turn in the dough; brush with melted butter; cover with a dry towel and set the bowl over a pan containing hot (not boiling) water, keeping the water hot. Let rise for 2 hours or more or until mixture has doubled in bulk. Then punch air out of center, punching only once. Let rise again for 30 minutes. Toss onto slightly-floured board and knead 1 or 2 minutes, or until dough is smooth, elastic and not sticky. Roll out to the thickness of ⅓ inch. Cut the dough with floured biscuit cutter; brush one-half of each round with melted butter; dip handle of a knife in flour and make a deep crease across the middle of each roll. Fold over and place in rows in a well-greased baking pan. Brush with melted butter and let rise until doubled in bulk. Bake in a very hot oven as directed until rolls are delicately brown. Serve warm.

NOTE: You may place a small pitted, cooked prune, a cooked dried apricot, a piece of ginger (preserves), or almost any kind of fresh or cooked fruit, well-drained, in the crease before folding.

The first "kitchen raider" was Julius Caesar who used to get up at

3 A.M. *for some bread and cheese, then return to bed to digest in peace.*

(487) PECAN ROLLS

YEAST METHOD

Makes about 2 dozen rolls. Oven temperature: 400° F.
Baking time: 18–20 minutes.

Prepare Crusty Rolls as in Recipe No. 466 and arrange in a pan prepared as follows:

Spread bottom of baking pan with a mixture of one part butter to two of sugar and sprinkle with pecan, walnut, or any desired nut meats, chopped. Roll dough after second rising and spread with butter; place over nut mixture and let rise until doubled in bulk. Then mark in squares with floured cutter and bake in a hot oven as directed until top is delicately browned. Serve warm.

(488) PENNSYLVANIA CINNAMON PECAN ROLLS

YEAST METHOD

Makes about 2 dozen rolls. Oven temperature: 350° F.
Baking time: 25 minutes.

Ever since the thirteen families of Crefelders and Mennonites arrived on the Concord at Philadelphia in 1683, the Pennsylvania Dutch have been noted for their food, and many of their recipes which have come down through the years represent a superior type of regional cookery whose fame has spread throughout the country. They were the first gourmets in America and the first dining club in the New World was organized in 1732 in Philadelphia, a city which became and remains a center for good food.

As early as 1725, Dutch farmers were building the huge Conestoga wagons with the typical boatlike curves of the wagon bodies hanging low in the middle which were later to be seen in increasing numbers as pioneers pushed their way westward. Loaded with food and grain for the Philadelphia markets, the Dutch farmers brought with them hearty appetites and a taste for the wholesome and even lavish fare of their kitchens. They were accustomed to good food, for there has never been a more tireless preserver, pickler, curer, spicer, canner or baker than the Dutch housewife. Very little escaped her expert touch; she got in the habit centuries ago of loading every table so liberally with "sweet and sours" that over the years it became a fixed tradition of hospitality for her to put on the table, especially for guests, precisely seven sweets and seven sours.

Often she would serve afternoon coffee with Cinnamon Pecan Rolls which were made as follows:

1½ cakes compressed yeast
½ cup lukewarm water
2 cups sweet milk, scalded, cooled to lukewarm
4 egg yolks, well-beaten
1¼ teaspoons salt
½ cup butter, melted
¾ cup granulated sugar
4½ to 5 cups bread flour, sifted twice
Melted butter (not too hot) for spreading
2 tablespoons granulated sugar
2 tablespoons brown sugar
1½ to 2 teaspoons powdered cinnamon
1 cup chopped pecan meats
Butter for tops

Dissolve yeast cakes in water and stir until dissolved. Stir in the milk, alternately with 2 cups of the flour. Beat briskly; cover with a light, dry towel and set over a pan containing hot (not boiling) water to rise until mixture bubbles and is half doubled in bulk; beat in the egg yolks with salt, butter and ¾ cup of granulated sugar.

Mix well and let rise until doubled in bulk, after adding the remaining sifted flour, or enough to make a stiff dough that can be handled and kneaded easily. When doubled in bulk, knead down until smooth, elastic and not sticky. Put in a greased mixing bowl; brush with melted butter; cover with a dry cloth and place over a pan of hot (not boiling) water until it rises. Then cut it down with your hands and allow to rise again to double in bulk.

Knead lightly (about ½ minute); roll out until dough is ¼ inch thick; spread with melted butter, then with granulated sugar, and sprinkle brown sugar on top of granulated sugar. Over the brown sugar sprinkle powdered cinnamon, adding more if desired. Now take one end of the dough and roll up like a jelly roll. With a sharp knife cut slices about an inch wide.

Grease a baking pan generously; sprinkle with a thin layer of granulated sugar, and over this spread pecan meats. Arrange the slices over the nuts; brush tops with melted butter to prevent hardening and allow to rise until doubled in size, in a warm place and covered with a dry towel. Bake in a moderate oven as directed. Remove from oven, let stand a few minutes, then turn upside down on a hot platter, thus getting a thick syrup with pecans on top of slices.

(489) POTATO WATER FEATHER ROLLS

PENNSYLVANIA DUTCH RECIPE—YEAST METHOD

Makes about 2½ dozen rolls. Oven temperature: 400° F. Baking time: 20 minutes.

NOTE: The potato water used in this recipe is that saved from potatoes cooked before.

- 1 cake compressed yeast
- ½ cup lukewarm potato water, strained
- ½ cup butter or lard
- 2 tablespoons granulated sugar
- 1¾ teaspoons salt
- 2 cups lukewarm potato water, strained
- 5 cups bread flour, sifted twice
- Melted butter for tops

Add crumbled yeast cake to the ½ cup of lukewarm potato water and stir until dissolved. Cream butter or lard with combined sugar and salt, stir into the remaining 2 cups of potato water, and when thoroughly blended stir in the yeast mixture. Blend well; then gradually add the flour, beating vigorously after each addition, until mixture is smooth and dough begins to leave the wooden spoon (about 5 or 6 minutes). Cover with a clean, dry towel; place pan over hot (not boiling) water and let rise until doubled in bulk. Then knock the dough down with your hands and let rise until it is again doubled in bulk. Place a spoonful of dough in each generously greased muffin pan, slightly warmed. Work quickly so as not to release air bubbles, handling as little as possible. Place muffin pans away from drafts in a warm place, covered; allow to rise again until doubled in bulk or dough fills the pans. Bake in a hot oven as directed. Serve warm with either jam, jelly, marmalade or preserves, as well as plenty of butter.

(490) POTATO WATER CARROT ROLLS

PENNSYLVANIA DUTCH RECIPE—YEAST METHOD

Makes about 2½ dozen rolls. Oven temperature: 400° F.
Baking time: 18–20 minutes.

2 cakes compressed yeast
½ cup lukewarm potato water, strained
1 cup cooked carrots, sieved
1½ cups lukewarm potato water, strained
2 whole fresh eggs, well-beaten
½ cup melted butter or lard
2 tablespoons granulated sugar
1 to 2 teaspoons salt
Sifted bread flour
Ice cold water for tops

Crumble yeast cakes in the ½ cup lukewarm potato water and stir until dissolved. Combine all remaining ingredients except the flour; beat well and combine with yeast mixture. Blend thoroughly, then add enough sifted bread flour to make a dough that kneads easily. Knead until smooth, elastic and not sticky. Turn into greased mixing bowl; brush top with shortening to prevent cracking; cover with a clean, dry, light towel and set over hot water to rise until doubled in bulk. Fill warm, greased muffin pans half full of dough; brush with shortening and cover. Stand it in a warm place or over hot water and let rise to doubled in bulk. Bake 10 minutes in a hot oven; quickly sprinkle with ice-cold water to make the rolls crusty, and continue baking 8 or 10 minutes longer until rolls are brown on top and bottom. Serve warm or cold.

NOTE: You may substitute sweet milk for potato water.

(491) PRUNE ROLLS

YEAST METHOD

Makes about 3 dozen rolls. Oven temperature: 400° F.
Baking time: 25 minutes.

2 cakes compressed yeast
¼ cup lukewarm sweet milk
½ cup granulated sugar
1 teaspoon salt
2 whole fresh eggs, well-beaten
1 cup sweet milk, scalded
5 cups (about) bread flour, sifted twice
Cooked, cold, pitted small prunes

Crumble yeast cakes into the milk. Combine all the remaining ingredients, except bread flour and prunes and add to yeast mixture. Gradually add the flour, using enough to make a dough stiff enough to handle, and beat vigorously until it is smooth. Brush with melted shortening; cover, place dough over a pan containing hot water and let rise until doubled in bulk. Turn out upon lightly floured board and knead until smooth, elastic and not sticky. Shape into small round rolls the size of a small egg. Place on greased baking sheet; press a prune in center of each; let rise to double in bulk and brush with butter. Bake in a hot oven as directed. Serve warm or cold.

(492) RAISED BRAN MOLASSES ROLLS

YEAST METHOD

Makes about 2½ dozen rolls. Oven temperature: 450° F. Baking time: 20 minutes.

2 cups sweet, rich milk, scalded
1 cup unsifted bran
3 tablespoons butter
½ cup molasses
2 scant teaspoons salt
1 yeast cake
¼ cup lukewarm water
1 whole fresh egg, well-beaten
5½ cups bread flour, sifted twice (about)

Combine the first five ingredients and blend thoroughly; let cool to lukewarm. Stir in the yeast cake dissolved in water and mixed with egg. Beat briskly, then gradually add flour, beating well after each addition, until smooth and thoroughly blended (use enough bread flour to make a stiff dough easily handled). Brush top of dough with melted shortening; cover with a light, clean, dry towel; place over a pan containing hot (not boiling) water, and allow to rise until doubled in bulk. Punch the dough two or three times with your closed hand, then cover and let rise until again doubled in bulk. Knead lightly a minute or so until smooth, satiny and not sticky. Shape in any desired form; place upon greased baking sheet; let rise again until doubled in bulk. Bake in a hot oven as directed. Serve warm or cold.

(493) RAISIN HONEY CLOVER LEAF ROLLS

YEAST METHOD

Makes about 2 dozen rolls. Oven temperature: 400° F. Baking time: 12–15 minutes.

1 cup sweet rich milk, scalded, cooled
2 cakes compressed yeast
¼ cup granulated sugar
1¾ teaspoons salt
1 whole fresh egg, well-beaten
½ cup melted lard or butter
1 cup parboiled, dried seedless raisins
2½ cups bread flour, sifted
2½ cups (about) additional bread flour, sifted

Dissolve yeast cakes in a little of the milk. Combine granulated sugar, salt, egg and melted fat; mix thoroughly, and add dissolved yeast cakes. Blend well; then add the first 2½ cups of flour and beat vigorously until sponge is smooth. Gradually add enough of remaining flour to make a dough easy to handle, alternately with the prepared, floured raisins. Knead about 3 minutes on a lightly floured board until dough is smooth, satiny, elastic and not sticky. Place in a greased mixing bowl; brush top with melted shortening; cover with a clean, light, dry cloth and allow to rise until doubled in bulk. Punch down; let rise again to double its bulk (about 40–45 minutes). Form balls the size of a large marble and place three in each greased muffin pan. Cover and let rise again until double in size. Brush with the following mixture:

½ cup strained honey
2 tablespoons butter, melted
⅓ teaspoon cinnamon

Then bake in a hot oven as directed until glossy and brown. Serve warm.

The dinner bell is believed to have originated in Sicily about 50 A.D. *when a cook pounded on a piece of metal to summon men working in a stone quarry.*

(494) REFRIGERATOR CINNAMON ROLLS

YEAST METHOD

Makes about 2½ dozen rolls. Oven temperature: 400° F.
Baking time: about 18 minutes.

NOTE: If slices are desired not too rich, boiling water may be used instead of milk. The spread of soft butter, brown sugar and cinnamon is left to the taste of the maker.

2 cups sweet milk, scalded
¼ cup granulated sugar
2¾ teaspoons salt (about)
2 tablespoons shortening
2 cakes compressed yeast
¼ cup lukewarm water
1 teaspoon granulated sugar
2 whole fresh eggs, well-beaten
8 cups (about) bread flour, sifted twice

Spread: Soft butter. Brown sugar, sifted. Cinnamon to taste.

Add the ¼ cup granulated sugar, salt and shortening to scalded milk; blend; cool to lukewarm. Crumble yeast cake into lukewarm water; add remaining sugar and eggs; then stir into the milk mixture. Gradually stir in the flour, adding just enough to make a dough which will follow the spoon. *Do not knead at all.* Cover with a light, clean, dry cloth and place over a pan containing hot (not boiling) water; let rise until doubled in bulk. Wrap in waxed paper and set in refrigerator until ready to use. Roll out a quarter of the dough, 1/4-inch thick, making a sheet 10 × 12 inches square. Spread with soft butter and sprinkle with sugar mixed with powdered cinnamon. Roll up like a jelly roll; cut into 3/4-inch slices and place in greased pan far apart to allow for expansion. Cover and let stand over hot (not boiling) water until slices are twice their size (about 4 hours). Bake in a hot oven as directed until delicately brown. Serve warm or cold.

(495) REFRIGERATOR CLOVER LEAF ROLLS

MODERN YEAST METHOD

Makes about 2 1/2 dozen rolls. Oven temperature: 425° F.
Baking time: 12–15 minutes.
Sponge standing: 30 minutes. First rising time: 2 hours (about).
Chilling time in refrigerator: 2–3 days.
Second rising time: 1 hour (about).

1 cake compressed yeast
1/4 cup lukewarm water
1/4 teaspoon granulated sugar
1/4 cup shortening
1/4 cup granulated sugar
1 scant teaspoon salt
1 whole fresh egg, well-beaten
1 1/3 cups sweet milk, scalded, cooled
5 cups (about) bread flour, sifted twice
2 or 3 tablespoons melted butter for tops

Crumble yeast cake into lukewarm water and stir until dissolved; stand in a warm place for 30 minutes (this is called sponge). Blend shortening, sugar and salt in mixing bowl; stir in combined egg and milk and add to the yeast sponge. Blend thoroughly; then stir in flour enough to make a dough that can be easily kneaded. Turn upon a slightly floured board and knead until smooth, elastic and not sticky, adding a little more flour if needed. Form into a large ball; cover; put over a pan containing hot (not boiling) water and let stand until doubled in bulk and very light. Knead dough again, about half a minute; brush with butter; place in a greased bowl; cover with waxed paper; secure with a string or still better with a rubber band and store in refrigerator. Every day knead the dough half a minute to drive off the gas.

When ready to make the rolls, knead the dough slightly, pinch off very small pieces and roll into balls an inch in diameter. Place 3 balls in each buttered muffin pan, having the pan one-half full. Brush with melted butter; cover with a light, clean, dry cloth; let rise in a warm place until doubled in bulk. Bake in a very hot oven as directed. Serve warm or cold.

In 1467 the Earl of Leicester created a bread sauce which he called "saucealiper."

(496) REFRIGERATOR HONEY ROLLS I

YEAST METHOD

Makes about 2½ dozen rolls. Oven temperature: 425° F.
Baking time: 12–15 minutes.

Use the same dough as in Recipe No. 495, prepared as indicated (that is, remaining 2 to 3 days in refrigerator before using). Roll dough quite thin (scant ¼-inch) in an oblong sheet. Spread with melted butter, strained honey and a sprinkling of granulated sugar. Roll up as for jelly roll; cut in one scant inch slices; place on a well-greased baking sheet or pan; let rise until very light (about 35 to 40 minutes). Bake in a very hot oven as directed. Serve warm or cold.

NOTE: You may spread parboiled, seedless raisins over the sprinkling of sugar, before rolling up dough. Or add chopped, blanched almonds, or any other nut meats, instead of raisins; or use both.

"Mormon Gravy" is made by frying pork or bacon in a pan and then mixing flour with the grease and letting it brown. Then if you are poor, you mix in water, or if you have a cow, you use milk. "Mormon Gravy" is eaten for breakfast, dinner or supper, with bread or potatoes.

An old Mormon grandma told me how she baked her bread: "Cook the bread until it has a hard, brown crust on it." On hard Mormon bread crusts, babies cut their teeth; debutantes masticate crusts to obtain pearly, beautiful molars. The tradition that "crusts make your hair curly" is faithfully upheld by Mormon mothers and children. Oldsters, especially, call for hard crusts, and often a pan of dough is rolled out thin in the pan and baked for "pa." This is known as "Pa's Bread."

To be accorded special favor, if elderly, is to be served the crusts and the heels of the loaves of bread. The crust craze was started by

Brigham Young who insisted: "Bread is the staff of life—especially, if it's browned well."

(497) REFRIGERATOR HONEY ROLLS II—MISSISSIPPI METHOD

YEAST METHOD

Makes about 2½ dozen rolls. Oven temperature: 400° F. Baking time: 20 minutes (about).

NOTE: Sieve warm mashed potatoes to get them very smooth.

- 2 cakes compressed yeast
- ½ cup lukewarm water
- ⅓ cup sweet milk, scalded
- ⅔ cup shortening
- ⅔ cup strained honey
- 1 cup warm mashed potatoes
- 1 teaspoon salt
- 2 whole fresh eggs, well-beaten
- 6½ to 7 cups bread flour, sifted twice

Crumble yeast cakes in lukewarm water; stir until dissolved. (You may add a generous teaspoon of granulated sugar to the yeast. This is optional.) To the milk add shortening, honey, mashed potatoes and salt and stir to blend thoroughly. Add dissolved yeast mixture after milk mixture has cooled to lukewarm. Mix well; let stand for about 20 minutes; then stir in the eggs. Add the flour gradually (using just enough to make a dough easily handled), beating vigorously after each addition. Toss upon a lightly floured board and knead for 8 to 10 minutes. Place, ball-like, in greased bowl. Brush with butter; cover and set in refrigerator until wanted, but no longer than 3 days, kneading one minute or so every day to drive off gas. When ready to use, pinch off a small piece of dough; shape in any desired form; place upon greased baking sheet; let rise until doubled in bulk and bake in a hot oven as directed.

(498) REFRIGERATOR POTATO ROLLS—DAKOTA METHOD

COMBINATION YEAST, BAKING POWDER AND SODA METHOD

Makes about 2½ dozen rolls. Oven temperature: 400° F. Baking time: 20 minutes.

- 2 cups sweet milk, scalded
- 1 scant cup warm mashed potatoes
- ½ cup granulated sugar
- ½ cup lard or butter
- 1 cake compressed yeast
- ¼ cup lukewarm water
- ½ teaspoon baking soda
- ½ teaspoon baking powder
- 1¾ to 2 teaspoons salt
- 4½ to 5 cups bread flour, sifted twice

Combine milk, mashed potatoes, granulated sugar and lard (or butter) in a saucepan and bring just to a boil. Turn into mixing bowl; let cool to lukewarm. Crumble yeast cake into lukewarm water; stir until dissolved and add to milk-potato mixture. To the flour add soda, baking powder, and salt and sift together. Gradually add flour mixture to the first mixture, beating briskly after each addition until smooth. The dough should be rather stiff. Cover with a clean, light, dry towel; place over a pan of hot (not boiling) water and let stand about one hour or until dough doubles in bulk. Place in refrigerator, still covered, until wanted. When ready to bake, cut off the amount needed, roll out; shape or cut into rolls and place upon greased baking sheet. Let rise about two hours, or until light and doubled in bulk. Bake in a hot oven as directed. Serve warm or cold.

(499) REFRIGERATOR RING ROLLS

YEAST METHOD

Makes about 2 dozen ring rolls. Oven temperature: 400° F. Baking time: 18–20 minutes.

1/4 cup lard or butter	1/4 cup lukewarm water
1/4 cup granulated sugar	3/4 cup sweet milk, scalded
2 whole fresh eggs, well-beaten	1 scant teaspoon salt
1 cake compressed yeast	4 1/2 cups bread flour, sifted twice

Melted butter for tops

Important: Refrigerator bread or rolls need to stand about 30 minutes in a warm place before being handled to remove the chill.

Cream together shortening and sugar. Beat in the eggs. Crumble yeast cake into lukewarm water and stir until dissolved. Add to creamed mixture alternately with scalded milk which has been cooled to lukewarm and mixed with salt. Gradually add the flour, beating briskly after each addition, until smooth, adding more flour if needed to obtain a dough to handle easily. Cover; place in refrigerator until wanted, but no longer than 3 days. When ready to bake, remove from refrigerator; let stand about 30 minutes; roll out on lightly floured board to 1/3-inch and cut with floured doughnut cutter. Place on greased baking sheet; spread with melted butter; cover with a clean, light, dry towel and allow to rise in a warm place until doubled in bulk (about 2 1/2 to 3 hours). Bake in a hot oven as directed until delicately brown. Serve warm or cold.

Few words have a more peculiar origin than "etiquette." It really means "label," or "ticket"! . . . Once upon a time a certain Scottish gardener in charge of Louis XIV's garden at Versailles was much upset because the courtiers would walk on his precious flower beds. To keep them off, he placed notices in the shape of tickets, or labels —French "étiquettes"—at various spots in his beloved grounds with instructions to keep off. The haughty courtiers laughed them to scorn and would not deign to notice such instructions—till a hint came from high quarters that walks in future must be within the étiquettes laid down by the gardener. Thus originated the present word "etiquette."

(500) REFRIGERATOR SOUR CREAM ROLLS

Makes about 2 dozen rolls. Oven temperature: 400° F.
Baking time: 25–30 minutes.

NOTE: Sour cream is a goodly thing. It makes delicious gravies and salad dressings; it is fine whipped to use as a topping for soups; it can be substituted for sour milk in quick breads, cakes and cookies; and because one cup of heavy sour cream is about 40 per cent fat, it can take the place of part of the fat in such recipes. If sour cream is thinnish, use it as you would use rich sour milk. When you bake with sour cream, use soda alone or with baking powder for leavening.

In the following recipe, the dough may be stored in the refrigerator for as long as 4 or 5 days.

1 cake compressed yeast
½ cup granulated sugar
¾ cup butter
½ cup sweet milk, scalded
2 whole fresh eggs, well-beaten
1 cup sour cream (dairy-made)
4½ cups bread flour, sifted twice
1¼ teaspoons salt
1½ cups additional bread flour, sifted twice

Crumble yeast cake into mixing bowl, add sugar and stir together until yeast liquefies (no lukewarm water required to dissolve the yeast). Let stand about 20 minutes. Meanwhile combine butter and milk. Beat eggs and add to sour cream, blending thoroughly. Combine liquefied yeast, buttermilk mixture (cooled to lukewarm) and egg and sour cream mixture. Blend thoroughly. Turn the flour over the first mixture all at once and beat briskly for 8 or 10 minutes (automatic mixer good for the purpose). Place dough in covered mixing bowl and allow to stand overnight in refrigerator before using, to mellow and ripen.

The next day, let the dough rise over hot water, covered with a light towel, to double its original bulk or more. Knead in 1½ cups of additional bread flour. Flour board slightly; roll out into two sheets about ¼-inch thick; spread with a thin layer of additional sour cream; sprinkle with brown sugar to taste (2 or 3 tablespoons); add a few nut meats, chopped. Roll lengthwise as for jelly roll; cut in slices 1½ inches thick. Place in generously buttered (no other shortening should be used) muffin pans lined with brown sugar, chopped nut meats and a dot of butter; set in a warm place to rise to double their bulk. Bake in a hot oven for 20 minutes; reduce heat to moderate, and continue baking 5 or 8 minutes longer, or until slices are delicately brown. Serve warm or cold.

In 1541 Michelangelo Buonarroti, the famous Florentine painter, derived inspiration from a meal of a dozen onions and bread.

(501) REFRIGERATOR WHOLE WHEAT ROLLS

YEAST METHOD

Makes about 2½ dozen rolls. Oven temperature: 400° F.
Baking time: 18 minutes (about).

- 2 cups sweet milk, lukewarm
- 2 cakes compressed yeast
- ½ cup granulated sugar
- 2¼ generous teaspoons salt
- ½ generous teaspoon baking soda
- 3 cups bread flour, sifted once
- 4 cups (1 quart) unsifted whole wheat flour
- 2 large whole eggs, well-beaten
- ¼ cup melted shortening (preferably lard or butter)

Scald milk and let cool to lukewarm; crumble in the yeast cakes and stir until thoroughly dissolved; add sugar and salt. Mix well. Combine soda with flour and sift together over the unsifted whole wheat. Mix well. Gradually stir flour mixture into the yeast mixture, alternately with eggs, beating vigorously until dough is smooth. Lastly stir in briskly the melted shortening. Turn dough into a large, greased mixing bowl; cover with a light, clean, dry cloth and place in refrigerator until needed. When ready to bake, knead dough until smooth, elastic and not sticky. Shape into rolls according to fancy and place on a greased baking sheet; cover with a cloth and let rise in a warm place until doubled in bulk. Bake in a hot oven as directed until delicately browned. Serve warm or cold.

(502) SOUR CREAM ROLLS—MIDWEST METHOD

YEAST METHOD

Makes about 3 dozen rolls. Oven temperature: 400° F.
Baking time: 18 minutes.

1 cake compressed yeast
¼ cup lukewarm water
2 cups heavy dairy-made sour cream, scalded
3 tablespoons granulated sugar
1¾ generous teaspoons salt
¼ generous teaspoon baking soda
5 cups (about) bread flour, sifted twice
Melted butter for tops

Crumble yeast cake into lukewarm water and stir until dissolved. To the sour cream add sugar, salt and soda; stir; cool to lukewarm; add yeast mixture; blend thoroughly; then stir in half of the flour, and stir briskly until smooth. Add enough of the remaining flour to make a soft dough, easy to knead; turn out on lightly floured board and knead for 5 minutes, or until dough is smooth, satiny, elastic and does not stick to the hands. Roll out ½-inch thick; cut into small rounds with floured cutter or pinch off pieces the size of a small egg and shape into desired form; place close together on well-greased baking pan or sheet; brush with melted butter; cover with light cloth and allow to rise until doubled in bulk (about 2 hours), in a warm place or over hot water. Bake in a hot oven as directed until delicately browned. Serve warm or cold.

NOTE: Buttermilk plus 3 tablespoons of melted shortening may be used instead of sour cream.

In 1794 patrons of New York's only hostelry, the City Hotel, had to bring their own vegetables, their own bread and pay extra for having vegetables cooked.

(503) SQUASH ROLLS

YEAST METHOD—REFRIGERATOR

Makes about 2½–3 dozen rolls. Oven temperature: 375° F.
Baking time: 25–30 minutes.

NOTE: Parsnips, turnips, or pumpkin may be used instead of squash.

1 cup steamed, baked or canned squash sieved rather dry
½ cup granulated sugar
1½ teaspoons salt
1 cup sweet milk, scalded
1 cake compressed yeast
¼ cup lukewarm water
½ cup melted shortening
2 teaspoons grated lemon rind
5 cups (about) bread flour, sifted twice

Combine sieved squash, sugar, salt and milk and blend well, beating vigorously until smooth. Cool to lukewarm. Crumble yeast cake into lukewarm water, stir until dissolved, add to squash mixture; blend well, adding the grated lemon (or orange, grapefruit, or lime) rind. Add half of the flour and beat briskly until smooth. Beat in the melted shortening, alternately with remaining bread flour. Cover with a light, clean, dry cloth; place over a pan of hot (not boiling) water and let rise until doubled in bulk. Cover dough with waxed paper, then with a clean, dry, light towel and place in refrigerator over night. When ready to bake, remove dough from refrigerator at least 2 hours before rolling out; shape into rolls and place on a greased baking sheet; let rise, covered, until doubled in bulk, and bake in a moderately oven as directed until delicately brown. Immediately after removing from oven, brush with melted butter and serve warm or cold.

(504) SUPPER BOW-KNOT ROLLS

YEAST METHOD

Makes 2½ dozen rolls. Oven temperature: 375° F.
Baking time: 20–25 minutes (about).

NOTE: You may shape dough into tea rings, coffee cake, crescents, plain rolls, etc., instead of bow-knot rolls. You may also ice tops, using your favorite icing recipe, and while icing is still soft, sprinkle it with chopped nut meats, shredded almonds, or shredded coconut.

2 cakes compressed yeast
¼ cup lukewarm water
¼ cup butter
½ cup granulated sugar
1 scant teaspoon salt
1 cup sweet milk, scalded, cooled to lukewarm
2 whole fresh eggs, well-beaten
5 cups bread flour, sifted twice
Melted butter for tops

Crumble yeast cakes into lukewarm water; stir until dissolved. Combine butter, sugar and salt with scalded milk; cool to lukewarm then stir in the beaten eggs. Gradually add flour, stirring and beating well after each addition, until smooth. When all the flour has been stirred in, beat briskly for a minute. The dough should be stiff enough to be easily kneaded. Turn out on lightly-floured board and knead until glossy, elastic and not sticky. Place in greased mixing bowl, put bowl over hot water; cover with a dry towel, and allow to rise until doubled in bulk (about 2 long hours). Then, punch down; make bow-knots from pieces of rolled dough cut into strips about 6 inches long and ½ inch in diameter. Place each bow-knot on greased baking sheet; cover with a light towel; let rise until doubled in bulk, and bake in a moderate oven as directed. Brush with melted butter and serve warm or cold.

(505) SWEDISH TEA ROLLS

"PINWHEEL ROLLS"—YEAST METHOD

Make the same dough as in Recipe No. 504. When dough has risen to double its bulk, knead for 3 or 4 minutes on lightly floured board; roll out to about ½ inch thickness; spread first with softened butter, then with granulated sugar mixed with powdered cinnamon, and over this sprinkle grated lemon or orange rind to taste. Roll up like a jelly roll; cut into slices one inch thick; let rise to double in bulk; then bake in a hot oven as directed. Serve warm.

While writing, Anatole France, the French satirist, used to nibble on white bread, claiming that by so doing, he was much more inspired and could write better.

(506) TOMATO JUICE ROLLS

YEAST METHOD

Makes about 2 dozen rolls. Oven temperature: 400° F.
Baking time: 12–15 minutes.

1 cup tomato juice, scalded
2 tablespoons granulated sugar
½ generous teaspoon salt
2 tablespoons butter
1 whole fresh egg, well-beaten
1 cake compressed yeast
3 tablespoons lukewarm water
1 teaspoon granulated sugar
3½ to 4 cups bread flour, sifted

Add the 2 tablespoons of granulated sugar, salt and butter to the tomato juice; blend well; cool to lukewarm, then beat in the egg. Crumble yeast cake into lukewarm water; stir until dissolved and add the remaining teaspoon of granulated sugar. Blend well and stir into tomato juice mixture. Gradually add the flour, beating briskly after each addition until smooth. Turn dough into a greased bowl; brush lightly with melted butter; cover with a light, clean dry towel; place the bowl over one containing hot (not boiling) water and let rise until doubled in bulk. Then punch dough twice; turn upon a lightly-floured board and knead until smooth, elastic, satiny and not sticky. Roll out about ½-inch thick; shape into desired form; place on greased baking sheet; cover again with a towel and let stand in a warm place, or over hot water, to rise until doubled in bulk. Bake in a hot oven as directed. Serve warm.

(507) TOMATO BUTTERFLY ROLLS

YEAST METHOD

Makes about 2 dozen rolls. Oven temperature: 400° F.
Baking time: 12–15 minutes.

NOTE: These "butterfly" rolls may be made with sweet milk, buttermilk, or sour milk. If buttermilk or sour milk is used, add ½ teaspoon of baking soda.

Use the same dough as indicated for Recipe No. 506, or doubling ingredients if more rolls are required. When risen once, punch down the dough and let "rest" for 10 minutes. Roll out in a rectangular sheet ¼-inch thick; brush generously with melted butter and roll up, jelly roll fashion; cut roll into 1½-inch slices; press center of each roll down with handle of knife to give "butterfly" effect; place slices on a greased baking sheet; cover with a towel, and allow to rise until doubled in bulk. Bake in a hot oven as directed until slices are delicately brown. Remove from oven, brush at once with melted butter, and sprinkle with chopped pistachio nut meats.

In 51 B.C. Athenian judges were ordered to eat wheaten loaves only on holidays and barley cakes at other times, "to bring them nearer the people."

Scones

. . . Kentucky, oh Kentucky,
How I love your classic shades,
Where flit the fairy figures
Of the star-eyed Southern maids;
Where the butterflies are joying
'Mid the blossoms newly born;
Where the corn is full of kernels,
And the Colonels Full of Corn!
—*Will Lampton*

SCONE RECIPES

(508) ORIGINAL SCONE RECIPE

If you look up scones in some of the highly indorsed cook books, you most likely will find a good practical recipe for tea biscuits *such as mother used to make*. But some good woman who was compiling a cook book, sometime, somewhere, hit upon a way out. She couldn't make that doggone recipe book look like anything but baking powder biscuits, so she cut them into triangles for scones, and now the average American believes that a scone is a triangular biscuit. We see those triangles sometimes in real Scottish bakeshops, but probably the canny Caledonian has found that Yankees expect their scones to be three-cornered.

Taken quite seriously the scone, to be a scone, is obviously and deliciously indigestible. The Scots are a hardy race, with an alimentary apparatus adapted to rations of oatcake and Scotch whisky neat, and they don't develop dyspepsia till they come to America—even though a certain author has said that Carlyle's sound and fury were due to his steady diet of oat porridge which he was too stubborn to give up. Say what you will, you must have a cast-iron, copper-riveted stomach to enjoy in fullest measure a feast of Scotch scones or English crumpets; but there are some of the pleasures of the table that are occasionally worth a few moments of remorse—and there's always the bicarbonate in the cabinet!

In the privacy of your kitchenette, take two cups of wheaten meal, as they call it on the other side of the big pond—or entire-wheat flour, or just plain bread flour if you can do no better—and combine it with a scant half-cup of butter, using knife blades or the tips of the fingers for the mixing. First, however, you'll have sifted or mixed a teaspoon of cream of tartar, a teaspoon of baking soda, and ½ teaspoon of salt with the flour. Two teaspoons of sugar may go in or stay out, according to taste. Scones will be scones, with or without the sugar.

When you have worked in the butter till the flour looks like coarse meal, add about three-quarters of a cup of cream or rich sweet milk—just enough to make a soft dough of good consistency. Mix thoroughly and very quickly; then pat it out on a floured board (handling it as lightly as possible) to the thickness of half an inch, cut into rounds, squares, triangles, or what you will, and pop them into a hot oven (400° F.) on a lightly floured skillet. As soon as they are risen and nicely tinted (ten or twelve minutes), fetch them forth, slit them neatly and spread soft butter between the halves.

Of course, you may add a little make-up by brushing the scones with yolk of egg before they are placed in the oven; you may also add one whole fresh egg to the dough to make it rich and yellow. You can do all these things to scones and they'll be scones, but don't try to make them fluffy or frivolous like some of the light and airy seafoam confections of the tea rooms. And if it happens that you've never talked about scones, or heard them talked about, just bear in mind that America may rhyme *scone* with *pone,* but the lads and lassies on the heather rhyme it with *brawn* and *fawn.*

When is a scone not a scone? The question has been asked facetiously and just as many times with gravity or vexation, and the answer comes not readily from any one of other than Scottish blood. Of a certainty you'll never find it in the dictionary, and least of all in any one of the encyclopaedic American cook books, except that, a scone—and I quote verbatim—"is a thin cake, baked on a griddle, as of oatmeal"!

(509) AMERICAN SCONES

BAKING POWDER METHOD

Makes about 18 scones. Oven temperature: 400–425° F.
Baking time: 12–15 minutes.

2 cups bread flour, sifted
½ teaspoon salt
1 tablespoon baking powder
3 tablespoons granulated fine sugar
A generous pinch powdered nutmeg
½ cup butter
1 whole fresh egg, well-beaten
½ cup cold sweet rich milk

To the flour, add salt, baking powder, fine granulated sugar and powdered nutmeg and sift together into mixing bowl. Rub in butter (margarine may be used) as for pie, that is to a coarse meal, using a fork, the tips of your finger or a pastry blender. Then add combined egg and milk, gradually, until all the dry ingredients are dampened, making a soft dough (add an extra tablespoon or so of milk if needed). Turn the dough out on a lightly-floured board and knead lightly into an oblong form. Flatten this into a sheet about ½-inch thick and cut with a large, fluted round cutter (about 3 inches in diameter).

Mark each scone into quarters with the back of a knife but do not cut through. Brush with cold milk; sprinkle very lightly with granulated sugar; place on greased baking sheet and bake in a hot oven as directed. Serve as hot as possible with butter, jam, jelly, marmalade or preserves. Very fine for breakfast.

Scotch Scones were created in 1431, at the same time as the haggis, by an unknown Scottish genius.

(510) BUTTERMILK SCONES

NO BAKING POWDER USED

Makes about 18 scones. Oven temperature: 425° F.
Baking time: 12–15 minutes.

2 cups bread flour, sifted
1½ teaspoons cream of tartar
1 scant teaspoon salt
¾ teaspoon baking soda
¼ cup shortening (butter preferably)
1 whole large egg, well-beaten
1 scant cup buttermilk (very cold)

To the flour add cream of tartar, salt and baking soda and sift into mixing bowl; rub in shortening as for pie. Combine egg with cold buttermilk and mix lightly with first mixture. Turn out onto lightly-floured board; sprinkle a little flour over top; divide in 4 equal parts; pat each into a 4-inch round; then cut with floured cutter. Flatten each scone to about ½-inch thickness. Mark in quarters with the back of a knife; prick surface with the tines of a fork; place on greased baking sheet; brush with melted butter, then sprinkle with granulated sugar and bake in a very hot oven as directed. Serve as hot as possible with butter, jam, jelly, marmalade or preserves.

(511) CREAM SCONES I

BAKING POWDER METHOD

Makes about 18 scones. Oven temperature: 425° F.
Baking time: 12–15 minutes.

1 tablespoon baking powder
½ generous teaspoon salt
2 cups bread flour, sifted once
1 generous tablespoon granulated sugar
½ cup butter, margarine or lard
2 whole fresh eggs, well-beaten
½ cup light cream or evaporated milk
Melted butter for tops
Granulated sugar for sprinkling tops

Add baking powder, salt and granulated sugar to flour and sift into a mixing bowl; cut in butter or other shortening as for pie crust and add combined eggs and light cream or undiluted evaporated milk. Turn out upon lightly-floured board and knead a half minute. Divide dough in two equal parts, and roll into rounds about 6 inches in diameter, then cut into quarters. Place on greased baking pan; brush tops with melted butter; then sprinkle with granulated sugar. Bake in a hot oven as directed until delicately brown. Serve as hot as possible.

For eye-appeal brush tops with slightlv beaten egg white, omitting butter and sugar.

(512) CREAM SCONES II

BAKING SODA METHOD—VERY RICH

Makes about 18 scones. Oven temperature: 425° F.
Baking time: 12–15 minutes.

2 cups bread flour, sifted
1 teaspoon cream of tartar
1 teaspoon baking soda
½ generous teaspoon salt
2 teaspoons granulated sugar
½ scant cup butter
½ generous cup light cream or evaporated milk
Melted butter for tops
2 egg yolks, well-beaten

To the flour add cream of tartar, baking soda, salt and sugar and sift into mixing bowl; work in butter as for pie crust. Add light cream (or undiluted evaporated milk) mixed with the egg yolks and blend thoroughly. Pat dough out on lightly-floured board (handling as little as possible) to the thickness of ½-inch; cut into rounds, squares or triangles; place in a lightly floured iron skillet and bake in a very hot oven as directed or until delicately brown. Immediately after removing from the oven brush with melted butter and serve at once with jam, jelly, marmalade or preserves.

Scones! You'll find them in every English-speaking country. They may be sour and hardy as a typical Scot. They may be sweetened, spiced and enriched with dried fruits, large or small, round or triangular in shape, baked on a griddle, in a skillet or in the oven—but a scone is a scone "for a' that!"

(513) FRUIT SCONES

"AFTERNOON TEA SCONES"—BAKING POWDER METHOD

Makes about 18 scones. Oven temperature: 425° F.
Baking time: 12–15 minutes.

2 cups bread flour, sifted
1 tablespoon baking powder
½ teaspoon salt
A tiny pinch baking soda
2 tablespoons fine granulated sugar
⅓ cup butter or lard
1½ teaspoons grated orange rind
½ cup seedless raisins, parboiled, dried, chopped
2 whole fresh eggs, well-beaten
½ cup light cream or undiluted evaporated milk

To the flour add baking powder, salt, soda and fine granulated sugar and sift over grated orange rind and prepared seedless raisins. Blend well. Cut in shortening (preferably butter or lard) as for pie crust; then stir in combined eggs and light cream (or undiluted evaporated milk). Beat briskly until dough follows spoon around mixing bowl. Turn out upon lightly-floured board and knead a half minute or so. Roll out ½-inch thick; cut in fancy shapes, fluted rounds, triangles, rectangles, etc.; place upon lightly-floured baking sheet (ungreased); brush with melted butter and bake at once in a very hot oven, as directed until delicately brown. Serve warm.

You may brush with slightly beaten egg white instead of butter.

In 1805 a French battery under Napoleon's command, having used up all its shots, continued to fight by using stale, round, soldier's bread for bullets.

(514) GINGER MOLASSES SCONES

EGGLESS—BAKING POWDER METHOD

Makes about 18 scones. Oven temperature: 400° F.
Baking time: 18–20 minutes.

2 cups bread flour, sifted
1 tablespoon baking powder
½ teaspoon salt
2 teaspoons powdered ginger
2 tablespoons shortening
A pinch of baking soda
2 tablespoons molasses
½ generous cup cold sweet milk
Melted butter for tops

Combine the first four ingredients and sift into mixing bowl; cut in shortening as for pie crust. Stir baking soda into combined molasses and milk, and add to the dry, sifted ingredients. Blend thoroughly to make a soft dough easily handled. Turn out onto lightly floured board and knead a half minute or so; roll out ½-inch thick; cut into desired shapes; place on lightly-floured (not greased) baking sheet and bake in a hot oven as directed until well browned. Serve warm. Delicious!

(515) NUT MEAT SCONES

BAKING POWDER METHOD

Makes about 18 scones. Oven temperature: 425° F.
Baking time: 12–15 minutes.

2 cups bread flour, sifted
1 tablespoon baking powder
½ teaspoon salt
2 tablespoons granulated sugar
¼ cup butter, margarine or lard
½ cup chopped nut meats (any kind)
1 whole fresh egg, well-beaten
½ cup cold sweet milk
1 egg yolk (for brushing tops)
¼ cup chopped nut meats for tops

Combine the first four dry ingredients and sift into a mixing bowl; cut in shortening as for pie crust; then stir in the ½ cup chopped nut meats. Blend thoroughly. Combine egg with milk and stir into mixture just enough to mix thoroughly. Turn out upon lightly-floured board and knead a half minute; roll out to ¼-inch thickness; cut into diamond-shaped pieces and fold into triangles. Brush with slightly beaten egg yolk; sprinkle with remaining chopped nut meats and bake in a hot oven as directed. Serve warm.

(516) OATMEAL SCONES

OLD-FASHIONED SCOTCH METHOD—NO BAKING POWDER, SODA OR OTHER LEAVENING AGENT USED

Makes about 18 scones. Hot greased griddle.
Baking time: until brown on both sides.

Into a thick, cooked, cold oatmeal porridge, beat as much sifted bread flour as will enable it to be rolled out about ¾-inch thick. Cut into desired shapes and bake on a hot, greased griddle until brown on both sides. Split and spread plenty of butter on both sides. Serve hot with jam, jelly, marmalade, preserve, honey or maple syrup.

In 1651 canny Scots used bread baked in the form of boxes for use as containers in the pantry. When these bread-boxes were stale, they soaked them in water and ate them as a breakfast bread.

(517) POTATO SCONES

BAKING SODA METHOD

Makes about 2 dozen scones. Oven temperature: 400° F.
Baking time: 15 minutes.

2 cups bread flour, sifted
1 tablespoon baking soda
½ generous teaspoon salt
½ teaspoon baking powder
¼ cup butter or lard
2 cups cold mashed potatoes, sieved
½ generous cup sweet milk
1 whole fresh egg, well-beaten
Melted butter for tops

To sifted bread flour add soda, salt and baking powder and sift into mixing bowl. (Here you may add 1 or 2 teaspoons of granulated sugar.) Cut in butter or lard as for pie crust; mix in potatoes. Blend well. Combine egg with milk and add to mixture, blending thoroughly. Roll out on lightly floured board about ¾-inch thick; cut into desired shapes; place on greased baking sheet; brush with melted butter and bake in a hot oven as directed. Serve warm.

(518) RAISIN SCONES

BAKING POWDER METHOD

Makes about 18 scones. Oven temperature: 425° F.
Baking time: 12 to 15 minutes.

2 cups bread flour, sifted
1 tablespoon baking powder
½ generous teaspoon salt
1½ to 2 tablespoons granulated sugar
¼ cup butter, lard or margarine
2 whole fresh eggs, well-beaten
½ cup light cream or evaporated milk
½ cup seedless raisins, parboiled, dried and chopped
1 egg yolk, well-beaten, for brushing tops

To the sifted flour add baking powder, salt and sugar and sift into mixing bowl; cut in shortening as for pie crust. Combine eggs, milk and prepared raisins, stir well and add to first mixture. Blend thoroughly. Pat and roll out ½ generous inch thick; cut into any desired shape (rounds, squares, triangles, etc.); place on greased baking sheet; brush with beaten egg yolk; then sprinkle with additional granulated sugar and bake in a hot oven as directed. Serve hot; or split, toast and spread generously with butter.

In 1809 American pioneers west of the Alleghanies found wild turkey so plentiful that they used turkey as bread with their venison steaks.

Miscellaneous Bread Recipes

. . . We've got a cook that's awfully cross,
  Her name is Juliette.
She won't allow much fooling
When she is putting bread to set;
And today when I was hungry
And I stole a piece of dough,
She made me leave the kitchen
  When I didn't want to go. . . .

—Betty Sage

MISCELLANEOUS BREAD RECIPES

(519) HOT BREADS

When a young married man tells you, and keeps on telling you, that he has the finest little wife in the world, you may be pretty certain that, nine times out of ten, he means she makes good hot breads. There never was an accomplishment that appealed more to the masculine imagination, although, for that matter, accomplishment isn't just the right word, as men persist in regarding good hot bread-making, as one of the sweet womanly virtues—something which is inherent in the character, not just acquired, like playing the piano or violin.

The one bright spot in all this is the fact that bread-making is one of the simplest numbers in the whole kitchen repertory. There are a few difficult exceptions, of course, such as making croissants, or those elaborate Swedish coffee breads—some of which are the very devil to do—and raised breads take time; but simple, quick hot breads with short time baking get to be a mere "twist" of the work and no trick at all.

To vary the menu further, sometimes serve hot breads instead of a starchy vegetable. Corn meal muffins in place of potatoes with broiled chicken or ham; sweet potato buns rather than candied yams with a roast of pork—and so on indefinitely and appetizingly.

There are two rules you must bear in mind. First, you should stick to a good, reliable recipe, since bread-making is no time to experiment with bright ideas of your own; secondly, you should use judgment and your own sense of taste in deciding what bread goes best with what meat or fish or poultry.

Good as it is, brown bread can lower the rating of a fine, complicated sauce and hot rolls are not the bread to serve with a dish of beans. Put some thought and imagination on deciding what bread will best complement your entrée and then learn how to make that bread superlatively well.

(520) AARON'S BUNDLES

KIND OF MUFFINS

Makes 18 bundles or muffins. Oven temperature: 425° F. Baking time: 20–25 minutes.

2 cups bread flour, sifted
1 teaspoon salt
2 teaspoons baking soda
¾ cup dark molasses
¼ cup granulated sugar
½ cup lard or other fat, melted
¼ scant teaspoon allspice
¼ teaspoon nutmeg
¼ scant teaspoon cinnamon
1 whole fresh egg, lightly beaten
1 cup sweet cold milk
½ cup seeded or seedless raisins (about)

Sift flour once; measure; add salt and soda and sift twice. Mix molasses, sugar and melted fat; blend well, then add combined spices beaten into milk and egg together. Stir in flour all at once, beating well until smooth. Drop by tablespoons into greased muffin pans and put 4 or 5 raisins on top of each muffin. Bake immediately in a hot oven as directed. Serve hot with jam, jelly, marmalade, preserves, honey or maple syrup.

(521) AFTERNOON CHEESE SPLITS

Make your favorite baking powder biscuits and bake as usual. Split each biscuit, insert thin slices of cheese; sprinkle with paprika mixed with a little Worcestershire sauce and a little prepared mustard, cinnamon and a few grains of cayenne. Bake in a hot oven (400° F.) until cheese melts and runs over. Serve immediately.

(522) AFTERNOON COFFEE CAKES

YEAST METHOD

Makes about 1 dozen little cakes or rings. Oven temperature: 375° F. Baking time: 25 minutes (about).

2 cakes compressed yeast
¼ cup rich milk, lukewarm
1 cup rich sweet milk, scalded, cooled
¼ cup butter, melted, cooled
¼ cup each brown and granulated sugar
1 scant teaspoon salt
2 fresh eggs, slightly beaten
5 cups bread flour, sifted twice

Crumble yeast cakes into lukewarm milk (water may be used) in a bowl; add melted butter, salt and sugar to the cup of milk and mix thoroughly. Add enough flour to make a thick, smooth batter, mixing well, then stir in the yeast cake mixture. Mix thoroughly. Now add the slightly beaten eggs and enough flour to make a soft dough. Turn onto lightly floured board and knead until soft and satiny. Place in large greased mixing bowl, cover with a dry cloth and let rise until light or doubled in bulk. Punch down, then shape into 12 cakes or rings. Let the rings rise until doubled in bulk (35–40 minutes) and bake in a moderate oven as directed. You may ice or frost these delicious little rings when cold.

Englishmen of the fourteenth century indicated their wealth by the diameter of the silver meat or fish platters on their tables. The serving platters of the wealthy nobles averaged fourteen inches in width. The Royal Household meat or fish platters were eighteen inches wide.

(523) AMERICAN BRIOCHES I

YEAST METHOD

Makes about 1 dozen brioches. Oven temperature: 350° F. Baking time: 30 minutes (about).

1 cup sweet milk, scalded	1½ cups bread flour, sifted
¼ cup granulated sugar	2 whole fresh eggs, well-beaten
¾ teaspoon salt	½ cup butter, melted
1 yeast cake	1 teaspoon grated lemon rind
¼ cup sweet milk, lukewarm	A pinch ground nutmeg

2 cups bread flour, sifted (about)

To the cup of milk add sugar and salt. Let cool to lukewarm. Crumble yeast cake into the remaining lukewarm milk (water may be used) and add to milk-sugar-salt mixture. Stir in the 1½ cups flour. Beat until smooth. Cover with a dry, clean towel; put in a warm place and let rise until doubled in bulk (about an hour). Now add the eggs, alternately with mixed lemon rind and nutmeg. Mix thoroughly; then stir in, gradually, the remaining 2 cups of flour. Cover with a dry cloth and let stand in a warm place until doubled in bulk. Turn dough onto a lightly floured board and knead 2 minutes, adding more flour, if necessary to make a soft dough that you can handle easily. Knead until smooth, satiny and not sticky. Cut off small pieces of the dough and shape into balls about 1½ inches in diameter. Keep out a piece of dough about the equivalent of two balls. Shape these into small wedge-shaped bits. Cut a slit in the top of each ball of dough and insert a wedge, small end down. Place the balls on a generously greased baking sheet about 3/4 inch apart. Cover with a clean, dry, light towel and let rise 40–45 minutes or until light and doubled in bulk. Brush with beaten egg yolk and bake in a moderate oven as directed. Serve warm.

(524) AMERICAN BRIOCHES II

YEAST METHOD—SPONGE BEING PREPARED THE NIGHT BEFORE BAKING

Makes about 20 brioches. Oven temperature: 350° F.
Baking time: 25 minutes.

- 1 cup rich milk, scalded
- 2/3 cup butter, melted
- 1 generous teaspoon salt
- 1/2 cup granulated sugar
- Grated rind of medium-sized lemon
- 2 yeast cakes
- 1/2 cup lukewarm water or milk
- 5 whole fresh eggs, well-beaten
- 5 cups bread flour, sifted

Combine milk, butter, salt, sugar and grated lemon rind. Blend well; let stand until lukewarm. Crumble yeast cakes into lukewarm water or milk, stir until dissolved and add to first mixture. Beat briskly for 4 or 5 minutes. Cover with a dry, light towel; put in a warm place free from draft; let rise for 4 to 5 hours, then store in refrigerator over night. Next day, shape dough into balls the size of a small egg; place in generously buttered muffin pans. Put a tiny ball of dough on top of each and let rise until doubled in bulk. Brush with melted butter and bake in a moderate oven as directed.

Fine for Sunday breakfast. For afternoon tea, you may frost the same as coffee cake.

As early as 1693, Bulgarians considered garlic as a "lucky fruit"; they used it lavishly, even grinding it up in hot wine and bread dough.

(525) BLACKBERRY CHEESE STICKS

Makes about 2 dozen sticks. Oven temperature: 375° F.
Baking time: 10 minutes.

NOTE: Any kind of berries may be used.

2 cups bread flour, sifted
1 tablespoon baking powder
½ scant teaspoon salt
1 generous teaspoon granulated sugar
½ cup grated dry American cheese or Gruyère
3 tablespoons butter
⅔ cup (about) very cold sweet milk
1 cup washed, stemmed, drained blackberries

Combine flour, baking powder, salt and sugar and sift once. Cut in grated cheese, alternately with butter, mixing lightly with a fork, then gradually add the *very cold milk* (just enough to make a soft dough). Turn upon slightly floured board and knead a short minute; flatten to a scant ¼-inch in thickness. Sprinkle with prepared berries, then with a little sugar to taste, the amount depending upon sweetness of berries. Fold the dough half over, pressing it down gently at sides with the tines of a fork to keep in the berries. Cut into 4 or 5 strips; brush with butter or lightly beaten egg yolk; lift strips with a spatula onto greased baking sheet and bake in a moderate oven as directed until strips slip off the pan and are delicately browned. Serve hot with salad.

(526) BRIOCHES—FRENCH METHOD

Obviously there must be brioches and brioches, according to latitude and longitude, and the following recipe must be made as it is made in Paris. You use eggs for brioche—six, seven or eight—the more, the better! Here is how:

Taking 4 cups (1 quart) of sifted bread flour, add a cake of compressed yeast that has been dissolved in half a cup of lukewarm water and a teaspoon of granulated sugar. Use only as much of the flour as will make a soft dough which can be formed easily into a ball. Put the ball in a greased bowl and fill it with lukewarm water. Set the bowl in a warm place and within an hour the ball will have risen to the surface, light and buoyant. Put 2 cups of sifted bread flour in a large bowl and add ¼ pound of the best creamery butter you can lay your hands on, 2 tablespoons of sugar, ½ teaspoon salt and 2 unbeaten eggs. Mix and knead to a smooth paste, using as much milk as may be needed. Then add another ¼ pound of soft butter and 2 more eggs and repeat the mixing and kneading. When the paste is smooth and no longer sticky, juggle with it in the approved French manner, throwing it in the air and banging it on the slab or board till it becomes as smooth as marble. Add 2 more eggs and mix and beat again and continue the juggling and acrobatics until you are almost, but not quite, exhausted.

You must reserve enough strength for the task of incorporating the beaten paste with the ball of sponge, and 2 or 3 more eggs must be worked in. Knead the mass long and well and beat it to the original smoothness, but without the violent juggling; then set it away in a greased bowl, covered with a very light, clean, dry towel to rise to double its size. (Time depends on the temperature of the room. It may be 2 to 2½ hours.) When it is risen, beat it down again with closed fists and put it in the refrigerator to stand overnight, to mellow and ripen. The conventional brioche baking pans are usually bowl shaped and often fluted and there are several sizes.

To bake the brioche, mold enough of the dough into a ball to fill the pan half full; then make a criss-cross incision in the top of the ball and gently insert a smaller ball of the dough for the head or crown of the brioche. Set it in a warm place to double in size and cover; then brush it lightly with beaten egg yolk and bake in a moderate oven (350–375° F.) till it is brown and shining. The time depends upon the size of the brioche. For a large one, about 70 minutes; for individual ones 25–30 minutes.

It's possible for any clever cook to make brioches, but the importance of tradition and authority in any art is not to be taken lightly.

In the seventeenth century, the "bread and cake eating lady" was a familiar figure at English fairs. One such performer ate twelve pounds of cake and bread in less than thirty minutes at each of six daily performances.

(527) CHEESE STRAWS

Makes about 2 dozen straws. Oven temperature: 450° F.
Baking time: 7 to 8 minutes.

NOTE: To "curl" cheese straws, curve them in a circle as soon as they come out of the oven and are still hot. Parmesan or any other kind of cheese may be used.

1 cup bread flour, sifted
½ scant teaspoon salt
1 tiny pinch of cayenne pepper
¼ generous cup grated sharp American cheese
¼ cup butter (no substitute)
¼ cup ice water

Sift flour and measure; add salt and cayenne pepper and sift again in mixing bowl. Add grated cheese and mix until evenly distributed. Cut in the butter with two knives until mixture is the consistency of coarse meal. Sprinkle in ice water, just enough to make a stiff dough. Roll upon a lightly floured board into a thin sheet (about ⅛ inch). Cut into strips 4 to 5 inches long and about ⅜ inch wide. Chill in refrigerator 35 minutes, the longer the better, before baking. Place on an ungreased baking sheet and bake in a very hot oven as directed.

Fine served with salad, especially green ones or with afternoon tea.

(528) CINNAMON TEA STICKS

Makes about 3½ dozen sticks. Oven temperature: 350° F. Baking time: 5 to 6 minutes.

1 whole fresh egg, well-beaten
½ cup granulated sugar
½ generous teaspoon salt
A pinch of cayenne pepper
½ cup butter, creamed
2 cups bread flour, sifted
1 generous teaspoon baking powder
3 tablespoons granulated sugar
1 generous teaspoon ground cinnamon

Beat egg with the ½ cup sugar, salt and cayenne pepper until light; add creamed butter alternately with flour. Mix thoroughly and set in refrigerator until firm.

Roll out on lightly floured board and shape into pieces the size of little finger. Roll in mixed remaining sugar and cinnamon (more cinnamon may be added, if desired), flatten out slightly with broad spatula and arrange sticks, lifting them with spatula on a baking sheet about 2 inches apart and bake in a moderate oven as directed until delicately browned. Serve hot with salad or for afternoon tea.

In 1870 a New Yorker named Cornelius B. Spaulding led a movement to eat without knives, forks and spoons, claiming that dining with one's fingers would recapture the pioneer spirit. Very few people were interested.

(529) CORN STICKS

Makes about 2 dozen sticks. Oven temperature: 425° F.
Baking time: 12 to 15 minutes.

- 4 cups corn meal, sifted
- 4 cups bread flour, sifted
- 4 tablespoons baking powder
- 8 tablespoons granulated sugar
- A generous pinch cayenne pepper (optional)
- A generous pinch cinnamon (optional)
- 2 teaspoons salt
- 4 whole fresh eggs, well-beaten
- 1 quart rich sweet milk
- ¾ cup butter, melted

Sift flour and corn meal, then measure. Combine with baking powder, sugar, salt, cayenne pepper and cinnamon and sift in a mixing bowl. Beat eggs until light and foamy and add to milk and melted butter. Stir liquid into dry ingredients as quickly and briskly as possible. Turn batter into generously greased corn stick pans and bake in a hot oven as directed. Serve hot or cold.

(530) CORNISH YEAST SPLITS

Makes about 2 dozen splits. Oven temperature: 400° F.
Baking time: 20–25 minutes.

NOTE: These splits, in great favor in England, are usually served cold at tea time.

- 1 cake compressed yeast
- 2 tablespoons granulated sugar
- 4 cups bread flour, sifted
- ⅓ cup cinnamon
- ⅓ cup butter or substitute
- ¾ cup rich milk, lukewarm
- 2 whole fresh eggs, well-beaten with
- 2 tablespoons granulated sugar
- ½ cup cream, whipped
- ½ cup apricot or strawberry jam or marmalade

Crumble yeast, mix with sugar (first 2 tablespoons) and stir until mixture becomes liquid. To the flour add the remaining 2 tablespoons sugar and sift once, then add flour to yeast mixture. Cut in butter, creamed with cinnamon and salt and add combined milk and eggs. Mix well and rapidly to form a soft dough. Rub with melted butter; cover with a dry, clean, light cloth and allow to rise until doubled in bulk. Form small pieces of the dough into flat cakes; place on ungreased baking sheet; brush with melted butter and let rise until doubled in bulk. Bake in a hot oven as directed. When cold, split one side and insert either jam or marmalade mixed with whipped cream.

Italian inn keepers of the fifteenth century had a custom which suggests an idea for present-day food conservation. Diners were given wrappers in which to take home the surplus food which otherwise would remain on their plates.

(531) ENGLISH CORN PONES

APPROPRIATE FOR BREAKFAST, LUNCHEON OR DINNER

Makes about 1½ dozen. Oven temperature: 375° F.
Baking time: 20–25 minutes.

2 cups white corn meal	¾ teaspoon salt
2 tablespoons melted butter	¾ cup boiling water

Sweet cold milk

Combine corn meal and salt and scald with the boiling water, mixing thoroughly. Add melted butter (no substitute) and enough cold milk to form a rather stiff mush. Shape with the hands into oblong cakes about 3½ inches long and an inch thick. Place on buttered baking sheet and bake in a moderate oven as directed until a good, appetizing brown. Serve as hot as possible.

(532) FRENCH CROISSANTS

NATIONAL BREAKFAST BREAD OF PARISIANS

Makes about 1 dozen crescents. Oven temperature: 450° F.
Baking time: 20–25 minutes.

Into a mixing bowl sift 2 cups pastry flour, then combine with ½ generous teaspoon salt and ½ generous teaspoon of granulated sugar. Sift twice, then make a hole in the center and add 1 cake of compressed yeast, crumbled into ½ cup scalded rich milk, cooled to lukewarm and mixed with 1 egg yolk, well-beaten with 1 tablespoon lukewarm water and 1 tablespoon olive oil (may be omitted but the olive oil gives a rich flavor and helps yeast to rise, thus making the croissants more friable). Have all the ingredients cold.

Starting from center of the bowl, gradually bring the flour mixture into the liquid in the hole, a little at a time, moistening well with each addition. When all the flour is dampened, knead lightly on a scantily floured board. Shape into a round ball; sprinkle a little flour over top and make a cross with pastry cutter. Place the dough ball in a dry mixing bowl, cover with a light cloth, such as a cheesecloth, and let rise to double its bulk (about 2 hours). Toss onto a lightly floured board, knead very gently (about 3 minutes); roll out to 1/8-inch in thickness forming a large square. Place in center of this square 1/3 pound of the best creamery butter; fold each corner of the dough over the butter, square envelope-style; then give it two rollings as for puff paste. Repeat this process four times, allowing the dough to rest in refrigerator for 15 minutes each time.

Now put the dough into a cold earthen bowl, cover with a cloth wrung out in cold water and chill in the refrigerator for at least 30 minutes. After last rolling, roll out again to 1/8-inch in thickness in a large square; cut into 6-inch squares, then each square in two from corner to corner, making two triangles. Roll each triangle cigar-like, starting from the wide side of the triangle and finishing at the point, having center much thicker than ends. Shape into crescent by bringing ends almost together; arrange on lightly floured, thin baking sheet and let stand for one hour or more, until crescents double in bulk.

Brush each crescent with beaten egg yolk mixed with a little cold milk and bake 5 long minutes in a very hot oven (450° F.) to set the dough; decrease heat to moderate (350° F.) and continue baking 15 to 20 minutes longer, or until crescents are of a rich golden brown.

Crescents are at their best when eaten lukewarm. Reheated crescents are impaired in their delicate butter flavor and in texture.

(533) DANISH CRESCENTS

For Danish crescents, or breakfast crescents as they are more commonly called, proceed exactly the same as above (No. 532), but when ready to be baked, sprinkle with chipped almonds.

(534) HOMEMADE BAKING POWDER CRACKERS

ANY SHAPE DESIRED

Oven temperature: 450° F. Baking time: 10–12 minutes.

4 cups bread flour, sifted	1/2 cup melted butter
2 teaspoons baking powder	1 teaspoon salt
2 egg whites, stiffly beaten	2 cups cold sweet milk

To the flour add baking powder and salt and sift twice; gradually add milk, alternately with melted butter, beating briskly; then add stiffly beaten egg whites. The dough should be very stiff. Roll out to 1/5-inch in thickness; place on an ungreased baking sheet, after cutting in any desired shape, and bake in a very hot oven as directed. When cold, store in a container and keep in a dry, dark, cool place.

In 1640 any English apprentice baker who spoke disrespectfully of his master was not allowed to eat meat for a month.

(535) HOMEMADE GRAHAM CRACKERS

ANY SHAPE DESIRED

Oven temperature: 450° F. Baking time: 10–12 minutes.

1 cup sour heavy cream	1 teaspoon baking soda
½ cup granulated sugar	½ scant teaspoon salt
1 tablespoon butter	Graham flour to make a stiff dough

Mix the above ingredients, in order given, as thoroughly as possible. Roll out on lightly floured board to 1/5-inch in thickness and cut in squares, ovals or circles. Bake in a very hot oven as directed.

(536) HOMEMADE NUT AND DATE CRACKERS

Makes about 3 dozen crackers. Oven temperature: 350° F. Baking time: 12–15 minutes.

1 cup granulated sugar	1 cup bread flour, sifted
3 whole fresh eggs, well-beaten	1 cup nuts, ground
⅓ teaspoon salt	1 cup dates, ground

Stir sugar into eggs then add flour sifted with salt over mixed nuts and dates. Roll out on lightly floured board to 1/5-inch in thickness and cut into 2 squares. Place on an ungreased baking sheet and bake in a moderate oven as directed. When cold, store in a container in a cool, dry place.

(537) HOMEMADE SOFT PRETZELS

ANY SIZE DESIRED

Oven temperature: 400–425° F. Baking time: 10–12 minutes (about).

Pretzels have a religious origin. They were first made by monks; they were eaten on fast days; and they were given by priests to good children who learned all their prayers. The design represents folded arms in the attitude of prayer.

Pretzels are not, as many believe, the heavenly bread. The substance called *manna,* which is analogous in appearance and quality to the heavenly bread mentioned in Biblical history, is a saccharine exudation from leaves of certain species of larch, tamarisk and dwarf oaks found in Kurdistan and other parts of Asia Minor.

Manna consists chiefly of mucilaginous sugar which has a honey-like aromatic flavor and color and is largely used in sweet preparations. Its appearance depends entirely upon rains and dews during short spring and fall periods. Shaped like a large lemon seed, the *manna* is shaken off the leaves before sunrise and brought to market each morning. Climatic changes sometimes tend to give it a flaky appearance; and when the bloom is blown off by strong winds, it resembles a snow flurry. It is believed that hot weather and high atmospheric humidity cause the leaves to become overturgid and the plant sap to press the sweet liquid through the pores of the leaves where it accumulates and hardens in the form of drops.

There are two kinds of pretzels—the soft and the hard. The pretzel—hard or soft—is basically made out of a raised bread dough, treated to its bath in wood ash solution. Each pretzel baker jealously guards what he considers his secret. The soft pretzel, a delicious snack when fresh (and it must be fresh), is made merely with yeast, flour and water. The soft pretzel is round in cross-section and "fat."

The hard pretzel can be made from this simple dough, but shortening is usually added—even butter in the finer and more costly ones. The hard pretzel, as its name designates, is baked hard throughout. It is the pretzel that can be bought in tins and it keeps. The hard pretzel is always small in cross-section, about one-quarter of an inch.

Since the soft pretzel must be made fresh every day, and since, therefore, it is always made by small individual bakers and cannot be stored and shipped, it is found principally in cities in Pennsylvania where old pretzel bakers have set up small establishments.

2 cups water
1½ tablespoons salt
1 yeast cake
5 cups (about) bread flour, sifted

Heat water and dissolve salt in it; let cool to lukewarm. Soften yeast cake in ¼ cup lukewarm water and add to water-salt mixture. Sift flour into a mixing bowl; make a hollow in center of flour; add the yeast mixture and mix thoroughly, adding more flour if needed to make a soft dough but not sticky. Let rise in a warm place until doubled in bulk; covered with a dry cloth (about overnight). Toss dough onto floured board and knead until satiny and elastic. Take pieces of dough and roll them into strips about one foot long and one-half inch in diameter. These pretzel strips will be "rods" (about ½ inch in diameter and a foot long) ready for "bending" or "slinging." Grasp the ends with the fingers of each hand and give the "rod" a little pull; this will stretch the ends so that they will be a little smaller in diameter than the mid-point in the "rod." Then, watching the diagram, deftly "bend" the pretzel. No one can explain how to do this; it is a knack that must be acquired by practice. If you do not succeed at first, no harm is done, since the dough can be rolled into another "rod" and a second try made.

After the pretzels are "bent," they are laid on a board or piece of waxed paper to "set." The proper time can be ascertained by waiting until the pretzel in its unbaked state rises to about twice the cross section.

Now the pretzel is ready for its dip in boiling wood ash solution, if you wish to go through with this. If you do not, it can be brushed with an egg beaten up, yolk and white, and sprinkled with salt. This must be coarse salt and it must be sprinkled freely. The pretzel thus salted is placed on a generously greased baking sheet, put in a hot oven and baked as directed. Serve warm.

The hard pretzels are made in the same manner except that shortening is added to the dough. They bake very hard and crisp.

The object of giving a wood ash solution bath is simply to give pretzels a golden brown color and possibly make the salt stick better in large production. This wood ash solution is usually composed of 1 tablespoon of caustic soda to five gallons of water.

(538) HOMEMADE SODA CRACKERS

Makes about 3 dozen crackers. Oven temperature: 400° F.
Baking time: 12–15 minutes.

4 cups of bread flour, sifted
½ generous teaspoon baking soda
1 teaspoon salt
¾ cup sour milk
1 cup butter

To the flour add soda and salt; sift twice and cut in the butter. Gradually add just enough sour milk to make a stiff dough. Knead the dough thoroughly for 8 to 10 minutes; roll out on lightly floured board to about 1/5-inch in thickness and cut in rounds, squares, etc.

Punch holes with tines of a fork; place upon greased baking sheet and bake in a hot oven as directed.

A formal invitation to a dinner in fourteenth-century Rome informed the guest whether or not he was to furnish his own napkin.

(539) HOMEMADE YEAST CRACKERS

Makes about 4 dozen crackers. Oven temperature: 400° F.
Baking time: 8–10 minutes.

½ yeast cake
2 cups lukewarm water
1½ quarts bread flour, sifted
1 scant tablespoon salt
¼ cup cold milk, soured
⅓ cup lard
1 teaspoon baking soda

Make a sponge with yeast, water and flour at night. In the morning add the other ingredients in order given. Pound or knead, adding enough flour to make a very stiff dough. Fold over and pound with rolling pin. Continue until the dough is smooth, velvety and not sticky. Place on a lightly-floured board and roll out in a very thin sheet (1/5-inch in thickness or less). Immediately cut into squares, rounds, ovals, etc., and make holes with tines of a fork. Place upon ungreased baking sheet and bake in a hot oven as directed.

(540) HONEY TWIST

Makes about 8 portions. Oven temperature: 375° F.
Baking time: 25–30 minutes.

1 cup rich milk, scalded
¼ cup butter
½ cup granulated sugar
1 teaspoon salt
2 yeast cakes
¼ cup lukewarm water
2 whole fresh eggs, well-beaten
6 cups bread flour, sifted

Mix hot milk, shortening, sugar and salt thoroughly. Crumble yeast into lukewarm water and when milk mixture is lukewarm add the yeast and eggs. Beat in flour to make a soft dough. Turn upon a lightly floured board and knead 3 or 4 minutes or until smooth and not sticky. Form into a large ball and place in a greased bowl. Cover with a light, dry cloth and let rise until doubled in bulk. When light, shape into a long roll about one inch in diameter. Coil the roll into a greased cake pan, beginning at the outside edge and covering the bottom. Brush generously with honey; let rise until doubled in bulk and bake in a moderate oven as directed. Serve warm or cold.

(541) PEANUT BUTTER CORN STICKS

Makes about 1 dozen. Oven temperature: 425° F.
Baking time: 12–15 minutes.

1 cup bread flour, sifted
¼ cup unsifted corn meal
1 tablespoon baking powder
½ teaspoon salt
1 tablespoon granulated sugar (optional)
¼ cup peanut butter
1 whole fresh egg, well-beaten
¾ cup cold sweet milk

To the flour add corn meal, baking powder, salt and sugar and mix thoroughly. Cut in peanut butter to form a granular mixture as for pie crust. Combine beaten egg with cold milk and pour into the flour mixture. Mix only enough to dampen all flours. Fill sections of greased and heated iron corn-stick pans (muffin pans may be used) ⅔ full. Bake in a very hot oven as directed until firm and brown. Serve hot.

Old fashioned Maine housewives still "thribble the hulled corn," cooking it until the grains are three times their normal size and serving them with milk and sugar as a breakfast dish.

(542) RAGGED ROBINS

Makes about 24 from teaspoon. Oven temperature: 400° F.
Baking time: 12–15 minutes.

NOTE: These very old Southern corn meal drops are really delicious for luncheon or supper.

1¾ cups corn meal, sifted
1 cup bread flour, sifted
½ generous teaspoon salt
2 tablespoons baking powder
¼ cup butter or lard
1 cup cold sweet milk

Combine corn meal, bread flour, salt and baking powder and sift twice. Work in butter or lard with two knives or pastry cutter, as for pie crust. Add milk all at once; mix well to a dropping dough and drop from tip of tablespoon or a full teaspoon on greased baking sheet. Bake in a hot oven as directed. Serve hot.

Fine served with salad, creamed fish, meat hash, etc. For lamb hash, you may add to the sifted dry ingredients 1 scant teaspoon curry powder.

(543) RAISIN CORN MEAL STICKS

Makes about 18 sticks. Oven temperature: 450° F.
Baking time: 12–15 minutes.

2 cups corn meal, sifted
1 cup bread flour, sifted
1 tablespoon baking powder
1 teaspoon salt
¼ cup granulated sugar
1 cup very cold buttermilk
1 teaspoon baking soda
2 whole fresh eggs, well-beaten
¼ cup butter or lard, melted
⅔ cup seedless raisins, parboiled, dried

Combine corn meal and bread flour; add baking powder, salt and sugar and sift twice to ensure thorough blending. Combine very cold buttermilk, soda and eggs; beat briskly and add to dry mixture. Beat well for a minute; then add raisins and melted shortening. Stir until thoroughly blended. Fill greased, hot corn-stick pans level full and bake in a very hot oven as directed.

For a variation use brown instead of granulated sugar.

An old Oregonian game law permits fish to be caught using single kernels of corn as bait, but makes it a misdemeanor to feed fish on canned corn.

(544) SOUTHERN CORN STICKS

Makes about 1 dozen sticks. Oven temperature: 425° F.
Baking time: 18–20 minutes.

1 cup bread flour, sifted
1 cup yellow corn meal, sifted
2 tablespoons granulated sugar
2 teaspoons baking powder
1 scant teaspoon salt
⅔ cup very cold sweet milk
1 whole fresh egg, beaten
1 cup cream style canned corn
2 tablespoons butter, melted

Combine flour, corn meal, sugar, baking powder and salt and sift once in mixing bowl. Combine very cold milk, beaten egg, canned corn and melted butter. Mix thoroughly and quickly. Fill greased and hot corn stick pans (or muffin pans) ⅔ full and bake in a hot oven as directed. Serve as hot as possible.

(545) SPIDER CORN BREAD

Makes about 6 portions. Oven temperature: 425° F.
Baking time: 20 minutes.

- 1¼ cups corn meal, sifted
- 2 cups sour milk
- 1 teaspoon baking soda
- 1 scant teaspoon salt
- 2 whole fresh eggs, well-beaten
- 2 tablespoons butter

Combine corn meal, soda and salt and sift once; combine beaten eggs and sour milk and blend thoroughly. Add milk mixture gradually to dry mixture, blending well. Heat a spider and butter thoroughly on bottom and sides with the butter; turn mixture into hot spider; place in hot oven and bake as directed. Serve hot with baked beans, chowder, or for afternoon snack when split in two and filled with butter, jam, jelly, marmalade or honey.

(546) TEA HORNS

Makes about 3 dozen. Oven temperature: 350° F.
Baking time: 20–25 minutes.

- 3 cups bread flour, sifted
- 2 tablespoons powdered sugar
- ¾ lb. butter
- 1 scant teaspoon vanilla extract
- 2 egg yolks, beaten
- 1½ cups almonds, blanched, ground
- 2 egg whites, stiffly beaten
- ¼ cup powdered sugar, sifted

Combine flour with the 2 tablespoons of powdered sugar and sift once. Cut in the butter with two knives or pastry blender; add vanilla extract and egg yolks. Beat until smooth. Take a teaspoon at a time of dough and rolling in palm of hand shape into horns. Place the horns on generously buttered (no other shortening substituted) baking sheet; brush tops with well-beaten egg whites and sprinkle with ground almonds. Bake in a moderate oven as directed. Remove from oven, quickly sprinkle with remaining sifted powdered sugar; remove carefully from pan as the horns break easily. Cool before serving for afternoon tea, after school snack, or with dessert.

(547) TORTILLAS

FRYING METHOD

Tortillas are the staple national of the Mexican diet. They form the basis of the ordinary menu and countless other dishes are based upon them. They may be fried or baked. To bake tortillas, place a lump of *masa* (name given to the corn mixture) and rub it back and forth on a flat grinding stone with a rolling-pin until it becomes pliable and somewhat fluffy. A piece the size of a small egg is taken between the hands and patted back and forth until it is as thin as pie crust. It is then laid on a hot iron (usually heated by charcoal) and toasted.

Tortillas are made from corn or maize and nothing else; their palatability depends upon the way they are handled in the making. The corn should be white and is soaked with enough lime to soften the hull. This takes from five to six weeks. It is then thoroughly washed in clear water, drained, and ground, forming a paste. This is called *masa* and can be purchased at any Spanish or Italian food store.

The following recipe is a simple common one adaptable to the American kitchen. In Mexico, tortillas are made of coarse Indian corn ground on the *metate,* a special, square stone for the purpose.

2 cups sifted corn meal
1 tablespoon (scant) salt
1 tablespoon lard
Lard or oil for frying

Mix the ingredients, adding enough cold water to make a thin dough. Roll very thin and cut about the size of a coffee cup saucer. Fry in lard deep enough to float the tortillas. Do not allow them to brown; they are done when they begin to blister. Fry one at a time.

The famous *tamal* (*tamale* is the plural) of Mexico is always rolled in a tortilla before being wrapped in corn husk. The enchilada is also a rolled tortilla, usually stuffed with cheese and onions and with a chili sauce poured over it. The workingman at lunch uses it as a combination fork and spoon for the transportation of loads of beans from his lunch pail to his mouth; filled with beans—or almost anything else—and rolled, it becomes the *taca* of the better classes.

(548) TURNOVERS

Makes about 1 dozen. Oven temperature: 450° F.
Baking time: 15–18 minutes.

As a change from the conventional cup cakes for tea, serve these crispy turnovers filled with your own favorite jam, jelly, marmalade, preserves or cheese.

Cream ½ cup butter and work into it 3 packages of cream cheese, blending the two thoroughly. Add 1 teaspoon salt and 2 cups of bread flour (sifted) and mix well. Combine flour with cheese mixture a little at a time and work it in with a fork, adding a teaspoon or two of ice-water. Form the dough into a ball and chill.

For the turnovers, roll the cream cheese pastry out very thin and cut into 3-inch squares. Place 1 teaspoonful of any jam, jelly, marmalade or preserves in one corner of each square and fold the other half of the square over it to form a triangle. Press the edges together with the tines of a fork. Cut the tops of the turnovers to allow the steam to escape and bake on an ungreased pan in a very hot oven as directed until they are a golden brown. Serve cold.

During the Civil War General Stonewall Jackson's soldiers, when they were on the march, carried their frying pans with the handles thrust into the muzzles of their guns.

(549) VANOCKA BREAD

Makes 1 loaf. Oven temperature: 350° F.
Baking time: 1½ hours.

This delicious Bohemian bread gives a flair to any Christmas breakfast.

½ cup butter (no substitute)
4 cups bread flour, sifted
½ cup granulated sugar
⅓ teaspoon salt
1 teaspoon grated lemon rind
1 yeast cake
2 tablespoons bread flour
1 tablespoon granulated sugar
3 tablespoons very cold sweet milk
2 egg yolks, well-beaten
1 cup very cold sweet milk
⅓ cup seedless raisins
¼ cup blanched almonds
2 tablespoons candied citron
1 large fresh egg, slightly beaten

Work butter into flour sifted with salt as for pie crust. Add lemon rind. Mix crumbled yeast cake with 2 tablespoons of flour, the tablespoon sugar and the 3 tablespoons of cold milk. When bubbling, add to the first mixture. Turn the dough upon a lightly floured board and knead about half a minute. Add raisins, seeded or seedless, parboiled and dried, almonds and citron, cut very fine. Place the dough in a large bowl, cover with a dry cloth and let rise for 2 hours.

Now divide the dough into nine parts. Roll each part into a strand about 15 inches long, make a braid with four pieces and put it on a baking pan lined with a greased sheet of paper. On this braid put another braid made with three pieces and finally the last one, using the two remaining pieces of dough. Brush dough with slightly beaten egg. Let rise 1½ hours, covered and in a warm place. Brush again with slightly beaten egg yolk and white and sprinkle with chopped nut meats. Bake in a moderate oven as directed. Allow to cool before slicing.

In ancient Corinth little boys were permitted to eat with their parents. Girls, however, were barred from the parental meals until they were married.

(550) VIENNESE CHEESE BLINTZES

Makes about 6 generous servings. Browning time: 5 short minutes.

True to its name, "cottage" cheese probably originated with, or was mostly used by, the "cottager" or small farm-holder who thus thriftily utilized sour milk for his table. In old English manuscripts we find mention of *sawer ches* and curious drawings showing the housewife going through the various steps of making curds in her medieval kitchen. Known in the cuisine of many lands, this solid form of sour milk, or semi-cheese, as we might call it, enters into numerous famous as well as nourishing dishes. The special Easter dish of the Russians, *pascha,* is a well-blended mixture of cottage (or cream) cheese, pounded nuts and honey, packed into an ornamental wooden mold of tower shape; when unmolded and wreathed with paper roses, it occupies the center of the heavily-laden Easter dinner table.

The nursery rhyme tells us that "Little Miss Muffet sat on a tuffet, eating her curds and whey." In this most simple form, the curds were sprinkled with sugar and often eaten not only by children but by ex-children, especially those who believe that old age may be warded off by a more generous inclusion of sour milk.

The Viennese housewife prepares the famous Viennese Cheese Blintzes as follows:

½ lb. cottage cheese
2 whole fresh eggs, lightly beaten
½ cup cold water
A generous pinch of salt
1½ cups bread flour, sifted
3 tablespoons butter
1 cup cottage cheese
1 whole fresh egg, lightly beaten
1 teaspoon granulated sugar
½ teaspoon vanilla extract

Beat the half-pound of cottage cheese with the 2 beaten eggs; add the cold water, salt and flour, beating until smooth. The batter should be thin. Heat a heavy skillet; grease it slightly; pour in 2 tablespoons of batter, rolling the pan to cover the bottom thinly, and fry until brown on both sides, as you would for a pancake. Remove to a towel. Continue until all the batter is used. Spread each blintze with remaining cottage cheese, mixed with the remaining egg, sugar and vanilla (the vanilla may be omitted). Fold over and press together. When all pancakes have been filled, fry them in butter on both sides until slightly browned. Serve hot with butter instead of bread.

(551) WISCONSIN FAT RASCALS

A KIND OF MUFFIN IN GREAT FAVOR IN WISCONSIN

Makes about 8 rascals. Oven temperature: 400° F.
Baking time: 20 minutes.

Measure 2 cups of bread flour and sift again with 1 tablespoon baking powder, ½ teaspoon salt and ⅓ cup granulated sugar. Beat 1 whole fresh egg and combine with ¾ cup of rich sweet milk. Stir into the flour mixture. Then add 1 cup of blueberries washed, stemmed and dried and turn quickly into generously greased (preferably butter) muffin pans. Bake in a hot oven as directed. Serve very hot.

Instead of a spoon and sugar many Spaniards use the "Azucarillo," a stick of hardened sugar candy to flavor, stir and sweeten their drinks.

(552) YEAST BABA AU RUM—FRENCH METHOD

Serves 6 generously. Oven temperature: 400° F.
Baking time: 12–15 minutes.

This is a large bun, very popular among French people, found in almost any good bakery.

First combine ½ an ounce of fresh yeast, 1 tablespoon bread flour and a little milk. Work to a paste and leave it in a warm place. Soak in warm rum 1 cup of seedless raisins or seeded currants, or equal parts of both, washed and dried. Mix ¼ lb. of sifted bread flour (1 cup) and 3 strictly fresh eggs, added one at a time to make a smooth batter. Add the yeast mixture. Blend well. Work it and beat it with the hand until it comes up easily and makes a kind of thin rubbery band. Then add 4 tablespoons of butter, washed into a soft mass. All this takes about 20 minutes. Place the dough in a greased bowl, cover with a clean, light, dry cloth and keep in a warm place to rise until doubled in bulk. Punch down for half-minute and add the rum-soaked raisins or currants, a little salt and sugar to taste (a *baba* should be neither very salty nor sweet). Now beat the dough back to the rubbery consistency and fill small, generously buttered *baba* molds about half-full. Let the *babas* rest at least 15 minutes or until dough reaches almost to the top of molds; then bake in a hot oven as directed.

Turn out on a hot bread rack or slightly wet board and allow to cool. When cold, pour over them gradually a little sugar syrup to make them swell, and lastly some rum to taste. Some people flavor them with kirsch.

NOTE: Many food writers to the contrary, the *baba au rum* should never be eaten hot.

(553) YEAST COFFEE RING

Serves 6 generously. Oven temperature: 400–300° F.
Baking time: 20 minutes.

1 cup rich sweet milk, scalded
¼ cup butter
½ cup granulated sugar
1 teaspoon salt
1 yeast cake
¼ cup warm water
4½ cups bread flour, sifted
Softened butter
Sugar, cinnamon and nutmeg to taste
Raisins or currants

To the hot milk add sugar and salt and after mixing let cool to lukewarm. Dissolve the yeast cake in lukewarm water and add to milk; then stir in the flour. Allow to rise in a warm place until doubled in bulk. Toss on lightly floured board and knead a half-minute. Roll out about ¼-inch thick. Spread generously with softened butter; then sprinkle with mixed sugar and spices. Shape in ring, and place on buttered baking sheet; cover with a clean, light cloth and let rise until doubled in bulk. Bake immediately for 10 minutes in a hot oven; reduce the heat to moderate and continue baking 10 minutes longer. Remove from the oven and again brush with softened butter. Let cool and serve lukewarm.

(554) YEAST COFFEE RING

Serves 6 generously. Oven temperature: 375° F.
Baking time: 20–30 minutes.

Soften 2 cakes of yeast in ¼ cup of lukewarm water. Scald 1 cup rich sweet milk and add to it ½ cup of butter, ½ cup granulated sugar (or equal parts of granulated and brown sugar) and 1 scant teaspoon salt. Mix well. Cool to lukewarm; then add to it 2 cups bread flour, sifted. Stir in the softened yeast and 2 eggs, well-beaten with the grated rind of a washed medium-sized lemon, and beat briskly until smooth. Next add 3 additional cups of sifted bread flour (about 5 cups in all) or enough to make a soft dough. Turn out on a lightly floured board and knead until smooth, satiny and not sticky. Shape the dough into a ball, place in a greased bowl, cover with a dry, light cloth and let rise until doubled in bulk. Quickly punch down the dough and shape either in individual forms or in one large coffee cake. Let rise until doubled in bulk and bake in a moderate oven 20 minutes for individual cakes and 25–30 minutes for a large one. Serve cold.

(555) YEAST COFFEE STICKS

Makes about 1½ dozen. Oven temperature: 425–350° F.
Baking time: 20 minutes.

1 cake of compressed yeast
2 tablespoons lukewarm sweet milk
½ cup butter
1 cup bread flour, sifted
A generous pinch of salt
1 egg white, slightly beaten
½ cup blanched almonds, sliced thin
Granulated sugar

Crumble the yeast cake into lukewarm milk, stirring until dissolved. Cut butter into flour sifted with a generous pinch salt. Shape in a ball; then roll on lightly floured board with rolling pin until *leafy* in appearance. Add yeast-milk mixture and mix lightly to form a dough, kneading ½ minute on lightly floured board. Cut into small sticks 3½ to 4 inches long. Place on ungreased baking sheet; cover with a dry cloth and let rise for an hour in a warm place, away from drafts. Then brush each stick with slightly beaten egg white and sprinkle with sliced almonds. Bake in a hot oven for about 10 minutes; reduce heat to moderate and bake 10 minutes longer.

Delicious at tea time, luncheon time or for Sunday breakfast in place of coffee cake.

Drinking coffee was forbidden in sixteenth-century Constantinople. The ruling dictator believed that coffee stimulated thinking among the common people. The first offense was punished by a beating; the second offense by death.

(556) YEAST COFFEE RAISIN TWIST

Makes 1 large twist. Oven temperature: 400–350° F. Baking time: 40–45 minutes.

1½ cups rich sweet milk, scalded
1 yeast cake
⅓ cup granulated sugar or equal parts of granulated and brown sugar, or all brown sugar
¼ cup butter, melted
1 quart (4 cups) bread flour, sifted
1 teaspoon salt
½ teaspoon ground ginger
½ teaspoon ground nutmeg
½ teaspoon ground cinnamon
⅔ cup seedless raisins

Wash raisins, scald, and let stand in hot water for 15 minutes. Scald rich milk and cool to lukewarm. Crumble yeast cake into sugar and stir until dissolved. Then add to lukewarm milk with melted butter, 2 cups of the flour, salt and spices. Beat briskly, add remaining 2 cups of flour and mix well. Turn dough onto lightly floured board and knead gently until smooth, elastic, velvety and not sticky. Now add raisins, thoroughly dried, kneading them into the dough. Place dough in a generously greased bowl, brush with melted lard or butter and cover with a light, dry cloth. Let rise in a warm place 2½ to 3 hours or till doubled in bulk.

Now divide dough into two equal parts and from one part make four strips of even length and thickness. Braid them and lay them on a greased and lightly floured baking sheet. From ⅔ of the remaining dough, make three thinner strips, braid them and place on top of the first braid. From remaining dough make two small strips, twist them together and lay on top of the two braids. Cover with a light, dry cloth, let rise in a warm place ¾ hour longer, or until doubled in bulk, and bake 15 minutes in a hot oven. Reduce heat to moderate and bake 25 minutes longer. Serve warm or cold with jam, jelly, marmalade, preserves, honey or maple syrup.

In Arabia a woman may divorce her husband if he fails to keep her well supplied with coffee.

(557) YEAST COFFEE STREUSEL CAKE

Approximately 2 coffee loaf cakes. Oven temperature: 375° F. Baking time: 25 minutes.

2 yeast cakes
1 tablespoon granulated sugar
4 to 4½ cups bread flour, sifted
6 tablespoons lard, melted
½ cup granulated sugar
3 whole eggs, beaten
¾ teaspoon salt
1 cup scalded milk, cooled to lukewarm
¾ cup lukewarm water
Streusel

Dissolve yeast cakes by crumbling them in mixed lukewarm milk and water to which has been added the tablespoon granulated sugar; add 3 cups of flour and beat until smooth. Now add melted lard alternately with eggs, remaining sugar and balance of bread flour sifted with the salt, making a moderately soft dough. Toss upon lightly floured board and knead lightly (about 30 seconds). Place in greased bowl, brush with a little melted butter, cover with a dry towel and let rise to twice its bulk (about 2 hours). Now divide the dough in half, spreading each half in a pan 8″ × 11″, pressing into corners. Let rise about 1 hour, covered, in a warm place. Brush tops with beaten egg yolk diluted with half a tablespoon of milk; sprinkle with *streusel* and a little cinnamon to taste, and bake in a moderately hot oven as directed.

Streusel top dressing:

1 cup bread flour
1 cup sugar
½ cup butter

Work all together with fingers thoroughly and sprinkle over top of cakes before baking.

There is a certain satisfaction—even a thrill—in making things with your own hands. There is nothing that quite equals a warm, light, cozy kitchen and the rich smell of bread baking.

(558) YEAST NUT STICKS

Makes about 2 dozen sticks. Oven temperature: 425° F. Baking time: 12–15 minutes.

1 yeast cake
1 cup sweet milk, scalded, cooled
¼ cup granulated sugar or brown sugar
1 scant teaspoon salt
1 whole fresh egg, well-beaten
⅓ cup butter, melted
4 cups bread flour, sifted

Crumble yeast cake and slowly add milk cooled to lukewarm; stir until yeast is dissolved. Stir in sugar alternately with egg beaten with salt and half of the flour. Beat until smooth and free from lumps; add remaining flour, mix well, then add melted butter. Toss upon lightly floured board and knead until dough is smooth, elastic and not sticky. Place dough in greased bowl, cover with a light, dry cloth, set in a warm place and let rise until doubled in bulk. Punch dough, then roll out one inch thick, cut into strips and roll in chopped nut meats (any kind). Place in greased bread stick pan, brush with melted butter and let rise, covered, in a warm place, until doubled in bulk. Bake in a hot oven as directed. Serve warm or cold with coffee, chocolate or tea.

(559) YEAST RUM BABETTES—FRENCH METHOD

Makes about 2 dozen small babettes. *Oven temperature: 425° F. Baking time: 15–18 minutes.*

Delicious afternoon delicacies, shaped into buns, brushed with a mixture of rum and cream before baking.

3½ cups bread flour, sifted
½ cup confectioner's sugar
2 yeast cakes
1 tablespoon brown sugar
¾ cup heavy sweet cream
½ cup sweet butter
3 whole fresh eggs, well-beaten with
1 teaspoon grated lemon rind
1 tablespoon rum, mixed with
1 tablespoon sweet cream
1 scant tablespoon salt

Combine 1¼ cups of the flour with the salt; cut in the sweet butter as for pie crust; add the crumbled yeast cakes and brown sugar to the cream. Blend thoroughly and stir into the first mixture. Cover with a light, dry cloth and let stand 30 minutes. Then add the eggs, beaten again with the lemon rind and remaining bread flour. Stir until perfectly smooth. Set the dough in greased bowl, cover with a light, dry cloth and allow to rise in a warm place for about 1½ hours or until doubled in bulk. Then knead lightly in bowl (about 30 seconds).

Pinch off pieces the size of a hen's egg; shape into buns; place in buttered pan. Cover the pan with a dry, light cloth and let rise an hour. Now brush lightly with half of the rum and cream mixture. Bake in a hot oven as directed. As soon as the *babettes* are removed from the oven, spread thinly with a frosting made of the remaining rum and cream to which confectioner's sugar has been added. Serve cold.

Carolina tea, a member of the holly family, was the historical "Black Drink" of the Cherokee Indians.

(560) YEAST TEA RING—SWEDISH METHOD

Makes 1 large ring. Oven temperature: 375° F.
Baking time: 25–30 minutes.

Crumble 2 yeast cakes into ¼ cup lukewarm water. Scald 1 cup rich milk; add to it ¼ cup butter, ½ cup granulated sugar and 1 teaspoon salt. Blend well. This is the sponge. Cool the mixture to lukewarm; add enough sifted bread flour to make a thick batter; then stir in the yeast mixture and 2 well-beaten fresh eggs; beat briskly to blend. Now add enough sifted bread flour (about 5 cups) to make a soft dough; turn onto a lightly floured board and knead until smooth, satiny and not sticky. Place the dough in a greased bowl, cover wih a light, dry cloth and let rise in a warm place about 2 hours or until doubled in bulk. When the dough is light, punch it and roll into a rectangular sheet about ½-inch in thickness; brush with melted butter and sprinkle with a mixture of brown sugar and cinnamon. Roll up like a jelly roll and shape into a ring. Place the ring on a greased baking sheet and cut with the scissors at one-inch intervals almost through the ring. Turn each slice slightly on the side; cover and let rise until doubled in bulk. Bake in a moderate oven as directed. While warm, cover with confectioner's sugar frosting and sprinkle with finely chopped nut meats.

(561) YANKEE STEAMED HONEY BROWN BREAD

NO YEAST, BAKING POWDER, OR EGGS USED

Makes 2 large loaves. Oven temperature: (to warm up the bread after steaming): 400° F.

Steaming time: 2½ hours (about). Baking time: 15–20 minutes.

Combine 2¼ cups buttermilk, 1 cup strained honey and blend thoroughly. Add 2 cups unsifted whole-wheat, mixed with 1 teaspoon baking soda, 2 cups of sifted corn meal, 1 teaspoon salt, ½ generous teaspoon powdered ginger and a tiny pinch of nutmeg. Blend well while adding ½ cup seedless raisins, washed, parboiled then dried, alternately with ½ cup of chopped nut meats (any kind) and 1½ tablespoons of melted lard. Pour batter into two large covered molds or coffee cans which have been generously greased, filling them ⅔ full. Cover closely; place molds into a cheesecloth and tie. Place molds on rack in kettle of violently boiling water, having molds well covered with the water. Cover the kettle and steam steadily for about 2½ hours, keeping boiling water constantly covering the molds. Remove molds from water; uncover and bake in a hot oven for 15–20 minutes. Serve cold.

General Jean Cuvier-Prescet in 1613 paid the equivalent of 2000 dollars to obtain the services of a French chef who was reputed to be the best cinnamon bun baker in all France.

SOY FLOUR BREADS AND BISCUITS

(562) SOY FLOUR

Confucius eagerly advocated tea drinking in order to get his people to boil China's impure water, and the ancient saints and sages of all lands had much to say of health and hygienic principles; but diet came into its own as the potential means to peaceful and painless old age when science and salesmanship placed a radio receiving set in every home.

It is bewildering, however, to hear all the doctors, professors, dietitians, beauticians and what-noticians talking at once—with the morticians just around the corner. One centenarian owes his first hundred years to the little brown jug; another smashed the jug and found the elixir of life in the old oaken bucket. One man's good red meat is another's crimson and gory poison and the desperate listener to the radio and reader of health columns is worked up to the point of dashing out and guzzling off a cup of spinach juice, a pint of orange nectar or a quart of gin. One gets ideas, however, out of the flux, and it's the boast of modern education that it trains the mind to pick and choose. In books and periodicals and in numerous food columns, a lot has been said about the soy bean as an omnibus of nutrition and utility, with particular emphasis on its freedom from starch and its protein richness. Hence it was startling to hear a learned and estimable doctor say recently, in his regular and popular radio broadcast, that the starch content of soy beans was relatively high and that the overplump and the dyspeptic would do well to be wary of them. He intimated, with reference to those who had recommended soy beans, that anyone could assume the authority of a dietitian without much knowledge of the subject—which is a living truth! He was by way of putting the Department of Agriculture on the spot, however, for in its Farmer's Bulletin No. 1617, *Soy Bean Utilization,* issued January 1930 and revised March 1932, there is found on page 3, under the caption "For Human Food," the following statement:

". . . Investigations of the nutritive efficiency of the soy bean have shown that it contains both the water-soluble and the fat-soluble vitamin. It contains at the most but a slight trace of starch. Extensive experiments in North America and Europe indicate its value as the basis of food for persons requiring a low starch diet and for many years food companies have had on the market forms of soy bean flour prepared for persons requiring a diet of this kind."

And under the same head, on page 7, the analysis by the Bureau of Chemistry and Soils shows that soy beans have:

6.4 per cent moisture
4.8 per cent ash (or mineral salts)
39.1 per cent crude protein
5.2 per cent crude fiber
25.8 per cent nitrogen-free extract
18.7 per cent fat (or other extract)
35.6 per cent digestible protein
60.4 per cent digestible carbohydrate equivalent

And a footnote explains:

"The carbohydrate equivalent shown is the sum of the digestible crude fiber and nitrogen-free extract, plus 2.25 times the digestible fat."

Carbohydrates have horns and cloven hoofs to the avid general readers on health and weight-reducing and are understood broadly to include the dreaded starches and sugars. It's more than possible that the skittish laity have been frightened away from soy beans by the mere sight of the word *carbohydrate* in analytical charts; but the broadcasting doctor knows his chemistry and his misstatements can hardly be due to misunderstanding.

Our paternal Department of Agriculture is kindly disposed toward soy beans, and publishes two other bulletins: No. 1520, *Soy Bean Culture and Varieties,* and No. 1605, *Soy Bean Hay and Seed Production,* and for technical and statistical literature they are little short of romantic. From telling you that the new "Easycook" and "Hahto" varieties are as soft and tender as any other beans and how to make muffins with soy bean flour, they plunge deep into the intricacies of soy bean products and by-products. You learn not only that the soy bean provides meat and drink for the human race, but that in its lavish bounty it is prepared to furnish celluloid, glue, vegetable casein, soap, paint, printer's ink, varnish, rubber substitutes, linoleum, lubricants, candles and illuminating and fuel oil. And this vegetable Aladdin's lamp has been burning dimly but usefully in mysterious and inscrutable China since time was young, when Chinese paper and ink and the art of writing were yet to be thought of and invented.

"The Little Honorable Plant of China" has a useful history dating back five millenniums. In the year 2838 B.C., Emperor Shen-Nung, father of Chinese agriculture, listed some three hundred medicinal properties to be found in the soy bean. In Manchuria today, where two-thirds of the world's annual six million-ton crop is raised, it is a staple food. Soy beans furnished Orientals the proteins as well as minerals and vitamins lacking in a diet of rice; and although introduced into the United States in 1804 by a Yankee shipmaster, the soy bean was considered nothing but an oddity until 1890, when its commercial and food possibilities were recognized by the Department of Agriculture.

The little Chinese vegetable that looks like an insignificant lima bean and tastes like a nut is growing in importance as an American product largely because of Uncle Sam's efforts.

You will never find soy beans on the bill of fare of a Chinese restaurant as beans, and your Chinese waiter will be perplexed and bothered if you ask for soy beans as such; yet their essence and their substance are in the condiment cruets on the table, in the food served and in all manner of barrels, bottles, jars and packets on the shelves of Chinese grocery shops.

If you can figure how and why it is that thousands of Italian peasants *never* have enjoyed the luxury of spaghetti, or ravioli, or risotto, you may guess why millions of China's four hundred million people have *never* eaten or seen a soy bean. In one of the more recent Chinese famine years, some of the coolie families that were lucky enough to eat at all were found subsisting on weeds and tree sawdust, thistles and almost anything that could be chewed and swallowed. Five hundred thousand persons starved to death in that particular calamity and there is tragic irony in the fact that some of the rescued sufferers were fed on bean cake—the fibrous residue of processed soy beans pressed into bricks. Yet the soy bean is called a "universal provider" and it was grown extensively in China before Marco Polo started blazing trails for travelers; and its culture is said to be the economic foundation of the new industrial Manchuria. Cobblers go barefoot, dairy farmers deny themselves milk and butter and Chinese farmers perish as Manchuria exports about 115,000,000 pounds of soy beans and soy bean products to the United States in a single year. The approximate annual value is three million dollars—about 70 per cent of the whole world's supply of soy beans.

Henry Ford, American champion and prophet of the soy bean, sees it superseding dairy and beef cattle and turns it into oil and paint and wheels and gears for motor cars. He is reported to have said that a soy bean gear is stronger than a steel one. You won't find much soy bean hardware in a large city's Chinatown, even in New York, but stroll inquiringly through Mott, Pell, and Doyer Streets, and you may see how significantly the bean figures in everyday Chinese life. Fresh bean sprouts—some from soy and some from other beans—stand in large hampers in the shops; on the shelves around them are jugs and bottles of soy sauce in several grades and varieties, for the kitchen or the table.

In the more typically native shops, corresponding vaguely to our delicatessen stores, you will see *Teou-fu,* or *tofu,* made fresh daily, in cream-white cakes like Philadelphia cream cheese, kept cool and moist in pans of water. It is made from soy bean milk mush as cheese is made from cow's milk or goat's milk, and it was a staple commodity in Chinese cities more than two thousand years ago. The Chinese prepare it for breakfast, dinner or supper in many ways, and a favorite form is ready for you in the shops—*Tsa tofu,* the little cheeses fried in deep fat, that look like well-browned and rather robust doughnuts without holes. You can get them hot from the kettle and eat them with syrup or without; a Chinese laborer finds them sustaining and satisfying as a noon-hour meal. *Tofu nao* is of custard consistency and is eaten in soups and as a custard; *Chien chang,* or thousand-fold *tofu,* is made in thin layers rolled together and cut up like noodles for soup or fried in sesame oil. A brown, dry *tofu, Hsiang khan,* is colored and flavored with caramelized millet sugar and eaten with soups and salads. There are many forms of preserved *tofu cheese:* smoked, salted, spiced and packed in wine and brandy to be used in cooking or as a delicacy like cheeses of the Western World. *Yuba,* as old as soy beans from which it is made, is the dried creamy film from boiling soy milk, sold in flakes or sheets, or rolled into "bean sticks," and it has been one of the most popular commodities in China and Japan for centuries. It is rich in protein and fat, gives flavor to soups and made dishes and can be softened and dried by itself.

A Chinese grocer is mystified, sometimes curious, when an Occidental customer buys soy beans; for he thinks that only Chinese and Japanese know how to use them. Mention baked beans to him and you get a dead-pan reaction or a glance of lofty pity. Beans are not done that way in China, and China and the Chinese do not change. Nevertheless, Boston yellow or red soy beans are delicious and digestible, and a little Chinese soy sauce in the bean pot makes them even more so.

"Canned" soy beans were sold in China as early as 1800. Pickled in stone jugs, they were stored in the equivalent of the Chinese pantry.

Important: Soy bean flour cannot be used by itself in baking bread, cake or any other kind of baked products. It's a flour without gluten, and only about 12 per cent of available starch. The usual approximate proportion is ONE PART *of soy flour to* THREE PARTS *of flour; and such a mixture may be used to make any bread recipe found in this book or any kind of pastry or cake or cookie.*

Recent experiments by the U. S. Department of Agriculture, Research Division, Washington, D. C., have shown that when *5 per cent* of soy flour is added to *95 per cent* of flour, the protein efficiency, or body building factor, is *doubled.* When this is increased to *10 per cent,* the protein efficiency is *quadrupled.*

Soy bean flour in its natural state has a bitter flavor, decidedly unpleasant, and should *never* be used alone in any baked product.

(563) SOY FLOUR APRICOT BISCUITS

BAKING POWDER METHOD

Makes about 50 large biscuits. Oven temperature: 400° F.
Baking time: 15 minutes.

Sift twice ⅔ cup soy flour, 5 cups bread flour, ¼ cup baking powder and 1 tablespoon salt. Make a well in center and add 3 cups of sieved cooked apricot pulp alternately with ¾ cup of shortening and cut in well until mixture is of the consistency of coarse corn meal; then add all at once 1½ cups of cold milk and work or knead dough very lightly until evenly moistened. Turn out on floured board and pat out or roll to the desired thickness. Cut with a floured cutter and bake on ungreased sheet in a hot oven as directed.

(564) SOY FLOUR BACON BISCUITS

BAKING POWDER METHOD

Makes about 50 large biscuits. Oven temperature: 400° F.
Baking time: 15 minutes.

NOTE: Best results are obtained by pan broiling bacon, by placing a single layer in a cold skillet, turning the heat on low, and allowing it to cook very slowly until the bacon is crisp and golden brown. The fat is poured off as it accumulates so that the bacon will panbroil, not fry. The fat should be slightly opaque or yellow, not brown.

Sift together twice 1 cup soy flour, 9 cups bread flour, 1/2 cup baking powder, 1 generous tablespoon salt. Work in 3/4 cup bacon fat (drippings and cold) and 3/4 cups of finely chopped cooked bacon, cutting in well until mixture is of the consistency of coarse corn meal. Then add all at once 3 cups of cold milk. Work or knead mixture until evenly moistened. Turn out on floured board and pat out or roll to the desired thickness. Cut with floured cutter and bake on ungreased sheet in a hot oven as directed.

(565) SOY FLOUR BISCUITS (PLAIN)

MASTER RECIPE—BAKING POWDER METHOD

Makes enough for 25 servings. Oven temperature: 400° F.
Baking time: 15 minutes (about).

Sift together 3/4 scant cup soy flour, 3 cups bread flour, 1/3 cup baking powder, 1 rounded teaspoon salt, 1 1/2 tablespoons granulated sugar in mixing bowl. Work in 1/3 cup shortening until mixture is of the consistency of coarse corn meal. Make a well in center and add 1 pint (about) milk, to which has been added a thoroughly beaten egg. (The amount of milk required will vary, depending upon the strength of the bread flour being used.) Then work or knead mixture lightly until evenly moistened. Turn out on a floured board and pat out or roll to the desired thickness. Cut with a floured cutter and bake in a hot oven as directed.

As early as the sixteenth century B.C. *small dishes about the size of saucers were used as currency in northern China. A small pig was worth 130 of these dishes.*

(566) SOY FLOUR BUTTERMILK BISCUITS

BAKING POWDER METHOD

Makes about 50 large biscuits. Oven temperature: 400° F. Baking time: 15 minutes.

Important: For a browner crust, the top may be brushed with cold milk before baking. Some cooks prefer to brush the tops with melted butter as soon as they are removed from the oven.

Sift twice 3/4 generous cup of soy flour. Combine with 7 cups bread flour, 5 tablespoons baking powder, 1 tablespoon salt and 1/4 cup granulated sugar and sift twice again in mixing bowl. Work in 1 scant cup shortening until mixture is of the consistency of coarse corn meal. Make a well in center and add 3 cups of buttermilk, mixed with 2 teaspoons of baking soda. Work or knead mixture lightly until evenly moistened. Turn out on a floured board and pat out or roll to the desired thickness. Cut with a floured cutter and bake on ungreased baking sheet in a hot oven as directed.

(567) SOY FLOUR BUTTERSCOTCH BISCUITS

BAKING POWDER METHOD

Makes about 50 large biscuits. Oven temperature: 400° F. Baking time: 15 minutes.

Sift bread flour once and measure out 7 cups. Combine with 3/4 generous cup soy flour, 5 tablespoons baking powder, 2 3/4 teaspoons salt and 1/2 cup brown sugar and sift twice into mixing bowl. Work in 3/4 cup of shortening until mixture is of the consistency of coarse corn meal. Make a well in center and add 2 3/4 cups of very cold milk; work or knead mixture lightly until evenly moistened. Turn out on a floured board and pat out or roll to the desired thickness. Cut with a floured cutter and bake on ungreased baking sheet in a hot oven as directed, after brushing biscuits with butter and sprinkling with a little brown sugar.

Before 55 B.C. the use of ovens for baking was unknown in Rome. After the loaf of bread was kneaded, it was toasted either upon a warm hearth or bake-stone, as it was later called when made of metal. Thus was the griddle invented.

(568) SOY FLOUR CHEESE BISCUITS

BAKING POWDER METHOD

Makes about 50 large biscuits. Oven temperature: 400° F. Baking time: 15 minutes.

Important: You may roll and cut biscuits, store them in the refrigerator, then bake them as needed. They may be kept from 1/2 to 2 hours in a refrigerator if covered with a moisture-proof paper to prevent a crust forming on top. They should always be served hot and preferably as soon as they are taken from the oven. So it's wise to bake a batch, serve them hot and start another one immediately.

Sift once 5 1/3 cups of bread flour. Return to sifter and add 2/3 cup soy flour, 3 tablespoons baking powder, 1 rounded teaspoon salt and sift twice into mixing bowl. Work in 3/4 cup shortening until mixture is of the consistency of coarse meal, then work in 1 1/2 cups grated American cheese (other grating cheese may be used). Make a well in center and add 2 1/2 cups (about) of cold milk. Work or knead mixture very lightly until evenly moistened. Turn out on a floured board and pat out or roll to the desired thickness. Cut with a floured cutter and bake on ungreased baking sheet in a hot oven as directed.

(569) SOY FLOUR CREAM BISCUITS

BAKING POWDER METHOD

Makes about 50 large biscuits. Oven temperature: 400° F. Baking time: 15 minutes.

Important: Some people prefer to use pastry flour for biscuits, others use half-bread and half-pastry. Bran or whole wheat flour may be substituted for half of the bread or other flour, except soy flour; if you use whole wheat, do not sift but toss it lightly; then add the remaining dry, sifted ingredients.

Combine 3/4 generous cup of soy flour, 7 cups bread flour, 4 tablespoons baking powder and 1 tablespoon salt and sift twice into mixing bowl. Make a well in center and add all at once 1 quart of heavy cream whipped stiff with 1 teaspoon salt. Work or knead mixture very lightly until evenly moistened. Turn out on a floured board and pat out or roll to the desired thickness. Cut with a floured cutter and bake on ungreased baking sheet in a hot oven as directed.

VARIATIONS: Add to the whipped cream, before adding to dry ingredients, 1 generous teaspoon of grated lemon, orange, grapefruit or lime rind. Add to the whipped cream before adding to dry ingredients 1 scant tablespoon of powdered ginger, or 1 scant cup of chopped crystallized ginger.

If these biscuits are to be served with lamb, add to the whipped cream, before adding to dry ingredients 1 tablespoon of curry powder.

If these biscuits are to be served with fish, add $1/3$ teaspoon powdered saffron before mixing whipped cream with dry ingredients.

If biscuits are to be served instead of tea or coffee cake, add any of the flavoring extracts to the whipped cream before mixing it with dry ingredients, or: (a) 1 cup plumped, dried seedless raisins; (b) 1 cup finely broken nut meats (any kind); (c) 1 cup cooked, cold chopped cranberries; (d) 1 cup chopped figs, dates or a mixture of both.

(570) SOY FLOUR DROP BISCUITS

BAKING POWDER METHOD

Makes about 50 large biscuits. Oven temperature: 450° F. Baking time: 12 minutes.

Important: Drop biscuits may be prepared more quickly than regular or soy flour baking powder biscuits, so it is well to tuck this idea away for emergencies. Use the same ingredients as for any baking powder biscuits, but *add* more liquid so that it will be the consistency of muffin batter. The mixture should be stirred quickly and immediately dropped onto *greased* baking sheet or into greased muffin pans and baked in a very hot oven for about 12 minutes, time depending on size of drops, or until delicately browned.

Sift bread flour once and measure out 6 cups; add 6 tablespoons baking powder, $2\frac{1}{4}$ teaspoons salt, $1/4$ cup fine granulated sugar and $3/4$ generous cup of soy flour and sift twice into mixing bowl. Work in $3/4$ cup shortening until mixture is of the consistency of coarse corn meal; make a well in center and stir in 3 cups of milk mixed with 5 whole fresh eggs (well-beaten and strained); then work or knead mixture lightly until evenly moistened. Turn out on a floured board and pat out or roll to the desired thickness. Cut with a floured cutter and drop biscuits in muffin pans or onto an ungreased baking sheet. Bake in a very hot oven as directed, after brushing tops with melted butter, peanut butter, or any of the fruit butter desired (optional).

According to an old custom dating back to the fourteenth century, at harvest time an English farm hand had the right to choose his own menu and his employer was obligated to supply and prepare it.

(571) SOY FLOUR GINGER BISCUITS

BAKING POWDER METHOD

Makes about 50 biscuits. Oven temperature: 400° F.
Baking time: 15 minutes.

Important: Shortcakes may be made from a biscuit dough, although sugar is often added, and sometimes eggs to give a fine texture. Roll the dough one-half inch thick and cut into size desired. Brush the top of half of the circles with butter; then cover them with unbuttered circles of the same size. Bake in a hot oven (450° F.); then separate the two circles and put the fruit between. This applies to almost any kind of biscuit dough.

Sift 8 cups bread flour and measure out. Combine with 1 cup soy flour, ½ cup baking powder, 1½ tablespoons salt and sift twice into mixing bowl. Make a well in center and add ¾ cup shortening, working it in until mixture is of the consistency of coarse corn meal. Make a well again in center and pour in all at once 3 cups (about) of sweet cold milk mixed with 2 well-beaten fresh eggs; then work or knead mixture, adding gradually 1 cup finely chopped crystallized ginger, until evenly moistened. Turn out on a floured board and pat out or roll to the desired thickness. Cut with a floured cutter and bake in a hot oven as directed.

(572) SOY FLOUR MAPLE BISCUITS

BAKING POWDER METHOD

Makes about 50 biscuits. Oven temperature: 400° F.
Baking time: 15 minutes.

Sift bread flour and measure out 9 cups. Mix with 1 cup of soy flour, ½ cup of baking powder, 1½ tablespoons salt and sift twice into a mixing bowl; make a well in center and work in ¾ cup of shortening until mixture is of the consistency of coarse corn meal. Gradually add 1 scant cup of sifted maple sugar; blend thoroughly;

then moisten gradually with about 3 cups of cold milk. Knead mixture very lightly until evenly moistened. Cut with a floured biscuit cutter; place on ungreased baking sheet and bake in a hot oven as directed.

"Restaurant" is believed to have originated in the mid sixteenth century when medicinal soup and bread was called "restorant." One tavern famous for this soup and bread was called a "restaurant" by its patrons. Other taverns soon took up the name.

(573) SOY FLOUR PEANUT BUTTER BISCUITS

BAKING POWDER METHOD

Makes about 50 biscuits. Oven temperature: 400° F.
Baking time: 15 minutes.

Sift bread flour, measure 9 cups and sift again with 6 tablespoons baking powder, 1½ tablespoons salt and 1 cup soy flour and sift again into a mixing bowl. Make a well in center and work in 1 cup peanut butter until mixture is of the consistency of coarse corn meal. Again make a well in center and add 3 cups of cold milk. Knead mixture very lightly until evenly moistened. Turn out on a floured board and pat out or roll to the desired thickness. Cut with floured cutter and bake on ungreased baking sheet in a hot oven as directed.

(574) SOY FLOUR RAISIN BISCUITS

BAKING POWDER METHOD

Makes about 50 biscuits. Oven temperature: 400° F.
Baking time: 15 minutes.

NOTE: To have biscuits with a nice brown crust, brush them with a pastry brush dipped in milk.

Sift bread flour twice and measure out 5 cups. Combine with 2 tablespoons baking powder, ⅔ cup soy flour, 2¼ teaspoons salt and sift twice again into a mixing bowl. Blend in ½ cup melted shortening (not hot) until mixture is of the consistency of coarse corn meal. Make a well in center and add 3 cups of orange juice and 1 tablespoon of grated orange rind, alternately with 3 cups washed seedless raisins, floured. Knead mixture very lightly but thoroughly until evenly moistened. Turn out on a floured board and pat out or roll to the desired thickness. Cut with a floured cutter; place biscuits on ungreased sheet and bake in a hot oven as directed.

From as early as 400 B.C. Greek food merchants had their scales periodically checked by government officials and were punished if they gave false weight.

(575) SOY FLOUR SOUR MILK BISCUITS

BAKING POWDER METHOD

Makes about 50 biscuits. Oven temperature: 400° F.
Baking time: 15 minutes.

Sift and measure 9 cups of bread flour; combine with 1 cup soy flour, 5 tablespoons baking powder, 2 tablespoons salt and 1 tablespoon baking soda, and sift twice in mixing bowl. Work in ¾ cup shortening until mixture is of the consistency of coarse corn meal. Make a well in center and add 4 cups cold sour milk. Knead mixture very lightly until evenly moistened. Turn out on a floured board and pat out or roll to the desired thickness. Cut with a floured cutter and bake on ungreased baking sheet in a hot oven as directed.

(576) SOY FLOUR SWEET POTATO BISCUITS

BAKING POWDER METHOD

Makes about 50 biscuits. Oven temperature: 400° F.
Baking time: 15 minutes.

Sift bread flour twice, measure out 5 cups; combine with ¼ cup baking powder, ⅔ generous cup soy flour, 1 rounded tablespoon salt and sift twice in a mixing bowl. Work in ¾ cup of shortening until mixture is of the consistency of coarse corn meal. Make a well in center and add 3 cups of cold, mashed sweet potatoes. Blend thoroughly, then moisten with about 2 cups of buttermilk thoroughly mixed with 2 teaspoons of baking soda. Knead mixture very lightly until moistened throughout. Turn out on a floured board and pat out or roll to the desired thickness. Cut with a floured cutter; place biscuits on ungreased baking sheet; brush each biscuit with cold milk and bake in a hot oven as directed.

Do you know that the jewelers' "carat" owes its origin to a lowly bean, the fruit of an exotic tree which is native to southern Abyssinia, on the east coast of Africa?

This tree is known as the "kuara" or "sun-tree." When in blossom, its fruit and flowers are a beautiful coral red color. The fruit, a large red bean called "carat," has a little black spot on the side and hangs from the branch in a spherical pod of a pithy and fibrous substance as tough and hard as the bark of the tree. As these beans are always uniform in size and weight, the natives employed them many years ago as their standard for weighing gold, and the use and popularity of the fruit spread over the length and breadth of Africa, being readily accepted by both white and black traders—and by money changers. In time the practice passed from the Dark Continent to India where the shrewd native goldsmiths, who were without a standard, early adopted the carat as a medium and likewise applied it to the grading of all precious stones. This expression of the diamond and gold standards in terms of carats eventually grew into universal usage and continues today.

(577) SOY FLOUR WHOLE WHEAT BISCUITS

BAKING POWDER METHOD

Makes about 50 biscuits. Oven temperature: 400° F.
Baking time: 15 minutes.

Do not sift, but toss lightly 8 cups whole wheat flour with 1 cup of soy flour sifted with 4 tablespoons of baking powder and 1 rounded tablespoon of salt. Work in 1 cup of shortening until mixture is of the consistency of coarse corn meal. Make a well in center and add 3 cups of cold milk (orange or grapefruit juice with 1 tablespoon of grated rind may be substituted for milk, or if preferred 3 cups sour milk mixed with 2 teaspoons of baking soda). Work or knead mixture lightly until evenly moistened. Turn out on a floured board and pat out or roll to the desired thickness. Cut with floured cutter, place biscuits on ungreased baking sheet, brush each biscuit with cold milk and bake in a hot oven as directed.

(578) SOY FLOUR CINNAMON NUT BREAD

BAKING POWDER METHOD

Makes 1 loaf. Oven temperature: 350° F.
Baking time: 1 hour.

1 cup soy flour, sifted
1½ cups bread flour, sifted
2 tablespoons granulated sugar
1 scant teaspoon salt
1 scant tablespoon baking powder
1 teaspoon ground cinnamon
1 cup nut meats, chopped (any kind)
2 fresh eggs, well-beaten
1 cup sweet cold milk
4 tablespoons butter, melted

Combine soy flour, bread flour, sugar, salt, baking powder and cinnamon and sift together over chopped nut meats. Blend well. Add beaten eggs, mixed with milk and melted butter. Blend thoroughly and stir into flour-nut mixture. Allow this to stand in a generously greased loaf pan for 20 minutes; then bake in a moderate oven as directed. You may brush top of baked loaf with a little milk or butter as soon as removed from oven. Let cool before slicing.

In the fourteenth century Chinese noblemen used napkins of silk. Almost a yard in length, they were decorated with mottoes woven in gold.

(579) SOY FLOUR COFFEE TWISTS

BAKING POWDER METHOD

Makes about 12 twists. Oven temperature: 400° F.
Baking time: 12–15 minutes.

Sift 1¾ cups bread flour with ⅓ cup soy flour, 1 tablespoon granulated sugar, 1 scant teaspoon salt and 1 tablespoon baking powder in a mixing bowl. Rub in ½ cup lard (butter or margarine may be substituted) until mixture is of the consistency of coarse corn meal; then moisten with about ⅔ cup of rich cold milk or enough to make a soft dough. Turn out on a floured board and knead lightly to a smooth ball. Flatten the ball to ½-inch in thickness; then roll into an oblong. Spread lightly with softened butter or margarine and again spread with equal parts of orange marmalade mixed with chopped nut meats (any kind). Roll up; cut off strips ½-inch wide and twist into S-shaped rolls. Place on greased pan; brush with melted butter or margarine and bake in a hot oven as directed. Serve warm.

(580) SOY FLOUR GINGERBREAD

BAKING POWDER METHOD

Makes 1 loaf or square. Oven temperature: 300° F.
Baking time: 40–45 minutes.

There are many recipes for the spicy favorite of all ages and some call for an egg or more while others are eggless. Molasses and a combination of spices are, of course, essential ingredients for almost any gingerbread—soft, hard or rich.

Mix and sift twice the following ingredients: 1¾ cups sifted pastry flour, 1/4 cup soy flour, 3/4 teaspoon baking soda, 1 teaspoon baking powder, 1/2 teaspoon ground cinnamon, 1/3 teaspoon ground cloves, 1 rounded teaspoon ground ginger, 1/2 generous teaspoon salt and a tiny pinch of cayenne pepper (optional) in a mixing bowl. Blend thoroughly 1/4 cup sieved brown sugar, 3/4 cup of molasses and 1 large fresh egg, well-beaten. Stir into this 1 cup boiling sweet cider to which has been added 1/4 cup butter or margarine. When thoroughly blended, stir in the sifted dry ingredients, gradually, mixing well after each addition until well blended. Turn mixture into a well-greased cake pan or a 9-inch square pan and bake in a slow oven as directed.

Fine with whipped cream blended with equal parts of apple or other fruit sauce, jelly or marmalade.

(581) SOY FLOUR HOMEMADE BREAD

YEAST METHOD

Makes 2 loaves. Oven temperature: 375–400° F.
Baking time: 45–50 minutes.

Place 2 tablespoons of granulated sugar, 1 tablespoon salt and 2 tablespoons melted lard in mixing bowl. Gradually stir in 2 cups of rich, scalded (not boiling) milk, until sugar and salt are dissolved. Cool to room temperature. Meanwhile crumble 1 compressed yeast cake into 1/4 cup of warm water, stirring until yeast is dissolved, and add to milk-sugar mixture with 2 cups bread flour, sifted twice, beating hard for at least a minute. Then gradually add 2 more cups of sifted bread flour with 7/8 cup soy flour, stirring it constantly until a stiff dough forms. Turn the dough onto floured board and knead until it is smooth, elastic and not sticky (about 12–15 minutes), using the palms of the hands lightly floured and adding more sifted bread flour as needed to obtain a springy dough. Place the dough in a greased warm bowl; brush top lightly with melted lard; cover with a clean, light cloth and stand over hot water (not boiling) for about 4 hours or until dough has doubled in bulk. Then punch down in the bowl for about one minute. Again brush with melted lard and again let rise until doubled in bulk.

After this second rising, toss dough on lightly floured board and knead one minute; divide in two equal parts; knead each ball into a rectangle; fold over in half and seal edges by pressing with the flat of the fingers. Repeat this twice, the last time folding both ends toward center. Seal again by pressing with the flat of the fingers. Place the dough in greased pans, sealed edge down; brush tops with melted lard and allow to rise until doubled in bulk. (This makes three risings.) The dough should round over top of pan slightly. Bake in a hot oven as directed until crust is well browned and crisp and sides have shrunk slightly from pan. Turn over a rack, remove pans and when cold store wrapped in waxed paper in bread box.

The common mark of "X" on flour bags originated in the California gold-rush. It indicated the price, not the quality. Thus a sack marked "XXXX" showed that the price was forty dollars.

The rose petals with which Cleopatra strewed her dining table were more than decorative. Between courses, guests dipped the petals in small honey jars provided for that purpose and nibbled on the floral appetizers. More practical, Americans use the honey to make bread, such as:

(582) SOY FLOUR HONEY FRUIT BREAD

Makes 2 loaves. Oven temperature: 325° F.
Baking time: 1¼ hours (about).

Line bottoms of two greased loaf pans (9 × 5 × 3 inches) with waxed paper.

Cream ¼ cup of lard; gradually add 2 cups of liquid honey, beating constantly until thoroughly blended, adding while beating 2 well-beaten fresh eggs alternately with 3 tablespoons of grated orange rind. Set aside. Sift bread flour, measure out 4 cups and mix with ½ cup soy flour, 5 teaspoons baking powder, 1 generous teaspoon salt and 1 teaspoon baking soda and sift twice. Gradually add to the honey mixture alternately 1½ cups unstrained orange juice and 1½ cups of broken nut meats (any kind), previously floured. Pour into the prepared pans, having sides higher than the center, and bake in a very moderate oven as directed. Cool upon a rack and let stand one day before cutting.

In the seventeenth century in the Baltic States a girl could propose to a bashful youth by baking a loaf of bread and sending it to him. There was just one catch—the girl had to produce a witness who could testify that her intended bridegroom received the loaf while it was still warm.

(583) SOY FLOUR HOT CROSS BUNS

YEAST METHOD

Easter, like many another church festival, is a mixture of both pagan and Christian customs. In old Norse mythology, Easter was associated with the spring festival welcoming the rebirth of Nature and the awakening of the Earth. Indeed, the very word *"Easter"* is derived from an old Saxon word meaning "Rising."

Again, in India rabbits and eggs were symbols of reproduction and fertility and were important features of another festival closely corresponding in date to our Easter. This was a very old celebration and since rabbits and eggs were always associated with it, they were easily included in a Christian festival occurring at the same period of the year.

Every land and every district has quaint customs peculiar to the celebration of Easter. In the northern parts of England, for example, the men paraded the streets on Easter Sunday and claimed the privilege of lifting any woman they met three times from the ground and then demanding a kiss in payment! In Old Russia, when the Greek Orthodox Church was very strong, it was a rule that anyone could accost another in the streets and give him the triple kiss on the cheeks, saying meantime, the three words: "Christ Is Risen." Even the poorest peasant might so accost his Tsar, or Little Father. Some of us may also have heard the expression "kicking the gong around," but never suspected its origin. Who, for instance, ever heard of inviting for Easter morning as many people as possible to gather to kick pies, cakes and bread around, as well as full bottles of wine and liquor, resulting in a scramble as wild as any football scrimmage? Yet in certain villages in England, what is known as "bottle kicking" contests take place at the Easter celebration of the end of the long season of fasts.

In Poland a boiled pig's head elaborately decked with flowers is the principal food on the Easter table. Surrounding it are roast veal and hams, flanked by the popular Polish sausage highly spiced with garlic. Cakes of all kinds and Easter buns, adorned with sprigs of boxwood, are part of a feast that has for its centerpiece a large mold of butter in the form of the Paschal Lamb—fresh sweet butter makes its appearance in poor homes only on important occasions.

Hot cross buns belong to Easter as does turkey to Christmas and here is an old English recipe which the writer has arranged to use soy flour:

Makes 3 dozen rich buns. Oven temperature: 375–400° F.
Baking time: 20–25 minutes.

Sieve ½ cup each of brown and granulated sugar and combine with ½ cup of melted butter or margarine, 4 fresh egg yolks, well-beaten, and 2 cups scalded milk cooled to lukewarm; blend thoroughly. Crumble a cake of compressed yeast into ¼ cup lukewarm cider and stir until dissolved; then add yeast mixture to sugar-egg mixture, blending well. Set aside.

Sift bread flour (pastry flour may be used) and measure out 7¼ cups and add ¾ cup soy flour, 1½ teaspoons salt, 1 teaspoon powdered nutmeg, and 1 teaspoon of powdered cinnamon and sift twice. Add half of this flour mixture to the first mixture (*i.e.* sugar-egg-yeast mixture) and beat steadily for about 3 minutes or until it is smooth and thoroughly blended. Then stir in the remaining flour mixture and beat for 5 minutes or until very smooth and entirely free from lumps. Next fold in 4 egg whites beaten stiffly with ½ teaspoon salt, as you would for a cake. This will result in a very soft sponge. Cover with a light dry cloth such as cheesecloth and set aside in a warm place overnight.

Next day, early in the morning so as to have the buns hot for the breakfast table, proceed as follows: Toss the dough onto lightly floured board and punch it, using gradually ⅓ cup of sifted bread flour or pastry flour. Now roll the dough out to ½ inch in thickness and with floured biscuit cutter shape 4-inch rounds. Place the dough disks on a baking sheet, brushed with melted butter or margarine; cover again with a light dry cloth and allow to rise for an hour and a half until doubled in bulk. With the blade of a sharp knife, cut a cross on each disk, almost through it. At once bake in a hot oven as directed until buns are golden brown. Remove from the oven and brush each bun with a syrup made of 1 cup molasses and ½ cup water. Serve as hot as possible. If this entails too early rising, serve them for luncheon with tea or coffee and a fruit compote.

In ancient Greece only those who owned their own homes and paid at least five minae (a hundred dollars) in taxes per year were permitted to invite guests to dinner on Easter Sunday.

(584) SOY FLOUR MOLASSES OATMEAL WHOLE WHEAT BREAD

STEAMED METHOD

The Scots for generations have recognized oatmeal as a superlative food for building a sturdy race. They didn't know why, but they knew it was true. When old Sam Johnson got out his dictionary 150 years ago, in wisecracking humor he defined oats as a grain they fed to horses in England and to men in Scotland. To which a proud old Scot replied: "Aye, sir, as you must have noticed. What horses! What men!"

Porridge became "brose," or soup, when a large lump of butter was added and milk sufficient to make the consistency like that of a cream soup. When still more water was added, the porridge became "gruel," excellent for children and invalids. But it is perhaps in the wide classification of breads, cakes, cookies and baked goods that oatmeal really shows its possibilities. There's that highly satisfying and nourishing "quick" or loaf bread made with oats, which any mother should plan to bake at least once a week if she has a family of growing children.

Among the grains the only one used in great quantity without much processing is oats. Oats contain more vitamin B_1, more calories, more protein, more fat, more calcium, less starch, less phosphorus, less iron, and less niacin (nicotinic acid, the chief anti-pellagra factor) than wheat.

Makes 3 small loaves. Steaming time: 3 long hours.
Drying time (in oven): 15–20 minutes.

Mix thoroughly 1 cup soy bean flour with 1 cup oatmeal, 1 cup unsifted whole wheat, 2 teaspoons baking soda, 1 teaspoon salt and stir in ½ cup each of chopped nut meats (any kind) and chopped seedless raisins. Combine 2 cups sour milk or buttermilk with 1 cup of Grandma's molasses, blending well; then stir liquid into the flour mixture. Beat briskly for about 2 minutes; fill 2 generously greased coffee or baking powder cans a scant ⅔ full; adjust lids or covers tightly and steam steadily for 3 long hours in constantly, rapidly, boiling water. Cool before slicing with a string or thread as for any steamed bread. You may dry the bread by placing it in a moderate oven (375° F.) for 15–20 minutes.

(585) SOY FLOUR MUFFIN BATTER (PLAIN)

BAKING POWDER METHOD

Makes 12 medium-sized muffins. Oven temperature: 425° F. Baking time: 18–20 minutes.

Combine 1¾ cups sifted bread flour, ⅓ cup soy flour, 1 tablespoon baking powder, ½ generous teaspoon salt, and ¼ teaspoon (optional) powdered cinnamon and sift twice in a mixing bowl. Set aside while beating 1 extra large fresh egg with 2 tablespoons granulated sugar (if liked sweet); then beat this into 1 cup cold milk alternately with 3 tablespoons melted shortening. Make a well in center of flour mixture and pour milk mixture in it. Stir as vigorously as possible without spattering until ingredients are evenly dampened (about 15 seconds). Spoon batter into greased hot muffin pans, filling about ⅔ full. Stir the batter as little as possible while filling muffin pans. Bake in a very hot oven as directed until the crusts are golden brown and muffins firm to the touch or a toothpick inserted in the center comes out clean. Serve as hot as possible. These muffins will have a creamy color, a firm crumb and a very satisfactory flavor and texture. They will break well and keep fresh for at least two days.

For muffin variations, *see* Section on "Muffins."

In Elizabethan England exquisitely baked little fruit tarts were sold to the nobility for as much as fifty dollars.

(586) SOY FLOUR MUFFIN SURPRISE

BAKING POWDER METHOD

Makes 6 large muffins. Oven temperature: 400° F. Baking time: 20 minutes.

½ cup unsifted soy flour
½ teaspoon salt
1 generous teaspoon baking powder
2 egg yolks, well-beaten
⅓ cup cold water
2 egg whites, stiffly beaten
6 dried apricots, parboiled, drained

Butter 6 muffin pans generously and press in bottom of each pan a parboiled dried apricot, round face down. Set aside. Combine soy flour, salt and baking powder and sift into mixing bowl. To the beaten egg yolks add cold water and beat until thoroughly blended. Pour over flour mixture stirring just enough to moisten flour. Gradually fold in stiffly beaten egg whites; then spoon carefully over apricots in the pans, filling 2/3 full, and bake in a hot oven as directed until muffins are firm and brown on top. Serve hot with butter or your favorite jam or marmalade.

(587) SOY FLOUR NUT BREAD

BAKING POWDER METHOD

Makes 1 loaf. Oven temperature: 350–375° F.
Baking time: 1 hour (about).

Measure out 2¼ cups sifted bread flour and add ¼ cup of soy flour, 2 tablespoons granulated sugar (or brown sugar), 1 scant teaspoon salt, 1 tablespoon baking powder and ½ generous teaspoon ground cinnamon. Sift over 1 cup of nut meats, chopped (any kind). Blend thoroughly and set aside. Beat 2 fresh eggs well; then beat them into 1 cup of rich sweet milk, adding while beating 3 tablespoons melted shortening. Gradually add the flour mixture to milk mixture and blend well. Pour into greased, floured loaf pan; let stand for about 20 minutes in a warm place, covered with a cloth; then bake in a moderate oven as directed. Remove from oven, brush with butter, place on a cooling rack and when cold store in bread box.

Rationing "cards" issued in Athens in 490 B.C. *were slabs of marble that had to be presented in person to obtain food and drink, orders for which were inscribed thereon.*

(588) SOY FLOUR OATMEAL BREAD

YEAST METHOD

Makes 2 loaves. Oven temperature: 375° F.
Baking time: 1 hour (about).

Combine 2 cups of oats with 2 cups of boiling water and let stand 5 minutes, stirring occasionally; then stir in ¼ cup of molasses. Set aside covered with a cloth. Crumble 2 cakes of compressed yeast into ½ cup lukewarm milk and when dissolved, stir well into oat mixture.

Measure 1½ cups sifted bread flour once; then combine with ½ cup of soy flour and ½ generous teaspoon salt and sift over the oat mixture. Blend thoroughly; stir in 2 tablespoons melted shortening and another cup of molasses. Beat a minute or so until smooth and cover with a light, dry cloth. Keep in a warm place until doubled in bulk; then punch the sponge down and add 3 cups of sifted bread flour and combine with ½ cup soy flour and sift again. Blend thoroughly; cover to allow to rise until doubled in bulk. Shape into 2 loaves; place in greased, floured loaf pans and again allow to rise, covered until doubled in bulk. Bake in a moderately hot oven as directed. Cool on rack and when cold store in bread box.

Perfumers and apothecaries now supply society with its scents and restoratives, not without profit, but the heroines of Thomas Love Peacock and Mrs. Radcliffe rolled their own pomanders; and when the family budget couldn't stand the strain of gold or ivory gadgets, an orange stuck full of cloves was esteemed as better than nothing.

In the days of this writer's infancy and earliest recollections a small brown globe had a place among the curious knick-knacks on the family's parlor cabinet, and it exhaled at close range a subtle fragrance that might now be described by a romantic writer as "intriguing." It was in the mustn't-touch class of household treasures, and was nothing more nor less than an ancient orange which some patient and devoted grandmother or aunt had jabbed full of cloves. It had been in the cabinet time without mind, it now seems, and was shown to favored visitors as a particular curiosity; for the full symmetry of the embalmed orange had been retained and the aromatic incense of spice and oil of orange still hung faintly in the air about it. A good and careful child was sometimes permitted to touch it and attempt an estimate of the number of cloves involved in the composition, but it was never quite determined by hundreds or by thousands.

And now, after all the years, we are told that the clove-studded oranges were commonplace keepsakes in the romantic sun-dial and herb-garden era, and that they figured importantly among the simplest forms of the ubiquitous and cherished pomanders of Georgian and early Victorian days. A pomander was fully as important and necessary in those times as the cigarette case of today. It was smart to carry a pomander as elegant and costly as the purse would allow, and the pomander's strong-smelling contents not only perfumed the air of drawing-room or club, but warded off dread fevers and distempers and sent all the witches and evil spirits of those hazardous days a-packing.

To make pomanders, select firm oranges and stick cloves into the skin of the orange until the rind is completely covered, about 1/8 of an inch apart. Don't stick the cloves in rows because the skin may crack. Then roll it in a mixture of equal parts of orris root and ground cinnamon. Pat in as much of the powdered mixture as will adhere to the orange. Wrap the pomander in tissue paper for a week or so. This gives the cinnamon mixture time to coat the orange and add its fragrance. Then remove the paper, shake off the loose powder and the pomander is ready for use in drawers or in linen shelves. To hang in a closet, crochet a loose circular cradle or tie a ribbon crisscross around the pomander, looping it so it may be hung. Your pomander is ready to give pleasure for a whole year.

Almost everyone likes oranges and the morning glass of orange juice makes its appearance on countless breakfast tables. Bread made with orange is really delicious. It is made as follows:

(589) SOY FLOUR ORANGE BREAD

BAKING POWDER METHOD

Makes 1 loaf. Oven temperature: 325° F.
Baking time: 1 hour (about).

Cream 2 tablespoons of butter with 1/4 cup granulated sugar (or equal parts of dark brown and granulated sugar). Continue creaming while adding 1 large fresh egg, well-beaten with 1/2 teaspoon each of ground cinnamon, cloves and ginger. Set aside. Measure out 1 3/4 cups of sifted bread flour, combine with 1/4 cup of soy flour, 1 teaspoon salt, 1 tablespoon baking powder and a tiny pinch of nutmeg and sift into a mixing bowl containing 3/4 cup of broken nut meats (any kind). Blend well. Gradually, moisten flour and nuts with butter-spice-egg mixture and stir in 1 scant cup of unstrained orange juice. Mix thoroughly. Pour batter into a greased loaf pan and bake in a moderate oven as directed. Remove from pan and cool on rack. When cold wrap in waxed paper and store in bread box.

Evidence indicates that as primitive man had no flour, he made a kind of bread out of crushed acorns or beechnuts. To rid them of bitterness, he soaked the nuts in water. Then the mass was taken up, squeezed into a solid cake and dried in the sun. The Egyptians made bread from wheat, spelt, durra, kneading it with their feet. This struck Herodotus, the Greek historian who visited Egypt, as odd.

"Dough they knead with their feet," he observed, "but use their hands for clay."

We know that ancient Pompeii boasted professional bakers; for excavations in the buried city have turned up loaves of bread bearing imprints of the baker's name, presumably as a guaranty of purity and weight at the time of sale. When Constantine abolished slavery, experienced bakers became scarce. To restore the supply, the Emperor Trajan founded a college of millers and bakers. A London baker's guild, divided into the Company of White Bakers and the Company of Brown Bakers, was formed in 1155. The brotherhoods were not unified until 1509.

DIETETIC BREADS

(590) DIETETIC BREADS

Food constitutes the chief item of the living expenses of the people of this country and of Europe. The health and strength of all of us are intimately dependent upon our diet. Yet few of us know much about what our food contains, how it nourishes us, whether or not we are economical or wasteful in buying and preparing it for use, and whether or not the food we eat is rightly fitted to the demands of our bodies. The result of our ignorance is great waste in the purchase and use of food, loss of money, and injury to health. The reason for this ignorance is simple enough. Fifty years ago no man knew what our bodies and our foods were composed of; how the different nutritive ingredients of the food served their purposes in nutrition; how much of each of the ingredients was needed to supply the demands of people of different age, sex, and occupation; and how best to adjust the diet to the wants of the user. We do not today know as much about these things as we ought. For that matter, we never shall be able to lay down hard-and-fast rules to apply to all cases, because of the differences between individuals in respect to their demands for nutriment and the ways in which their bodies can make use of different kinds of foods. But the research of the past fifty years has brought a great deal of definite information. Nearly all of the exact inquiry in this direction has been done in Europe. We are only beginning it in the United States.

The subject of dietetic breads has not received the attention it deserves, and it is to be regretted that in the curriculum of medical colleges it is usually either omitted or is disposed of briefly at the end of a course in general nutrition.

Among these special breads are the following:

Aerated Bread, which keeps fresh longer than other varieties. It has a peculiar taste which, however, is liked by some.

Zwieback is a thoroughly dry form of bread which is very wholesome for invalids and children and is excellent for "dunking" by all.

Gluten Bread is made from gluten flour. It is very useful where there is a tendency to obesity, and it is also given to diabetics under a doctor's direction. It may be toasted like white or graham bread. It is made by washing wheat flour in such a manner as to remove the starchy granules in whole or in part, leaving the gluten behind. Such bread is certain to contain more or less starch and may have a little sugar. It is usually much more difficult to chew than regular bread and unless well-prepared, it is not very palatable. Some of it is unpleasantly tough and stringy. It is difficult to panify but it may be aerated. Gluten biscuits are therefore more palatable than the bread unless special formulas and treatment are used. Gluten flour is also used for thickening broths, egg puddings, etc. Consult your doctor before using it.

Fromentine, a French product, is another form of diabetic flour made from wheat germ. It contains less starch than mature wheat but has an oil which is purgative and prevents proper panification, causing the bread to sour easily. It is usually used in diabetic cases and under the advice of a doctor.

Swedish Rye Bread is a most palatable and wholesome health bread made from the entire rye, according to the Swedish process, in flat, round disks about 10 inches in diameter with a small hole in the center. It is excellent for children, especially when placed in a moderately hot oven (325° F.) for a few minutes. It requires thorough mastication and contains valuable food elements. It can be bought in any of the large cities of the United States. Consult your doctor before using this bread.

Following are a few dietetic breads which may be made at home. All the above can be bought in health stores.

(591) DOCTOR SEEGEN'S ALMOND BISCUITS

FOR DIABETICS

Makes about 8 biscuits. Oven temperature: 300° F.
Baking time: 30 minutes (about).

Blanch ¼ pound of sweet almonds and chop coarsely. Put them through food chopper, using the finest blade or pound in a mortar. Place the resulting paste into a linen bag and steep it in boiling water to which has been added 1 teaspoon of lemon juice or mild vinegar for 20 minutes so as to remove all the sugar contained in the paste; mix this paste thoroughly with 6 tablespoons of sweet butter, creamed with 2 whole fresh eggs. Next add the yolks of 3 fresh eggs and a tiny pinch of salt and stir with rotary beater. Fold in 3 egg whites, stiffly beaten with a small pinch of salt and divide mixture into 8 biscuits. Place in buttered muffin pans and bake in a slow oven for about 30 minutes or until biscuits are golden brown. Serve cold.

(592) DOCTOR EUSTACE SMITH'S BARLEY JELLY

FOR STOMACH TROUBLE

Put 2 tablespoons of washed pearl barley into a pint and a half of cold water and slowly boil down to a pint (2 cups); strain through a fine cloth and let the liquid settle into a jelly in a cool place. Two teaspoons of this jelly, dissolved in 8 ounces of warmed (not boiled) and sweetened milk, are enough for a single feeding, and such a meal may be allowed twice a day.

(593) DOCTOR CHRYSTIE'S BREAD JELLY

FOR OBESITY

Pour boiling water on 4 slices of stale bread and let it soak for an hour. Drain thoroughly, squeezing gently; add fresh cold water, and boil down until a thick mass is obtained which becomes jellylike on cooling. May be eaten with milk or cream and a little sugar.

(594) UNFERMENTED WHOLE WHEAT BREAD

Makes 2 loaves. Oven temperature: 350–375° F.
Baking time: 1 hour (about).

Beat ½ cup olive oil steadily, adding 1¼ cups of cold water, a little at a time until an emulsion is formed resembling the beaten whites of eggs. When all the water has been added, sprinkle 7 cups (about) of unsifted whole wheat flour very quickly over the entire emulsion, so as to hold all the air confined in the mixture. Make a stiff dough, adding more flour as needed; knead thoroughly until smooth, elastic and not sticky. Let the dough stand over night, or at least 6 hours, covered and in a cool place, and then knead again before forming into loaves. Bake in a moderate oven as directed.

(595) UNLEAVENED FLAKED WHOLE WHEAT BISCUITS

DROPPING METHOD

Makes 24 biscuits. Oven temperature: 425° F.
Baking time: 12–15 minutes.

4 cups whole wheat flakes
¼ cup honey
¾ teaspoon salt
1 cup nut cream
3 egg whites
3 egg yolks

Beat whites and yolks of eggs separately; thoroughly mix together the yolks, nut cream and honey; then fold in the stiffly beaten egg whites with salt, alternately with wheat flakes. Drop by spoonfuls on greased pans and bake until light brown as directed.

(596) UNLEAVENED FRUIT BREAD

Makes 2 small loaves. Oven temperature: 350° F.
Baking time: 30 minutes (about).

2 cups of cold water
1 cup cracked wheat
1 cup seedless raisins
½ cup pitted dates, chopped fine
½ cup dried figs, chopped fine
¾ scant teaspoon salt
A generous pinch cinnamon
1 cup nut cream
½ cup strained honey

Soak cracked wheat in water overnight; add the other ingredients in the morning and mix thoroughly. Steam steadily in double boiler for 2 hours; then shape into small loaves and bake in a moderate oven as directed until dry. Cool before slicing. Fine with jam, marmalade or preserves.

Lest his foreign chef lose his way when shopping for groceries, Prince Charles Radziwill in 1772 bought the entire Paris street between his home and the market.

(597) UNLEAVENED WHOLE WHEAT FRUIT CRACKERS

Makes about 24 small crackers. Oven temperature: 350° F.
Baking time: 12 minutes (about).

1 lb. (about) unsifted whole wheat flour
½ cup almond butter
A tiny pinch of nutmeg
¾ teaspoon salt
¾ cup cold water
½ cup seedless raisins, ground figs or dates

Dissolve almond butter by adding a little water at a time; mix well until water is used. Add salt and nutmeg and all the flour that can be kneaded in. Knead dough 10 to 15 minutes; roll out until 1/8 of an inch thick and cut into equal parts. Spread one part with seedless raisins, ground figs or dates; then place the other piece of dough upon the fruit; press together with rolling pin and perforate partly through with a fork at frequent intervals. Cut into 24 pieces of any desired shape and bake in a moderate oven as directed until a light brown color.

In 1695 when "Civilité," a book of etiquette á la Emily Post was published, readers were informed that it was no longer good manners to wipe their fingers on the bread.

TOASTS

(598) TOAST

An expert on culinary matters distinguishes three kinds of toast: soft golden toast which requires very fresh bread and must be toasted quickly; the crisp and brown, which is the same but toasted by low heat; and the dry and crunchy, which is made with stale bread and cooked by very slow heat. Preference is a matter of taste —and of teeth. Other kinds of toast might be added, such as the paper-thin sort which is credited to Dame Nellie Melba; milk toast, appreciated by both invalids and the well; and the special toast preferred by gourmets, which is surmounted juicily by a plump-breasted quail.

Only one kind of toast is shunned by men of discernment. It is the kind that begins "Mr. Chairman" and only after forty minutes of platitudes ends with "Gentlemen, I give you ——." It's a pity that this sort of thing was ever permitted to disgrace the name of toast.

However, if none other will say it, I'll say it: Our toast is N.G. It may be that the bread is partly to blame, but generally it is the cook's fault. In any case, something awful happens in our kitchens and at the table where mechanized toast is everlastingly a part of the breakfast.

What does the dictionary say: "*Toast*—Sliced bread browned at a fire," a definition of six words that is interpreted by the modern school of cookery to have at least sixty meanings, most of them calculated to disorganize far and wide the practice of toast making.

From all sources I hear widespread complaints about this article of diet—its texture, its resistance and its close resemblance to hardware. During a long childhood—years before my second childhood—in our house, bread was quite unlike anything now classified as food. My mother was a born toaster, accomplishing wonders with a plain iron, wood-burning stove. In the present era I find that many housewives have perfected a process by which plain white bread, light as a feather, can be turned into a square of tiling or a piece of linoleum. While this composition has the color of toast and will even absorb butter, if applied quickly, it will withstand much wear and tear—unless one has the trepidity to dunk and inhale it before the moistened end detaches itself from the main structure and falls into one's lap. Certain specimens of toast resist even dunking and once allowed to cool in a toast rack become absolutely inedible.

Moreover, in the preparation of hors d'oeuvre or "snacks" served with cocktails, it has been discovered that this vitrified toast, cut into cubes with a cold chisel, may be made to serve as a base for caviar, sliced smoked salmon, sardine paste and frankfurters.

Many the guest who, after biting indiscreetly into such a collection of holdovers, snatches his hat and makes a hurry call on the nearest dentist, or in the cause of social service licks off the top layer and leaves the cornerstone in a convenient ash tray. Better thus than to roam among the guests for an afternoon chewing a toast cud innocently selected from a tray of delicacies alleged to stimulate appetite and thirst.

It may well be that this generation of toast eaters should look partly for relief to the bakers, who are more concerned with the appearance of a loaf than with its final conversion into toast; but the toast maker is the real culprit, for delectable toast can be made.

In a recent interesting survey it was found that the average person consumes between 30 and 40 per cent of his daily bread in the form of toast. Why, it may be asked, is so much bread eaten in this form? What might they do if the toast were good?

It has likewise been scientifically proved that pleasant anticipation causes the digestive juices to flow more freely and hence results in an increased or "whetted" appetite. That is why, in order to be enjoyed and properly digested, all food should be so prepared as to tempt taste or appetite. Here the factors of appearance, texture, taste, and aroma or odor, all come into play—the food must look, chew, taste and smell good. Now what happens to a slice of bread when it is toasted, either by the old-fashioned way of holding the slice on a long toasting-fork over a coal or wood fire or in a broiler or electric toaster? When bread is toasted, some of the starch of the wheat is dextrinized, some of the sugars are caramelized and some of the proteins are parched. These chemical reactions make changes, not only in the texture and digestibility of the bread, but specifically in its flavor.

For a slice of ideal toast, "piping-hot," has first an appetizing golden-brown color; a smooth, crunchy toasted surface; a tender or soft "crumb"; a pleasing nut-like odor; and a taste that is slightly sweet and suggestive of the wheat kernel itself.

The origin of toast is lost in the mists of antiquity. Some inspired writer ought to do for toast what Charles Lamb did for roast pig: that is give us at least a plausible theory of how it came to be. Most probably the actual inventor will never be known and it is best so, for monuments would be erected to him, or her, at every cross-road adding intolerably to our traffic problems. Toast is the *sine qua non* of every American breakfast, luncheon, dinner or supper. Every *materfamilias* knows that the quickest way to get the men-folk out of bed in the morning is not to jangle a bell, but to open the kitchen door a chink and let the fumes of toast, bacon and coffee, like incense, pervade the house.

However, even with an electric toaster, making toast is not always the simple job you would think it might be. A few secrets that have been discovered by questing cooks are passed on here:

If you have an automatic toaster, try this method of keeping toast *piping hot* longer; turn the dial on the toaster to "light," as far as it will go, and toast the slices once very lightly. Remove from the toaster and when ready to serve toast lightly once more. The result will surprise and please you.

Toast in large quantities is best made in the broiler. Here you can make as many as nine slices of toast at one clip. Pre-heat the broiling oven at moderately hot (400° F.); then place the rack with the bread on it about five inches below the flame. Toast the bread until a golden brown on one side, turn and toast half a minute. The second side toasts quicker because the bread is thoroughly hot by this time. Butter quickly and serve at once, or use it dry as you wish. This method is recommended especially if you are making toasted sandwiches or toast to serve with eggs, creamed food, etc. For *canapés,* toast on one side only.

To serve toast, either buttered or dry, cut it diagonally in half and arrange the slices overlapping in two rows on a hot plate. A folded napkin placed on the plate first will absorb the steam from the hot bread and keep the toast more crisp. If it has to stand for a few minutes—which shouldn't be—cover it with a folded napkin and place in a warm oven.

Bread Patty Cases are easy to make. Cut three rounds of sliced bread. Cut holes in the center of two of them and place on the first slice. Brush with a mixture of egg and milk and bake in a moderate oven (325–350° F.) until brown.

Toasted Hearts are easy to do. Lay a paper heart pattern on two-inch thick slices of firm, unsliced bread. Cut around paper pattern with sharp knife, making a bread heart. Hollow out each bread heart, leaving a side wall and bottom a scant 3/8 inch thick. Brush all surfaces with melted butter. Bake in a moderate oven (350° F.) until golden brown (about 12 minutes). Fill with any creamy food. Use extra scraps of bread for bread pudding, scalloped dishes or stuffing.

Bread Basket comes very handy to serve creamed food. Trim crusts from a whole loaf of uncut bread. Hollow out the center, brush with melted butter and bake in a moderate oven (350–375° F.) until a delicate brown.

A palace ordinance issued by Louis XVI of France dictated that the toast and the meat should be brought to the royal table in this manner: Two guards march in front, followed by the beadle, then the maître d'hotel, after him the head pantryman, then the head steward of the kitchen carrying the meat and behind him the assistant kitchen steward carrying the toast, followed by two guards.

TOAST RECIPES

(599) ALMOND JAM TOAST

(Appropriate for breakfast, luncheon, afternoon tea, snack, or light supper)

De-crust and toast as many slices of bread as required. Toast on both sides. Butter while very hot; spread with your favorite jam, marmalade or jelly on one side and sprinkle over the jam slivers of blanched, toasted almonds. Serve hot.

Variation—Substitute heated poppy seeds for almonds.

Centuries ago in many lands, particularly Persia, the mourning of the death of a great man was often emphasized by having his horses as well as his family and friends shed tears during the funeral procession. It was done by placing mustard seeds in the nostrils of the animals. After the funeral, the family and friends used to eat chunks of toasted bread dipped in perfumed wine.

(600) APPLESAUCE BACON TOAST

(Appropriate for Sunday breakfast, afternoon snacks or a light supper)

De-crust as many slices of bread as required. Toast on both sides. Spread first with a little butter, then with applesauce and crisscross top of each slice with 2 slices of crisp bacon. Serve hot.

(601) BACON CHEESE TOAST

(Appropriate for breakfast, light luncheon or supper)

Remove crusts from as many slices of bread as required. Place a thin piece of American cheese on each slice; then add one or two slices of bacon and place under the flame of the broiling oven until bacon is brown and cheese melted. Serve bubbling hot. Worcestershire or mixed mustard will add a suggestion of Welsh rabbit.

(602) BROILED BURGER TOAST

(Appropriate for breakfast, luncheon or supper)

Toast as many slices of bread as required (without trimming the crusts) on one side only. Spread untoasted side lightly with butter mixed in equal parts with prepared mustard and cover with ground raw beef. Season top with salt, pepper and a dash of cinnamon (optional) and broil under the flame of the broiling oven until meat is slightly browned and the juice oozes out. Serve at once.

(603) BUTTERSCOTCH TOAST

(Appropriate for breakfast, afternoon tea or coffee or evening snack)

Toast narrow strips of day-old bread on one side. Spread untoasted side with a mixture of equal parts of butter (or margarine) and dark brown sugar creamed together as for hard sauce. Toast under the flame of the broiling oven until hot and bubbly. Serve at once.

Variation—Add a little grated lemon or orange rind to butter and brown sugar mixture.

King Arthur is said to have invented the round table so no one of his knights could feel he was sitting "at the foot of the table."

(604) BUTTERSCOTCH TOAST PINWHEELS

(Appropriate for breakfast, afternoon tea or coffee or evening snack)

Remove the crusts from a fresh loaf of bread and cut in lengthwise slices. Spread with soft butter; sprinkle with dark brown sugar; roll up each long slice like a jelly roll; wrap each roll in waxed paper and keep in refrigerator overnight. Cut each roll in three parts and toast under the flame of the broiling oven until lightly browned. Serve immediately.

(605) CALAVO ROLLED FRIED TOAST

MAKES ABOUT 6 ROLLS

(Appropriate for breakfast, luncheon, light supper or after-theatre snack)

Trim off crusts of 6 slices of day-old bread cut very thin. On each slice lay lengthwise two thin short slices of calavo, or avocado, of medium size, peeled; sprinkle over the fruit, salt, pepper and nutmeg to taste and roll up like a jelly roll. Secure with toothpicks; dip each roll into a mixture of one well-beaten egg and 4 tablespoons of cold milk, seasoned to taste with salt and white pepper and brown the rolls on all sides in 4 generous tablespoons of butter or margarine. Drain on absorbent paper, remove toothpicks and serve piping hot with a jug of maple syrup or honey.

In ancient Rome when the art of eating was really an art, chef's salaries ran into "gastronomical" figures. Cooks made as much as the equivalent of forty thousand dollars a year! (Those were the days of Emperor Vitellius whose simple "meals" cost as much as fifteen thousand dollars.)

(606) CELERY CHEESE TOAST LUNCHEON

SERVES 6

(Appropriate for luncheon, light supper or midnight snack)

Into a saucepan put 2 cups of chopped celery, using green leaves and stalks; 1 small onion, chopped fine; a thin slice of garlic, mashed; 1 tablespoon of chopped chives; 1 medium green pepper, chopped fine, 4 strips of bacon, grilled then chopped; salt, pepper and nutmeg to taste and barely cover with fresh or canned beef bouillon, scalded. Cook until vegetables are tender and most of the liquid evaporated. Mix well 3/4 cup of grated American or Swiss cheese with 1 1/2 tablespoons flour and add gradually to vegetables, stirring constantly until cheese is melted and mixture thickened. Pour over 2 well-beaten fresh eggs, stir well for 3 or 4 minutes and serve on 6 slices of buttered toast. Sprinkle with a little minced parsley or chives.

(607) CHERRY TOAST

SERVES 6

(Appropriate for a light luncheon, afternoon tea, light supper or dessert)

Bring to the boiling point 2 cups of canned red pitted cherries with 1/3 cup of granulated sugar mixed with 2 1/2 tablespoons of flour, stirring almost constantly with a wooden spoon. Stir in 1/3 teaspoon of cinnamon (may be omitted). Dip 6 slices of bread in a mixture of 2 well-beaten fresh eggs, 1 tablespoon of granulated sugar and

1 cup of cold sweet milk, seasoned with a few grains of salt to taste, and brown the bread on both sides in about 1/3 cup of butter or margarine (amount of fat depending on how the bread absorbs the butter). Place toast on hot, individual plates and divide cherry mixture over the slices of toast. Serve immediately.

(608) COCONUT TOAST

(Appropriate for afternoon tea or coffee)

Toast on one side as many slices of bread as needed; then cut in strips. Spread the untoasted side with a mixture of equal parts of butter or margarine, confectioner's sugar and shredded coconut. Brown in a hot oven (400–425° F.) or under the flame of the broiling oven. Serve hot.

(609) CINNAMON BANANA TOAST

SERVES 6

(Appropriate for afternoon tea or coffee or as an afternoon snack)

De-crust 6 slices of bread; toast and spread quickly while very hot with butter. Have ready 1 large or 2 small bananas peeled and sliced. Overlap slices of banana on toast; sprinkle lightly with cinnamon sugar made by mixing 2 tablespoons each of cinnamon and brown sugar; place under the flame of the broiling oven and heat for a minute or two until tops are delicately brown. Serve immediately.

Edward VI of England had a court artist whose duty it was to make sketches each day of the dishes the royal chef prepared in the kitchen. The king then chose his evening meal from the drawings shown to him.

(610) CINNAMON FRENCH TOAST

(Appropriate for breakfast, especially Sunday, afternoon tea or coffee)

Mix 2 beaten strictly fresh eggs, 1/2 scant cup of granulated sugar, 2 cups of cold sweet milk, 1/2 scant teaspoon salt and 2 generous teaspoons of ground cinnamon. Dip slices of bread (any kind, even fruit bread) in this and then in flour. Fry in hot, deep fat until golden brown on both sides and serve hot with jelly, jam, marmalade, preserves, honey or maple syrup.

(611) CINNAMON TOAST

(Appropriate for breakfast, especially Sunday, afternoon tea or coffee)

Cinnamon toast is perfect for tea, but alas, it is seldom we find it really good.

Toast bread slices on one side only. Have ready a mixture of 1 cup soft brown sugar and 2 (or more) tablespoons ground cinnamon. Butter bread slices on the untoasted side, spread with a thick layer of sugar-cinnamon mixture and place under broiler a good 5 inches below the flame. Let it toast very, very slowly until the sugar is melted and bubbling and the bread delicately browned and crisp, but not burned on the edges. Remove from the oven at once, cut in strips and serve as quickly as you can run with it to the table. *Further Suggestions:* Remove crusts, since they may burn; increase cinnamon to taste (some like up to 4 tablespoons); put small bits of butter on top of cinnamon-sugar mixture.

(612) CINNAMON HONEY TOAST

(Appropriate for breakfast, especially on Sunday or with afternoon tea)

Toast slices of bread on one side; butter the untoasted side with honey and sprinkle with cinnamon to taste. Place slices under the flame of the broiling oven and heat slowly until bread is nicely brown. Serve at once.

The "Kitchen Guard" of Louis XIV of France consisted of eight soldiers. Four of them served the royal table and the other four with drawn swords provided an escort between kitchen and dining room.

(613) CINNAMON MAPLE TOAST— VERMONT METHOD

(Appropriate for breakfast, especially on Sunday, afternoon tea, coffee or cocoa)

Cream together equal parts of butter and shaved maple sugar with ½ generous teaspoon cinnamon (more, according to taste) for each slice. Toast one side of bread; spread mixture on the untoasted side. Place five inches below the flame and toast slowly until delicately browned and bubbling. Serve at once.

(614) CINNAMON PINEAPPLE TOAST

(Appropriate for breakfast, light luncheon or with afternoon tea, coffee or cocoa)

Toast on both sides as many bread slices as are needed. Spread with softened butter, then with 1 generous tablespoon drained, crushed pineapple for each slice and sprinkle with 2 teaspoons mixed brown sugar and cinnamon (for each slice); place 5 inches below the flame of the broiling oven and heat until mixture bubbles. Serve at once cut in 2 or 3 strips. A little grated lemon rind enhances the flavor of the pineapple.

(615) CORN SYRUP TOAST—SOUTHERN METHOD

SERVES 6

(Appropriate for breakfast or with afternoon tea, coffee or cocoa)

Beat 2 large or 3 small fresh eggs slightly; add 1 tablespoon of white corn syrup, a few grains of salt and 2 cups of cold sweet milk and beat again until smooth. Dip bread slices (12 for 6 servings) into milk mixture and fry in butter in frying pan, turning slices once or twice. Serve immediately.

Leave something on your plate for the cat and your stomach will benefit.—French Proverb

(616) DEVILED HAM FRENCH TOAST

SERVES 6

(Appropriate for Sunday breakfast, afternoon tea or light supper)

Toast lightly 12 slices of white bread; spread butter on one side; then spread thinly with deviled ham (one can will serve 6). To 2 lightly beaten strictly fresh eggs add 2 teaspoons ground cinnamon, 1/4 teaspoon salt and 2 cups of cold sweet milk; beat again until smooth. Put two slices together as a sandwich, dip both sides in milk-egg mixture and sauté in butter until nicely browned on both sides. Serve at once.

(617) ENGLISH MUFFIN TOASTED BRUNCH

(Appropriate for a light luncheon, afternoon snack or light supper)

Tear apart—don't cut—as many English muffins as needed. Spread with soft butter creamed with a little onion juice to taste and a pinch of nutmeg. Cover with a little maple sugar, then with a slice of sharp American or Swiss cheese. Toast under the flame of the broiling oven until cheese melts and bubbles. Serve at once.

(618) ENGLISH TOAST

SERVES 2

(Appropriate for a light luncheon, afternoon snack, or light supper)

Lightly toast 2 slices of bread on both sides. Butter on one side and then spread with a mixture of 3 tablespoons of cream cheese and 1 tablespoon orange marmalade. Put under the flame of the broiling oven, 6 inches below the flame and toast slightly. Serve immediately.

(619) FRENCH GRIDDLE TOAST

SERVES 6

(Appropriate for breakfast, light luncheon or supper)

Beat 3 strictly fresh eggs slightly; add 2 tablespoons of granulated sugar and 1/3 teaspoon salt. Strain into a shallow dish. Cut 6 half-inch slices of one loaf day-old bread; remove crusts. Dip slices of bread in the egg-milk mixture, turning them until liquid is well absorbed. Brown both sides on a hot, well-greased griddle or frying pan. Remove to hot plate and sprinkle lightly with fine powdered sugar. Serve with jelly, jam, marmalade, preserves, honey or maple syrup.

In 1880 Czar Alexander II of Russia was nearly killed by a bomb in his great winter palace in St. Petersburg (Leningrad today). The guards searched the thousand-odd rooms, but did not find the anarchist. However, they did discover, in an unused boudoir on an upper flour, a peasant and his cow and several loaves of bread. Both of them had lived there a number of years.

(620) FRENCH TOAST

SERVES 6

From the standpoint of genuine goodness as well as for economy, French toast stands as one of America's favorite breakfast and luncheon dishes. For breakfast it may be served plain to accompany bacon and eggs or fried liver and bacon, and often it is used as the main part of the meal with jam, marmalade, honey, maple syrup, etc.

The preparation is very simple and it is an excellent way to utilize stale bread. In France French toast is called *pain perdu* ("lost bread") and is very popular as a dessert.

Allow one slice of bread for each serving. For six servings beat 3 fresh eggs slightly and add 1 cup of rich sweet milk, or half milk and half thin cream (undiluted evaporated milk may be used); season with ½ teaspoon salt, a fresh grating of nutmeg (this is a "must") and a dash of white pepper, and 1 teaspoon of granulated sugar. Dip each slice of bread (toasted or not) into mixture, being careful not to get the bread sodden as it will break, and brown on both sides in plenty of hot butter. Serve, well-drained on a folded napkin. Sprinkle freely with confectioner's sugar, if served for dessert or breakfast.

For a luncheon or supper dish, unsweetened French toast will be just the thing. Use any left-over piece of fish, carefully boned, chicken, meat, ham or cheese minced. Spread one slice of the bread with any one of these, cover with another slice; dip in egg-milk mixture (unsweetened) and brown as for French toast, *i.e.* on both sides until delicately browned. Seasonings, will of course, depend upon the filling of these sandwiches. Serve as hot as possible.

(621) FRENCH TOASTED LOAF

SERVES 6

Cut a loaf of French bread in diagonal slices, but not all the way through. Spread every slice with butter creamed with a little mustard, prepared horseradish, anchovy paste, mashed sardines, or any left-over meat, fish, poultry, or cheese, finely ground. Tie together and heat loaf thoroughly in a hot oven (400° F.). Serve hot. Delicious as an accompaniment of green salad.

(622) GINGER TOAST

(Appropriate for breakfast, luncheon, afternoon tea, coffee or cocoa)

De-crust as many slices of bread as required and toast on both sides. Cut each slice into 3 or 4 strips; butter lightly and spread with a mixture of finely chopped preserved ginger, a few drops of lemon juice to taste, a little powdered sugar and water—all cooked to the consistency of marmalade. Serve very hot.

Between each dinner course in seventeenth-century England, serv-

ants made the rounds of male guests with clay pipes, tobacco, fire tongs and a dish of burning coals so that a brief smoke might be had. This was supposed to aid digestion.

(623)

JELLY CUP TOAST

SERVES 6—TWO APIECE

(Appropriate for breakfast, luncheon or light supper)

Cut the crusts neatly from thin slices of white fresh bread; butter both sides with butter creamed with equal parts of finely ground almonds, previously blanched and toasted. Fit each slice in a buttered muffin pan, so that a little cup is formed. Bake in a very hot oven (425–450° F.) 5 or 6 minutes or until browned to a crisp. Remove from oven and fill each cup with your favorite jelly, jam, marmalade or preserves. Serve hot.

(624)

JOCKO TOAST

SERVES 4

(Appropriate for luncheon, supper, green salad and after-theatre snack)

Remove crust from a long French loaf. Cut into 8-inch, narrow strips, one or two inches wide; rub liberally with garlic; then toast in a hot oven (400° F.). Quickly brush with plenty of butter and serve as hot and garlicky as possible. That's all, but please do try this toast! A revelation, especially as an accompaniment for roasted dark meat. This Jocko toast, when cold and cut into small cubes (butter omitted), adds "oomph" to any kind of green or vegetable salad.

(625)

KIPPERED TOAST

SERVES 6

(Appropriate for breakfast, light luncheon or supper or snack)

Flake enough canned kippered herring to obtain 1½ cups, and place in a shallow saucepan with ⅔ cup tomato juice, 1 generous teaspoon onion juice, and a dash of pepper, nutmeg and cayenne. Let simmer over a low flame for 5 or 6 minutes. Meantime, trim the crusts from 6 slices of white bread, cut diagonally; toast on both sides to a golden brown; butter generously and lay on a hot platter.

Beat 6 eggs slightly with a fork, add 1/4 generous cup of scalded heavy cream seasoned with a few grains of salt and white pepper. Stir into the hot kipper mixture. Cook until thick and creamy, stirring almost constantly and scraping from the bottom of the pan. Remove from the fire and pour over toast. Sprinkle with finely chopped parsley or chives and garnish platter with lemon slices and crisp, green young watercress.

(626) MELBA TOAST

This paper-thin toast may be served as a side dish with almost any kind of soup and salad; or spread with butter, cream cheese, jam, jelly, ground cooked fish (carefully boned), meat, poultry or game. It may be served hot or cold. To make it, you need a stale loaf of bread—the staler the better.

Slice bread, white preferably, as thinly as possible and remove the crusts. Cut either in two or four pieces; arrange on a dry baking sheet and bake in a very slow oven (250° F.) until pieces are evenly browned and crisp on both sides. This toast may be made in large quantity and stored in a dry, cool place in an airtight container.

Lunches were carried to meetings in handkerchiefs or small leather bags by members of our first Continental Congress.

(627) MILK TOAST

SERVES 1

(Old-fashioned Method)

Trim the crusts from 2 or 3 slices of bread and toast very dry. Spread with butter while hot. Bring 1 1/2 to 2 cups of rich milk (or half-milk and half-cream) to a boil. Cream 2 tablespoons of butter with 1 tablespoon of flour and drop by small pieces into the simmering milk. Season to taste, and dip each slice of toast into the milk mixture. Quickly lay the toast in a soup plate, and pour the boiling, seasoned milk over it. With old-fashioned milk toast, made as above, it is the rule to serve a small jug of boiling thin cream (or undiluted evaporated milk). Very nourishing.

(628) ORANGE TOAST—FLORIDA METHOD

SERVES 2

(Appropriate for breakfast, light luncheon, supper or midnight snack)

Spread 2 slices of freshly toasted bread with creamed butter and cut into narrow strips. Divide the strips between two soup plates. Keep hot. Remove pulp and juice from 4 Florida oranges, add 1 tablespoon grated orange rind (or still better, shredded orange rind), free from white membrane, and ¼ generous cup of granulated or brown sugar. Bring to the boiling point and pour over the toast strips in soup plate. Serve dusted with a little nutmeg.

(629) ORANGE TOAST—HOME MANNER

SERVES 3

(Appropriate for breakfast, light luncheon, supper or snack)

Combine ¼ cup of unstrained orange juice, 2 scant teaspoons of grated orange rind and ¼ cup of granulated sugar; blend thoroughly. Spread on buttered toast and broil 5 or 6 inches below the flame until browned. Remove quickly and sprinkle over each slice 1 teaspoon of blanched, toasted, ground almonds. Serve as hot as possible.

Two hundred pounds of almonds are used to make one quart of almond milk, an esteemed delicacy of the Arabs in Morocco.

(630) ORANGE TOAST—CALIFORNIA METHOD

(Appropriate for breakfast or afternoon tea, coffee or cocoa)

Remove crust from as many slices of white bread as desired and toast; butter, while hot, on one side only; spread with orange marmalade and serve immediately.

While California produces an abundance of oranges today, it is said that in 1875 they were so scarce that they sold for eighty-five cents apiece.

(631) PARSLEY BUTTER TOAST

(Very appropriate to serve with almost any hot dish)

Parsley was one of the few seasonings grown in England before the Norman Conquest, the others being garlic, onions, leeks, sage, and thyme. The Greeks made wreaths and decorative garlands of it, dedicating it to the gods. During the time of Pliny there was not a sauce or a salad served without parsley. Its smell was supposed to absorb the intoxicating fumes of wine and thus prevent the usual effects of overindulgence.

Horace includes parsley in one of his odes:

I have a cask of Alban wine,
Phyllis, that counts its years at nine,
And parsley in my garden grounds
For garlands, ivy too abounds
To deck thy shining tresses. . . .

Parsley was well liked in Cornwall in England, where it was used mostly in parsley pies for which, unfortunately, we have no recipe. A bowl of minced parsley on the table, to sprinkle as desired on salads, vegetables, meats or fish, is a good idea. One ounce of parsley will supply an adult's vitamin C needs for a day. You can't eat parsley by the fistful, but why not include larger quantities of this inexpensive green in almost all your bread dough?

Slice French loaf crosswise. Spread each slice with parsley butter made by creaming to a soft paste equal parts of butter and finely chopped parsley and adding while creaming 1 teaspoon of unstrained lemon juice for each 1/4 cup of mixture. Place pieces of bread (each slice about 4 inches in length and the width of the loaf) on a baking sheet and toast in a very slow oven (250–275° F.) until butter mixture is absorbed and the bread nicely toasted. Serve hot on a folded napkin or paper doily.

(632) PEANUT BUTTER TOAST

(Appropriate for breakfast, luncheon or supper as well as afternoon snack)

Toast as many slices of bread as required and spread with a mixture of equal parts of butter and peanut butter creamed together. Serve hot.

(633) PORTUGUESE TOAST

SERVES 6

(Appropriate for breakfast, light luncheon, dinner or supper and afternoon snack)

Beat 3 strictly fresh eggs lightly; add 1 1/2 cups sifted bread flour with 1/2 generous teaspoon salt and 1 teaspoon baking powder. Mix thoroughly until smooth. Add enough tomato juice (about 1 scant cup) to make a batter thick enough to spread. Dip 6 slices of bread in the batter and sauté in a frying pan containing enough smoking olive oil, butter or lard so that the slices of bread float in it; brown on both sides. Arrange on a hot platter, sprinkle with mixed sugar and cinnamon in almost equal parts and serve very hot. Nourishing and intriguing.

(634) RUSKY TOAST

(Appropriate to serve with soups and salads)

Trim off crusts of stale bread slices; cut in triangles and spread on a baking sheet or oven rack; allow to dry, like Melba toast (No. 626) slowly in a low oven (250–275° F.) for about 25 minutes, turning frequently. When brittle-dry and gold-tinged, store them in an airtight container. This may be called "Thrifty with Style."

In medieval Europe tablecloths were known as "carpets" and carpets were often used as tablecloths.

(635) RUSSIAN RYE BISCUIT MILK TOAST

SERVES 6

(A meal in itself)

In bread-making qualities, rye approaches wheat more nearly than does any other grain, and is in fact the only grain that can be used alone successfully in yeast breads. The proteins of rye are similar to, though not identical with, those of wheat, and in food value the two grains are about the same. But rye flour makes a more sticky and less elastic dough than wheat flour. Rye flour is marketed in four general grades: dark; light; medium; and straight. The dark flour includes some of the outer part of the grain; the light flour, the inner part of endosperm; and the medium grade is usually a blend of the dark and the light. The straight grade is all the flour produced in the milling of rye, and normally consists of about 30 per cent dark flour and 70 per cent light flour. Ordinarily the medium and straight-grade flours can be used interchangeably.

Sift 1 cup rye meal and 2 cups of bread flour with 4 teaspoons baking powder and ½ generous teaspoon salt, add 2 tablespoons of butter and mix until smooth; then add sufficient milk to make a dough as for baking powder biscuits. Turn out on lightly floured board and roll to ½ inch in thickness; cut with floured biscuit cutter and bake in a hot oven (450° F.) for about 10 minutes or until biscuits are golden brown.

Meanwhile scald 2 quarts of rich sweet milk in double boiler; add 2 tablespoons butter and 2 tablespoons flour moistened in ½ cup cold milk, and add gradually to milk, stirring constantly until milk thickens. Season to taste with salt and a generous pinch of saffron. Keep hot.

Split rye biscuits in two, crosswise, and toast cut sides to a golden brown. Arrange 3 or 4 halves of biscuits in soup plates and pour the milk mixture over them. Serve at once.

Macaroni with grated cheese was a popular dish in England in Chaucer's day. However it was eaten as a dessert or savoury.

(636) SOUTH CAROLINA MOLASSES TOAST

SERVES 6

Split open 6 cold baking powder biscuits and place in a shallow baking pan, cut side up. Pour over enough dark molasses to barely cover; place pan in a moderate oven and let stay until biscuits are crisp and yet slightly softened with the molasses. Serve hot.

(637) TARTARE TOAST

SERVES 6

(Appropriate for luncheon, dinner, supper or for picnicking or camping)

Toast lightly on one side 6 slices of bread ¾ inch thick. Scoop out the crumbs from the untoasted side, without piercing the toasted side. Break a fresh egg into the cavity of each slice; add enough raw, chopped beef (Hamburger) to cover the egg and the entire surface of the slices to a thickness of ⅜ of an inch. Season to taste with salt, pepper and nutmeg; sprinkle with melted butter and brown under 6 to 7 inches below flame of broiling oven. When a light crust forms on the tops, serve immediately.

The meat should be very rare. It may be mixed with a little dry mustard or Worcestershire sauce. Serve on a platter garnished with 6 lettuce cups filled with a generous teaspoon each of finely chopped onion and hard-cooked egg white dusted with paprika. Pass the tomato catsup along!

(638) TOASTED CHEESE ROLLS—TRAPPER'S MANNER

SERVES 6

(Appropriate for breakfast, light luncheon or light supper or snack)

Hollow out 6 French round rolls. Brush with bacon drippings and place on a baking sheet. Toast in a slow oven (275–300° F.) until golden brown and crisp. Keep hot. Meanwhile, cook 2 cups of grated American or Swiss cheese, ½ cup undiluted evaporated milk, a few grains of cayenne and nutmeg over boiling water until smooth, stirring it almost constantly. Fold in 1 cup of shredded dried beef, 1 tablespoon prepared horseradish and ½ teaspoon dry mustard. Blend thoroughly; fill the hollows of the six rolls, heat well and serve at once.

(639) WAFFLED RAISIN BREAD CINNAMON TOAST

(Appropriate for breakfast, luncheon, supper or snacks. Should be served very hot)

Trim the crusts from slices of raisin bread and brush both sides with butter. Place slice or slices in center of hot waffle iron and close. When nicely browned, spread with cinnamon to taste and serve immediately.

(640) WATER TOAST

(Very appropriate the morning-after-the-night-before)

Dip slices of very dry, crisp toast quickly in boiling salted water, allowing 1 teaspoon salt to 1 pint water. Spread slices with butter and serve at once. For this kind of toast, you'll need to work very rapidly lest the toast fall to pieces when removed from the water bath!

(641) WELSH TOAST

(Appropriate for breakfast or supper)

Butter the cut end of a loaf of bread; then slice very, very thin, Melba style, repeating until you have all the slices required. Place the thin buttered slices in a slow oven (250–275° F.) and toast slowly until crisp and light brown. Remove from the oven and quickly butter again. Serve very hot.

The average ancient Roman meal was divided thusly: (1) The appetizer (asparagus, oysters and eggs). (2) Water and napkins (for guests to clean their hands). (3) Course A (meat, fish and fowl; vegetables). (4) Intermission. (5) Course B (salted meal and wine). (6) Course C (sweet cakes and apples). Then they would say: "Ab ovo usque ad mala," or a meal complete "from eggs to apples"—instead of "from soup to nuts."

INDEX

INDEX

THIS INDEX IS ALPHABETIZED WITHIN EACH SECTION

BISCUIT RECIPES

BREAD RECIPES

BUN RECIPES

MUFFIN, GEM AND JOHNNY CAKE RECIPES

POPOVER RECIPES

ROLL RECIPES

SCONE RECIPES

MISCELLANEOUS BREAD RECIPES

SOY FLOUR BREADS AND BISCUITS

VISUAL ILLUSIONS: THEIR CAUSES, CHARACTERISTICS, AND APPLICATIONS, Matthew Luckiesh. Thorough description and discussion of optical illusion, geometric and perspective, particularly; size and shape distortions, illusions of color, of motion; natural illusions; use of illusion in art and magic, industry, etc. Most useful today with op art, also for classical art. Scores of effects illustrated. Introduction by William H. Ittleson. 100 illustrations. xxi + 252pp.
21530-X Paperbound $2.00

A HANDBOOK OF ANATOMY FOR ART STUDENTS, Arthur Thomson. Thorough, virtually exhaustive coverage of skeletal structure, musculature, etc. Full text, supplemented by anatomical diagrams and drawings and by photographs of undraped figures. Unique in its comparison of male and female forms, pointing out differences of contour, texture, form. 211 figures, 40 drawings, 86 photographs. xx + 459pp. 5⅜ x 8⅜. 21163-0 Paperbound $3.50

150 MASTERPIECES OF DRAWING, Selected by Anthony Toney. Full page reproductions of drawings from the early 16th to the end of the 18th century, all beautifully reproduced: Rembrandt, Michelangelo, Dürer, Fragonard, Urs, Graf, Wouwerman, many others. First-rate browsing book, model book for artists. xviii + 150pp. 8⅜ x 11¼. 21032-4 Paperbound $3.50

THE LATER WORK OF AUBREY BEARDSLEY, Aubrey Beardsley. Exotic, erotic, ironic masterpieces in full maturity: Comedy Ballet, Venus and Tannhauser, Pierrot, Lysistrata, Rape of the Lock, Savoy material, Ali Baba, Volpone, etc. This material revolutionized the art world, and is still powerful, fresh, brilliant. With *The Early Work,* all Beardsley's finest work. 174 plates, 2 in color. xiv + 176pp. 8⅛ x 11.
21817-1 Paperbound $3.75

DRAWINGS OF REMBRANDT, Rembrandt van Rijn. Complete reproduction of fabulously rare edition by Lippmann and Hofstede de Groot, completely reedited, updated, improved by Prof. Seymour Slive, Fogg Museum. Portraits, Biblical sketches, landscapes, Oriental types, nudes, episodes from classical mythology—All Rembrandt's fertile genius. Also selection of drawings by his pupils and followers. "Stunning volumes," *Saturday Review.* 550 illustrations. lxxviii + 552pp. 9⅛ x 12¼. 21485-0, 21486-9 Two volumes, Paperbound $10.00

THE DISASTERS OF WAR, Francisco Goya. One of the masterpieces of Western civilization—83 etchings that record Goya's shattering, bitter reaction to the Napoleonic war that swept through Spain after the insurrection of 1808 and to war in general. Reprint of the first edition, with three additional plates from Boston's Museum of Fine Arts. All plates facsimile size. Introduction by Philip Hofer, Fogg Museum. v + 97pp. 9⅜ x 8¼. 21872-4 Paperbound $2.50

GRAPHIC WORKS OF ODILON REDON. Largest collection of Redon's graphic works ever assembled: 172 lithographs, 28 etchings and engravings, 9 drawings. These include some of his most famous works. All the plates from *Odilon Redon: oeuvre graphique complet,* plus additional plates. New introduction and caption translations by Alfred Werner. 209 illustrations. xxvii + 209pp. 9⅛ x 12¼.
21966-8 Paperbound $5.00

DESIGN BY ACCIDENT; A BOOK OF "ACCIDENTAL EFFECTS" FOR ARTISTS AND DESIGNERS, James F. O'Brien. Create your own unique, striking, imaginative effects by "controlled accident" interaction of materials: paints and lacquers, oil and water based paints, splatter, crackling materials, shatter, similar items. Everything you do will be different; first book on this limitless art, so useful to both fine artist and commercial artist. Full instructions. 192 plates showing "accidents," 8 in color. viii + 215pp. 8⅜ x 11¼. 21942-9 Paperbound $3.75

THE BOOK OF SIGNS, Rudolf Koch. Famed German type designer draws 493 beautiful symbols: religious, mystical, alchemical, imperial, property marks, runes, etc. Remarkable fusion of traditional and modern. Good for suggestions of timelessness, smartness, modernity. Text. vi + 104pp. 6⅛ x 9¼.
20162-7 Paperbound $1.25

HISTORY OF INDIAN AND INDONESIAN ART, Ananda K. Coomaraswamy. An unabridged republication of one of the finest books by a great scholar in Eastern art. Rich in descriptive material, history, social backgrounds; Sunga reliefs, Rajput paintings, Gupta temples, Burmese frescoes, textiles, jewelry, sculpture, etc. 400 photos. viii + 423pp. 6⅜ x 9¾. 21436-2 Paperbound $5.00

PRIMITIVE ART, Franz Boas. America's foremost anthropologist surveys textiles, ceramics, woodcarving, basketry, metalwork, etc.; patterns, technology, creation of symbols, style origins. All areas of world, but very full on Northwest Coast Indians. More than 350 illustrations of baskets, boxes, totem poles, weapons, etc. 378 pp.
20025-6 Paperbound $3.00

THE GENTLEMAN AND CABINET MAKER'S DIRECTOR, Thomas Chippendale. Full reprint (third edition, 1762) of most influential furniture book of all time, by master cabinetmaker. 200 plates, illustrating chairs, sofas, mirrors, tables, cabinets, plus 24 photographs of surviving pieces. Biographical introduction by N. Bienenstock. vi + 249pp. 9⅞ x 12¾. 21601-2 Paperbound $4.00

AMERICAN ANTIQUE FURNITURE, Edgar G. Miller, Jr. The basic coverage of all American furniture before 1840. Individual chapters cover type of furniture—clocks, tables, sideboards, etc.—chronologically, with inexhaustible wealth of data. More than 2100 photographs, all identified, commented on. Essential to all early American collectors. Introduction by H. E. Keyes. vi + 1106pp. 7⅞ x 10¾.
21599-7, 21600-4 Two volumes, Paperbound $11.00

PENNSYLVANIA DUTCH AMERICAN FOLK ART, Henry J. Kauffman. 279 photos, 28 drawings of tulipware, Fraktur script, painted tinware, toys, flowered furniture, quilts, samplers, hex signs, house interiors, etc. Full descriptive text. Excellent for tourist, rewarding for designer, collector. Map. 146pp. 7⅞ x 10¾.
21205-X Paperbound $2.50

EARLY NEW ENGLAND GRAVESTONE RUBBINGS, Edmund V. Gillon, Jr. 43 photographs, 226 carefully reproduced rubbings show heavily symbolic, sometimes macabre early gravestones, up to early 19th century. Remarkable early American primitive art, occasionally strikingly beautiful; always powerful. Text. xxvi + 207pp. 8⅜ x 11¼. 21380-3 Paperbound $3.50

A HISTORY OF COSTUME, Carl Köhler. Definitive history, based on surviving pieces of clothing primarily, and paintings, statues, etc. secondarily. Highly readable text, supplemented by 594 illustrations of costumes of the ancient Mediterranean peoples, Greece and Rome, the Teutonic prehistoric period; costumes of the Middle Ages, Renaissance, Baroque, 18th and 19th centuries. Clear, measured patterns are provided for many clothing articles. Approach is practical throughout. Enlarged by Emma von Sichart. 464pp. 21030-8 Paperbound $3.50

ORIENTAL RUGS, ANTIQUE AND MODERN, Walter A. Hawley. A complete and authoritative treatise on the Oriental rug—where they are made, by whom and how, designs and symbols, characteristics in detail of the six major groups, how to distinguish them and how to buy them. Detailed technical data is provided on periods, weaves, warps, wefts, textures, sides, ends and knots, although no technical background is required for an understanding. 11 color plates, 80 halftones, 4 maps. vi + 320pp. 6⅛ x 9⅛. 22366-3 Paperbound $5.00

TEN BOOKS ON ARCHITECTURE, Vitruvius. By any standards the most important book on architecture ever written. Early Roman discussion of aesthetics of building, construction methods, orders, sites, and every other aspect of architecture has inspired, instructed architecture for about 2,000 years. Stands behind Palladio, Michelangelo, Bramante, Wren, countless others. Definitive Morris H. Morgan translation. 68 illustrations. xii + 331pp. 20645-9 Paperbound $3.00

THE FOUR BOOKS OF ARCHITECTURE, Andrea Palladio. Translated into every major Western European language in the two centuries following its publication in 1570, this has been one of the most influential books in the history of architecture. Complete reprint of the 1738 Isaac Ware edition. New introduction by Adolf Placzek, Columbia Univ. 216 plates. xxii + 110pp. of text. 9½ x 12¾. 21308-0 Clothbound $12.50

STICKS AND STONES: A STUDY OF AMERICAN ARCHITECTURE AND CIVILIZATION, Lewis Mumford.One of the great classics of American cultural history. American architecture from the medieval-inspired earliest forms to the early 20th century; evolution of structure and style, and reciprocal influences on environment. 21 photographic illustrations. 238pp. 20202-X Paperbound $2.00

THE AMERICAN BUILDER'S COMPANION, Asher Benjamin. The most widely used early 19th century architectural style and source book, for colonial up into Greek Revival periods. Extensive development of geometry of carpentering, construction of sashes, frames, doors, stairs; plans and elevations of domestic and other buildings. Hundreds of thousands of houses were built according to this book, now invaluable to historians, architects, restorers, etc. 1827 edition. 59 plates. 114pp. 7⅞ x 10¾. 22236-5 Paperbound $3.50

DUTCH HOUSES IN THE HUDSON VALLEY BEFORE 1776, Helen Wilkinson Reynolds. The standard survey of the Dutch colonial house and outbuildings, with constructional features, decoration, and local history associated with individual homesteads. Introduction by Franklin D. Roosevelt. Map. 150 illustrations. 469pp. 6⅝ x 9¼. 21469-9 Paperbound $5.00

THE ARCHITECTURE OF COUNTRY HOUSES, Andrew J. Downing. Together with Vaux's *Villas and Cottages* this is the basic book for Hudson River Gothic architecture of the middle Victorian period. Full, sound discussions of general aspects of housing, architecture, style, decoration, furnishing, together with scores of detailed house plans, illustrations of specific buildings, accompanied by full text. Perhaps the most influential single American architectural book. 1850 edition. Introduction by J. Stewart Johnson. 321 figures, 34 architectural designs. xvi + 560pp.
22003-6 Paperbound $4.00

LOST EXAMPLES OF COLONIAL ARCHITECTURE, John Mead Howells. Full-page photographs of buildings that have disappeared or been so altered as to be denatured, including many designed by major early American architects. 245 plates. xvii + 248pp. 7⅞ x 10¾. 21143-6 Paperbound $3.50

DOMESTIC ARCHITECTURE OF THE AMERICAN COLONIES AND OF THE EARLY REPUBLIC, Fiske Kimball. Foremost architect and restorer of Williamsburg and Monticello covers nearly 200 homes between 1620-1825. Architectural details, construction, style features, special fixtures, floor plans, etc. Generally considered finest work in its area. 219 illustrations of houses, doorways, windows, capital mantels. xx + 314pp. 7⅞ x 10¾. 21743-4 Paperbound $4.00

EARLY AMERICAN ROOMS: 1650-1858, edited by Russell Hawes Kettell. Tour of 12 rooms, each representative of a different era in American history and each furnished, decorated, designed and occupied in the style of the era. 72 plans and elevations, 8-page color section, etc., show fabrics, wall papers, arrangements, etc. Full descriptive text. xvii + 200pp. of text. 8⅜ x 11¼.
21633-0 Paperbound $5.00

THE FITZWILLIAM VIRGINAL BOOK, edited by J. Fuller Maitland and W. B. Squire. Full modern printing of famous early 17th-century ms. volume of 300 works by Morley, Byrd, Bull, Gibbons, etc. For piano or other modern keyboard instrument; easy to read format. xxxvi + 938pp. 8⅜ x 11.
21068-5, 21069-3 Two volumes, Paperbound $10.00

KEYBOARD MUSIC, Johann Sebastian Bach. Bach Gesellschaft edition. A rich selection of Bach's masterpieces for the harpsichord: the six English Suites, six French Suites, the six Partitas (Clavierübung part I), the Goldberg Variations (Clavierübung part IV), the fifteen Two-Part Inventions and the fifteen Three-Part Sinfonias. Clearly reproduced on large sheets with ample margins; eminently playable. vi + 312pp. 8⅛ x 11. 22360-4 Paperbound $5.00

THE MUSIC OF BACH: AN INTRODUCTION, Charles Sanford Terry. A fine, nontechnical introduction to Bach's music, both instrumental and vocal. Covers organ music, chamber music, passion music, other types. Analyzes themes, developments, innovations. x + 114pp. 21075-8 Paperbound $1.50

BEETHOVEN AND HIS NINE SYMPHONIES, Sir George Grove. Noted British musicologist provides best history, analysis, commentary on symphonies. Very thorough, rigorously accurate; necessary to both advanced student and amateur music lover. 436 musical passages. vii + 407 pp. 20334-4 Paperbound $2.75

JOHANN SEBASTIAN BACH, Philipp Spitta. One of the great classics of musicology, this definitive analysis of Bach's music (and life) has never been surpassed. Lucid, nontechnical analyses of hundreds of pieces (30 pages devoted to St. Matthew Passion, 26 to B Minor Mass). Also includes major analysis of 18th-century music. 450 musical examples. 40-page musical supplement. Total of xx + 1799pp.
(EUK) 22278-0, 22279-9 Two volumes, Clothbound $17.50

MOZART AND HIS PIANO CONCERTOS, Cuthbert Girdlestone. The only full-length study of an important area of Mozart's creativity. Provides detailed analyses of all 23 concertos, traces inspirational sources. 417 musical examples. Second edition. 509pp. 21271-8 Paperbound $3.50

THE PERFECT WAGNERITE: A COMMENTARY ON THE NIBLUNG'S RING, George Bernard Shaw. Brilliant and still relevant criticism in remarkable essays on Wagner's Ring cycle, Shaw's ideas on political and social ideology behind the plots, role of Leitmotifs, vocal requisites, etc. Prefaces. xxi + 136pp.
(USO) 21707-8 Paperbound $1.75

DON GIOVANNI, W. A. Mozart. Complete libretto, modern English translation; biographies of composer and librettist; accounts of early performances and critical reaction. Lavishly illustrated. All the material you need to understand and appreciate this great work. Dover Opera Guide and Libretto Series; translated and introduced by Ellen Bleiler. 92 illustrations. 209pp.
21134-7 Paperbound $2.00

BASIC ELECTRICITY, U. S. Bureau of Naval Personel. Originally a training course, best non-technical coverage of basic theory of electricity and its applications. Fundamental concepts, batteries, circuits, conductors and wiring techniques, AC and DC, inductance and capacitance, generators, motors, transformers, magnetic amplifiers, synchros, servomechanisms, etc. Also covers blue-prints, electrical diagrams, etc. Many questions, with answers. 349 illustrations. x + 448pp. 6½ x 9¼.
20973-3 Paperbound $3.50

REPRODUCTION OF SOUND, Edgar Villchur. Thorough coverage for laymen of high fidelity systems, reproducing systems in general, needles, amplifiers, preamps, loudspeakers, feedback, explaining physical background. "A rare talent for making technicalities vividly comprehensible," R. Darrell, *High Fidelity*. 69 figures. iv + 92pp. 21515-6 Paperbound $1.35

HEAR ME TALKIN' TO YA: THE STORY OF JAZZ AS TOLD BY THE MEN WHO MADE IT, Nat Shapiro and Nat Hentoff. Louis Armstrong, Fats Waller, Jo Jones, Clarence Williams, Billy Holiday, Duke Ellington, Jelly Roll Morton and dozens of other jazz greats tell how it was in Chicago's South Side, New Orleans, depression Harlem and the modern West Coast as jazz was born and grew. xvi + 429pp.
21726-4 Paperbound $3.00

FABLES OF AESOP, translated by Sir Roger L'Estrange. A reproduction of the very rare 1931 Paris edition; a selection of the most interesting fables, together with 50 imaginative drawings by Alexander Calder. v + 128pp. 6½x9¼.
21780-9 Paperbound $1.50

AGAINST THE GRAIN (A REBOURS), Joris K. Huysmans. Filled with weird images, evidences of a bizarre imagination, exotic experiments with hallucinatory drugs, rich tastes and smells and the diversions of its sybarite hero Duc Jean des Esseintes, this classic novel pushed 19th-century literary decadence to its limits. Full unabridged edition. Do not confuse this with abridged editions generally sold. Introduction by Havelock Ellis. xlix + 206pp. 22190-3 Paperbound $2.50

VARIORUM SHAKESPEARE: HAMLET. Edited by Horace H. Furness; a landmark of American scholarship. Exhaustive footnotes and appendices treat all doubtful words and phrases, as well as suggested critical emendations throughout the play's history. First volume contains editor's own text, collated with all Quartos and Folios. Second volume contains full first Quarto, translations of Shakespeare's sources (Belleforest, and Saxo Grammaticus), Der Bestrafte Brudermord, and many essays on critical and historical points of interest by major authorities of past and present. Includes details of staging and costuming over the years. By far the best edition available for serious students of Shakespeare. Total of xx + 905pp.
21004-9, 21005-7, 2 volumes, Paperbound $7.00

A LIFE OF WILLIAM SHAKESPEARE, Sir Sidney Lee. This is the standard life of Shakespeare, summarizing everything known about Shakespeare and his plays. Incredibly rich in material, broad in coverage, clear and judicious, it has served thousands as the best introduction to Shakespeare. 1931 edition. 9 plates. xxix + 792pp. 21967-4 Paperbound $4.50

MASTERS OF THE DRAMA, John Gassner. Most comprehensive history of the drama in print, covering every tradition from Greeks to modern Europe and America, including India, Far East, etc. Covers more than 800 dramatists, 2000 plays, with biographical material, plot summaries, theatre history, criticism, etc. "Best of its kind in English," *New Republic*. 77 illustrations. xxii + 890pp.
20100-7 Clothbound **$10.00**

THE EVOLUTION OF THE ENGLISH LANGUAGE, George McKnight. The growth of English, from the 14th century to the present. Unusual, non-technical account presents basic information in very interesting form: sound shifts, change in grammar and syntax, vocabulary growth, similar topics. Abundantly illustrated with quotations. Formerly *Modern English in the Making*. xii + 590pp.
21932-1 Paperbound **$4.00**

AN ETYMOLOGICAL DICTIONARY OF MODERN ENGLISH, Ernest Weekley. Fullest, richest work of its sort, by foremost British lexicographer. Detailed word histories, including many colloquial and archaic words; extensive quotations. Do not confuse this with the Concise Etymological Dictionary, which is much abridged. Total of xxvii + 830pp. $6\frac{1}{2} \times 9\frac{1}{4}$.
21873-2, 21874-0 Two volumes, Paperbound $7.90

FLATLAND: A ROMANCE OF MANY DIMENSIONS, E. A. Abbott. Classic of science-fiction explores ramifications of life in a two-dimensional world, and what happens when a three-dimensional being intrudes. Amusing reading, but also useful as introduction to thought about hyperspace. Introduction by Banesh Hoffmann. 16 illustrations. xx + 103pp. 20001-9 Paperbound $1.25

POEMS OF ANNE BRADSTREET, edited with an introduction by Robert Hutchinson. A new selection of poems by America's first poet and perhaps the first significant woman poet in the English language. 48 poems display her development in works of considerable variety—love poems, domestic poems, religious meditations, formal elegies, "quaternions," etc. Notes, bibliography. viii + 222pp.
22160-1 Paperbound $2.50

THREE GOTHIC NOVELS: THE CASTLE OF OTRANTO BY HORACE WALPOLE; VATHEK BY WILLIAM BECKFORD; THE VAMPYRE BY JOHN POLIDORI, WITH FRAGMENT OF A NOVEL BY LORD BYRON, edited by E. F. Bleiler. The first Gothic novel, by Walpole; the finest Oriental tale in English, by Beckford; powerful Romantic supernatural story in versions by Polidori and Byron. All extremely important in history of literature; all still exciting, packed with supernatural thrills, ghosts, haunted castles, magic, etc. xl + 291pp.
21232-7 Paperbound $2.50

THE BEST TALES OF HOFFMANN, E. T. A. Hoffmann. 10 of Hoffmann's most important stories, in modern re-editings of standard translations: Nutcracker and the King of Mice, Signor Formica, Automata, The Sandman, Rath Krespel, The Golden Flowerpot, Master Martin the Cooper, The Mines of Falun, The King's Betrothed, A New Year's Eve Adventure. 7 illustrations by Hoffmann. Edited by E. F. Bleiler. xxxix + 419pp. 21793-0 Paperbound $3.00

GHOST AND HORROR STORIES OF AMBROSE BIERCE, Ambrose Bierce. 23 strikingly modern stories of the horrors latent in the human mind: The Eyes of the Panther, The Damned Thing, An Occurrence at Owl Creek Bridge, An Inhabitant of Carcosa, etc., plus the dream-essay, Visions of the Night. Edited by E. F. Bleiler. xxii + 199pp. 20767-6 Paperbound $1.50

BEST GHOST STORIES OF J. S. LEFANU, J. Sheridan LeFanu. Finest stories by Victorian master often considered greatest supernatural writer of all. Carmilla, Green Tea, The Haunted Baronet, The Familiar, and 12 others. Most never before available in the U. S. A. Edited by E. F. Bleiler. 8 illustrations from Victorian publications. xvii + 467pp. 20415-4 Paperbound $3.00

MATHEMATICAL FOUNDATIONS OF INFORMATION THEORY, A. I. Khinchin. Comprehensive introduction to work of Shannon, McMillan, Feinstein and Khinchin, placing these investigations on a rigorous mathematical basis. Covers entropy concept in probability theory, uniqueness theorem, Shannon's inequality, ergodic sources, the E property, martingale concept, noise, Feinstein's fundamental lemma, Shanon's first and second theorems. Translated by R. A. Silverman and M. D. Friedman. iii + 120pp. 60434-9 Paperbound $2.00

SEVEN SCIENCE FICTION NOVELS, H. G. Wells. The standard collection of the great novels. Complete, unabridged. *First Men in the Moon, Island of Dr. Moreau, War of the Worlds, Food of the Gods, Invisible Man, Time Machine, In the Days of the Comet.* Not only science fiction fans, but every educated person owes it to himself to read these novels. 1015pp. (USO) 20264-X Clothbound $6.00

LAST AND FIRST MEN AND STAR MAKER, TWO SCIENCE FICTION NOVELS, Olaf Stapledon. Greatest future histories in science fiction. In the first, human intelligence is the "hero," through strange paths of evolution, interplanetary invasions, incredible technologies, near extinctions and reemergences. Star Maker describes the quest of a band of star rovers for intelligence itself, through time and space: weird inhuman civilizations, crustacean minds, symbiotic worlds, etc. Complete, unabridged. v + 438pp. (USO) 21962-3 Paperbound $2.50

THREE PROPHETIC NOVELS, H. G. WELLS. Stages of a consistently planned future for mankind. *When the Sleeper Wakes,* and *A Story of the Days to Come,* anticipate *Brave New World* and *1984,* in the 21st Century; *The Time Machine,* only complete version in print, shows farther future and the end of mankind. All show Wells's greatest gifts as storyteller and novelist. Edited by E. F. Bleiler. x + 335pp. (USO) 20605-X Paperbound $2.50

THE DEVIL'S DICTIONARY, Ambrose Bierce. America's own Oscar Wilde—Ambrose Bierce—offers his barbed iconoclastic wisdom in over 1,000 definitions hailed by H. L. Mencken as "some of the most gorgeous witticisms in the English language." 145pp. 20487-1 Paperbound $1.25

MAX AND MORITZ, Wilhelm Busch. Great children's classic, father of comic strip, of two bad boys, Max and Moritz. Also Ker and Plunk (Plisch und Plumm), Cat and Mouse, Deceitful Henry, Ice-Peter, The Boy and the Pipe, and five other pieces. Original German, with English translation. Edited by H. Arthur Klein; translations by various hands and H. Arthur Klein. vi + 216pp.
20181-3 Paperbound $2.00

PIGS IS PIGS AND OTHER FAVORITES, Ellis Parker Butler. The title story is one of the best humor short stories, as Mike Flannery obfuscates biology and English. Also included, That Pup of Murchison's, The Great American Pie Company, and Perkins of Portland. 14 illustrations. v + 109pp. 21532-6 Paperbound $1.25

THE PETERKIN PAPERS, Lucretia P. Hale. It takes genius to be as stupidly mad as the Peterkins, as they decide to become wise, celebrate the "Fourth," keep a cow, and otherwise strain the resources of the Lady from Philadelphia. Basic book of American humor. 153 illustrations. 219pp. 20794-3 Paperbound $2.00

PERRAULT'S FAIRY TALES, translated by A. E. Johnson and S. R. Littlewood, with 34 full-page illustrations by Gustave Doré. All the original Perrault stories—Cinderella, Sleeping Beauty, Bluebeard, Little Red Riding Hood, Puss in Boots, Tom Thumb, etc.—with their witty verse morals and the magnificent illustrations of Doré. One of the five or six great books of European fairy tales. viii + 117pp. 8⅛ x 11. 22311-6 Paperbound $2.00

OLD HUNGARIAN FAIRY TALES, Baroness Orczy. Favorites translated and adapted by author of the *Scarlet Pimpernel.* Eight fairy tales include "The Suitors of Princess Fire-Fly," "The Twin Hunchbacks," "Mr. Cuttlefish's Love Story," and "The Enchanted Cat." This little volume of magic and adventure will captivate children as it has for generations. 90 drawings by Montagu Barstow. 96pp.
(USO) 22293-4 Paperbound $1.95

THE RED FAIRY BOOK, Andrew Lang. Lang's color fairy books have long been children's favorites. This volume includes Rapunzel, Jack and the Bean-stalk and 35 other stories, familiar and unfamiliar. 4 plates, 93 illustrations x + 367pp.
21673-X Paperbound $2.50

THE BLUE FAIRY BOOK, Andrew Lang. Lang's tales come from all countries and all times. Here are 37 tales from Grimm, the Arabian Nights, Greek Mythology, and other fascinating sources. 8 plates, 130 illustrations. xi + 390pp.
21437-0 Paperbound $2.75

HOUSEHOLD STORIES BY THE BROTHERS GRIMM. Classic English-language edition of the well-known tales — Rumpelstiltskin, Snow White, Hansel and Gretel, The Twelve Brothers, Faithful John, Rapunzel, Tom Thumb (52 stories in all). Translated into simple, straightforward English by Lucy Crane. Ornamented with headpieces, vignettes, elaborate decorative initials and a dozen full-page illustrations by Walter Crane. x + 269pp. 21080-4 Paperbound **$2.00**

THE MERRY ADVENTURES OF ROBIN HOOD, Howard Pyle. The finest modern versions of the traditional ballads and tales about the great English outlaw. Howard Pyle's complete prose version, with every word, every illustration of the first edition. Do not confuse this facsimile of the original (1883) with modern editions that change text or illustrations. 23 plates plus many page decorations. xxii + 296pp.
22043-5 Paperbound $2.75

THE STORY OF KING ARTHUR AND HIS KNIGHTS, Howard Pyle. The finest children's version of the life of King Arthur; brilliantly retold by Pyle, with 48 of his most imaginative illustrations. xviii + 313pp. 6⅛ x 9¼.
21445-1 Paperbound $2.50

THE WONDERFUL WIZARD OF OZ, L. Frank Baum. America's finest children's book in facsimile of first edition with all Denslow illustrations in full color. The edition a child should have. Introduction by Martin Gardner. 23 color plates, scores of drawings. iv + 267pp. 20691-2 Paperbound $2.50

THE MARVELOUS LAND OF OZ, L. Frank Baum. The second Oz book, every bit as imaginative as the Wizard. The hero is a boy named Tip, but the Scarecrow and the Tin Woodman are back, as is the Oz magic. 16 color plates, 120 drawings by John R. Neill. 287pp. 20692-0 Paperbound $2.50

THE MAGICAL MONARCH OF MO, L. Frank Baum. Remarkable adventures in a land even stranger than Oz. The best of Baum's books not in the Oz series. 15 color plates and dozens of drawings by Frank Verbeck. xviii + 237pp.
21892-9 Paperbound $2.25

THE BAD CHILD'S BOOK OF BEASTS, MORE BEASTS FOR WORSE CHILDREN, A MORAL ALPHABET, Hilaire Belloc. Three complete humor classics in one volume. Be kind to the frog, and do not call him names . . . and 28 other whimsical animals. Familiar favorites and some not so well known. Illustrated by Basil Blackwell. 156pp. (USO) 20749-8 Paperbound $1.50

EAST O' THE SUN AND WEST O' THE MOON, George W. Dasent. Considered the best of all translations of these Norwegian folk tales, this collection has been enjoyed by generations of children (and folklorists too). Includes True and Untrue, Why the Sea is Salt, East O' the Sun and West O' the Moon, Why the Bear is Stumpy-Tailed, Boots and the Troll, The Cock and the Hen, Rich Peter the Pedlar, and 52 more. The only edition with all 59 tales. 77 illustrations by Erik Werenskiold and Theodor Kittelsen. xv + 418pp. 22521-6 Paperbound $3.50

GOOPS AND HOW TO BE THEM, Gelett Burgess. Classic of tongue-in-cheek humor, masquerading as etiquette book. 87 verses, twice as many cartoons, show mischievous Goops as they demonstrate to children virtues of table manners, neatness, courtesy, etc. Favorite for generations. viii + 88pp. 6½ x 9¼. 22233-0 Paperbound $1.50

ALICE'S ADVENTURES UNDER GROUND, Lewis Carroll. The first version, quite different from the final *Alice in Wonderland,* printed out by Carroll himself with his own illustrations. Complete facsimile of the "million dollar" manuscript Carroll gave to Alice Liddell in 1864. Introduction by Martin Gardner. viii + 96pp. Title and dedication pages in color. 21482-6 Paperbound $1.25

THE BROWNIES, THEIR BOOK, Palmer Cox. Small as mice, cunning as foxes, exuberant and full of mischief, the Brownies go to the zoo, toy shop, seashore, circus, etc., in 24 verse adventures and 266 illustrations. Long a favorite, since their first appearance in St. Nicholas Magazine. xi + 144pp. 6⅝ x 9¼. 21265-3 Paperbound $1.75

SONGS OF CHILDHOOD, Walter De La Mare. Published (under the pseudonym Walter Ramal) when De La Mare was only 29, this charming collection has long been a favorite children's book. A facsimile of the first edition in paper, the 47 poems capture the simplicity of the nursery rhyme and the ballad, including such lyrics as I Met Eve, Tartary, The Silver Penny. vii + 106pp. (USO) 21972-0 Paperbound $2.00

THE COMPLETE NONSENSE OF EDWARD LEAR, Edward Lear. The finest 19th-century humorist-cartoonist in full: all nonsense limericks, zany alphabets, Owl and Pussycat, songs, nonsense botany, and more than 500 illustrations by Lear himself. Edited by Holbrook Jackson. xxix + 287pp. (USO) 20167-8 Paperbound $2.00

BILLY WHISKERS: THE AUTOBIOGRAPHY OF A GOAT, Frances Trego Montgomery. A favorite of children since the early 20th century, here are the escapades of that rambunctious, irresistible and mischievous goat—Billy Whiskers. Much in the spirit of *Peck's Bad Boy,* this is a book that children never tire of reading or hearing. All the original familiar illustrations by W. H. Fry are included: 6 color plates, 18 black and white drawings. 159pp. 22345-0 Paperbound $2.00

MOTHER GOOSE MELODIES. Faithful republication of the fabulously rare Munroe and Francis "copyright 1833" Boston edition—the most important Mother Goose collection, usually referred to as the "original." Familiar rhymes plus many rare ones, with wonderful old woodcut illustrations. Edited by E. F. Bleiler. 128pp. 4½ x 6⅜. 22577-1 Paperbound $1.00

TWO LITTLE SAVAGES; BEING THE ADVENTURES OF TWO BOYS WHO LIVED AS INDIANS AND WHAT THEY LEARNED, Ernest Thompson Seton. Great classic of nature and boyhood provides a vast range of woodlore in most palatable form, a genuinely entertaining story. Two farm boys build a teepee in woods and live in it for a month, working out Indian solutions to living problems, star lore, birds and animals, plants, etc. 293 illustrations. vii + 286pp.

20985-7 Paperbound $2.50

PETER PIPER'S PRACTICAL PRINCIPLES OF PLAIN & PERFECT PRONUNCIATION. Alliterative jingles and tongue-twisters of surprising charm, that made their first appearance in America about 1830. Republished in full with the spirited woodcut illustrations from this earliest American edition. 32pp. 4½ x 6⅜.

22560-7 Paperbound $1.00

SCIENCE EXPERIMENTS AND AMUSEMENTS FOR CHILDREN, Charles Vivian. 73 easy experiments, requiring only materials found at home or easily available, such as candles, coins, steel wool, etc.; illustrate basic phenomena like vacuum, simple chemical reaction, etc. All safe. Modern, well-planned. Formerly *Science Games for Children.* 102 photos, numerous drawings. 96pp. 6⅛ x 9¼.

21856-2 Paperbound $1.25

AN INTRODUCTION TO CHESS MOVES AND TACTICS SIMPLY EXPLAINED, Leonard Barden. Informal intermediate introduction, quite strong in explaining reasons for moves. Covers basic material, tactics, important openings, traps, positional play in middle game, end game. Attempts to isolate patterns and recurrent configurations. Formerly *Chess.* 58 figures. 102pp. (USO) 21210-6 Paperbound $1.25

LASKER'S MANUAL OF CHESS, Dr. Emanuel Lasker. Lasker was not only one of the five great World Champions, he was also one of the ablest expositors, theorists, and analysts. In many ways, his Manual, permeated with his philosophy of battle, filled with keen insights, is one of the greatest works ever written on chess. Filled with analyzed games by the great players. A single-volume library that will profit almost any chess player, beginner or master. 308 diagrams. xli x 349pp.

20640-8 Paperbound $2.75

THE MASTER BOOK OF MATHEMATICAL RECREATIONS, Fred Schuh. In opinion of many the finest work ever prepared on mathematical puzzles, stunts, recreations; exhaustively thorough explanations of mathematics involved, analysis of effects, citation of puzzles and games. Mathematics involved is elementary. Translated bv F. Göbel. 194 figures. xxiv + 430pp. 22134-2 Paperbound $3.50

MATHEMATICS, MAGIC AND MYSTERY, Martin Gardner. Puzzle editor for Scientific American explains mathematics behind various mystifying tricks: card tricks, stage "mind reading," coin and match tricks, counting out games, geometric dissections, etc. Probability sets, theory of numbers clearly explained. Also provides more than 400 tricks, guaranteed to work, that you can do. 135 illustrations. xii + 176pp.

20335-2 Paperbound $1.75

MATHEMATICAL PUZZLES FOR BEGINNERS AND ENTHUSIASTS, Geoffrey Mott-Smith. 189 puzzles from easy to difficult—involving arithmetic, logic, algebra, properties of digits, probability, etc.—for enjoyment and mental stimulus. Explanation of mathematical principles behind the puzzles. 135 illustrations. viii + 248pp.
20198-8 Paperbound $1.75

PAPER FOLDING FOR BEGINNERS, William D. Murray and Francis J. Rigney. Easiest book on the market, clearest instructions on making interesting, beautiful origami. Sail boats, cups, roosters, frogs that move legs, bonbon boxes, standing birds, etc. 40 projects; more than 275 diagrams and photographs. 94pp.
20713-7 Paperbound $1.00

TRICKS AND GAMES ON THE POOL TABLE, Fred Herrmann. 79 tricks and games—some solitaires, some for two or more players, some competitive games—to entertain you between formal games. Mystifying shots and throws, unusual caroms, tricks involving such props as cork, coins, a hat, etc. Formerly *Fun on the Pool Table.* 77 figures. 95pp. 21814-7 Paperbound $1.25

HAND SHADOWS TO BE THROWN UPON THE WALL: A SERIES OF NOVEL AND AMUSING FIGURES FORMED BY THE HAND, Henry Bursill. Delightful picturebook from great-grandfather's day shows how to make 18 different hand shadows: a bird that flies, duck that quacks, dog that wags his tail, camel, goose, deer, boy, turtle, etc. Only book of its sort. vi + 33pp. 6½ x 9¼. 21779-5 Paperbound $1.00

WHITTLING AND WOODCARVING, E. J. Tangerman. 18th printing of best book on market. "If you can cut a potato you can carve" toys and puzzles, chains, chessmen, caricatures, masks, frames, woodcut blocks, surface patterns, much more. Information on tools, woods, techniques. Also goes into serious wood sculpture from Middle Ages to present, East and West. 464 photos, figures. x + 293pp.
20965-2 Paperbound $2.00

HISTORY OF PHILOSOPHY, Julián Marias. Possibly the clearest, most easily followed, best planned, most useful one-volume history of philosophy on the market; neither skimpy nor overfull. Full details on system of every major philosopher and dozens of less important thinkers from pre-Socratics up to Existentialism and later. Strong on many European figures usually omitted. Has gone through dozens of editions in Europe. 1966 edition, translated by Stanley Appelbaum and Clarence Strowbridge. xviii + 505pp. 21739-6 Paperbound $3.50

YOGA: A SCIENTIFIC EVALUATION, Kovoor T. Behanan. Scientific but non-technical study of physiological results of yoga exercises; done under auspices of Yale U. Relations to Indian thought, to psychoanalysis, etc. 16 photos. xxiii + 270pp.
20505-3 Paperbound $2.50